The Other Side of Western Civilization

Readings in Everyday Life

Third Edition

Volume I

The Ancient World
to the Reformation

Edited by

Stanley Chodorow

University of California, San Diego

HARCOURT BRACE JOVANOVICH, PUBLISHERS

San Diego   New York   Chicago   Atlanta   Washington, D.C.

London   Sydney   Toronto

For Peggy

ISBN: 0-15-567651-2
Library of Congress Catalog Card Number: 83-81993
Printed in the United States of America

Picture Credits:

p. 6, Anderson/EPA; page 80, Courtesy of University Library, Utrecht; page 148, EPA; page 230, Saolne, EPA; page 322, Alinari/EPA.

Copyrights and acknowledgments:

BASCOM   Exerpts from *Deep Water, Ancient Ships* by Willard Bascom. Copyright © 1977 by Willard Bascom. Reprinted by permission of Doubleday & Company, Inc.   WESTERMANN   Reprinted by permission of the Polish Institute of Arts & Sciences of America, *Polish Revue*.   JONES   From *The Green City* by A. H. M. Jones (1940). Reprinted by permission of Oxford University Press.   POMEROY   Reprinted by permission of Schocken Book Inc. from *Goddesses, Whores Wives, and Slaves* by Sarah B. Pomeroy. Copyright © 1975 by Sarah B. Pomeroy.   JONES   From *The Conflict between Paganism and Christianity in the Fourth Century*, edited by Arnaldo Momigliano, © Oxford University Press, 1963. Reprinted by permission of Oxford University Press.   THOMPSON   Reprinted by permission of the author from "The Passio S. Sabae and Early Visigothic Society," copyright 1955 by E. A. Thompson.   CHANEY   From *The Cult of Kingship in Anglo-Saxon England* by William Chaney. Reprinted by permission of the author and Manchester University Press.   POWER   From *Medieval People* by Eileen Power (Methuen & Co., 1924). Reprinted by permission of Associated Book Publishers, Ltd.   CHAZAN   From *Medieval Jewry in Northern France* by Robert Chazan. Reprinted by permission of Johns Hopkins University Press. PRAWER   Reprinted by permission of Joshua Prawer.   PAINTER   From *William Marshal* by Sidney Painter. Reprinted by permission of Johns Hopkins University Press. BURKE   From *Life in the Castle in Medieval England* by John Burke, London, B. T. Batsford Ltd., 1978.   McLAUGHLIN   From *The History of Childhood*, Lloyd DeMause, editor. Copyright © 1974, The Psychohistory Press. Reprinted by permission of the publisher, Atcom, Inc.   MURRAY   From "Religion Among the Poor in Thirteenth-Century France" by Alexander Murray. Reprinted by permission of the publisher from *Traditio*, Vol. 30 (1974). Copyright © 1974 by Fordham University Press.   BARBER   Reprinted by permission of Malcom Barber; The Historical Association.   SUMPTION   From *Pilgrimage: An Image of Medieval Religion* by Jonathan Sumption, Rowman & Littlefield, 1975.   HILTON   From *Bond Men Made Free* by Rodney Hilton. Copyright © 1973 by Rodney Hilton. Reprinted by permission of Viking Penguin, Inc.   KEEGAN   From *The Face of Battle* by John Keegan. Copyright © 1976 by John Keegan. Reprinted by permission of Viking Penguin, Inc.   STRAUSS   Excerpts from Gerald Strauss, *Nuremberg in the Sixteenth Century*, © 1966 by John Wiley & Sons. Revised edition © 1976 by Indiana University Press. Reprinted by permission of Indiana University Press.   LYTLE   Excerpts from Guy Fitch Lytle, "Patronage Patterns and Oxford Colleges," in *The University Society, Vol. I: Oxford and Cambridge from the 14th to the Early 19th Century*, ed. Lawrence Stone. Copyright © 1974 by Princeton University Press. Reprinted by permission of Princeton University Press. CIPOLLA   From *Cristofano and the Plague*, © 1973 by Carlo M. Cipolla. Reprinted by permission of the University of California Press.   DAVIS   Exerpted from *Society and Culture in Early Modern France: Eight Essays* by Natalie Zemon Davis with the permission of the publishers, Stanford University Press. © 1973, 1975 by Natalie Zemon Davis.   BRUCKER From *Renaissance Florence* by Gene Brucker. Copyright © 1969 by Gene Brucker. Reprinted by permission of John Wiley & Sons, Inc.   ROSS   From *The History of Childhood*, Lloyd DeMause, editor. Copyright © 1974, The Psychohistory Press. Reprinted by permission of the publisher, Atcom, Inc.

Preface

The Third Edition of *The Other Side of Western Civilization*, Volume I, like the previous two editions, describes and evokes the experience of living in premodern times. This new edition, however, reflects the trends in scholarship published since 1979. A third of the selections are new to this work. The progress of social history is demonstrated by the replacement of pieces written in the premodern period by the works of contemporary historians who have tried to re-create the life and attitudes of the past. This progress is also demonstrated by the inclusion of some articles which were published a generation ago, but which have now been given renewed value by recent work. The selections have been arranged chronologically to fit the organization of the majority of Western civilization and humanities courses, but a second table of contents provides a topical arrangement.

Courses in Western civilization necessarily focus on events and trends or ideas and culture. Interdisciplinary courses in the humanities, which have become increasingly popular, concentrate on great books and works of art, music, and drama. This book is designed to help students understand the social and institutional world in which events happened, ideas were expressed, and art was created. The readings do not merely add color to the basic picture, however. They deal with fundamentally important aspects of past life.

Four selections represent the increasing interest that scholars have given to popular religion. Two selections treat the character of travel in the premodern world. Other pieces describe life in cities, the condition of women, the ideas and practices of child-rearing in medieval Europe and Renaissance Italy, the world of the peasant, the common soldier's experience of battle in late medieval Europe. Taken together, the readings describe the commonplace existence that formed the context in which great rulers, thinkers, and artists of Western civilization lived and effected historically significant changes.

A number of people provided guidance and assistance in the preparation of the book. I want to thank Jeremy duQ. Adams, Southern Methodist University; Elizabeth E. R. Brown, Brooklyn College of the City University of New York; Charles Hamilton, San Diego State University; and Jeffrey B. Russell, University of California, Santa Barbara. These critics gave me valuable advice and helped significantly in shaping the book. I am indebted to Drake Bush of Harcourt Brace Jovanovich for his encouragement and aid. I want also to thank my editor, Jack Thomas, for his helpful criticism and editorial guidance.

Finally, I thank my wife, Peggy. She is not only a source of encouragement and criticism, the usual things; her own intense, productive work schedule and her success provide a model and a goad that cures indolence and sharpens the mind.

—Stanley Chodorow

Contents

Topical Table of Contents

Introduction

The aim of this third edition, as of the first two, is to provide insight into the character of premodern society. Focusing on the social life of western Europe from the time of the Greek city-states through the Renaissance and Reformation, the selections present a composite picture of the activities of the social classes and professions in both urban and rural life.

Social history was first written by the Enlightenment *philosophes*, who reacted strongly against the ancient historiographical tradition that equated history with the history of politics and government. Critics like Voltaire, who called for a history of men to replace the history of kings, ministers, and courts, inspired writers like Montesquieu to describe and explain the social personalities of national groups. Others, in Germany as well as in France, began to write about the cultural history of Europe—the history of art and literature as well as of society. But, even when they were ostensibly writing it the *philosophes* were really uninterested in history. For them, history was only a source of evidence for proving the truth of their conviction that the human race was progressing toward the realization of its rational capacity.

In the late eighteenth and early nineteenth century, Goethe, Herder, Hegel, and other thinkers reacted against this attitude. In the eighteenth century, the progress of the human race had culminated in the reign of terror of the French Revolution. Humanity had not escaped its history of irrationality and violence; it had only continued in its ancient course. These writers, the romanticists, thought that society is as much a product of its past as an adult is a product of his childhood and adolescence. For them, historical studies provided the key to understanding the present. The historical work of the romanticists therefore treated the whole past: Social and economic history, cultural history, linguistics, and the history of religion became integral parts of the study of the past.

Yet the historical field that gained most from the new valuation of historical study was the old mainstay of the genre, political history. Most extant documents and narrative sources derived from political action and concerned political organization. Methods for dealing with the cryptic sources on which social history could be founded took much longer to develop than did methods for handling the literary products of the governing elite. Real progress in social history was not made until the 1920s, when Marc Block and Lucien Febvre founded the so-called *Annales* school—named for the journal in which they published studies of social and economic history. Inspired by Bloch and Febvre, current social historians have studied the social structures that provided the context in which politics, artistic creation, and other human endeavors took place.

The development of various fields of historical scholarship has paralleled increasing interest in certain periods of history. Nineteenth-century historiography, founded on the romanticists' reaction to the Enlightenment, took a striking interest in the medieval period. This interest contrasts sharply with the attitude of the Renaissance humanists and Enlightenment *philosophes*. The humanists had coined the phrase "Middle Ages" as a pejorative description of the long period of European history that separated them from the ancient world. The *philosophes* shared the humanists' attitudes toward the supposed barbarism and superstition associated with medieval society. But nineteenth-century historians increasingly discovered that the origins of modern European institutions and ideas were to be found in the medieval communities that succeeded to the power of Rome during the sixth century. In fact, in English universities, the professorial chairs of modern history, which were established in the middle of the nineteenth century, have usually been held by medievalists; today there are over eighty major centers of medieval studies in the United States and Canada. The structure of this book reflects this interest in European history by focusing attention on the life of the Middle Ages.

Although most courses on Western civilization begin with ancient Israel or Mycenaean Greece, the social life of the ancient peoples of these countries is not, strictly speaking, relevant to the development of European society. The ancient Greeks lived in a different world—geographically, economically, and politically—from that of the European peoples whose social and economic institutions formed the basis for modern society. The societies of archaic Greece and the ancient Near East were antecedents of European society and provided ideas and attitudes that influenced the formation of modern western society, but they were not a part of the edifice itself. The effect of Roman social life on the development of European society was, of course, much greater than that of Greece, nonetheless, before Europe became a distinct civilization, its social and economic foundations were profoundly transformed by the Germanic invasions. The urban life of the Roman Empire virtually disappeared during the fifth and sixth centuries, and although most modern Italian and many northern European cities were founded on the Roman *urbes* that had existed on their locations, the character and even the plan of these later towns bears little relation to the Roman installations. In rural areas also, the influx of Germans changed the nature of Roman society. The provincial nobility continued to exist beside the German aristocracy, but the two groups increasingly became one through conflict and intermarriage—and the Germanic pattern of life soon dominated both groups. The peasantry also changed through intermarriage and cultural amalgamation.

The organization of the book focuses on this medieval transformation of Western society. There are five broad chronological periods. The first treats the ancient world, the next three the medieval world, and the last the Renaissance–Reformation period. In choosing articles for the first section, I have focused on those aspects of ancient life that had the greatest effect on the development of Western society and culture. The emphasis on the Middle Ages reflects my conviction that the changes that occurred during this long period were of fundamental importance in the formation of Western society. Selections on peasant life, travel, religious life, and the experiences of the elite form the core of these sections. The last part emphasizes urban life, which, in the Renaissance–Reformation period, set the pattern for social and cultural values.

In Part I, "The Ancient World," Willard Bascom's "Ancient Ships and Shipping" lays the foundation for our understanding of one of the most important aspects of Western civilization—its inescapable experience and preoccupation with the sea. The sea became the physical setting for the adventure through which men achieved heroic stature, and heroic character was important not only in the face of wild nature or war, but in the social setting, the *polis*, which the hero had left and to which he would return. In "Sanitation and Safety in the Greek City," A. H. M. Jones describes the physical organization of the *polis*, and in "The Condition of Slaves in Greek Society," William Linn Westermann treats the absolutely unheroic segment of ancient society. Turning to Roman society, Sarah B. Pomeroy provides a basic description of the society while assessing the position of women in it. She also shows how historians use the scanty remains of ancient civilization to construct a coherent historical account. The final article of this part places Christianity in its early historical milieu, the Roman empire, to show how it overcame obstacles to its acceptance by the populations outside of Palestine. In the first three centuries of this era, many cults competed for the faith of empire's population. A. H. M. Jones assesses the social background of the victory of Christianity in this contest.

The selections in Part 2, "The Early Middle Ages," deal primarily with the history of social groups that evolved after the barbarian invasions. The first two articles treat the Visigoths of southern Russia and the Anglo-Saxons of England—barbarians themselves—and provide a basis for understanding important aspects of medieval social life and ideas. Eileen Power's description of a typical medieval peasant enlivens generalizations about the formation of the medieval and early modern peasant classes. Robert Chazan's article illuminates both the life of the Jews in northern Europe and the life of the medieval cities. In the final selection, Joshua

Prawer views upper-class society from a special perspective by examining the society of the knights who established the kingdom of Jerusalem in the early twelfth century.

Part 3, "The Peak of Medieval Civilization," treats the everyday experience of the society on which rested the flowering of medieval art, architecture, and intellectual life, as well as commerce and government. The first article describes the training of a knight, whose special skills made him both a protector of and a menace to medieval communities. In the second selection, John Burke describes life in the aristocratic household. Next, Mary Martin McLaughlin describes the experiences of mothers and children. Alexander Murray relies on the handbook of a thirteenth-century Dominican preacher for a view of the religious attitudes and practices of his audience, the lower and middle classes of the cities. Malcolm Barber's article on the heresy scare of 1321 continues this concern with popular religion and its social and political effects.

Part 4 covers the late medieval period, the fourteenth and fifteenth centuries. During this period, Europeans suffered from pestilence and war, and the selections tell us much about the experience of these terrors. In the first article, R. H. Hilton analyzes the causes and characteristics of the widespread uprisings of peasants, which occurred with increasing frequency and violence from the late thirteenth century on. In the second selection, John Keegan evokes the reality of medieval warfare for the common soldier. In "The Organization of the Late Medieval City," Gerald Strauss describes the laws regulating urban life. These regulations grew during the medieval period because of the increasing size and complexity of social and commercial activities as well as the continuing challenge to organized life posed by famine, war, and plague. In the final article of this part, Guy F. Lytle examines a crucial period in the history of the university, a peculiarly medieval institution that has survived nearly intact into the modern world. He shows that the problem of finding employment for university graduates is nothing new, and that in the fourteenth century as more recently, a decrease in the number of positions available to graduates profoundly affected the structure of the university.

The final section covers the Renaissance–Reformation period, the sixteenth and seventeenth centuries. In his piece, Carlo Cipolla describes the institutions of public health, which the towns developed to meet the continuing threat of bubonic plague. Natalie Z. Davis turns our attention to religious change and tries to assess the effect of the Reformation on the lives of individuals, particularly women. In "Cultural Patronage in Renaissance Florence," Gene Brucker considers the reasons why the society of Florence attracted and supported the new artistic and intellectual culture more than any other city-state in Italy. Finally, James Bruce Ross gathers material on child-rearing and parent-child relationships in the urban society of Renaissance Italy. The significance of childhood in an

urban setting is very great, for just as the family life of the rural aristocracy set the standards for child-rearing and early socialization in the Middle Ages, the urban, middle-class family was the model for the
Renaissance–Reformation world—and became the model for the modern
world.

BIBLIOGRAPHY

For a history of the historian's discipline and the way its focus has
changed, see Herbert Butterfield, *Man on his Past: The Study of the History
of Historical Scholarship* (Cambridge, Eng., 1940). See also Fritz Stern,
The Varieties of History: From Voltaire to the Present (Cleveland, 1956).
When he died in 1979, Butterfield had almost completed a work on the
origins of historical writing. The book was published by Adam Watson; in
The Origins of History (New York, 1981), Butterfield studied the development of historical consciousness from ancient Mesopotamia to the Renaissance, including brief chapters on Islamic and Chinese historical writing.
The great social historian Marc Bloch wrote an appraisal of his craft which
was found among his papers and published as *The Historian's Craft* (New
York, 1953). In 1971, two numbers of *Daedalus*, published by the American Academy of Arts and Sciences, were devoted to an assessment of the
discipline and fields of history; see *Daedalus*, Vol. 100 (1971), Nos. 1–2.

PART 1

The Ancient World
5th Century B.C. — 5th Century A.D.

The Ancient World

The five selections of Part 1 treat the social life of ancient Greece and Rome. At the beginning of the fifth century B.C., Greece was the center of Western civilization, extending its influence over the entire Mediterranean world. Athens used its navy and commercial power to establish a far-flung empire of city-states. Aligned against this maritime empire was the Peloponnesian League, a confederation of Greek cities led by Sparta. The cities of both these configurations possessed a great deal of cultural and economic homogeneity. This pan-Hellenism reflected the great importance of seafaring, for links among the Greek communities around the Mediterranean and Black seas were maintained through continual communication by sea. In fact, the ancient world was a Mediterranean world because sea travel was one of is salient characteristics; some historians have explained the transition from the ancient to the medieval period as a result of the collapse of Mediterranean shipping. In the first article, Willard Bascom examines the character of the ships and shipping that played this important role.

The society of a Greek city was controlled by its male citizens, whether the community government was democratic or oligarchic. But the society of the towns included many other elements beside citizens. The *metics*, or foreigners, formed a large class of merchants, artisans, and laborers, who played important roles in the economic and social life of the cities, but who were excluded from a direct role in politics. Then many persons of substance, although of low status, were former slaves or descendants of them. In the second article, William Linn Westermann uses the institution of slavery in the western hemisphere as a comparative framework for a detailed analysis of the condition of slaves in ancient Greece.

The cities continued to dominate the Greek world of the eastern Mediterranean and its dependencies elsewhere, even after the Macedonians had destroyed the independence of the city-states and built their own empire. In the third selection, A. H. M. Jones investigates the character of the Greek cities under the successors of Philip and Alexander of Macedonia and under the Romans. The Romans, although they retained the values of their primitive agricultural society, built an empire based on cities, which developed under the influence of the Greeks.

In ancient biographies of the Roman emperors, their relations with women hold an important place. Clearly some women exercised extraordinary behind-the-scenes power, but the sources reveal little about the normal conditions of women's life. In the fourth selection, Sarah B. Pomeroy successfully uses this scanty material as the basis for an evaluation of the place of women in Roman society. The selection not only adds much to our knowledge of this aspect of

Roman life, but reveals the problems historians have in trying to use ancient sources.

The final selection treats a question that has puzzled historians since the eighteenth century: Why did Christianity win the competition among the many religions of the Roman empire to become first the dominant faith and then the official one? Edward Gibbon dedicated a famous chapter of his *Decline and Fall of the Roman Empire* (1782) to this problem, and nearly every eminent historian of the empire has taken it up anew. In this piece, A. H. M. Jones gives his answer to the question.

BIBLIOGRAPHY

For a broad introduction to ancient seafaring, see Lionel Casson, *The Ancient Mariners* (New York, 1959), and *Ships and Seamanship in the Ancient World* (Princeton, 1971). For more specialized studies, see William Culican, *The First Merchant Venturers* (New York, 1966); W. L. Rodgers, *Greek and Roman Naval Warfare* (Annapolis, Md., 1964); George Bass, ed., *A History of Seafaring Based on Underwater Archaeology* (London, 1972).

On ancient cities, see A. Zimmern, *The Greek Commonwealth* (Oxford, 1911); R. E. Wycherley, *How the Greeks Built Cities* (London, 1949); and Raphael Sealey, *A History of Greek City States, ca. 700–338 B.C.* (Berkeley, 1976). For western cities, see Russell Meiggs, *Roman Ostia* (Oxford, 1960); and A. Boëthius, "Urbanism in Italy," *The Classical Pattern of Modern Western Civilization* (Copenhagen, 1958).

For the social context of the life of women in ancient Rome, see W. W. Fowler, *Social Life at Rome in the Age of Cicero* (New York, 1909); Jerome Carcopino, *Daily Life in Ancient Rome* (New Haven, 1940); P. A. Brunt, *Social Conflicts in the Roman Republic* (New York, 1971); and Ramsay MacMullen, *Roman Social Relations, 50 B.C. to A.D. 284* (New Haven, 1974). On women, see M. I. Finley, "The Silent Women of Rome," in *Aspects of Antiquity* (London, 1965), pp. 129–42; and J. P. V. D. Balsdon, *Roman Women* (London, 1962).

For the history of Christianity in the Roman Empire, see W. W. Fowler, *The Religious Experience of the Roman People* (London, 1911); T. R. Glover, *The Conflict of Religions in the Early Roman Empire* (London, 1909); Samuel Angus, *The Mystery Religions and Christianity* (London, 1925) is the best work on the mystery cults. See also, Erwin R. Goodenough, *The Church in the Roman Empire* (New York, 1931); Harold Mattingly, *Christianity in the Roman Empire* (New York, 1967); and the articles in A. Momigliano, ed., *Paganism and Christianity in the Fourth Century* (Oxford, 1963).

Ancient Ships and Shipping

WILLARD BASCOM

Willard Bascom studies ancient ships with the eye of a professional oceanographer and amateur underwater archeologist. Seafaring skills and oceanographic knowledge are of primary importance in this historical study, for the men of Crete, Phoenicia, and Greece, and the sailors of Carthage, Rome, and medieval Europe wrote little about their sea trade or the technology that made it possible. To know something of this very important part of the experience and of the economies and politics of these peoples, we must know about their life on the Mediterranean—"mare nostrum," our sea, as the Romans called it.

The ancient sailors left almost no records, the substructure underlying the myths and literature of the ancient world is plain only to those who are familiar with the ancient shipping routes and with the places of refuge or danger around the Mediterranean. The adventures of Jason and the Argonauts, for example, relate to the experiences of Greek sailors in the Black Sea. In the *Odyssey*, Homer makes the real world of the ancient mariners the geography of a symbolic journey toward self-knowledge and self-realization. Aeneas, the model Roman in Vergil's epic, arrived at his destiny in Italy by a route patterned on that of Odysseus, and the tests of the sea were universalized by Vergil, as they were by Homer, into the basic tests of every human life. If we jump many centuries and many cultures north, we see that seafaring remained a crucial aspect of life and the poetic vision of Germanic life. The mythic figures of Siegfried and Brunhild lived in a world in which land and sea were nearly equal parts; Beowulf's world was similar. In the Icelandic sagas, a long spell of adventure on the sea was the final step of the maturation before a man assumed the burdens of marriage, fatherhood, and political life.

None of these observations about the importance of the sea and seafaring in literature is new to those who study the actual history of the ancient and medieval worlds. Since the middle of the nineteenth century, adventurers and archeologists have tried with substantial success to identify the Homeric and Germanic sea routes as well as those of even earlier peoples. Thor Heyerdahl is probably the best known of these explorers. But Bascom wants to shift our attention away from the re-creation of ancient sea voyages to the study of ancient ships themselves. He argues that modern recovery techniques, which he has had a great part in developing, will make the study of ancient ships more fruitful than ever before.

His argument rests on two assertions. First, he points out that the ship, particularly the merchant ship that plied the Mediterranean routes for months on end, was a microcosm of society. The sailors took with them all the necessaries of life: food, implements, and portable pastimes. Thus, recovery of a downed ship should reveal more about the daily life of its particular civilization than any but the most remarkable and extensive excavations on land. Second, he argues that wrecks retrieved from deep water will produce by far the best archeological evidence for the study of ancient civilizations—and that the wrecks are there, in the hundreds if not the thousands. Recent advances in underwater archeology have all been concentrated on shallow-water excavations, where the action of waves and changes in the coastline have destroyed or dismantled much of what was once there. At great depths, where the water is still and marine life sparse or nonexistent for lack of oxygen, ships containing a veritable catalogue of Mediterranean civilization from the Bronze Age, the first great age of seafaring, to the sixteenth century wait to be lifted from the ocean floor. Bascom's book is intended to introduce students of the premodern world to the new techniques of sea recovery and to argue for a program that will put this technology into operation. His survey of what we already know about ancient ships and shipping is part of that argument.

The earliest known picture of seagoing warships was carefully carved on the tomb of a Pharaoh named Sahure in 2450 B.C.—two hundred years after Pharaoh Sneferu's forty ships brought cedars from Lebanon in the first recorded sea trade. The tomb drawing showed a fleet of troop transports carrying the Pharaoh's soldiers to some port in Asia. The ships look to be over thirty meters long, propelled by oars as well as sails. Obviously, they were the product of long years of development.

During the second millennium B.C., the people of the Aegean showed their strength at sea. The Minoans of Crete built a very high level of civilization, with cities and palaces that show no signs of defensive works. One explanation is that they relied on the same kind of "wooden walls" the oracle recommended to the Greeks during the Persian war a thousand years later. These wooden walls were fighting ships, ready to defend the island against all intruders. Thucydides wrote that "Minos is the first to whom tradition ascribes the possession of a Navy." According to Lionel Casson, "Their bold programs of overseas exploration and colonization, their far flung trade and their unwalled cities presupposes the existence of a great fleet." About 1500 B.C., the Minoan culture seems to have suddenly disintegrated. One hypothesis is that the great sea wave from the explosion of the volcano at Santorin wiped out the defending warships on the beaches and in the harbors along the northern coast. At any rate, by 1450 B.C. the fleet that had maintained order was gone and the chaos of sea raiders prevailed.

The Mycenaean Greeks then moved across the narrow channel from the Peloponnesus in strength and took over Crete, its colonies, and its commerce. Presumably they used warships, or at least troop transports,

From Willard Bascom, *Deep Water, Ancient Ships* (New York: Doubleday, 1976), pp. 39–51, 53–57, 65–68.

and readily subdued the Minoans, who were unprepared for land war. Mycenaean sea power rose quickly but faded in a few hundred years, leaving little trace. We do not know what their ships looked like; the record of those ships if it exists, is on the sea floor.

As the Mycenaean grip on the seas began to slip, the rovers and pirates of Lycia (in southwestern Asia Minor) and the nearby isles—presumably Cyprus, Rhodes, and the Cyclades—banded together and formed raiding parties that swept the shores of the eastern Mediterranean. These rovers were contemporaries with the ones who became known as the "Sea Peoples," whose great, final sea battle with Ramses III, in 1194 B.C., is recorded in considerable detail on a famous relief at Medinet Habu, in the Nile delta. Ramses won decisively, apparently by some ruse, and now the Mediterranean stage was set for the Phoenicians.

One thinks of the Phoenicians as explorers and traders, which they certainly were, but they also seem to have been largely responsible for many early developments in fighting ships. In order to maintain their famous coastal cities (Sidon, Tyre, Byblos) against raiders, as well as protect their merchantmen, the Phoenicians must have had a considerable navy. Certainly, they ventured to distant, unfriendly shores and dominated the eastern Mediterranean from 1100 to 800 B.C., although few details of their ships of that period are known. Later, in the fifth century, they minted coins showing fighting ships that were equivalent to those of the Greeks.

The first Greek ships of which we have a reasonably clear picture are the ones described by the poet Homer in the eighth century B.C. He told of the galleys of the Trojan War, in the Bronze Age, several hundred years earlier. The ships he described seem to have been a combination of those traditionally associated with Jason's Argonauts and the ships Homer saw about him. They were penteconters, long and slender, swift and black, painted with pitch except for the bow eyes. Such ships would have been about twenty meters long, low in the water and undecked. They were similar to, but probably less graceful than, the Viking ships of two thousand years later. They were built either for trading or raiding, as suited the captain's fancy. Such ships must have been light and strong, to permit frequent beachings and occasional portage. The rowing crew was fifty men, half on each side, one oar per man, and one steering oar on each side of the stern. There were also a mast and sail that could readily be stepped and rigged if there were a following wind. The crew would haul in on the forestays, raising the mast into its slot and tightening the backstay. Then they would hoist the single cross yard. The sail was square, probably of linen patches sewn checkerboard fashion between strengthening leather thongs, and supported from the yard, against which it was furled. The sail was raised and lowered by a series of lines called brails that looped around the foot, or bottom of the sail, so that it could be shortened by gathering it upward to the wooden yard, somewhat like a venetian blind.

Because the wind was contrary much of the time, the ship was often rowed. One such ship became known as the "hundred-handed giant of the Aegean"—a very apt description of fifty men rowing—not at all the mythical monster portrayed by some romantic artists. The ship would have been about wide enough to allow two men to sleep end to end on each rowing bench. With such accommodations, it is no wonder they preferred to go ashore every night to sleep on some soft beach where they could forage for food and build fires. Warships were not intended for good living even though the men that crewed them were sea rovers and adventurers used to rough conditions. Provisions, water in goatskin bags, and weapons were stowed under benches. It must have been a hard life.

The oars were about four meters long and were levered against thole pins (vertical wooden pins that serve as lever points for the oars), being secured there by leather straps so that when the men dropped them to fight or to handle the sail the oars would not slide off and drift away. The steering oars, operated from the short, raised afterdeck, were also partly supported by leather thongs. Perhaps there was a sternpost, against which the steersman could brace himself. Because these ships were so low in the water, there may also have been a low rail along the sides to which some kind of a temporary screen of cloth or leather could be rigged — much as the Norsemen used shields two thousand years later to keep out the wind, the blown spray, and small waves. . . .

Most warships, from earliest times until after the battle of Lepanto, in 1571, were galleys. They were driven by men's muscles, pulling on oars. Although most fighting ships of early times carried masts and sails for long passages at sea, sails were not dependable enough for fighting. Men were much better-disciplined than the wind.

Most of the naval engagements of the ancient world were probably fought within a mile or so of shore. This is because the ships were essentially land-based fighting tools. They were manned by soldiers and commands by generals. In fights between ships, ordinary swords, missiles, and spears were used and the tactics were like those on land. The soldiers slept and ate on shore, drawing the ship up on a sandy beach every night, stern first, ready to shove off in a hurry to do battle. On long cruises, headed for some distant rendezvous with an enemy fleet, they tended to follow the shore lines and stay within sight of land rather than strike off across the sea. When they sailed, they could only run before the wind or with it on the beam, because of the flat-bottomed hull and square sail.

Doubtless, there were numerous times when these early warships had to cross wide passages out of sight of land—either rowing or under sail—and this they did only when necessary and always with trepidation.

When King Nestor and his men returned to Greece from the Trojan War, in about 1200 B.C., he directly crossed the Aegean from Lesbos to Euboea, a distance of a hundred and ten miles, instead of the customary flitting from island to island for nightly camp-outs. At three knots, even on a somewhat zigzag course, this risky voyage took less than two days, but the expedition members were so pleased to reach the new shore safely they made a great sacrifice to Zeus. This episode unwittingly reveals quite a bit about the dangers to warships at sea in the Bronze Age. Since Nestor's courage is undoubted, there must have been a very bad record of ship losses, perhaps caused by the sudden violent winds and poor stability, to have made him so concerned. Possibly he wasn't certain about which direction to take, or he thought the sky would be cloudy and obscure the stars so he could not navigate, or he thought his boats had too little freeboard to survive a storm. Clearly, Nestor and his associates thought their open penteconters (which probably were loaded with booty and souvenirs) had a good chance of sinking as they crossed the deep water headed for home. Perhaps some did.

There are certain difficulties in training a large crew of men to row a ship. Anyone who has watched naval cadets rowing whaleboats, or crewmen from a large passenger liner practice with lifeboats in a quiet harbor, has an inkling of the problem. Those are small craft with six to twelve rowers. Until the crew has had considerable practice, there is a great likelihood of "catching a crab" (the oar not digging deeply enough into the water and suddenly skittering along the surface when the power stroke is carelessly applied) or getting out of synchronization and tangling oars. In larger ships, with hundreds of rowers, it would be difficult to keep all the rowers in good health and a high state of training; there must have been many "crabs," bumped oars, and other foul-ups. Certainly a lot of practice was required to co-ordinate the actions of hundreds of men so that they rowed effectively in unison. The rowers had to learn to start and stop quickly, and to turn the ship in its own length by packing down on one side and pulling ahead on the other. But, in warships, they rowed as though their lives depended on it. Which they did.

War upon the sea in the early days, once it had developed beyond the stage of looting and taking slaves from coastal cities, had as its ultimate objective the control of sea-borne commerce. Piracy was the first step, but control of the trade routes and the establishment of colonies by a formal military machine were vital to expansion. The sea was the most convenient highway of the irregularly shore-lined Mediterranean, and the destruction of the ships of a city-state could cut off its food supplies and its colonies. The need for greater speed and power in sea battles led to the development of several new rowing schemes: several men on each oar, oars of different lengths on one slanted bench, and a second tier of oars mounted on the fighting deck above. The latter type of ship, the bireme, improved the speed without increasing the length or width.

Sometime in the ninth century B.C., the ram was invented. This led almost immediately to the development of the *triere*, or trireme as it is popularly known.

The trireme was a three-banked warship made specifically for fighting with the ram. It was a fast ship because it was slender and yet carried many more rowers than previous ships. This was made possible by the use of an outrigger beam to hold tholepins a bit above and outboard of the upper deck level. This arrangement permitted an entire new bank of rowers to be added without requiring longer oars or widening the hull. With this outrigger beam serving as an oar fulcrum, the oars of the upper rowers could reach out over the two banks of oars below. Now, using a one-man one-oar scheme, it was possible to add thirty-one men on each side (top row only—there were twenty-seven men in each of the other rows) and give the ship an additional ten horsepower of driving force. All oars were the same length, and the men were arranged in rows on half levels so that each bank of oars was at its most effective height. It was also necessary to position the oars so the individual rowers were not exactly one above the other. They were staggered a little so that each man (and each oar) had maximum space. One has to visualize the oar positions and motions in three dimensions for the diagrams to make sense. An additional advantage of increasing the number of rowers in the same length of ship was that this design also increased the number of fighters that could be quickly brought to bear on the enemy. The outrigger beam also squared up the deck shape with a sort of fence that held protective shields.

One limitation on going further with the idea of more oars upward and outward was ship stability—the extra weight high above the slim hull would have made it top-heavy. If there were a rush of armed men to one side to engage the enemy, such a ship would heel sharply and perhaps capsize.

Greek oared ships were carefully constructed and were much admired for their craftsmanship. The wood used for hull planking was mainly oak and poplar, often as much as eight centimeters (three inches) thick, carvel-fitted. This means the planks were joined edge to edge and held there by the mortise-and-tenon system of rectangular cavities with fitted pegs. The planks were also nailed to reinforcing ribs so the structure was secured together in two ways and would not fly apart on ramming or flex and leak after beaching. To make sure that the planks held together, it was customary to tie them together before a battle with several sets of girding cables which went completely around the ship. Before these came into use, many a ramming must have sunk the rammer as well as the intended victim.

The development of the ram reached its peak when the Athenians decided to put emphasis on a ship that would depend mainly on skillful ship handling. The ship itself, instead of the soldiers aboard, became the weapon. If it could be maneuvered to ram and sink an enemy ship, this would save much of the trouble of hand-to-hand fighting and war would be less personal.

There was real significance in the shift of strategy from trying to kill the enemy's men to that of trying to kill his ships. This had much the same kind of effect on naval warfare that the first cannon had much later. No one could ignore the new threat, and all navies began to build triremes.

Triremes were built ruggedly—able to ram or to survive ramming and, after repair, to fight another day. On many occasions, triremes were holed and capsized but remained afloat. The next day, they were towed ashore to be repaired and used again.

A good deal is known about the Greek trireme because, as the leading kind of warship for several hundred years, it was repeatedly described by historians, painted on vases, and sculptured in bas-reliefs. Unfortunately, these pictures are invariably a side view of the bow or stern of the ship and no complete representation has survived. As a result, no one knows exactly how the men were arranged or what a complete trireme looked like. The artists found that if all men and oars were shown there was too much detail, so it was customary to draw many of the oars but only a few men—and those greatly oversized.

We know what the three banks of rowers were named: thranites had the uppermost and most tiring position, zygites were between decks, and thalamites were in the lowest position (with their oars just above the water). We also know the size of Athenian triremes, because the foundations of the boathouses and launchways are still in existence. Visitors to Piraeus today can peer in basement windows on the harbor drive and see remnants of the slipways that once held these ships. Based on their size and configuration, the triremes that used them must have had flat bottoms and could not have been longer than forty meters or wider than seven. The records of the shipyard that built them, carved on stone tablets, were found lining a Piraeus storm sewer a few years ago. They list the exact amount of equipment issued to the ships: size and quantity of oars, anchors, sails, and line.

Although there must have been many varieties and sizes of triremes, most authorities agree that one set of dimensions and number of rowers predominated. The standard trireme of 500 B.C. was about thirty-five meters long, three and a half meters in the beam (five, including the outriggers) with a loaded draft of one meter and about 1.2 meters of freeboard. This meant these ships were very long and slender (fineness of 10:1), which is necessary for speed. In fact, they must have been much like an oversize racing shell, since they were light enough to be launched and dragged ashore by their crews.

The lowest oars were only about half a meter above the water line, so the hole where they penetrated the hull was sealed by a leather bag which could be bound to the oar to keep the water out. These ships had 170 rowers, each pulling an oar about 4.2 meters long. This arrangement, which permitted the use of short, standard-length oars, made the trireme a convenient ship to operate. The idea of standardized oar length for large numbers of ships suggests that somewhere there must have been a substantial production line turning out matched, interchangeable oars.

Each man was responsible for his own equipment: sword, shield, oar, and seat cushion. Sun awnings and spray shields were part of the ship's equipment, intended to keep the men as comfortable as possible.

Nearly every night, the ships were drawn up on some beach and drain plugs pulled to release the bilge water and keep the bottom planks from becoming soggy and rotten. Because the ships were light and slim, there was no way for the men to remain aboard; besides, very small amounts of stores and water were carried. This also meant that when away from their regular bases the crews had to forage for food and find entertainment; presumably, this often meant seizure and rape.

Although triremes were meant to be rowed in battle, each ship had a mast and sail that were used when there was a considerable distance to go and a wind on the stern quarter. If a battle was expected, the bulky mast and sail were left on shore. In fact, it was so much the custom for early warships to leave the sails and masts ashore, that carrying them into battle, even though they were stowed below, was regarded as a sign of cowardice, since it implied the intention to leave the battle early. Mark Antony's decision to take sails along into the great naval battle at Actium, in which he and Cleopatra VII were defeated by Octavian is said to have demoralized his forces and contributed to his losing that battle.

The circumstances of life in the trireme fleet were not at all like most people imagine. First of all, the rowers of ancient Greece were all free men—never slaves—and no whips were used. Stroke beat was kept by a flutist, probably because the high-frequency tootling was easy to hear above the rumble and splash of the oars. Rowers who were not soldiers were well paid, with extra pay for the men who pulled the uppermost, thranite oars, where the work was hardest and the danger greatest.

Triremes were not good sea boats; in fact, they were unusable in heavy weather and a great many more were lost in storms than in battle. They were so susceptible to loss in bad weather that they rarely operated in the winter months.

Historians have noted that for one reason or another pairs of galleys were sometimes lashed together and a single sail was hoisted. On some occasions, this may have been a ruse to make the enemy think he had half as many ships to deal with. However, it seems possible this was intended to improve stability, since each hull would prevent the other from rolling over. In time, this technique may have evolved into the catamaran warships that Professor Casson has postulated.

Examples of Warship Losses in Battles and Storms

Year B.C.	Combatants		Location	Number of Ships Involved	Number of Ships Lost
	Winner	Loser			
535	Phoceans	Carthaginians and Etruscans	Corsica	180	100
480	Greeks	Persians	Salamis	1300	200
419	Syracuse	Athens	Harbor of Syracuse		350
333	Alexander	Tyre	Tyre Harbor	260	45
322	Macedonia	Athens	Amorgos (Sporades)	400	
306	Greeks	Egypt	Salamis, Cyprus		80
260	Rome	Carthage	Mylae	250	50
256	Rome	Carthage	Ecnomus	680	54
255	Rome	Carthage	Cape Hermaeum (storm)	620	284
255	Rome	Carthage	Camorina, Sicily		250
249	Rome	Carthage	Battle at Carthage and storm at Camorina	2 fleets	80
241	Rome	Carthage	Aegates Islands, Sicily	200	50
230	Rome	Illian pirates	Turkish straits	200	90
42	Agrippa	Sextus	Naulochus, Sicily	600	60
31	Octavian	Antony and Cleopatra	Actium, Gulf of Corinth	900	100

Another action that was taken to prevent these long ships from capsizing was to add ballast. Ballast may not always have been used on fighting triremes, but it was certainly used on troop transports and heavier galleys that were not intended to be drawn up on the beach. The ballast was usually in the form of sand or gravel carried in boxes in the bilges that could be removed separately to lighten the ship. Wet-sand ballast was used to keep wine jugs safe and cool as well as improve the ship's stability.

This is significant to the archaeologist. Unballasted wooden ships built for maneuvering and ramming would be "sunk" only in the sense they would fill with water and become unusable. Probably, the hulk would remain awash until it drifted ashore, was towed away, or became waterlogged and sank. But with ballast aboard, in addition to the weight of provisions in jugs, the ship fittings, the arms and armor, missiles for catapults, and souvenirs or booty from the enemy, there was a good chance a warship would go to the bottom immediately, taking these fascinating artifacts with it.

In the fourth century B.C., an arms race began when the city of Syracuse developed *tetreres* ("four-rowed" ships) to beat the Athenian *trieres* (or triremes). Although the changes in ship design came slowly at first, soon every navy in the ancient world was involved in building "fives," "eights," "tens," "thirteens," and so on up to a "forty." It is a marvelously intricate story of shifting naval power and how it was applied through great fleets of rowed ships. Ship weight, power, and stability increased at the expense of speed and convenience. Ramming became less important and instead battles were fought with catapults that flung rocks and arrows. Once again, ships grappled with each other and the rowers engaged in hand-to-hand fighting. Ptolemy II of Egypt eventually built the most powerful fleet in ancient times, which included four "thirteens," fourteen "elevens," thirty "nines," thirty-seven "sevens," and seven "fives." Unfortunately, we do not know what those numbers signify, because the exact meaning of the ending "eres," or "rowed," is lost. Presumably it is some combination of the number of tiers of oars and men on an oar.

Eventually the race subsided. After the battle of Actium, in 31 B.C., Rome ruled the Mediterranean and once again used triremes in its home fleet. In the course of the various struggles for power, especially that between Rome and Carthage, thousands of these ships were sunk. An estimate is that five thousand warships went down in deep water in ancient times. If one can be found, many of the above questions can probably be answered. . . .

Less is known about the merchant ships of the ancient world than about the warships, although there were a great many more of them. They were the slow, solid workhorses of the sea; "round ships," they were called, to distinguish them from the slender fighting craft, which were the "long ships." The fate of nations hung on how well each kind of ship did its job, but the glamorous warships were the better recorded. Information on the merchant ships that carried the trade goods cheaply and slowly from port to port is very sketchy. The appearance of seagoing merchant ships in the sixth century B.C. is known because one unusually fine Greek black-figured bowl was carefully illustrated with two scenes of a pirate ship chasing and preparing to board a merchantman. In the first scene, the unsuspecting trading ship rides high in the water with the sail on its single mast mostly reefed. Beamy and slow compared to the sleek and menacing pirate galley, it is an easy prize, idling along with a single crewman manning the steering oars. The large rectangular opening into the cargo hold takes up most of the deck space, and its high rim rises above the deck level to keep waves sloshing over the deck from reaching the cargo below. The sides of the cargo hatch show a pattern that seems to be lashings that hold down a covering tarpaulin. Aft of the helmsman, on the upcurved sternpost, there is the customary short ladder to be used by men to get off and on a beached or anchored ship. Another ladder-like structure, which runs the length of the ship, was probably used as a gangplank for carrying cargo from ship to shore.

In the second scene, the trader's crew has become aware they are an intended victim; the sail is down, filled with wind, pulling. But the merchantman cannot keep ahead of a pirate craft using both sails and oars. Probably the rest of the trader's crew are below, praying and getting weapons ready. Their life expectancy is short, or at least unhappy, because the pirates will likely make slaves of any who survive the take-over. . . .

Because changes in ship design have traditionally come slowly, this simple hull and sail design remained in use for many centuries. Although no good drawings of the trading ships used for the next five centuries have survived, in the first century A.D. similar vessels are portrayed by Roman artists in paintings on house walls, mosaics at Pompeii, and bas-reliefs in stone. They are still beamy and round, steered with a pair of oars, and have a single, large mainsail supplemented with a smaller sail farther forward. Their after deck was a little higher, the over-all size was often larger, but the appearance and sail-handling methods were about the same.

No doubt, a sailor of 500 B.C. could have stepped aboard a ship built six hundred years later and unhesitatingly sailed it to its next port. He would check out the rigging, noting that the mainsail hung from a yard made of a pair of saplings whose butts were lashed together. The top of the sail would be securely bound to the yard with twine made of esparto grass, and its foot on each side would be bound to lines (the mainsheets) that came back to be secured to chocks within the helmsman's reach. By adjusting the length of the lines, hauling in the lee sheet, and slackening the windward one, a lone sailor could set the sail on a small ship. As the ship came to anchor or if a storm threatened, the mariners aboard would shorten sail, raising it by means of brail lines. The free end of these lines was secured to a transverse bar, also convenient to the steersman; the other end went up over the top of the yard, loosely down in front of the sail, and up behind the sail to be secured to the yard. By shortening these brail lines, the sail could be crumpled upward against the yard.

Steering by means of a pair of nearly vertical steering oars, one on each side of the stern, was the standard method throughout ancient times. These oars were supported in pairs of sockets by leather thongs so that they need only be rotated about their own axes to exert a rudder-like effect. At a convenient height, a short "tiller" bar projected from each oar at right angles so that the helmsman could easily twist the oar in its socket. To steer left (to port), he would push the tiller bar in his right hand ahead and pull back on the one in his left (the bars were always moved in opposite directions to keep the oar blades parallel). This gave a lot of rudder surface and was probably quite convenient. Moreover, it was a good thing to have a second rudder so the ship was not out of control if one oar snapped or the guides holding it in place gave way.

In order to ease the forces acting on the rudder, many early sailing ships carried a small sail forward on a steep bowsprit. This spritsail, or *artemon,* was used to keep the ship from yawing—sliding sidewise and forward down the face of an overtaking wave into a dangerous position. Since these ships sailed well only when running before the wind, the pull of the *artemon* kept the bow ahead of the ship. Probably it was the only sail used during storms, since it would keep the vessel from getting sidewise to the wind and waves and being overwhelmed by a breaking wave. In any case, it made the helmsman's job an easier one.

Another common feature was the boarding ladder, which shows in many of the old drawings of both war and merchant ships. These ladders enabled the men to climb aboard when the ship was on the beach or in the shallows close to it. It was carried at the stern (which is logical, since ships beached their rounded after-ends first) and secured at its midpoint to the upswept sternpost. If a ladder was properly balanced, it could easily be swung down, used, and pushed up out of the way again.

Merchantmen also used long, ladder-like walkways for loading and unloading cargo. Significantly these are not shown on the ships after harbors with vertical stone piers came into use and a ship could tie up alongside and load or unload directly. But, in the days when cargoes were transferred across the beaches at the heads of small bays, the ship was securely moored just off the beach in very shallow water and the ladder was used as a bridge.

Like the warships, merchant vessels were beached for repair during the winter months. The bottoms were scraped to clean off the sea growth and then charred by holding blazing faggots against them to reduce marine-borer attack. The most seriously damaged planks were replaced. Teredos, the wooden hulls' worst enemy, took a heavy toll of ship bottoms that were not sheeted with lead beneath the water line. The lead was usually secured with copper tacks over a sealing fabric that was soaked in pitch or tar. If water became trapped between the lead sheeting and the planking, the wood would rot where it could not be seen, weakening the hull and sometimes causing it to break up in a storm. The results could be as bad as if borers had been there.

Many ancient ships were coated with tar and pitch and painted with colored wax to seal small holes and protect the wood against deterioration. Although the hulls were usually black from the tar, they often had bright-colored eyes and sternposts; red, violet, and gold seem to have been favored for superstructure decoration. Sails of linen or leather were sometimes assembled from multicolored patches or painted with symbols....

The number of ships in use in ancient times that could have sunk along the trade routes is of great interest to the archaeologist. Fred Yallouris, a native of the island of Chios and student of classics, estimated how many ships had been in use in ancient times as follows: "The lifespan of the merchant ship must have been around 40 years. The numbers we have suggest that in the fifth and fourth centuries B.C., well over 30,000 merchant ships of all sizes could have been built. Allowing for a lower building rate in the tenth to sixth centuries B.C., say 45,000, and an increase in the third to first centuries B.C., say 80,000, we arrive at an amazing 155,000 as the approximate number of merchant ships that sailed from 1000 B.C. to the beginning of the Christian era. If we were to extend our period of interest to include all the ships which sailed from the fourth millennium B.C. down to about 500 A.D., and also include warships, then that number could easily reach half a million."

Almost every port had some type of shipbuilding activity, but the larger ports, with greater merchant and naval fleets, dominated ship construction. We know that Tyre, Piraeus, Rhodes, Corinth, Alexandria, and Rome were great shipbuilding centers, but we do not know how many ships they produced. However, there are data on the docking capacity of some ports. Piraeus had, by 331 B.C., 372 docks in its three basins and could accommodate hundreds of ships, as could the harbors at Syracuse, Carthage, Rhodes, Alexandria, and the ports of Rome. The capacities of medium-sized ports such as Chios, Samos, Smyrna, Miletus, Antioch, Sidon, Tyre, Massilia, and Cyrene probably ranged from fifty to a hundred and fifty ships. The hundreds of smaller ports could probably harbor from twenty to fifty vessels.

There must have been close to four hundred ports in the Mediterranean by the end of the fourth century B.C. The average capacity of all these was probably around forty ships. Assuming that an average port was filled to about half capacity every night in the sailing season, we might reckon that from eight to ten thousand merchant ships could have been in use on the Mediterranean and the Black seas throughout the fifth and fourth centuries. The number could well have reached fifteen thousand at the height of Rome's commercial activities in the second and first centuries. . . .

Navigation must have been a serious problem for the early mariners. Although the development of navigational know-how cannot be traced precisely, we know that by the end of the fifth century B.C. most of the techniques that sailors would use for the next two thousand years were known. Of the later tools, only the magnetic compass was missing. Mainly, the early ships must have navigated by dead reckoning combined with the captain's memory.

Dead reckoning simply means that the skipper keeps track of the ship's course, its speed, and the elapsed time. From these data, he calculates how far the ship has gone and in which direction. For old sailing ships, which followed the wind and did not have a compass, a clock, or a good chart, the answer must have been, at best, a rough approximation. But perhaps because Mediterranean sailing distances are not great, the ancient mariners found their way fairly well. After years of apprenticeship, a sailor would learn the routes and how best to sail each leg of a voyage in each season. He would judge the ship's speed by tossing chips of wood overside and set its direction relative to the sun or stars if he could see them.

The knowledge of how and where to sail through the complex islands of the Aegean or across the Mediterranean to another country was largely kept in the captain's head. This special knowledge was his job security, and probably he did not want it written down so that someone else could replace him. On voyages of exploration, when new trading partners for valuable commodities were being located, the courses and distances were carefully guarded strategic secrets. At times, Phoenician vessels were followed by the ships of other countries eager to find where they traded for rare products. It is said that on more than one occasion Phoenician captains deliberately ran their ships through very dangerous waters and sometimes wrecked them in order to wreck the following ship or at least throw it off the track. Their country reimbursed them for the loss when they finally made it home.

By the fourth century B.C., a geographer named Scylax the Younger wrote a book (the Periplus), which gave the first published sailing directions for the Mediterranean. It contained the names of ports, rivers, and headlands, directions and distances from point to point, where to get water, and other useful information. Any charts of that time that may have existed were probably lost in the fires at the library of Alexandria in 47 B.C. and A.D. 640, or disintegrated over the ages.

Although there is virtually nothing in ancient literature that can tell us how many ships were lost at sea, there is no doubt that shipwrecks were a common phenomenon in antiquity. The Romans developed a code of maritime laws that eventually grew into a compendium called the Rhodian sea laws. It regarded pirates, fire, and wreck as the three normal maritime dangers, and had laws concerning all three. Three kinds of pirates were described: ". . . those who attack the merchantmen in open sea or lurk for them in harbors. Secondly there are the land-robbers, who cut a ship's cables or steal its anchors, or snap up a merchant or passenger or sailor who happens to go on land. Thirdly, there are the wreckers, and these do not merely plunder ships which have been driven ashore, but sometimes lure them to destruction by displaying false lights."

The danger of fire on board was always present. Although there is no way of ascertaining how many ships were lost in this way, it is evident from the strict laws regarding fires on board ship that loss of ship by fire was quite common.

Shipwreck was the usual way to lose a ship, however, and the sea laws discuss running aground, breaking up on the rocks, collision with other ships, seams opening up, and foundering in open water. A few excerpts from the sea laws will be of interest.

No. 28: "If a ship is hindered in the loading by a merchant or partner, and the time fixed for loading passes, and it happens the ship is lost by reason of piracy or fire or wreck, let him who caused the hindrance make good the damage."

No. 26: "If a ship in sail runs against another ship which is lying at anchor or has slackened sail, and it is day, all the damage shall be charged to the captain and those who are on board. Moreover let the cargo too come into contribution. If this happens at night, let the man who slackened sail light a fire. If he has no fire, let him shout. If he neglects to do this and a disaster takes place, he has himself to thank for it, if the evidence goes to this. . . ."

No. 45: "If in the open sea a ship is overset or destroyed, let him who brings anything from it safe to land receive instead of reward, the fifth part of that which he saves."

The Condition of Slaves in Ancient Greek Society

WILLIAM LINN WESTERMANN

The ancient society of the Mediterranean was a slave society. In the society of classical Greece, even citizens of quite modest income or land holdings had a few slaves, and nearly all the personal servants, of which there were very many by modern standards, even by nineteenth century standards, were slaves. In the fourth century B.C., Demosthenes, the great Athenian orator, noted that even people whose income barely put them into the bracket that paid the war tax owned at least one slave, usually a female servant. One of the largest subjects of Roman law, a system of jurisprudence that rivals modern systems in both scope and sophistication, was the law of slavery. The Roman attitude toward slavery is indicated by the biographer of St. Martin of Tours (†A.D. 396), who described Martin as leading a very ascetic life; he had only one slave orderly.

In Athens of the fifth and fourth centuries B.C., where the ideal of human freedom found its first and most lasting expression, slaves may have numbered as many as 80–100,000. This is, of course, an estimate, and it rests on little hard evidence, but even the most conservative of estimates would make the number 20,000, about one for each citizen of the *polis*.

In fact, the citizens of Athens, those who had the leisure to devote their time to the affairs of the state, were supported by the work of slaves. The wealth of the classical city-states was based in land, and the great landowners, who were also the leading citizens, farmed their properties with slaves. In fact, one historian, while recognizing that most agricultural work was done by free men, has argued that slave labor was dominant in Greek agriculture because the majority of crops produced for the market came from the large estates on which slaves did the work.

But slavery was not limited to agriculture or to the mines, another source of wealth in Greek society. Nearly every household had one or more slaves—the prefect of Rome under Nero (A.D. 54–68) is recorded to have had 400—who performed a great many tasks that we would find surprising. There were few independent institutions for carrying out functions that we now consider public or quasi-public, like education. Consequently, household slaves were tutors for children, secretaries, treasurers, and managers of their masters' businesses. One of the striking features of Greek and Roman society was that, aside from politics, there were no professions or jobs reserved for free men or for slaves. Virtually every craft and job had in it persons of both statuses. This does not, however, mean many slaves were pleased with their lots. Runaway slaves were a constant problem in the Greek world, and the 20,000 slaves said to have escaped from Athens in the last decade of the Peloponnesian war took with them skills essential to the city's economy.

Slaves were foreigners—in fact, the Greeks often referred to slaves as barbarians, their standard word for non-Greeks. It was assumed that people, particularly women, captured in war would be taken home as slaves, and some of the most prized slaves were captured in wars fought by the Greeks. But most slaves came through the slave market and, like the African slaves much later, were captured to be sold into slavery, not taken prisoner in a war. The slaves who worked the mines and the great estates seem to have come from this extensive trade and were not viewed in the same way as those who served as bankers and teachers. In this article, William Linn Westermann describes the nature of slavery in the Greek world, attempting to show the variety of functions performed by slaves and the course of the "careers" of slaves.

Of what type was the Greek institution of slavery? What were the characteristics peculiar to it which induced Alfred Zimmern, many years ago, to write an article which posed this question as its title: "Was Greek Civilization Based on Slave Labor?" Zimmern deserves great credit for having raised the problem in this new form as to how slavery presented itself to the inhabitants of the Greek city-states of the Mediterranean area. His argument is that Greek civilization did not display those conditions "which are the natural result of a system of slave labour." The specific conditions which underlie slavery, or develop from it, as he gives them, are taken directly from J. E. Cairnes's book upon "Slave Power." It must be understood that Cairnes restricts slavery as an economic institution to one form, one structure, with unvarying characteristics and a fixed set of requirements necessary for its continuation. This he did despite the fact that he knew, and specifically asserted, that ancient slavery is not to be compared with modern Negro slavery, which was the especial field of his observations.

Out of his observations of American Negro slavery as social and economic organism Cairnes abstracted a list of tendencies which, he claimed, were typical of slave societies. The slave system of any locality is, however, invariably an inextricable part of, and an expression of, that culture within which it exists. In its own degree it helps to determine the cultural coloration of its time and place; but to a far greater extent it tends to reflect the general features of the total culture. The differences which the slave institution may develop in any two contemporary and neighboring slave states may be so great that, as systems, they are morphologically incomparable and their social impacts and results completely different. In

From William Linn Westermann, "Slavery and the Elements of Freedom in Ancient Greece," *Quarterly Bulletin of the Polish Institute of the Arts and Sciences in America*, January 1943, pp. 1–16.

antiquity, for example, the differences between contemporary forms of enslavement appear conspicuously in the slave situations as known to us at Athens in its "classical" period of the fifth and fourth centuries B.C. and in the Cretan town of Gortyn at the same time.

Having taken the "typical" conditions set up by Cairnes as requirements in a true slave state, and not finding these in the Greek world, Zimmern concluded that Greek society was not a slave society. Yet there is no doubt in his mind that the Greeks kept slaves. He attempts to get himself out of this contradiction by a process of re-defining enslavement under two forms, chattel slavery and apprentice slavery. The chattel slave he regards as a possession, something owned, which itself cannot own. As soon as a slave is permitted to own property or make a contract, says Zimmern, he is no longer a chattel. He becomes a human being; and as such he has escaped from bondage.

There has seldom been in history, I should say, any slave-holding community in which the theoretical slave—that is, a thing totally devoid of legal personality and without possessions of his own—has really existed in the actual practise of that community. Only in the confinement of prisons can men be totally deprived of all their freedoms, and hence totally enslaved. This inability to coerce human beings into a situation of total slave subjection produces a fundamental contradiction inherent in the very structure of the institution of slavery. It was this inescapable contradiction which compelled Aristotle to acknowledge that a dichotomy existed between the freedom of man in nature and the enslavement of man in law.

Zimmern is to be credited with calling attention to the fact that the slaves of the Greeks lived close to the border of that wide space which exists between slavery and freedom. His phrase "apprentice slavery" is unfortunately chosen. The idea probably came to him from his observation of the Abolition Act as applied in the British colonies in the West Indies beginning August 1, 1834. This provided for an actual change of status of the negro slaves of the West Indies from slavery into apprenticeship and out of apprenticeship into the status of free men. By coining the phrase "apprentice slavery" Zimmern provided himself with an escape from the dilemma of a non-slave society which kept slaves; but the avenue of escape leads the reader into a state of mental confusion where two totally incompatible things are merged. Apprenticeship is a method of teaching some manual dexterity or mental skill by the age old process of imitation, instruction and directed practise. Apprentice status is always contractual, whether by an indenture or verbal agreement. Slavery is a status in which the enslaved can make no contract for himself.

The dominant form of Greek city-state slavery was non-praedial, meaning that it was not agricultural slavery either of the plantation or of the ranch type. Its foremost characteristic was its extensive use in the handicrafts. The practical results of this fact were simple ones. The skilled workmen in the industrial city-states, because of the type of the urban residences of the time, lived apart from their masters. This is a matter of deduction from archaeological observations. There are, it is true, but few Greek city-states of the fifth or fourth centuries which have been preserved for excavation. In the best example of such cities known to us the houses, even those of the well-to-do town residents, furnished rooms for "no more than three slaves—household servants." No example of slave barracks has, to my knowledge, been found in any of the older Greek cities so far excavated; and there is no mention known to me in Greek literature of any barracks for those slaves who were held in private ownership. The Greek phrase applied to these workers who lived away from their masters was χωρὶζ οἰκοῦντεζ [those living apart]. This is to be understood in its simple and most literal meaning. They "lived apart" from their owners, that is to say, in other residences.

Another descriptive phrase applied to these workmen was μισθοψοροῦντα σώματα, "pay-bringers" if one is to be literal. Living where they could these were the fellows who frequented the Anakeion, the temple of the Dioscuri on the north side of the Acropolis, as their special hangout. The degree of supervision and control to which these unfree workmen would be submitted would vary with the individual slave owner. Since these "pay earners" were incapable of letting out their own services under a legally binding contract, this must always have been done by the owner. There is some reason to believe, however, that the degree of freedom granted the unfree "pay-earners" in the search for work and in their conduct of their jobs was very large.

Highly instructive for the kind of life followed by these slaves is a single brief paragraph about an Athenian politician named Timarchus. It is his slaves which interest us, not his political or personal morality, both of which have been grievously befouled by the orator Aeschines. Timarchus inherited, along with a house south of the Acropolis and a plot of land at Alopeke, eleven or twelve slaves. Nine or ten of these were "leather cutters." This may mean that all of them were shoe makers. At any rate, Timarchus leased their craft skill to a single shop owner who paid him three obols per day for their use as a group. Each of these craftsmen slaves brought to Timarchus a return of two obols per day out of their wages. The rest of what they earned was their own.

Two more highly specialized workers belonging to Timarchus remain to be considered. One of these was a woman slave "skilled in working Amorgos cloth," who carried into the market the fine products of her loom. It is not possible to determine who furnished this skilled craft worker with her raw materials. Probably she bought the goods herself. Certainly she wove the cloths and sold them in the market. The chances are that she sold them to a local dealer, not to the ultimate consumers.

This is the best deduction from the phrase, "she carried them into the market." The second of these two slaves was a male, an embroiderer. Nothing is said about his work.

This entire group of "pay bringers" has been made to live and move before our minds by a group of shattered inscriptions long known and much disputed as to some of their meanings. These seem to present lists recording the offerings of silver bowls dedicated to the god in accordance with a law which was passed at Athens, apparently before the death of Lycurgus in 323 B.C. Three classes of Attic residents appear in these lists. The slaves are distinguished by having no father's name given. They are recorded as living in a certain town or deme. The second class is that of the metics, or resident aliens. Their distinguishing mark in these lists is that they invariably are said to be from a certain deme, "from Ceramicus" or "living in Ciriadae," which, again, indicates the actual location of their domiciles. Sometimes their patronymics are given, sometimes not. The third class comprises the Athenian citizens, always distinguishable by their deme registration. This would, in some cases, also indicate their places of residence, but not always, because the Athenian citizen inherited his deme connection and retained it throughout his life no matter where his residence might be. For my purpose of proving cases where slaves lived elsewhere than their owners, the citizen slave owners cannot be decisive. For this reason the cases of metic slave holders alone are used. The very fact that the demal residence of these slaves is recorded is, in itself, proof that they usually lived elsewhere than their masters. Otherwise the master's residence would suffice for both master and slave. The following examples will be enough to prove the point:

| (I G II, 2 1) | Slave | | Metic Owner | |
	Name	Residence	Name	Residence
1553, 18–20	Plinna	Piraeus	Astynomus	Oe
1567, 15–6	Lysias	Piraeus	Hegemon	Ceramicus
1569, 3–7	Mania	Collytus	Cerycides / Aristocles	A Theban Cydathene
1570, 85–6	Olympis	Melite	——emus	Collytus
1576, 40–3	Eutychus	Alopeke	Soterides	Ciriadae

A papyrus recently published, may here be quoted because it throws a beam of light upon the high degree of actual freedom of movement enjoyed by these slaves who lived where they desired and paid in a quantum of their earnings to their masters. It comes from Egypt and from the first century A.D. Nevertheless it is, in my judgment, fairly representative of the liberties accorded to the "pay-bringers" of Athens in the fifth and fourth centuries B.C.

A young man named Nilus writes, presumably from Alexandria, to his father who lived up the river at Oxyrhynchus. At the time of writing he was hearing lectures and studying with tutors, with whom he was not satisfied. It is the method of financing his education which is so striking. He claims that he has become despondent to the point where his health has been affected; and he states the reason, somewhat cryptically. People who do not bring in any money, (he says) and do not do anything to correct that fact, ought not to mix in his affairs. Then he becomes specific: "For earlier, Heracles—may the wretch die wretchedly—was useful, bringing in some obols day by day; but now when he was imprisoned by Isidorus, as he deserved to be, he has fled and gone up the river, as I believe, to you. Understand that he is a person who will not ever hesitate to intrigue against you. For he was not ashamed to spread reports joyfully in the city about the matter in the theater and to chatter lies such as a prosecutor in court would not tell, and that too when he suffered nothing that he deserved, but when he was released did everything like a free man. Nevertheless, if you do not send him (back) you will be able to turn him over to a carpenter, perhaps. For I hear that a young man makes two drachmas a day. Or bind him to some other work at which he will earn more money, so that his pay, when collected, may be sent to us from time to time. For you know that Diogas, too, is learning his letters."

The man Heracles certainly was a slave and a typical "pay-earner." Obviously carpentry was a trade at which he had some proficiency and earning power. He had been sent away with two lads, and his earnings above his own expenses were assigned to them as a part of their support during their period of study.

Two peculiarities of Greek city-state slavery distinguish it, by the looseness of its structure, from any other system of bondage known to me. The first is displayed for us most clearly in its practise at Athens. It is the custom of purchase by the city-state of slaves who were employed in its bureaucratic services. This was, in itself, not unusual in antiquity. The Romans used *servi publici*, both in imperial and in municipal services, upon a wide scale. But where else than in Greece will one find a purchased group of public slaves used as a police force, armed, and with powers of arresting the free? In the attempt to conceive a Negro police force in our southern states before slavery was abolished one may find a measuring rod for the immense disparities which may exist between one form of slavery and another. The second peculiarity is the existence of benefit clubs called *eranoi*, a social institution peculiar to the Greeks alone in antiquity, although it followed them in their emigrations into other lands. One of these types of club advanced money to slaves which they, in turn, used for the purchase of their freedom. This practise was already developed in Attica in the fourth century B.C. In the lists of the silver bowl dedications by emancipated slaves which were cited above, no less than fourteen examples of such loans appear. Since the manumissions of the freedmen or freedwomen of these documents remained subject to voidance through legal process so long as the debt to the loaning group was not repaid, these *eranoi*, as clubs, seem more analogous to temporary loan associations than to any other organization that occurs to me.

In the case for which Demosthenes wrote the prosecuting speech against the morally reprehensible, but charming, slave prostitute, Neaera, the girl had been bought out of a bordello in Corinth by two young men. When they wished to marry they did not want her about in some bawdy house in the town. They proposed that she buy her freedom and leave the city. Neaera, thereupon, collected contributions from some of her lovers, "bringing together an *eranos* for her freedom." The head of her benefit club was an Athenian named Phrynion who took the money already collected and made up the remainder required for the manumission price.

Let us place beside the literary evidence which I have already cited two cases attested by the Athenian silver bowl dedications of the late fourth century. The astonishing ease of manumission for industrial workers will thereby become even more clear.

"Nicias, dealer in frankincense, dwelling in Piraeus, having defeated Philocrates the Eleusinian, son of Epicrates, and an association of contributors (the loan group) headed by Theophrastus, son of Bathylus, of the deme of Cholargus, (has dedicated) a bowl worth 100 drachmas."

Nicias was the slave. He had run a retail incense shop as a "pay-bringing" slave and no doubt, continued in that business after he became a freedman. Eventually, we may surmise, he paid off his debt to the *eranos* group of Theophrastus and Company.

Again: "Bion, gem engraver, living in Melite (deme), having defeated Chaerippus, son of Chaeredemus of (the deme) Halae, and an association of contributors headed by Chaerippus of Halae, (has dedicated) a bowl worth 100 drachmas."

In this case the owner of the skilled gem worker, Bion, had himself formed the manumission loan group. Presumably he was its largest contributor since it bears his name.

What sort of slavery is this? What are its characteristics? Western scholars bring with them fixations upon the subject which derive from Negro slavery. In seeking answers to these questions, therefore, we must first discard all of the paraphernalia of modern slavery and all of the cannelized habits of thought upon slavery which we moderns carry about with us. What did the Greeks think of the slave system with which they were familiar? If we can ascertain that, we can, at least, try to see the slave structure as it appeared to them and think about it as they would think.

To the Greeks slavery was one of many forms of bondage and not, necessarily, the worst of these. Isocrates said that the Spartans enslaved the souls of their Perioeci no less than they enslaved those of their slaves, (meaning the Helots). Aristotle speaks more exactly to our purpose, which is to determine the rigidities and the flexibilities of the Greek idea of slavery. These, if we can isolate and examine them, should reflect the flexibilities and rigidities of the system which gave birth to their idea of it. Aristotle says: "The (free) workman in the meaner handicrafts has a kind of limited slavery." His point is that the slave may, by association with his master, partake of his quality of excellence, his *areté*. The free workman, who has no such association of dependence, is in this respect worse off, in his limited slavery, than the full slave.

However we may define the word "slave," slavery is a status which carries with it a series of limitations upon the options or choices, permitted to the enslaved person. This is exactly the way in which the Greeks envisaged slavery. In the Delphic inscriptions recording slave manumissions which are to be found in volume II of Collitz-Baunack, *Sammlung der griechischen Dialekt-Inschriften* [Collection of Greek Dialect Inscriptions], four liberties of the person are constantly reiterated as comprising the substance of the freedom which the present freedman had not enjoyed before his emancipation. These are highly significant.

1. He is to be his own representative, his own master, in all legal matters, without need of intervention of a second party. This is the legal expression of freedom.

2. He is not subject to seizure as property. Said otherwise: No one dares lay a hand upon him.

3. He may do what he desires to do.

4. He may go where he desires to go. Or, in a variant form, he may live where he desires to live.

These are the four elements of liberty of the individual which to the Greek mind distinguished the non-slave from the enslaved. Reversing this, as one may look at a transparency in a window from the back as well as from the front, the major personal restrictions which determine full slave status are these:

1. In all legal actions the slave must be represented by his master or by some other person legally empowered by the owner.

2. He is subject to having hand laid upon him by anybody. That is, he is subject to seizure and arrest (the *manus injectio* of the Latin). This would apply, with particular emphasis to fugitive slaves.

3. He cannot do what he wishes, but must do what his master orders. This means that freedom of choosing his activities is denied to him.

4. He cannot go to those persons or places to which he may wish to go, live in the domicile in which he desires to live, or determine his *polis* residence and affiliation.

These four major freedoms of men found their best expression for antiquity in the formulas devised and stated by the astute priests of the Delphian Apollo in the terms of the manumission by fictitious sale to the god whom they served. These may be briefly summarized in this form: To be one's own master ($\kappa\upsilon\rho\iota\epsilon\acute{\upsilon}\omega\nu$). To be protected against seizure (except by due process of law). To have freedom of action. To have freedom of movement. In the Delphic manumission documents which I have checked, numbering over 750, the Greek verb used in expressing two of these freedoms, namely those of action and of mobility, is $\dot{\epsilon}\theta\acute{\epsilon}\lambda\epsilon\iota\nu$ [to be able] never $\beta o\acute{\upsilon}\lambda\epsilon\sigma\theta\alpha\iota$ [to wish]. The new freedoms are the abilities to fulfill emotional desires, those things which one's heart prompts one to do. This is the essential meaning of $\epsilon\theta\acute{\epsilon}\lambda\epsilon\iota\nu$ whereas $\beta o\acute{\upsilon}\lambda\epsilon\sigma\theta\alpha\iota$ would invoke the rational elements of planning and of provision for carrying out that plan. $o\dot{\upsilon}\kappa\ \dot{\epsilon}\theta\acute{\epsilon}\lambda\epsilon\iota\nu$ denotes a longing to do something without the right or the will power to accomplish it. What the slave does is, therefore, done unwillingly ($\ddot{\alpha}\kappa\omega\nu$). What the free man does he does of his own volition ($\ddot{\epsilon}\kappa\omega\nu$).

As displayed in the institution of the slave police at Athens, in the *choris oikountes*, the slave craftsmen of the industrial towns who lived their lives apart from their owners, and in the accepted formulae of the Delphic manumissions, slavery was not separated from freedom by a sharp dividing line. This is the essential of the freedman status, of the condition of the $\dot{\epsilon}\zeta\epsilon\lambda\epsilon\acute{\upsilon}\theta\epsilon\rho o\zeta$ in the Greek, of the *libertus* in Latin legal terminology. It is well known, obvious and generally accepted by scholars. What has *not* been sufficiently noted is that, to the Greek mind, freedom was not a unit but something divisible. They broke it down into four common denominators: its legal recognition; the unassailable quality which it granted to the manumitted; the right of choice of action, or activity; the right to move where one wished. It is important to note that freedman status was not only divisible in itself. Each of the three remaining freedoms, once the legal status was fixed, could be broken into, or impinged upon. A freedman might be in possession of any one, or any two, of the three elements other than legal recognition which were the necessary components of complete freedom. He might be possessed of only a part of any one of these three elements. Any one of these three might be restricted in its relation to himself. But if he was a freedman at all, the restrictions imposed must be legalized, either by a law of the city-state or by a legally recognized contract.

This statement is susceptible of definite proof, by analysis of some 170 Delphic manumission documents containing clauses by virtue of which the emancipated slave was still subject, legally, to certain bondage restrictions. These restrictions were imposed upon his freedom for a fixed term of years or for a flexible period often dependent upon the life expectancy of the manumittor. Their result was to make illusory in some degree a liberty which was unquestionably and legally granted. These are the manumissions with bondage arrangements termed *paramone* by the Greeks. Recognition of the divisibility of freedom settles for me a long controversy as to whether the paramonist, the freedman under bondage limitations, was still a slave or a free man during the term of his bonded services. Several of the Romanistic legalists have decided that the freedman obligated to *paramone* services was actually of slave status. The *paramone* clauses of the manumission document, under this view, introduced conditions which suspended the grant of freedom. This is wrong. By the manumittor's sale to the god and by the act of the slave in entrusting this sale to the god the slave became free. The error arose through the fact that the four elements of freedom were not understood. The slave became *legally* free by the act of sale to the god. Of the other three elements of freedom (freedom from attack or summary arrest, freedom of action, and freedom of movement) the ex-slave had, in these cases, only partial control. Hence his *eleutheria* must again be asserted as becoming operative at the end of the term of his obligatory services. Often this is stated with specific enumeration of all the four elements of personal liberty. This I can only assert here, after a rather exhaustive survey of the material involved. Its proof must await more detailed study and another opportunity for its presentation.

By isolating these four freedoms I have found a way, I believe, which will lead to a deeper understanding of the structure of the slave system of the Greek society of which this slave structure was a necessary and accepted part. Theirs was a society in which a man could be part free and part slave, ἡμίδουλος. Aristotle, in a passage which has been unnecessarily questioned and corrected, tells us that Clisthenes after the casting out of the tyrants "enrolled in the tribes many foreigners and slave metics." Now the χωρὶς οἰκοῦντες [those living apart] of the Greek industrial towns became clear to me. Legally they were slaves, of course; but *de facto* only partly δοῦλοι because they lived where they wished. The fourth freedom was already theirs. In the letter from Oxyrhynchus to his father the student Nilus used a significant phrase about the slave who was his "paybringer": ὡζ ἐλεύθεροζ πάντα ποιῶν. "He did everything like a free person." This pay-earning slave was free, in one at least, of the four elements which constituted enslavement, probably in two of them.

Certainly he had some degree of choice as to the nature of his work. Presumably he could live where he wished in the city in which he happened to be employed. . . .

This has been an attempt to approach slavery in Greek society by way of the slave ideology of the Greeks themselves as this is disclosed in the formulas originated and repeated through centuries by the powerful priesthood of Apollo at Delphi. Its chief results may be stated as follows:

Greek society was, of course, a slave society. Its slavery was of a type unfamiliar to Europeans and Americans of the last two centuries. It had no color line. (Therefore, *pace Aristoteles*, it had no single and clearly defined slave race or slave caste.) The person enslaved might well be one-quarter free, or three-quarters free, depending upon the personal inviolability and the options of activity and movement which might actually be granted him. Herein lies the explanation of the fact that the Greeks could conceive of "debtor slaves, who are free" and "free slaves of the unprivileged classes," σώματα λαικὰ ἐλεύθερα. In the metic class of the city-states the manumitted slave found a group into which, as freedman, he merged easily, without effort on his part or opposition from the group which he entered. There was an astonishing fluidity of status in both directions, from slavery to freedom as from freedom to slavery. This it is which, in large measure, explains the absence of slave revolts in the Greek classical period. Why should an enslaved person revolt if thereby he merely gains that which he might so easily obtain by the simple process of borrowing money for his emancipation and repaying that money?

As labor, slave workmen had a marked advantage over free labor in that the slave craftsmen were usually exempt from all levies for military service; and they were not distracted from their occupations by the many civic duties which engrossed the time of the citizens. Economic competition between the slave and the free laborer seems to have been a negligible problem, at least at Athens where we know Greek slavery best. This may be explained, perhaps, by the fact that the economic organization of the Greek world was, on the whole, an expanding one in the fifth and fourth centuries. The lack of complaints about the condition of the slaves in the fifth and fourth centuries is the best proof of a condition of equilibrium between contentment and discontent attained among them. Otherwise there would have been slave revolts such as did occur under the more maleficent latifundian system of Sicily and Italy in the first two centuries B.C. In the ancient situation slave labor never became exclusive in the labor market, nor even its dominant feature, except upon the *latifundia* of Sicily and Italy. Ancient society does not appear to me to have been particularly self-conscious about its slaves. Certainly it was never hysterical, not even emotionally excited about the slave institution. I fail to find any background of fear of slavery in its literature or in its life. No moral horror of the institution appears such as developed in the eighteenth and nineteenth centuries in the west. In this sense ancient society did not develop a social slave mentality. There is no equivalent in ancient Greek literature for the many speeches and pamphlets written by modern slave owners upon the economic validity of the slave institution.

Upon the basis of its particular type of slavery ancient society attained a notably high level of culture. The decline of this culture was roughly contemporary with the displacement of a free-and-slave labor system by an enforced and immobile working class, the colonate upon the land and compulsory labor under the guild system in the handicrafts. We come back to the problem of mobility, the fourth of the four freedoms of the Greek manumissions. *Libertas—nihil aliud est quam absentia impedimentorum motus,* [Liberty is nothing other than the absence of impediments to movement] said Hobbes. When by legal enactments a society imposes personal immobility upon great masses of men, then you have, indeed, created a system more deadly in its rigidity than the loose structure of Greek slavery ever was.

Sanitation and Safety in the Greek City

A. H. M. JONES

Cities were the focal points of Greek civilization, and volumes have been written about them. The Greeks themselves analyzed the different forms of government found among the cities; the economic life, populations, and culture of the cities have also been studied. This selection examines an aspect of Greek city life rarely treated and hard to get information about—the public services. A. H. M. Jones provides us with a glimpse of the ways the Greeks dealt with the familiar and mundane problems of urban life.

First, however, something should be said about the cities. Jones focuses less on the ancient Greek city-states and their colonies in the classical period than on the cities founded by Alexander the Great during the fourth century B.C. The Greeks had always extended their control over new territories by founding cities—a practice Alexander continued in the lands he conquered. But whereas the urban colonies of the eighth and seventh centuries B.C. had been set up primarily for commercial purposes, Alexander seems to have had a different aim. He attempted to ensure a mixture of Greeks and natives in the populations of his cities. Many historians think that he hoped to effect an assimilation of the newly conquered peoples into Greek culture. His cities continued to be Greek—propagators of Greek culture—throughout the Roman and Byzantine periods. Jones draws his material from these communities, in which he found a great continuity.

The public services which the cities provided for their inhabitants naturally varied both in scope and in scale according to their size and wealth. Ephesus and Smyrna, Nicomedia and Nicaea, Tarsus, Antioch, and Alexandria could offer to their citizens amenities and luxuries which the average large town, the capital of a province or of a judicial circuit, could not afford. These again lived on a grander scale than ordinary provincial cities, and among these last there were many gradations, from substantial towns, which took a pride in their games and public buildings, to humble rural communes, which, though officially dignified with the name of city, lacked the barest essentials of civic life—municipal offices, a

From A. H. M. Jones, *The Greek City* (Oxford: The Clarendon Press, 1940), pp. 211–19.

gymnasium, a theatre, a marketplace, and a public water-supply, to quote Pausanias' list. But despite these wide contrasts in achievement, the ideal to which all cities aspired was monotonously uniform. The spread of Hellenism through the near East was to a large extent the product of imitation, and the place of any city in the scale of civilization was gauged by its success in reproducing the culture of the universally acknowledged archetype, the cities of the Aegean basin. Architecture, athletics, music, drama, and education were cosmopolitan; and from Macedonia and Thrace through Asia Minor and Syria to Egypt the cities, one and all according to their varying resources, erected the same type of buildings, celebrated musical and gymnastic games with identical programmes, and provided for their citizens the same opportunities for physical and intellectual culture.

What is today considered the most elementary duty of any government, the maintenance of law and order, seems, from the absence of reference to it, to have been almost ignored by the Hellenistic cities. There was indeed in Ptolemaic Alexandria a commander of the night watch, but he was probably a royal officer; and in general police functions in cities governed by kings seem to have been fulfilled by their commandants. The only civic police on record in the Hellenistic age are the frontier guards of Miletus and Heraclea, one of whose duties it was to arrest runaway slaves. Under the principate many more civic police officers are recorded. These were of several types. Commanders of the night watch, perhaps based on the Alexandrian model, are found in the second century in several cities of Asia, and regularly in the Egyptian metropoleis of the third century. They commanded a corps of night watchmen, who in Oxyrhynchus, a modest town, numbered fifty or sixty: we possess a list of the posts to which they were assigned, seven to the principal temple, the Thoereum, six to the Serapeum, three to the theatre, two to the gymnasium, one to the Iseum, and the remainder one to each street. The watchmen were humble citizens, cobblers, potters, fullers, and the like, and were conscripted for the service, but apparently paid for their trouble.

Frontier guards are in the Roman period commonly found in Asia Minor. The magistrates in charge of this force were styled guards, and their men, the frontier guards, who were naturally mounted, were drawn from the sons of the gentry; at Apollonia of Caria a party of ten, with their cadet officer and the guard himself, were attended by six slaves, who served as grooms. The service was perhaps modelled on the Athenian ephebate, in which cadets in their second year of training garrisoned the frontier forts. It was their duty to tour the outlying villages of the city territory; a decree of the Phrygian Hierapolis forbids them to demand hospitality from the villagers over and above lodging, wood, and chaff, and reproves them for extorting "crowns" from the village headmen. Another inscription, probably also of Hierapolis, bears more directly on their duties: they are instructed to deal with shepherds who graze their flocks in other people's vineyards.

Neither of these forces was capable of dealing with serious crime; to suppress this was the duty of the wardens of the peace. This magistracy is found from the beginning of the second century throughout the Roman East, and was probably created on the order of the Roman government, which controlled appointments to it; irenarchs were not directly elected, but nominated by the provincial governor from a list submitted by the city. They commanded a force of mounted constables, and their principal activity seems to have been to hunt down brigands: they acted as examining magistrates, but had no authority to inflict punishment, sending up the delinquents whom they captured to the governor, with a *dossier* of the evidence against them. Their sphere of operations was the country-side. At Smyrna the irenarch pursued Polycarp, when he fled from justice into the country, whereas in a later persecution Pionius, who stayed in town, was arrested by another officer, the commander of the cavalry. This office, originally military, survived under the principate in a number of Asiatic cities, where no doubt, as at Smyrna, it sank to be the captaincy of the city police: the hipparch was also supported by mounted constables. Every city had its jail, where prisoners were confined pending their trial; the warders were normally public slaves.

What are today regarded as the municipal services *par excellence* are not very frequently mentioned in antiquity. They were in the larger cities at any rate entrusted to a special board, the controllers of the town, and what we know of them is largely derived from the Pergamene law defining the duties of this office: as this law, framed by one of the Attalid kings, was inscribed under the principate, it may be inferred that Hellenistic and Roman practice was uniform in this field. The first duty of the *astynomi* was the care of roads and bridges, both in the city itself and in its territory. They had to prevent encroachments on the public highway; the Pergamene law lays down minimum widths for country roads, thirty feet for a main road, twelve feet for a by-road. They had to remove obstructions; shopkeepers were allowed to display their wares outside their shops, but not in such a manner as to block the traffic. They had to prevent rubbish being tipped into the streets, and were themselves responsible for having them scavenged. They had finally to see to the maintenance of the surface. According to the legal authorities, landowners and householders were responsible in both country and town for the paving of the roads on which their property fronted, and the *astynomi* had to enforce this obligation and only as a last resort to give out the work to contract, claiming the expense, plus a fine, from the delinquents. It is difficult to believe, however, that the magnificent and unform paving which we see today in the principal streets of excavated cities was maintained by this system, and it seems likely that householders regularly commuted their obligations for a cash payment, and that the city undertook the work; we know that cities maintained gangs of public slaves for street paving.

The cities were very proud of their streets and spent enormous sums on them. The regular chequer-board system of town planning invented by Hippodamus of Miletus was universally admired in the Hellenistic and Roman periods, and not only were new cities laid out according to this scheme, but many old towns were gradually remodelled to conform to it. The principal streets were very generally flanked by colonnades which sheltered pedestrians from the rain in winter and from the sun in summer. Street lighting seems to have been something of a rarity; the brilliant illumination of Antioch by night was a source of great pride to its citizens, as two of them, Ammianus and Libanius, testify. Some few lights outside public buildings, like the brilliant festoon of hanging lamps outside the *praetorium,* were no doubt maintained by the city, but the ordinary street lamps by the occupants of the shops outside which they hung.

Another care of the *astynomi* was drainage. Progressive cities had a regular system of drains, running under the streets, which carried off both surface-water and sewage. Strabo remarks with surprise that Lysimachus' architects in building New Smyrna failed to provide any, so that the sewage had to flow along open gutters; Josephus praises the up-to-date system installed by Herod in Caesarea; and a century later Pliny, as governor of Bithynia, covered in a malodorous canal which served as the main drain of Amastris. It was the duty of the *astynomi* to see that the drains were maintained in good condition and cleaned; a gang of public slaves did this work. They had also to keep clean the public conveniences, which Pergamum and probably most large cities provided.

For their water-supply all ancient cities relied to some extent on wells and rain-water cisterns, and it was the duty of the *astynomi* to see that the owners of these kept them in good order. As late as the reign of Hadrian so flourishing a place as Alexandria Troas had no other source of supply, but in the Roman period an increasing number of cities built themselves aqueducts which tapped springs often many miles away. These great arched structures, of which many impressive ruins still survive, were enormously expensive, but they brought the advantages of pure, copious, and regular supply, which could moreover be distributed under pressure to all parts of the city; the last advantage was so much appreciated that at Arsinoe of Egypt, where there was no possible source of supply save the canal on which the city lay, a costly pumping-system was maintained. The public water-supply was devoted mainly to public buildings, such as baths, and to street fountains. These were often architectural features of great magnificence—the "nymphaea" of Syria were particularly splendid—and it was one of the duties of the *astynomi* to see that they were kept clean and in repair, and to prevent the citizens from washing clothes or watering animals in them. At Arsinoe only a few private institutions, such as a brewery and a Jewish synagogue, had a private supply. At Antioch many private houses indulged in this luxury, but Libanius suggests that the citizens were lucky in not having to queue up round the public fountains. Aelius Aristides implies that Smyrna was as well off in this respect as Antioch. At Alexandria many private houses had cisterns, fed by a system of underground channels from the Nile, but the common people had to draw their water direct from the river, there being no public fountains. Private users naturally paid a water rate, but this by no means covered the cost of the service.

Precautions against fire were as a rule most inadequate. Nicomedia in Trajan's reign had no apparatus and no brigade; and, though Pliny saw to it that in future hoses and hooks (for pulling down adjacent buildings and thus isolating the outbreak) should be available, he was unable to persuade the emperor to allow him to establish a volunteer fire brigade, such as existed in many Italian cities. The reasons which Trajan gave for his refusal were based on local circumstances; Bithynia, and Nicomedia in particular, was a hotbed of faction, and any association would inevitably be turned to political ends. But a story in the life of Polycarp reveals that in Smyrna also at this date, though apparatus was provided, the general public were expected to turn out to extinguish fires. This suggests that the imperial government, at this time at any rate, uniformly forbade the formation of fire brigades in eastern cities; there is no evidence that it later changed its policy.

Astynomi are not very frequently mentioned, and it is probably that in many smaller cities their functions devolved on the controllers of the market. The market was normally a paved square, surrounded by colonnades, onto which opened shops. The city drew a considerable revenue from the rents of these shops, and from leasing sites for stalls, which were regularly placed between the columns of the colonnades; and it was the duty of the *agoranomi* to keep the fabric in repair and to collect the rents. They fixed the hours at which the market opened and closed, and proclaimed them by ringing a bell. They had further to inspect the quality of the goods exposed for sale, and to see that correct weights and measures were used. For this purpose standard weights and measures were kept in their office and those used by traders were tested and stamped by them. The *agoranomi* also enforced currency laws, controlling the rate of exchange, a complicated matter when almost every city issued its own copper coins for local use and these bore no fixed relation to the gold and silver currencies of various standards minted by kings and important cities, or later by the imperial government.

But these were the least onerous duties of the board. It was also required to regulate the hiring of casual labour, enforcing the payment of wages and performance of work as stipulated, but not apparently interfering with the rate of wages or labour conditions. Finally, it was the duty of the *agoranomi* to see that an adequate supply of provisions was put on the market at a fair price: vivid evidence of what was expected of them is afforded by a series of inscriptions in the market of Ephesus, recording the names of *agoranomi* "under whom there was plenty and fair dealing," and appending the prices which prevailed in their year of office. The means adopted to secure this happy state of affairs varied according to circumstances. *Agoranomi* were authorized to fix prices by decree and in some cases did so. At Cyzicus, for instance, when Antonia Tryphaena was financing great public works and there was an influx of labour, the *agoranomi* were instructed by the city to punish any tradesman who raised his prices by disfranchising or deporting him and boarding up his shop and placarding his offence upon it. This was a special measure to meet an emergency, but other inscriptions prove that the *agoranomi* of Messene in the first century B.C. and of Pergamum in the second century A.D. regularly fixed the prices of certain wares.

Such measures, however, could for obvious reasons be applied only to home-grown produce, and in dealing with importers less drastic methods were used. Delos in the third century B.C. ruled that importers of firewood must declare their prices on arrival to the *agoranomi*, who could compel them to fulfil their undertaking by banning sale at a higher price and meanwhile charging them for the stall which they occupied. The same law forbade sale by importers to middlemen: Hadrian similarly at Athens endeavoured to keep down prices by eliminating unnecessary middlemen—importers were allowed to sell to local dealers but no further resale was permitted. In times of scarcity, however, no mere regulations were of avail to prevent prices from rising, and in these circumstances not a few public-spirited *agoranomi*, especially in the Roman period, are recorded to have taken the heroic course of entering the market themselves and underselling the dealers, bearing the loss out of their own pockets.

The most critical question was the supply of corn, which was at once the staple foodstuff, especially for the poorer classes, and was subject to the most violent fluctuations of price. Some larger cities, whose territories were not suited to the production of corn, regularly depended on supplies imported from overseas, and their position was peculiarly insecure: owing to the very high cost of transport imported corn was always dear, and any disturbing factor, a crop failure in one of the producing areas, storms at sea, or political troubles, might raise the price above the purchasing power of the humbler classes. As early as the fourth century B.C. many cities of the Aegean adopted special measures to secure a regular supply. The system was to establish a capital fund which was lent each year to merchants on condition that they used it to import corn to the city. This system ensured a regular supply in normal times, but it did not cope with times of serious shortage. Even cities which were normally supplied from their own territory or the immediate neighbourhood not infrequently got into difficulties: if the local harvest failed, merchants who imported corn to supply the deficiency charged much higher prices than the local population was used to paying.

In such emergencies a persuasive *agoranomus* might occasionally induce a merchant to sell below the inflated market price: not a few Hellenistic decrees are preserved which heap honours and privileges on such generous merchants. Local landowners also often came forward and either sold at a cheap rate or distributed free the corn from their estates. But often the city took action: a fund was raised by public subscription or by an extraordinary levy, and corn-buyers were appointed to purchase corn with this sum and retail it below cost.

The *sitonae*, originally extraordinary officers, had already in some cities, such as Delos, which depended entirely on imported corn, become a permanent institution in the second century B.C. In the Roman period they were almost universal; by the second century A.D. they were established, under the name of directors of the corn supply, even in the metropoleis of Egypt. The cities thus undertook as a normal part of the administration not merely the supervision of the corn market but the actual supply of corn. They did not always have to rely exclusively on purchase; for some had the right of levying corn from all landowners in their territory, and most drew some rent in corn from public lands. Usually, however, they had to buy in the open market, and many are recorded to have possessed standing funds for the purchase of corn, administered by special treasurers. It would seem that these funds were capital sums, which the *sitonae* spent each year on buying corn, and repaid as the corn was sold, and that the corn supply did not ordinarily involve the government in a loss. When there was a shortage, however, the richer citizens were expected either to give corn to the city or subscribe additional sums for its purchase, and public-spirited *sitonae* often sold corn at below cost price; thus at Magnesia on the Maeander a *sitones* boasts that he lost 5,000 denarii, and at Aphrodisias a father and two sons call themselves "*sitonae* of the 10,000 denarii which they themselves gave."

It is unlikely that the *sitonae* went very far afield for their corn save in exceptional cases. For an inland city import of corn from any distance was quite impracticable owing to the prohibitive cost of transport. The most that the *sitonae* could try to do in a famine was to buy up local stocks and put them on the market at a moderate price, and in this they were often embarrassed by the avarice of the landowners, who withheld their corn from the market, hoping for a rise. In Domitian's reign Antioch of Pisidia had to appeal to the provincial governor, who ordered all landowners in the territory to sell their entire surplus stock to the *emptores coloniae* at one denarius the bushel (the normal price was about half this sum), and at Aspendus Apollonius of Tyana is alleged to have achieved the same result by the sheer force of his personality: the anecdote is interesting as showing how much even maritime cities relied on local production. Import from Egypt was, it must be remembered, subject to imperial licence, which was very sparingly granted to the cities. It is recorded among Hadrian's great benefactions to Ephesus that he allowed shipments of corn from Egypt, and a *sitones* of Tralles relates with very great pride that he "bought the sixty thousand bushels of corn from Egypt which was conceded to his native city by our lord Trajanus Hadrianus Augustus and advanced out of his own pocket the price of the corn and all the expenses incurred up to its arrival."

Having supplied the corn, the cities naturally maintained a very strict control on the millers and bakers, lest they should turn the cheap supply to their own profit. At Ephesus the city council was so exacting that it provoked a strike among the bakers, who were however soon brought to heel by the proconsul. At Oxyrhynchus the directors of the corn supply themselves leased mills and had the corn ground, and it would seem that the city also bought the monopoly of baking from the Roman government and operated its own bakeries.

The most direct contribution of the cities to the department of public health was the maintenance of salaried public doctors. Some Greek cities had employed doctors from a very early age, and in the Hellenistic period the practice became general. Under the principate almost every city had a number of official doctors; Antoninus Pius limited their number to ten for metropoleis of provinces, seven for capitals of assize districts, five for ordinary cities. The principal business of these doctors was to give medical attention to the citizens; they were apparently allowed to take fees but were not expected to confine their attentions to those who could pay. They also served as police doctors, certifying the authorities of the causes of deaths, when suspicious, and of the injuries sustained by plaintiffs in alleged cases of assault. They often also gave instruction in medicine: at Perge a public doctor is praised for the excellent lectures that he gave in the gymnasium, and at Ephesus under the principate they were members of the medical faculty of the local "museum" or university, and took a prominent part in the annual competitions which were held in surgery, instruments, and, it would appear, a prepared thesis and an unprepared problem set by the examiners.

Under the heading of public health may also be reckoned the public baths, of which most cities maintained several, besides those attached to the gymnasium. A charge was made for admission, but it was very small and by no means covered the cost of upkeep: fuel for the heating of the public baths was a large item in the city budget, and there were also the salaries of the bath attendants and stokers, usually public slaves, and the cost of the water. Oxyrhynchus ingeniously made a little money by leasing out the post of cloakroom attendant: stealing the clothes of bathers was a very popular form of petty larceny, and the attendant no doubt made a good thing out of tips. Oil was not normally provided for bathers, but public-spirited citizens often supplied it gratis to all comers on festal occasions.

Women in Roman Society

SARAH B. POMEROY

Until very recently, historians who studied women in Roman society were usually interested in them only as they related to men. This bias goes right back to the ancients themselves. Plutarch and Suetonius studied the character of imperial women to reveal the character of imperial men. Ancient legal sources have the same bias. Although they reveal a considerable amount about the legal position of women, Roman legal writings and laws nearly always focused principally on the legal status, authority, and responsibilities of men. A survey of the legal sources reveals that the classical Roman law of the late Republic and early Principate strictly limited the independence of women, requiring that their property be administered by men —either their husbands or guardians— and keeping them in a position of legal subjugation to their fathers or husbands. By the time of Justinian, however, a woman's dowry was protected from her husband's mismanagement or appropriation, and her power to act on her own behalf had increased. If a man alienated or diminished his wife's property, she could take action against him for damages. Thus, in late imperial times, women possessed significant legal rights, although their status would not meet the standards of equality being set today.

Sarah B. Pomeroy works with the same sources as other social historians, but she asks new questions of these sources. She finds ways of discovering a great deal not only about the women of upper-class families, but also about lower-class women, particularly slaves. Her study reveals much about Roman families, home life, and social relations.

The momentum of social change in the Hellenistic world combined with Roman elements to produce the emancipated, but respected, upper-class woman. The Roman matron of the late Republic must be viewed against the background of shrewd and politically powerful Hellenistic princesses, expanding cultural opportunities for women, the search for sexual fulfillment in the context of a declining birthrate, and the individual assertiveness characteristic of the Hellenistic period. The rest of the picture is Roman: enormous wealth, aristocratic indulgence and display,

From Sarah B. Pomeroy, *Goddesses, Whores, Wives, and Slaves* (New York: Schocken Books, 1975), pp. 153–55, 158–61, 164–66, 168–69, 190–95, 195–97.

pragmatism permitting women to exercise leadership during the absence of men on military and governmental missions of long duration; and, as a final element, a past preceding the influence of the Greeks—a heritage so idealized by the Romans that historical events were scarcely distinguishable from legends, and the legends of the founding of Rome and the early Republic were employed in the late republic and early Empire for moral instruction and propaganda. The result was that wealthy aristocratic women who played high politics and presided over literary salons were nevertheless expected to be able to spin and weave as though they were living in the days when Rome was young. These social myths set up a tension between the ideal and the real Roman matron, and were responsible for the praise awarded a woman like Cornelia, who lived in the second century B.C.

Among Roman matrons, Cornelia was a paragon. We are told that she turned down an offer of marriage from a Ptolemy. A widow, she remained faithful to the memory of her husband, Tiberius Sempronius Gracchus, to whom she had borne twelve children. She continued to manage her household and was praised for her devotion to her children's education. Only three of her children survived to adulthood, but through her two sons, Tiberius and Gaius Gracchus, Cornelia exercised a profound influence on Roman politics. Some say that she goaded her sons to excessive political zeal by insisting that she was famous as the daughter of Scipio Africanus—conqueror of Hannibal—rather than as the mother of the Gracchi. It was even rumored, though much after the fact, that, with the aid of her daughter Sempronia, Cornelia suffocated Scipio Aemilianus, Sempronia's husband, because he opposed the legislation of Tiberius Gracchus. This allegation did not tarnish Cornelia's reputation. She endured the assassination of both her adult sons with fortitude, and continued to entertain foreign and learned guests at her home in Misenum. She was herself educated, and her letters were published. A bronze portrait statue inscribed "Cornelia, daughter of Africanus, mother of the Gracchi," was erected in her honor by the Romans and restored by the Emperor Augustus.

The Letter of the Law . . . and the Reality

Looking beyond the picture of Cornelia—independent, cultured, self-assured even in her widowhood—we find a long history of Roman legislation affecting women especially in the areas of guardianship, marriage, and inheritance.

The weakness and light-mindedness of the female sex (*infirmitas sexus* and *levitas animi*) were the underlying principles of Roman legal theory that mandated all women to be under the custody of males. In childhood, a daughter fell under the sway of the eldest male ascendant in her family, the *pater familias*. The power of the *pater familias* was without parallel in Greek law; it extended to the determination of life or death for all members of the household. Male offspring of any age were also subject to the authority of the *pater familias*, but as adults they were automatically emancipated upon his death, and the earliest Roman law code, the XII Tables (traditionally 451–450 B.C.), stated that a son who had been sold into slavery three times by his father thereby gained his freedom. Among females, however, the only automatic legal exemption from the power of the *pater familias* was accorded those who became Vestal Virgins, a cultic role reserved for a very few.

Upon the death of the *pater familias*, the custody over daughters (and prepubertal sons) passed to the nearest male relative (agnate), unless the father had designated another guardian in his will. Guardianship over females was theoretically in force until the time of Diocletian (reigned A.D. 285–305), but this power was gradually diminished by legal devices and ruses and by the assertiveness of some women interested in managing their own concerns. A guardian was required when a woman performed important transactions, such as accepting an inheritance, making a testament, or assuming a contractual obligation, and all transactions requiring *mancipatio* (a ritual form of sale), including selling land and manumitting a slave. But if the guardian withheld approval, a woman could apply to the magistrate to have his assent forced, or to have a different guardian appointed.

By the late Republic, tutelage over women was a burden to the men acting as guardians, but only a slight disability to women. The virtuous Cornelia managed a large household and is not reported to have consulted any male guardian even in her decision to turn down Ptolemy Physcon's proposal of marriage. Similarly, a century later, much is said about the financial transactions of Terentia, Cicero's wife, but nothing about her guardian.

The legislation of Augustus provided a way for women to free themselves of the formal supervision by male guardians. According to the "right of three or four children" (*jus liberorum*), a freeborn woman who bore three children and a freedwoman who bore four children were exempt from guardianship. This provision incidentally impaired the juridical doctrine of the weakness of the female sex, by expressing the notion that at least those women who had demonstrated responsible behavior by bearing the children Rome needed could be deemed capable of acting without a male guardian.

The right of three children was not a response to demands from liberated women yearning to free themselves from male domination, nor did it act as much of an incentive. As we have seen, the famous women of Roman society who had wanted to be free of the influence of guardians had managed to do so before the reign of Augustus, and without the tedious preliminary of bearing three children. Moreover, papyri from Roman Egypt, where women were less sophisticated, show a large number of women proudly announcing that they have gained the *jus liberorum*, but nevertheless availing themselves of male assistance when they transact legal business. Even after a law of Claudius in the first century A.D. abolished automatic guardianship of agnates over women, the majority of guardians or men who were present at transactions of women possessing the *jus liberorum* and who signed documents in behalf of illiterate women continued to be male relatives.

The laws of guardianship indicate that the powers of the *pater familias* surpassed those of the husband. The *pater familias* decided whether his daughter would remain in his power, or would be emancipated from his power to that of another man, and if so, who would be her guardian. The guardian was not necessarily a relative, nor was the married daughter inevitably in the power of her husband. The *pater familias* decided whether or not she would be married according to a legal form that would release her from the authority of her father and transfer her to the power (*manus*) of her husband. If the marriage was contracted with *manus*, the bride became part of her husband's family, as though she were his daughter, as far as property rights were concerned.

A wife could become subject to a husband's *manus* in three ways: either by the two formal marriage ceremonies known as *confarreatio* (sharing of spelt—a coarse grain), and *coemptio* (pretended sale), or by *usus* (continuous cohabitation for a year). In ancient times, a vital feature of *manus* marriage for the bride was the change in domestic religions. A family's religion was transmitted through males, and the *pater familias* was the chief priest. Upon marriage, a girl renounced her father's religion and worshiped instead at her husband's hearth. His ancestors became hers. The guardian spirit of the *pater familias* (known as the *genius*) and that of the *mater familias* (the *juno*) were worshiped by the household. Conversely, the woman married without *manus* was not a member of the husband's agnatic family, and hence theoretically excluded from the rites celebrated by her husband and children. In that case, she would continue to participate in her father's cult. . . .

The testimony on the issue of the husband's powers in comparison with those of the blood relatives varies. Dionysius of Halicarnassus—who, like Livy, wrote during the reign of the Emperor Augustus—states that, according to the laws of Romulus, married women were obliged to conform themselves to their husbands, since they had no other refuge, while husbands ruled over their wives as possessions. Plutarch gives the additional information that, according to the regulations of Romulus, only the husband could initiate a divorce, and then only on the grounds that his wife had committed adultery, poisoned his children, or counterfeited his keys. If he divorced his wife for another reason, she took half his property; the other half was consecrated to the goddess Ceres.

Dionysius of Halicarnassus further confuses the question by stating that her husband, after taking counsel with a woman's relations, could inflict capital punishment on a wife guilty of adultery, or of drinking, since drinking inspired adultery. The elder Pliny relates that a married woman was forced by her family to starve herself to death because she had stolen the keys to the wine cellar, but it is not clear whether "family" refers to the husband or blood relatives.

So it is uncertain whether the husband had the right to kill the wife, or merely to divorce her, or to kill her only with the agreement of her male relatives. In 186 B.C., when thousands of men and women were sentenced to death for participating in Bacchic rites, the women were handed over to their blood relatives or to those who had authority (*manus*) over them to be executed in private. But here, each husband merely carried out the execution ordered by the state. He did not himself condemn her.

What does emerge from this investigation is the concept that when "wives had no other refuge," as Dionysius puts it, or when they were totally under the authority of their husbands, as envisioned by Cato, marriages were more enduring. This power of husbands over wives—if, in fact, it had ever been prevalent in early Rome—was idealized and became an element in the marriage propaganda of Stoics and Augustan authors, both concerned with promoting marriage among their contemporaries.

What is also striking to anyone who lives in a society where a father's control over a daughter terminates when she reaches the age of majority, but where certain other laws make the wife subordinate to the husband, is that the situation may have been reversed at Rome, and the husband's authority more ephemeral than that of the father and blood kin. Thus, even in *manus* marriage, the bride's blood relatives continued to be involved in her guidance and welfare. The surveillance over her drinking is only one aspect of this. Some legends point to continued involvement by fathers of married women: among them are the raped Lucretia's appeal to both her father and husband and their joint vengeance in her behalf, and the story of the Sabine fathers who, when coming to reclaim their pregnant married daughters, were told by them that they did not want to be forced to choose between their fathers and husbands. . . .

Divorce was easily accomplished, theoretically at the initiation of either or both parties to the marriage. Beginning in the late Republic, a few women are notorious for independently divorcing their husbands, but, for the most part, these arrangements were in the hands of men. As we have seen, divorce could be initiated by fathers whose married children were not emancipated from their authority. We may note a parallel to Classical Athenian law, where the father retained the right to dissolve his daughter's marriage. . . . Not until the reign of Antoninus Pius was it made illegal for fathers to break up harmonious marriages. If the marriage had involved *manus*, then the *manus* had to be dissolved, but this situation was infrequent. The major concern was the return of the dowry, as it had been in Classical Athens and Hellenistic Egypt. If the husband were divorcing the wife for immoral conduct, he had the right to retain a portion of her dowry; the fraction varied according to the gravity of her offense. A few husbands did attempt to profit by this procedure.

In divorce, children remained with their father, since they were agnatically related to him, but, as we have seen in our discussion of *manus*, blood relationship was an important bond. Thirty-seven years after her divorce from Augustus, Scribonia voluntarily accompanied her daughter Julia into exile. After his parents had been divorced, and he himself adopted into another family, Scipio Aemilianus shared his wealth with his mother. Marcia had been divorced by the younger Cato because he wanted to let his friend Hortensius breed children with her. Nevertheless, after the death of Hortensius she remarried Cato, probably motivated by a wish to look after her daughters by him while Cato went off to join Pompey. After her divorce from Claudius Nero to marry Augustus, Livia's children by her first marriage lived with their father, but following his death they joined their mother.

Most of the divorces we read about were prompted by political or personal considerations. No reason was legally required, but sterility of the marriage was often a cause, and a barren marriage was considered to be due to the wife. Sulla divorced Cloelia for alleged infertility. However, a woman who died at the end of the first century B.C. won extravagant praise from her husband for offering him a divorce after a barren marriage that had lasted forty-three years. She is called, "Turia," though her name is not definitely known. Her funerary encomium describes her heroism in her husband's behalf during the civil wars, and then praises her self-effacing offer to divorce her husband on the condition that she—with her fortune—would continue to stay with him and be as a sister, and treat his future children as though they were her own. Her husband indignantly turned her down, preferring to remain married although his family line would thereby become extinct. This is one of the many interesting aspects of the document. The husband regards his preference for his wife and married life over his duties to perpetuate his family line as untraditional, yet by this period morally acceptable, indeed commendable.

Some men divorced their wives for flagrant adultery. Thus, Pompey divorced Mucia, and Lucullus divorced Claudia; Caesar divorced Pompeia because her notorious involvement with Publius Clodius at the rites of the Bona Dea, which were supposed to be confined to women, created a scandal. Caesar was High Priest at the time, and proclaimed that "the High

Priest's wife must be above suspicion." We have little information on wives' divorcing husbands for adultery. This may have been due to a double standard, or to the discretion of some adulterous husbands, or the upper-class men's opportunities for involvement with women of lower social classes — liaisons that were accepted as not threatening to legitimate marriages.

Augustus declared adultery a public offense only in women. Consistent with the powers of the *pater familias*, the father of the adulteress was permitted to kill her if she had not been emancipated from his power. The husband's role, as we have seen in other areas of Roman law, was more limited than the father's. The husband was obliged to divorce his wife, and he or someone else was to bring her to trial. If convicted, she lost half her dowry, the adulterer was fined a portion of his property, and both were separately exiled. According to the Augustan legislation, a wife could divorce her husband for adultery, but she was not obliged to, and he was not liable for criminal prosecution. The law may have been more stringent than the real situation, for the jurist Ulpian later commented: "It is very unjust for a husband to require from a wife a level of morality that he does not himself achieve." Stoic theory as well condemned adultery in either man or wife. The younger Cato, a man of Stoic and Roman principles, carried the doctrine still further: he believed that sexual intercourse was only for the purpose of begetting children. Since he had a sufficient number of children and Marcia was worn out by childbearing, his second marriage to her was chaste. No doubt the long absences from home imposed by the civil wars facilitated Cato's continence in his relations with his wife during the five-year duration of the remarriage.

Like the Augustan rule on adultery, the regulation on criminal fornication (*stuprum*) perpetuated a double standard. No man was allowed to have sexual relations with an unmarried or widowed upper-class woman, but he could have relations with prostitutes, whereas upper-class women were not allowed to have any relations outside of marriage. Under some emperors, the penalties for breaking these laws were very severe. Augustus himself exiled both his daughter and granddaughter for illicit intercourse and forbade their burial in his tomb. Some upper-class women protested against the curtailment of their freedom by registering with the aediles (magistrates whose duties included supervision of the markets and trade) as prostitutes. Then the laws of *stuprum* would not apply to them, but such women were excluded from legacies and inheritance. In any case, this legal dodge was eliminated when Augustus' successor, Tiberius, forbade women whose fathers, grandfathers or husbands were Roman knights or senators to register as prostitutes.

Rape could be prosecuted — under the legal headings of criminal wrong (*iniuria*) or violence (*vis*) — by the man under whose authority the wronged woman fell. Constantine was explicit about the guilt of the victim. In his decision on raped virgins, he distinguished between girls who were willing and those who were forced against their will. If the girl had been willing, her penalty was to be burned to death. If she had been unwilling, she was still punished, although her penalty was lighter, for she should have screamed and brought neighbors to her assistance. Constantine also specified capital punishment for a free woman who had intercourse with a slave, and burning for the slave himself. This penalty was the outcome of a perpetual concern that free women would take the same liberties with slaves as men did. These liaisons were a real possibility, since unlike Athens, where women lived in separate quarters, in Rome wealthy women were attended by numerous male slaves, often chosen for their attractive appearance. The legendary virtuous Lucretia, according to the Augustan historian Livy, was so intimidated by Tarquin's threat that he would kill her and a naked slave side by side in bed that she submitted to Tarquin's lust. Though raped, she was technically an adulteress; therefore she made the honorable decision to commit suicide.

Augustan legislation encouraged widows, like divorcées, to remarry. There was some tension between the emperor's concern that women bear as many children as possible and the traditional Roman idealization of the woman like Cornelia who remained faithful to her dead husband. The epitaphs continue to praise the women who died having known only one husband (*univira*), some of whom easily earned this recognition by dying young. The ideal of the *univira* and the eternal marriage was strictly Roman, and without counterpart in Greece. Two lengthy encomia of upper-class women of the Augustan period—one of "Turia," the other of Cornelia, wife of Lucius Aemilius Paullus—stresses this ideal. In both cases, the women predeceased their husbands, who composed or commissioned the encomia. Even Livia, the widow of Augustus, although she had had a previous husband, was praised for not remarrying. Virgil, writing the national Roman epic, depicts a disastrous climax to Dido's decision not to remain faithful to her dead husband. In Rome, unlike Athens, a woman could lead an interesting life without a husband, as Cornelia, mother of the Gracchi, did in entertaining guests and pursuing her intellectual interests. But Cornelia earned praise because she bore twelve children first, and then chose not to remarry.

A further refinement of the ideal-wife motif stresses that not only should a woman have only one husband, but she ought not to survive him—especially if he has been the victim of political persecution. Thus Arria, the wife of A. Caecina Paetus, upbraided the wife of another member of her husband's political faction for daring to continue to live after seeing her own husband murdered in her arms. She also advised her own daughter to commit suicide if her husband predeceased her. When

Arria's own husband was invited to commit suicide during the reign of Claudius, she plunged the dagger into her own breast to set an example, and spoke her celebrated last words, "It does not hurt, Paetus." . . .

Facts of Birth, Life, and Death

Marriage and motherhood were the traditional expectation of well-to-do women in Rome as they had been in Greece. The rarity of spinsters indicates that most women married at least once, although afterward a number chose to remain divorcées or widows.

Augustus established the minimum age for marriage at twelve for girls and fourteen for boys. The first marriage of most girls took place between the ages of twelve and fifteen. Since menarche typically occurred at thirteen or fourteen, prepubescent marriages took place. Moreover, sometimes the future bride lived with the groom before she had reached the legal minimum for marriage, and it was not unusual for these unions to be consummated. Marriages of young girls took place because of the desire of the families involved not to delay the profit from a political or financial alliance and, beginning with the reign of Augustus, so that the bride and groom could reap the rewards of the marital legislation, although some of the benefits could be anticipated during the engagement. Sometimes one motive outweighed another. Thus there are cases of dowerless daughters of the upper class who nevertheless found social-climbing men so eager to marry them that the husbands surreptitiously provided the dowry, to save the pride of the girl's family. Another factor which we have traced back to Hesiod was the desire to find a bride who was still virginal.

Most upper-class Roman women were able to find husbands, not only for first marriages but for successive remarriages. One reason for this, apparently, was that there were fewer females than males among their social peers. As in Greece, this disproportion was the result of the shorter lifespan of females, whose numbers fell off sharply once the child-bearing years were reached. There were the additional factors of the selective infanticide and exposure of female infants and, probably more important, a subtle but pervasive attitude that gave preferential treatment to boys. . . . This can be surmised from a law attributed to Romulus that required a father to raise all male children but only the first-born female. This so-called law of Romulus — while not to be accepted at face value as evidence that every father regularly raised only one daughter — is nevertheless indicative of official policy and foreshadows later legislation favoring the rearing of boys over girls. The attitude may be criticized as short-sighted in face of the manpower shortage continually threatening

Rome; the policy of Sparta, where potential childbearers were considered as valuable as warriors, should be compared.

The law of Romulus incidentally shows that it was not inconvenient for a daughter to be automatically called by the feminine form of her father's name (*nomen*). But it was awkward when the father decided to raise two daughters, who thus had the same name, like Cornelia and her sister Cornelia. The Romans solved the problem with the addition of "the elder" (*maior*) or "the younger" (*minor*). In families where several daughters were raised, numerals, which in earlier times may have been indicative of order of birth, were added (e.g., Claudia *Tertia* and Claudia *Quinta*). A wealthy father might decide to dispose of an infant because of the desire not to divide the family property among too many offspring and thereby reduce the individual wealth of the members of the next generation. Christian authors such as Justin Martyr doubtless exaggerate the extent to which contemporary pagans engaged in infanticide, but, on the other hand, it is clear that this method of family planning was practiced without much fanfare in antiquity. An infant of either sex who appeared weak might be exposed; in his *Gynecology* Soranus, a physician of the second century A.D., gives a list of criteria by which midwives were to recognize which newborns should be discarded and which were worth rearing. In deciding to expose a daughter, the provision of a dowry was an additional consideration. However, there was enough of a demand for brides, as we have mentioned, to make even the occasional dowerless bride acceptable.

Additional evidence for a dearth of females in the upper classes is that in the late Republic some men were marrying women of the lower classes. We know of no spinsters, yet upper-class women are not known to have taken husbands from the lower classes. Studies of tombstones generally show far more males than females. This disproportion is usually explained away by the comment that males were deemed more deserving of commemoration. Such a factor might discourage the erection of tombstones for those low on the social scale, but at least among the wealthier classes—the very group where small families were the trend—we could expect that, once having decided to raise a daughter, her parents would commemorate her death. In our present state of knowledge we cannot finally say that women were actually present in Rome in the numbers one expects in an average pre-industrial society, and that their lack of adequate representation in the sepulchral inscriptions is totally ascribable to the social invisibility; but it should be noted that the existence of masses of women who are not recorded by the inscriptions is, at most, hypothetical.

The traditional doctrine, enforced by Roman censors, was that men should marry, and that the purpose of marriage was the rearing of children. The example of Hellenistic Greece, where men were refusing to marry and consequently children were not being raised ... , had a subversive influence on the ideal, although Stoicism affirmed it. A decrease in fecundity is discernible as early as the second century B.C., a time when the production of twelve children by Cornelia became a prodigy—probably because her son Gaius harped on it—although only three lived to adulthood. Metellus Macedonicus, censor in 131 B.C., made a speech urging men to marry and procreate, although he recognized that wives were troublesome creatures. The speech was read out to the Senate by Augustus as evidence that he was merely reviving Roman traditions with his legislation.

Augustus' legislation was designed to keep as many women as possible in the married state and bearing children. The penalties for nonmarriage and childlessness began for women at age twenty, for men at twenty-five. Divorce was not explicitly frowned upon, provided that each successive husband was recruited from the approved social class. Failure to remarry was penalized, all with a view to not wasting the childbearing years. Women were not able to escape the penalties of the Augustan legislation as easily as men. A man who was betrothed to a girl of ten could enjoy the political and economic privileges accorded to married men, but a woman was not permitted to betroth herself to a prepubescent male.

But the low birth rate continued, and the Augustan legislation on marriage was reinforced by Domitian and reenacted in the second and third centuries A.D. It appears that women as well as men were rebelling against biologically determined roles. One reason for the low birth rate was the practice of contraception. . . .

Abortion is closely associated with contraception in the ancient sources, and sometimes confused with it. Keith Hopkins suggests that the reason for the blurring of abortion and contraception was the lack of precise knowledge of the period of gestation. Some Romans believed that children could be born seven to ten months after conception, but eight-month babies were not possible. A contributing factor in the failure to distinguish between contraception and abortion was that some of the same drugs were recommended for both. Abortion was also accomplished by professional surgical instruments or by amateur methods. Ovid upbraids Corinna: "Why do you dig out your child with sharp instruments, and give harsh poison to your unborn children."

The musings of philosophers on when the foetus felt life and whether abortion was sanctionable will not be reviewed. In a society where newborns were exposed, the foetus cannot have had much right to life, although it is true that in the early Empire the execution of a pregnant woman was delayed until after the birth of her child. Literary testimony, including Seneca, Juvenal, and Ovid, shows both that some men were dismayed about abortions and that some upper-class women and courtesans had them. Not until the reign of Septimius Severus was any legislation enacted curtailing abortion, and this was merely to decree the punishment of exile for a divorced woman who has an abortion without her recent husband's consent, since she has cheated him of his child. In the reign of Caracalla, the penalty of exile (and death if the patient dies) was established for administering abortifacients, but this law was directed against those who traded in drugs and magic rather than against abortion itself.

Medical writers were concerned as well with methods of promoting fertility in sterile women and with childbirth. The writings of Soranus, a physician of the second century A.D., cover a sophisticated range of gynecological and obstetrical topics. He did not adhere to the Hippocratic Oath which forbade administering abortifacients, but stated his preference for contraception. At a time when wealthy women usually employed wet-nurses, Soranus declared that if the mother was in good health, it was better that she nurse the child, since it would foster the bonds of affection. Of interest are his recommendations for the alleviation of labor pains, his concern for the comfort of the mother, and his unequivocal decision that the welfare of the mother take precedence over that of the infant. In childbirth, most women who could afford professional assistance would summon a midwife, although if the procedure was beyond the midwife's ability, and funds were available, a male physician would be employed. In Rome the skilled midwives, like the physicians, were likely to be Greek. Midwives not only delivered babies, but were involved in abortions and other gynecological procedures, and as we have mentioned, they were supposed to be able to recognize which infants were healthy enough to be worth rearing.

Women—even wealthy women with access to physicians—continued to die in childbirth. Early marriage, and the resultant bearing of children by immature females, was a contributing factor. Tombstones show a marked increase in female mortality in the fifteen-to-twenty-nine-year-old group. In a study of the sepulchral inscriptions, Keith Hopkins claims that death in childbirth is to some extent exaggerated by the reliance upon evidence from tombstones. He suggests that women dying between fifteen and twenty-nine were more likely to be commemorated, because their husbands were still alive to erect tombstones. In his sample he found that the median age for the death of wives was 34; of husbands, 46.5. J. Lawrence Angel's study of skeletal remains in Greece under Roman domination shows an adult longevity of 34.3 years for women and 40.2 for men. Stepmothers are mentioned more than stepfathers, though this may reflect not only early death of mothers but the fact that children stayed with their father after divorce. . . .

How can we know about the lives of lower-class women—slaves, ex-slaves, working women, and the poor? The literature does tell us the ways in which the lower classes pleased or displeased their social superiors. The sepulchral inscriptions that owners of slaves or members of the lower classes had carved for their associates and themselves give the messages they wanted to announce to posterity. Thus an epitaph may include not merely the name of the deceased, but the name of her owner or former owner if she were a slave or freedwoman (especially if she had belonged to an important family), the name of her husband, the duration of her marriage and the number of children in the family, her age at death, and her métier.

For the present chapter I have drawn heavily on the recent study of P. R. C. Weaver of the slaves and freedmen of the imperial household, which includes statistics on a control group of nonimperial slaves. Also of immense value have been S. M. Treggiari's studies of slaves and freedmen of the late Republic and the early Empire. But the essential questions of how it felt to be a female slave among the Romans, and whether —if one were an ordinary slave—it was worse to be male or female, cannot be answered.

The Exploitation of Slaves

The Roman household (*familia*) included not only kinsmen legally dependent on the head of the family, but also slaves. The number of slaves of course varied according to the means of the family, but even humble families might own a few. There is more abundant documentation on the slaves of the wealthy, as is true of the wealthy themselves. Wealthy families owned thousands of slaves, living on their various holdings, and the household of the emperor (*familia Caesaris*) was probably the largest. Owners of slaves invested in human property with the expectation that certain services would be performed, and that their own wealth would thereby be increased and their personal comfort enhanced. The complexities of Roman slavery were such that a woman might gain more prestige by marrying a slave than a free person, and that slaves and ex-slaves might be more highly educated and enjoy greater economic security than the freeborn poor.

The variety of the jobs held by female slaves was more limited than those of the males. Some women were enslaved only in adulthood, either by kidnappers or pirates, or because they were camp followers or ordinary citizens where the Romans made a conquest. In a population of captive Greeks, the Romans would find male scholars, historians, poets, and men with valuable skills. Owing to the limitations of women's education, a freshly captured woman may have been at most a midwife, an actress, or a prostitute. Most women did not have any training beyond the traditional household skills. In slavery, as in freedom, they could work as spinners, weavers, clothesmakers, menders, wetnurses, child nurses, kitchen help, and general domestics. The household duties of female slaves in Rome differed somewhat from those we observed in Greece. Because Roman engineers devised mechanical methods for transporting large quantities of water, Roman slave women did not carry water to the same extent that Greeks had done. Moreover, in Rome, unlike Greece, all clothing was not made at home. In addition, female slaves were given special training in the wealthy Roman home and worked as clerks, secretaries, ladies' maids, clothes folders, hairdressers, haircutters, mirror holders, masseuses, readers, entertainers, midwives, and infirmary attendants. Children born into slavery in a wealthy Roman home thus stood a fair chance of receiving some education.

Some female slaves, like males, were employed as attendants to enhance the splendor of the mistress's entourage when she went out of her home. Such slaves would clear the way before their owner. If her mistress was traveling on a litter, a female slave would put her sandals on for her and place a footstool next to the litter before the mistress alighted. A slave might carry a parasol for a mistress who was taking a walk. Naturally, slaves' functions on a farm or country estate would have differed from those in the urban household, but less is known about rural slave women. However, Cato the Censor does list the duties of the *vilica*, the chief housekeeper, a slave woman who held a supervisory position of great responsibility, subordinate to a steward who was a male slave.

Women were always employable for sexual purposes, either in addition to their other domestic responsibilities, or as a primary occupation. The master had access to all his slave women. Scipio Africanus favored a particular slave girl, and when he died, his wife Aemilia, far from being vindictive, gave the girl her freedom. Cato the Censor, who was an authority on Roman virtue, was visited nightly by a slave girl after his wife died, and the emperors Augustus and Claudius consorted with numerous slave girls with the wives' explicit approval. Slave women were also available for sexual relations with the male slaves in the house, with the master's permission. Cato, who was always interested in financial gain, charged his male slaves a fixed fee for intercourse with his female slaves.

Employment in the sex trade brought great profit to the owners of female slaves. Women worked as prostitutes in brothels or in inns or baths open to the public. Exposed baby girls and daughters sold by their parents were raised for this trade. In this same category, but at a higher level, were the women trained to work as actresses and entertainers of all types. Actresses sometimes appeared nude and performed sexual acts on stage. However, actresses were not invariably employed sexually. Eucharis, a young performer who had been given her freedom sometime before her death at the age of fourteen performed in the chorus at respectable public games given as "Greek theater," and is described as "learned" and "skilled" in her epitaph.

Marriage, Manumission, and the Law

The fact of slavery disqualified a person from entering into a formal Roman marriage, but two slaves might have an informal marital arrangement known as "cohabitation" (*contubernium*). Although the usual incest regulations applied just as if it were legal marriage, this arrangement had no legal validity: the children of the union were considered illegitimate, and the woman could not be accused of adultery. But to the slaves themselves the marriages were valid, and in the epitaphs the partners refer to each other as husband and wife. It was in the master's interest to promote family life among his slaves, for it improved morale and produced slave children who were the master's to keep in his household or to dispose of as he wished. Slaves tended to marry other slaves, and were likely to marry within their master's *familia*. With permission, a slave might marry a slave from another *familia* or a free person. However, if a male slave married a female outside his master's *familia*, the master lost the profit that might be gained from the offspring, since the children belonged to the mother if she were free, or to her master if she were a slave. Hence such a marriage might not be permitted. There was no security in a slave marriage — either partner or the children might be sold to another owner or moved to a different property owned by the original master. Broken marriages left no record. But sepulchral inscriptions show that many slave marriages survived over long periods of time, regardless of changes in habitation or changes in status from slave to freed of one or both of the partners. In lives subject to the whims of others, the stability of the marriage bond was welcome.

The study of imperial slaves and freedmen shows that almost half the marriages of freedmen whose duration is mentioned lasted at least thirty years. Moreover, their wives had married young, like the aristocrats discussed in the previous chapter. In order that the statistics on the duration of marriage be consistent with those on the age of death of wives, it is necessary to remember Keith Hopkins' hypothesis that the age of death of wives who die young is more likely to be recorded on a tombstone. . . . Over half the wives of imperial slaves and freedmen were dead before thirty, with the highest proportion dying between twenty and twenty-five. Of the nine married women buried in the tomb of a wealthy family, the Statilii, studied by Susan Treggiari, five had died at age twenty or younger. The mortality was probably even higher among the slaves belonging to poorer families.

The Roman household employed a far larger number of male slaves than female. Among children of imperial slaves and freedmen, the proportion is sixty or more per cent male, and among the adults the proportion of males is far higher, owing to the nature of the work of this elite group of civil servants. Susan Treggiari's study of the slaves and freedmen of Livia and of the Volusii likewise shows a ratio of roughly three males per female, with a slightly larger proportion of female slaves in a household owned by a woman than in the slave household belonging to a male owner. On the estates of the fictional Trimalchio were born thirty boys and forty girls in a single day. These statistics, like much in the *Satiricon*, are intended to be ludicrous, but nevertheless it is interesting to observe that all the slaves at Trimalchio's dinner are male. Boy babies were retained to fill posts as their fathers were manumitted or died, but excess female children were disposed of in various ways. Some were sold to work as domestics in small households, many probably to brothels; others were perhaps exposed to die or be picked up by a slave-trader. Still others were given by the master to male slaves as marriage partners, with the expectation that children would be produced who would be the master's property; some girls were purchased by male slaves from their own funds. Perhaps Aurelia Philematium, a freedwoman who died at forty, was one of these girls. Her epitaph states that her freedman husband took her "to his bosom" when she was seven, and was like a father to her. Apparently he was kind to her when she joined the household, and then married her. That this marriage could have been consummated when the bride was only seven is not impossible.

Slaves were allowed to amass their own personal savings (*peculium*), and could use this money to buy other slaves. When a male slave purchased his wife, she had the status of a personal slave (*vicaria*) to her husband-owner—although, strictly speaking, like all her husband's possessions she belonged to his master—and the disaster of being sold to separate households was less likely. This arrangement also offered a path of upward mobility for the slave husband, since his master might free the slave's wife sooner than a valuable and industrious male slave. . . .

Females could win their freedom through routes other than marriage. As we have mentioned, slaves were allowed to amass their own personal savings with a view to repaying their purchase price. A woman employed in domestic work would have less opportunity to collect tips than a male slave in an influential post, and her savings would grow rather slowly, although the master's favorite bedmate might receive gifts, and a lady's maid would be given tips from her mistress' lovers. On the other hand, as she grew older and less attractive her value decreased, whereas the value of a highly trained male slave increased with years. Thus a woman might eventually be able to purchase her own freedom. In addition, Columella, who in the first century A.D. wrote a treatise on farming, considered that a slave woman had repaid her purchase price by bearing four children to be her master's property. Some urban slaves might get away with fewer than this number. Freedom was often granted to slaves voluntarily by owners, or by last testament. The manumission of the actress Eucharis may be attributable to the good will of her owner; for example, the slave girl may have been granted freedom as she lay ill. A married couple might be manumitted simultaneously, or the partner who was freed first could amass enough funds to buy the partner still in slavery and manumit him or her.

When both husband and wife had been slaves together, and the wife was a freedwoman, the husband could in turn be manumitted by marriage. However, a freeborn woman who freed a male slave and married him was disapproved of, and such marriages were outlawed by Septimius Severus (reigned A.D. 193–211).

The motives leading a freeborn woman or freedwoman to marry a slave are an indication of the complexity of slave society. Male slaves of the emperor or of important Roman families in administrative posts held positions of prestige and economic security. The wife had a good chance of being buried in the tomb of her husband's *familia*, and a place of burial was a concern to all Romans. The free woman who married an imperial slave was, in a sense, improving her status, while her husband also improved his. To the owner of the male slave, however, such an arrangement was detrimental, since the children were the property of the mother. Moreover, the prejudice against a free woman cohabiting with a slave extended even to slaves of high position within the slave hierarchy. There a decree of the Senate was passed in A.D. 52 that discouraged freeborn and freedwomen from marrying slaves by reducing such a wife to the status of slave or freedwoman of her husband's master. This regulation was aimed at slaves of the imperial household. The loss of status gave the husband's master — the emperor in particular — financial advantages in regard to the wives and children of his male slaves.

In contrast to male slaves, female slaves in upper-class families were less likely to marry above their station. Females, even in important households, were used only for domestic service and did not hold positions of influence. There was therefore little incentive for freeborn men or freedmen outside their households to unite with them. In a lower-class family a female slave could be freed to marry her master, but in senatorial or imperial households this route of upward mobility was closed. Men of senatorial status could not marry freedwomen, although they could, of course, cohabit with them.

A few female members of the imperial household attained positions of influence as the freedwoman concubines of emperors. These relationships were known publicly, often of long duration, and not a cause for scandal except when the woman misbehaved. Vespasian, Marcus Aurelius, and Antoninus Pius — all emperors of good reputation — lived with concubines after the death of their wives. They already had heirs to their throne, and, by choosing to live with women whom it was impossible for them to marry, they may have intended to avoid the squabbles between heirs descended from different wives which . . . characterized the Hellenistic monarchies.

The Social Background of Christianity in the Roman Empire

A. H. M. JONES

Native Roman religion was family-oriented, and the civic religion, as it developed, continued to rely heavily on the *gentes*, or clans. It was a practical and patriotic religion devoted to appeasing the gods who controlled the harvest, war, and civic affairs. Religious leadership was vested in a college of priests drawn from the best families and headed by the *pontifex maximus*, or highest priest. With the expansion of Rome's power, the priesthood gained political influence because it controlled the religious calendar. Public business could not be conducted on holidays, and the constant necessity of adjusting the imperfect Roman calendar gave the priesthood considerable power over the timing of public action. If a crucial vote on public policy was about to be taken, for example, the priests could impose a long cooling-off period by adjusting the calendar and declaring a holiday.

Notwithstanding this power, the priesthood remained remarkably independent during the difficult years of the late Republic. Julius Caesar did not appropriate the position of *pontifex maximus* when he became *dictator*, and Augustus, his successor, did not take the title until 13 B.C., when the holder of the office died. Thereafter, however, the title and the power of the *pontifex* was held by the emperor, and this continued even after Constantine embraced Christianity.

As the political power of the old Roman priesthood increased, the hold of the old religion over the Roman populace decreased. As the city became the center of power and commerce in an ever-widening empire, leading Romans began to show contempt for the superstitions of the old cults. After the establishment of Roman hegemony over Greece in 196 B.C., the influence of eastern religions permanently altered Rome's religious culture. Greek slaves and traders carried to Rome cults that had come to Greece from Thrace an Phrygia. These were the mysteries, cults through which men and women were initiated into a communal, mystical religious experience. As the old social associations broke down or atrophied in the altered circumstances of Roman imperial life, the new cults filled the need for community, order, and hope.

The great influx of mystery cults coincided with the early decades of the Principate founded by Augustus. Augustus and Tiberius, the first two emperors, were religiously conservative, bent on restoring the ancient glory and customs of Rome. Yet even they favored the mystery cult of the Great Mother, and their successors increasingly favored or at least condoned the establishment of the other mysteries. Two of Rome's most ancient and famous churches, San Clemente and Santa Maria in Trastevere, were built over the ruins of Roman houses in which there had been Mithraic shrines. There were thousands of such sanctuaries throughout the city and the empire.

This was the religious milieu in which the Apostles and their disciples began to preach Christianity. In fact, early Christianity resembled the mystery cults in its organization. Christian churches were like cells made up of relatively few members each and organized under the Roman laws governing private associations. Though the number of Christians grew, they did not gather together in one large community, but continued to meet in small groups. The persecutions that began in earnest during the third century drove these communities underground and made them seem even more mysterious than before. Hostile outsiders suspected Christians of crude antisocial activities, and the secrecy of the communities only enhanced this image. Similar criticism was leveled at other cults; for many Romans, all of them were subversive and perhaps even savage.

Who then became Christians? It used to be said that Christianity was a religion of the poor and uneducated. This view stemmed, it seems, from the relative obscurity of the religion in its first three hundred years and from the anti-intellectual remarks of some of its early leaders. Historians concluded that if the religion had attracted the elite of imperial society, it would have left some trace in the literature of the period, for the Roman upper classes were a literary elite. Also, the attitude of such early Christians as Tertullian (†ca. 225) toward classical learning indicated that the Christians were at odds with the dominant culture, and it was presumed that the leaders of imperial society would not be attracted to such an apparently anti-Roman religion. Recently, historians have challenged these presumptions. The evidence of archeology and the reassessment of the literary evidence have led them to conclude that the new religion from Palestine won converts in all classes. In the following article, A. H. M. Jones examines the social milieu of Christianity just when it began to expand rapidly and when it met the last significant resistance from conservative pagans in the senatorial class of the empire.

Christianity has always had its appeal for all sorts and conditions of men. Long before the conversion of Constantine made it politic for the ambitious to profess the emperor's religion, there were Christian senators and soldiers, and even Christian professors. But it remains true that for one reason or another Christianity was at the end of the third century more widely diffused in some areas and classes of society than in others. This fact makes a study of the social background against which Christianity fought its battle with paganism essential for a proper understanding of that struggle.

From A. H. M. Jones, "The Social Background of the Struggle between Paganism and Christianity," *The Conflict between Paganism and Christianity in the Fourth Century,* A. Momigliano, ed. (Oxford: The Clarendon Press, 1963), pp. 17–37.

Christianity was at this date far stronger in the Greek-speaking provinces of the empire than in the Latin-speaking areas. This was, of course, mainly due to the fact that it had originated in an eastern province, and that its earlier missionaries were Greek-speaking. Missionary activity, it is true, was at a very early date extended to the West, but it was at first confined to the colonies of Greek-speaking immigrants in Rome and other large towns. Latin-speaking Christianity first emerges at Carthage towards the end of the second century, but at this period the Church at Lyons was still mainly composed of Greek-speaking orientals, and the Roman Church continued to use Greek down to the third century, and perhaps even later. Even in the fourth century, to judge by the density of bishoprics, the western provinces lagged far behind the eastern. There were areas, such as peninsular Italy and Africa, where Christianity was widely diffused, but in northern Italy, and still more in Gaul, Spain, and Illyricum, many quite important towns still lacked a bishop in the early fourth century.

In the second place Christianity was still in the fourth century a mainly urban religion. This was partly due to the methods whereby Christianity was diffused. The early missionaries moved from city to city and rapidly spread the gospel over a very wide area, but at the expense of leaving the intervening countryside untouched. The early churches were thus urban communities, and they tended to remain so. There was in most parts of the empire a sharp cleavage between town and country: in many areas the peasants did not speak either of the two dominant languages of the empire, but still used their old Coptic, Syriac, Thracian, Celtic, or Berber tongues. Communication must then have been difficult even if urban Christians had taken more interest in their rural neighbours.

But the slow progress of Christianity in the rural areas is also to be attributed to the inherent conservatism of the peasantry. Peasants have at all times and in all places resisted change and clung stubbornly to their traditional way of life. Even in the sixth and seventh centuries, when they had for the most part long been converted, the Church in Gaul and Spain, as repeated canons of the contemporary councils show, had great difficulty in suppressing the old rites whereby they had from time immemorial warded off pests and promoted the fertility of their flocks and fields.

There are, of course, exceptions to this generalization. As early as the reign of Trajan Pliny notes, with some surprise, it would seem, that 'the contagion of this superstition has permeated not only the cities but also the villages and countryside'. It would appear that during the latter part of the third century Christianity became dominant in the rural areas of Africa and Egypt. It has been pointed out that in both countries pagan dedications at rural shrines come to an abrupt end in the middle of the third century. This in itself is not very good evidence, for at that troubled period inscriptions in general became very sparse. But it is perhaps permissible to argue back from later conditions. The story of the Donatist controversy makes it plain that by the 340's Christianity was dominant in rural Africa: the Circumcellions, who were certainly peasants, were already by this period a power in the land. In Egypt the scandal of the broken chalice reveals that at a slightly earlier date there was a well-established system of rural parishes in Mareotes. If one goes back a generation to the time of the Great Persecution, Africa and Egypt stand out sharply in our record for the number of their martyrs and confessors, and it might be inferred that the exceptional stubbornness of the Christian resistance in these areas was due to the fact that the peasant masses, who were made of tougher stuff than the townsmen, had adopted the new faith.

The evidence that the African and Egyptian peasantry were already predominantly Christian by the beginning of the fourth century, is admittedly tenuous. By contrast there is in other areas strong evidence that at much later dates paganism was still strong in the countryside. The Life of Martin of Tours reveals that in the later decades of the fourth century rural temples and festivals were flourishing in Gaul. Rather later John Chrysostom appealed to the Christian landlords of Constantinople to take some interest in the spiritual welfare of their tenants, and to win them to the faith by endowing priests and building churches on their estates. Even in the age of Justinian John of Ephesus, as the result of a prolonged missionary campaign in the rural areas of Asia, Caria, Lydia, and Phrygia— districts among the first to be evangelized—found 80,000 pagans to baptize. In the West, at the end of the sixth century, Pope Gregory the Great found that in Sardinia there was a substantial number of peasants, including tenants of the church, who paid the governor of the island a regular *douceur* to secure his connivance for their pagan worship.

In the third place Christianity had made relatively little progress among the aristocracy, or indeed among the educated upper classes in general. This was not for want of trying, for the Church early appreciated the importance of winning converts in governing circles. But among the upper classes the education which they had received created a strong resistance to the new faith. It must be remembered that in its early days Christianity was a more uncompromising faith than it later became, and had not yet acquired that wide variety of appeal which make it all things to all men. Christians regarded the old gods with fear and aversion: they were evil and active demons and any contact with them was dangerous. This being so, many believers felt that classical culture, permeated as it was with paganism, was to be rejected *in toto*: to study it was, if not sinful, playing with fire.

There was, it is true, in the third and even in the second century, a number of cultivated Christians who managed to accommodate their faith to classical culture, but the feeling long lingered that the two were incompatible. In Jerome's famous dream the Heavenly Judge answered his plea 'Christianus sum' by the stern retort 'Ciceronianus es, non Christianus', and even at the end of the sixth century Pope Gregory the Great severely reproved the Bishop of Vienna for teaching grammar: 'one mouth cannot contain the praises of Christ with the praises of Jupiter.' This feeling must have been far stronger in the early fourth century, when the synthesis of Christianity and classical culture was still in its infancy, and it formed a very real stumbling-block to men who had been brought up to reverence the poets, philosophers, and orators of Greece and Rome.

In the second place we must not forget that Christianity was in its early days a vulgar religion. Not only were most of its adherents persons of low degree and little or no education, but its holy books were uncouth and barbaric, written in a Greek or Latin which grated on the sensibilities of any educated man, bred up on Menander and Demosthenes, or Terence and Cicero. It is difficult for us to appreciate how serious an obstacle this was. On the one hand, we are accustomed to Biblical language, and venerate the Authorized Version as among the noblest monuments of English prose. And in the second place we find it hard to realize the immense importance attached in antiquity to verbal form. But under the Roman empire higher education was almost exclusively devoted to rhetoric, the art of correct and elegant speech, and the men who were the products of that education naturally tended to attach more importance to the form than to the content of what they read. Jerome himself confesses that when he weakly indulged himself by reading Plautus he found the Hebrew prophets very unpalatable. When Julian forbade Christians to teach the classics, and contemptuously ordered them 'to go to the churches of the Galileans and expound Matthew and Luke', only two Christian professors took up his challenge. But even they felt that the Christian scriptures were in their crude form impossible as a vehicle of education and proceeded to rewrite them as epic poems, Attic tragedies, and Platonic dialogues. In this mental climate it was difficult for any educated man to accept the new faith.

For members of the senatorial aristocracy there was yet another obstacle. Senators, believing themselves to be descendants of the republican nobility, and holding the republican magistracies and priesthoods, felt themselves to be the inheritors and guardians of the ancient traditions of Rome. Rome had grown to greatness under the protection of the old gods whom she so piously cherished: 'this worship brought the world under my sway', Symmachus pictures her pleading, 'these rites repelled Hannibal from the walls and the Senones from the Capitol'. It was difficult for men bred in these traditions to believe that Jupiter Optimus Maximus was a malignant demon.

It is very difficult to estimate how far, despite these adverse factors, Christianity had by the beginning of the fourth century penetrated into the upper classes. The edict of Valerian, laying down special penalties for senators and *equites Romani* who refused to conform, suggests that as early as 257 there were some Christians in these classes. The canons of the council of Iliberris, probably held shortly before the Great Persecution, lay down penances for Christians who as provincial *sacerdotes* or municipal *duoviri* or *flamines* take part in pagan rites or celebrate games. This would imply that there were not a few Christians among the curial class in Spain, and, indeed, among its richest and most prominent members, who held not only the highest municipal offices and priesthoods, but even the supreme honour of the provincial high priesthood. But it would seem likely that in the upper strata of society Christians were in a very small minority. The old senatorial families certainly remained predominantly pagan done to the latter part of the fourth century.

The main strength of Christianity lay in the lower and middle classes of the towns, the manual workers and clerks, the shopkeepers and merchants. It is significant that the city of Cyzicus (that is its council) sent an official delegation to Julian to ask for the restoration of its temples, while Eleusius, the bishop who had destroyed them, was supported by the workers in the local mint and government clothing factory. There were also Christians among the humbler decurions. The social range of the curial class was very wide, and while leading decurions of the great cities ranked not far below senators in birth, wealth, and culture, many humbler members of the council, especially in the smaller towns, were modest farmers or craftsmen with no pretension to culture. Diocletian even ruled that illiteracy was no bar to curial status.

But here again it is impossible to generalize, for there were sharp local variations whose reasons we often cannot fathom. There were some towns where the bulk of the population was early Christian, but there were others which long remained solidly pagan. In Mesopotamia Edessa was Christian even in the third century, but at Carrhae paganism was still dominant long after the Arab conquest. In Syria Antioch was strongly Christian in Julian's day, but the Apamenes defended their temples with spirit in the reign of Theodosius the Great. Palestine was in general a Christian province in the fourth century, but at Gaza the Christian community was still only a handful when Porphyry became their bishop in 395, and the temples, despite Theodosius' penal laws, were still open and the pagan cult overtly celebrated.

Let us now consider the bearing of these facts on the conflict of religions in the fourth century. The economy of the Roman empire was to an overwhelming extent agricultural. The vast majority of its inhabitants were peasants, and its wealth was almost entirely derived from their labours. The state drew, it would seem, over 90 per cent. of its revenue from taxes levied on land and on the agricultural population. The upper classes derived almost all their wealth from rents paid by peasant tenants.

Despite their immense numerical preponderance, however, and their vital economic importance, the opinions of the peasantry did not count for anything. They were merely a vast inert and passive, if stubborn, mass. This is demonstrated by their passive attitude when in the course of the fourth century pagan rites were banned and the temples closed or destroyed. Very occasionally they might lynch a tactless missionary or offer resistance to the destruction of their shrines. But recorded instances of violence are very rare, and pagan townsmen seem to have been far more active in defending their temples. This was no doubt partly because the laws against paganism were even more laxly enforced in the countryside than in the towns, but on the whole the peasantry seem to have submitted quietly to authority. This is not to say that they readily abandoned their ancestral rites and beliefs. Christianity gradually conquered the country-side, it is true, but it was a very slow process, by no means complete even in the sixth century. But the peasantry offered a passive resistance only, stubbornly carrying on their ancient worship, overtly if, as often was the case, the authorities did not bother to interfere, or could be bribed to turn a blind eye, or surreptitiously if the law was enforced.

It follows from what I have said that the proletariat of the towns, and the shop-keeping and mercantile class, were numerically and economically insignificant. They were far outnumbered by the peasantry, and the only tax which they paid, the *collatio lustralis*, was a very small item in the budget. Except for the workers in the mints and the arms and clothing factories, they were not essential to the state. On the other hand, they had greater opportunities for expressing their views and making them felt. They could and did shout slogans in the theatre and at other public gatherings, and if such demonstrations did not produce the desired result, they could riot. In the absence of any adequate police, riots, especially in the larger cities, often assumed dangerous proportions, and troops had to be used to quell them.. In this way the urban poor exercised an influence which was not justified by their numbers and economic importance. But they were not more than a nuisance, and could be suppressed whenever the government chose by a relatively small display of force.

An obviously much more important element was the army. The army was in the fourth century recruited, in what proportions we do not know, from three main sources—the sons of serving soldiers and veterans, peasants conscripted from the countryside, and barbarians from beyond the frontiers of the empire. Prima facie, then, it should at the beginning of the century have been overwhelmingly pagan. There were, of course, some Christian soldiers even in the third century. There are a few genuine acts of military martyrs, and in 298 the proconsul of Africa could retort to a Christian conscientious objector: 'There are Christian soldiers who serve in the armies of our lords Diocletian and Maximian, Constantius and Maximian.' But this, it may be noted, was said in Africa, where, as we have seen, the peasantry were probably already converted to the new faith. The famous Theban legion, if it is not a myth, will also have come from an exceptional area, Egypt. But by and large there must have been very few Christians in the army when Constantine decided to paint the [☧] monogram on the shields of his soldiers before the battle of the Milvian Bridge. The barbarians were still pagan, and so were the bulk of the peasantry, especially in the favourite recruiting grounds of the army, Gaul and Illyricum. We have, in fact, a little piece of evidence that the army which two years later, under the protection of the labarum, fought and won the war against Licinius, which was in Constantine's propaganda a crusade against a pagan tyrant, was still pagan. A curious law in the Theodosian Code has preserved the acclamations of the veterans discharged after the victory. 'Auguste Constantine, dei te nobis servent' is what they shouted, and the offensive words were not emended to 'Deus te nobis servet' until Justinian re-edited the law for insertion in his Code.

How far the army became christianized as the fourth century progressed it is very difficult to say. Its intake must have remained predominantly pagan. Christianity, as we have seen, made slow progress in the countryside, and the bulk of the peasant conscripts must have continued to belong to the old faith. With the conversion of the Goths and other east German tribes, some of the barbarian recruits will have been Christians, but the bulk of the barbarians in the fourth century seem to have come from the Franks and Alamans, who were still and long remained heathens. The army might have been expected to be a powerful force on the pagan side of the struggle.

Actually it played a purely passive role. It obeyed with equal loyalty Constantine and his sons, Julian the Apostate, and his Christian successors. It may be that military discipline and the habit of obedience were stronger forces than religious conviction. But what little evidence there is suggests rather that soldiers conformed more or less passively to the prevailing religion of the state whatever it might be for the time being. Julian seems to have inherited from Constantius II an army which was superficially at any rate largely Christian. His statement in his letter to Maximus that the bulk of the Gallic army, which he was leading against Constantius, worshipped the gods, reads like a boast of the achievement and implies that in the brief period since his proclamation he had changed the religious tone of the troops. Gregory Nazianzen's description of his insidious propaganda once again implies that Julian found the army of the East full of Christians, and its tone suggests that his success in winning the troops back to the old religion was considerable. Yet when Julian was dead the army accepted the Christian Jovian without ado, if without enthusiasm, and acclaimed Valentinian, who had publicly demonstrated his devotion to the new religion by resigning his commission under Julian.

The religious indifference of the army in an age when religious passions ran so high is a curious phenomenon. The explanation would seem to be that the army consisted of men torn from their normal environment and plunged into a new world where everything was unfamiliar. In his own village the peasant clung stubbornly to the immemorial beliefs and customs of his community, but when he was delivered over to the recruiting officers and marched to a distant province and posted among a heterogeneous crowd of strangers, he lost his bearings. His old gods were far away, and bewildered he accepted the prevailing worship of the army. The situation of barbarian recruits was similar. They too were plunged into an alien environment, and the majority seem to have been assimilated to it, losing touch with their tribesmen at home, and adopting Roman ways, and with them the prevailing Roman religion.

There were still at the end of the fourth century and at the beginning of the fifth some high-ranking German officers who retained their pagan faith despite many years in the Roman service—the Frank Arbogast and the Goths Fravitta and Generid: but the two last are noted as exceptional. Under a succession of Christian emperors the general tone of the army must have become more and more Christian. The sons of soldiers and veterans would have been normally brought up in the new religion, and barbarian and peasant recruits would have been quickly assimilated. It is noteworthy that when Arcadius had to employ military force to effect the arrest of John Chrysostom, he used a regiment of newly recruited Thracians. He may have feared that his more seasoned troops might have had scruples about dragging a bishop from the altar, and therefore have employed new recruits who were still pagans.

To turn to the upper classes, the old senatorial order, though it retained immense wealth and social prestige, had ceased in the latter part of the third century to possess much political influence. Under Gallienus, if we are to believe Aurelius Victor, senators had been excluded from military commands, and Diocletian, in his reorganization of the empire, relegated them to a very minor role. The prefecture of the city and the two proconsulates of Africa and Asia were still reserved for senators, and they could serve as *correctores* of the Italian provinces and of Achaea, but apart from these dignified but practically unimportant posts they took no part in the administration of the empire, which was entrusted to men of equestrian rank. The equestrian order thus became in effect the official aristocracy of the empire, and it was greatly increased in numbers. For not only did Diocletian's reforms involve the creation of many new posts, military and administrative, but many who aspired to the social prestige and legal privileges of the order secured admission to it by the grant of honorary offices or of the titular ranks of *egregius, centenarius, ducenarius,* or *perfectissimus.*

Constantine was less hostile to the senate, increasing the number of posts reserved for senators, admitting them to other high administrative offices, and enrolling them among his *comites.* At the same time he began

to expand the order, granting senatorial rank to many of his higher equestrian officers, and to others whom he favoured. His policy was carried on
by his sons, and gained momentum, so that by the middle of the fourth
century it had become normal for all the higher civilian offices to carry
senatorial rank: that is, on the one hand, senators by birth were eligible
for them, and, on the other hand, men of lower degree appointed to them
thereby became senators. The same policy was under Valentinian and
Valens applied to the higher military offices. The result was that the
equestrian order, limited to a decreasing number of lower-grade posts,
waned in power and prestige, and the socially ambitious no longer aspired
to be enrolled in it. The senatorial order, on the other hand, became once
more the official aristocracy of the empire, but it was at the same time
vastly inflated in numbers and profoundly modified in character. Not only
was it swelled by those who entered it by tenure of civilian, and later military, offices. Those who had previously aspired to the equestrian order
now strove by the tenure of honorary senatorial offices or the grant of the
clarissimate to make their way into the senate. This influx into the senate
threatened to deplete the municipal aristocracy of the empire, the curial
order, and the imperial government made periodic efforts to check it. But
its efforts were not very whole-hearted, and no regulations were proof
against interest and bribery. The senatorial order continued to expand,
particularly in the eastern half of the empire, where Constantius II, in his
efforts to build up his own senate in Constantinople to parity with that of
Rome, enrolled thousands of new members.

The new senators were drawn from very various origins. A very
large number, as was only natural, came from the upper ranks of the
curial class, the old families of the provincial and municipal aristocracy.
According to the prevailing standards of the day such men were in virtue
of their birth, wealth, and education fitted to hold the civilian offices and
eminently eligible for admission to the senatorial aristocracy. Moreover,
they possessed the social connexions and the money to press their claims
effectively. Both official posts and senatorial rank were normally obtained
by the interest of great men about the court, and this interest had often to
be bought by hard cash. Men of position and wealth obviously had advantage in making the necessary contacts, and recompensing their patrons
adequately for their services.

But a considerable number of the new senators, including many who
rose to the highest rank, came from lower in the social scale. There were
those who rose through the army by the tenure of the office of *magister
militum, comes rei militaris,* or *dux.* Many of these military men were barbarians, but there were not a few Romans, and as the army in the fourth
century offered a *carrière ouverte aux talents,* some of these were of quite
humble origins. We happen to know of two peasants who rose from the

ranks to high commands, Arbetio, who as *magister peditum* was long one of the most influential men in the court of Constantius II, and the elder Gratian, the father of Valentinian and Valens, who achieved the rank of *comes rei militaris.* Such cases were relatively rare, but there must have been a considerable number of senators whose fathers had started life as simple peasants.

The bar was also an avenue whereby able and ambitious men of humble origin could rise. It was the practice for the military and civilian administrators to select rising young barristers to serve as their judicial assessors, and after tenure of two or three such posts they were normally appointed to a provincial governorship, and might rise to the praetorian prefecture. Libanius laments that the law had become such a popular profession that humane studies were falling into neglect. Men of liberal education no longer got the jobs, they all went to barristers; and as a result the young men despised rhetoric and flocked to Berytus to the law schools. Not all barristers, of course, were men of humble origin: wealthy *curiales* and even senators did not disdain the profession. But it was possible for men of very modest status to climb to the top of the tree. Maximinus, who ultimately became praetorian prefect of the Gauls and one of Valentinian's right-hand men, was the son of a very low-grade civil servant, a financial clerk in the provincial office of Valeria.

If the promotion of barristers provoked Libanius' indignation, the rise to power of palatine civil servants, in particular of imperial notaries, roused him to a white heat of fury. What an age, he exclaims more than once, when a shorthand clerk becomes praetorian prefect. It was the function of the imperial notaries to keep the minutes of the consistory, and they were in the early fourth century simple clerks, whose only qualification was a knowledge of shorthand, and were normally men of very humble status. But from their intimate association with the emperor and his ministers they had great opportunities for advancement. They were employed for confidential missions, were appointed to the palatine ministries, and sometimes rose to the highest office of state. In one of his speeches Libanius gives a list of men who had thus risen from stenographers to senators. It includes many of the great names of the eastern half of the empire during the middle fourth century: Ablabius, Constantine's great praetorian prefect, consul in 331; Datianus, consul in 358; and four of Constantius II's praetorian prefects—Philippus, consul in 348, Taurus, consul in 361, Elpidius, and Domitianus. And of these, he declares, Datianus was the son of a cloakroom attendant in a bath, and Philippus of a sausage-maker, while Ablabius started as a clerk in a provincial office, and Domitianus' father was a manual worker.

The senatorial order thus became during the course of the fourth century a very mixed body. Its composition and structure differed in East and West. At Rome there was a strong nucleus of ancient families which claimed descent from the Gracchi and the Scipios. Tenuous as these claims might be, their members regarded themselves and were accepted as aristocrats of the bluest blood, and enjoyed immense inherited wealth. Many of them were content to hold the ornamental offices which they regarded as their due, and took no active part in the government of the empire. But some, like the great Petronius Probus, played an active part in politics. In the West the senatorial order had two main foci. Rome was the titular capital of the empire and the official seat of the senate. Here the old families reigned supreme. But the administrative capital of the emperor was no longer Rome but the imperial *comitatus*, wherever the emperor might be for the time being, at Milan, Paris, or Sirmium. Here members of the old families were less at home, and were outnumbered by new men who had risen in the emperor's service.

In the East there was no such division. Constantinople was both the centre of government and the seat of the senate, and the *comitatus* and the senatorial order were closely intertwined, with the result that the court dominated the senate. Moreover, at Constantinople there was no hard core of ancient families. As Libanius with rather heavy irony puts it: 'the whole senate does not consist of nobles whose ancestors for four generations back and more have held offices and served on embassies and devoted themselves to the public service.' Constantius II no doubt enrolled all senators who were already domiciled in his dominions, but they can have been few and undistinguished. The *élite* of the Constantinopolitan senate was formed of men like Philippus and Taurus who had risen to high office from quite humble origins: it was the descendants of such men who in the fifth and sixth centuries were the aristocracy of the eastern empire.

These facts have their bearing on the religious struggle, for the religion of senators was to some extent determined by their social origins. In the eastern parts the upper layer of the order was mainly composed of men who had risen from the strata of society most strongly impregnated by Christianity, the lower middle class and even, if Libanius is to be believed, the proletariat of the towns. In fact most of the leading men in the East in the fourth century were so far as we know Christians; the two principal exceptions were Themistius, who owed his advancement to his repute as a philosopher, and Tatian, a barrister, who after a long administrative career rose to be praetorian prefect. Many of them were no doubt Christians before their rise to power, and those who were not had not been conditioned against Christianity by a rhetorical education, and found little difficulty in accepting the faith of the court.

The great bulk of the eastern senators, who came from the upper layer of the curial order, would have been more divided in their allegiance. They came from families which cherished their Hellenic heritage, and higher education for long retained a strongly pagan colour in the East. Most of the great rhetoricians and philosophers were pagans in the fourth century, and even in the fifth and sixth centuries many remained so. Zacharias of Mytilene in his life of Severus of Antioch gives a striking picture of university life at Alexandria, where he and Severus were students, in the last quarter of the fifth century. Not only, it seems, were most of the professors pagans, but so were a large proportion of the students, and he tells lurid tales of the hidden temple where they conducted their secret rites. Even in the sixth century Athens, which remained the leading university town of the East, was still strongly pagan in tone until Justinian expelled the philosophers.

The persistence of paganism among the cultured classes of the East must not then be underestimated. Even in the second half of the sixth century a purge conducted by Tiberius Constantine revealed the existence of many crypto-pagans among the aristocracy. But the furious outcry raised by Julian's law against Christian professors shows how deeply Christianity had penetrated among the educated classes by the middle of the fourth century, especially in the eastern half of the empire. It was not only that there were many Christian teachers, including so celebrated a figure as Prohaeresius, who lost their posts. There were evidently a vast number of Christian parents who regarded a rhetorical education as essential for their sons, but feared that under Julian's régime the schools would become militantly pagan. It is probable that by this time only rather old-fashioned and puritanical Christians felt any objection to a classical education as such, and many pious parents did not even scruple to send their sons to professors who were well known to be pagan; John Chrysostom was sent to Libanius by his mother, a devout Christian. In these circumstances many of the *curiales* promoted to the senate of Constantinople may have been Christians and the influence of the court and of the higher aristocracy must have converted many waverers. On the whole, the senate of Constantinople was probably from its origin a predominantly Christian body.

In the West, on the other hand, the old families remained on the whole faithful to their traditional religion down to the end of the fourth century, and since they dominated Roman society, the senate at Rome was strongly pagan. This is amply demonstrated by the petitions which it officially presented to Gratian and Valentinian II for the restoration of the altar of Victory and of the Roman priesthoods.

How far the senatorial order as a whole was predominantly pagan or Christian it is more difficult to say. Ambrose in 384 claimed that 'the *curia* is crowded with a majority of Christians', and in 382 Pope Damasus, as a counterblast to the official request of the senate for the restoration of the altar of Victory, was able to organize a monster petition of Christian senators, who protested that they had given no such mandate, did not agree with such requests of the pagans, and did not give their consent to them. It is obviously impossible at this distance of time to discover the truth behind the rival propaganda of the two sides. From the fact that only two years after Damasus had got up his petition the senate again sent an official request to the emperor it is clear that at Rome the Christian opposition was weak, whether because Christian senators resident in the city were actually in a minority or because they were for the most part relatively humble members of the order, who dared not stand up to the great aristocrats. From the language of the petition it would appear that its signatories had not attended the meeting at which the resolution was voted. This may mean that they had not dared to voice their opposition openly. But it is more likely that Damasus obtained his 'innumerable' signatures by sending a round robin to non-resident senators. These would have been for the most part new men, and among them the proportion of Christians would have actually been higher.

At the court at Milan the balance, as the rejection of the senate's pleas showed, inclined to the Christian side. But the decision was by no means a foregone conclusion, and it needed all Ambrose's zeal and eloquence to sway the consistory.

These facts account in a large measure for the very different course which the struggle took in East and West. In the East the pagan opposition was never a serious political force. It was in both senses of the word academic. The leaders of paganism were almost all professors, Maximus, Themistius, Libanius, and the rest. The strongholds of paganism were the university towns, foremost among them Athens. It survived longest among students and intellectuals. Moreover, in the pejorative sense of the word the pagan opposition was academic. It was unorganized and ineffectual, finding expression only in speeches and pamphlets. When Theodosius the Great closed the temples and banned pagan cult, there was no serious opposition apart from the heroic but futile attempt of the philosopher Olympius to hold the Serapeum at Alexandria with a band of enthusiasts. Pagans thereafter contented themselves with furtively practising their rites in secret and nourishing apocalyptic dreams of the return of the old gods. As late as the reign of Zeno great excitement was caused among the pagan intellectuals of Asia Minor when the Neoplatonist philosopher Pamprepius became master of the offices to the pretender Leontius. They began to offer sacrifice openly on his behalf and an oracle was circulated that the span allotted by fate for Christianity had come to an end and that the old gods would come into their own again. Needless to say, their hopes were quite unfounded. Leontius, or rather his patron, the Isaurian general Illus, made no move in favour of paganism.

This weakness of paganism is partly accounted for by their numerical inferiority in the East. More important, however, than the question of mere numbers was that of political leadership. There was in the East no hereditary aristocracy bred up in the old ways to lead the opposition. The governing class at Constantinople was largely composed of parvenus drawn from the classes where Christianity was strongest, and the senate was from its first formation predominantly Christian in tone.

It cannot be claimed that the pagan opposition was very much more effective in the West, but here the Roman aristocracy did at least make an official stand for the old religion, and its representations, though rejected, were taken into serious consideration. What is more significant, a pretender at the end of the fourth century thought it worth while to make concessions to the pagan sentiments of the senate. Eugenius, though himself a Christian, if not a very fervent one, restored the altar of Victory and handed over the endowments of the Roman priesthood to pagan senators. This rather half-hearted gesture met with a vigorous response, and the Roman aristocracy, led by Flavian, the praetorian prefect of Italy, threw themselves wholeheartedly into the struggle on Eugenius' behalf. They, too, dreamed of a pagan restoration, but their dreams had rather more substance than those of their eastern fellow believers.

It may be claimed that the social changes of the third and fourth centuries were an important factor in the triumph of Christianity in the empire as a whole. When Constantine staked his faith on the god of the Christians in 312, he was on all human calculations making a very rash venture. Christians were on any reckoning a small minority, particularly in the West, where the struggle with Maxentius was to take place, and they mostly belonged to classes which were politically and militarily negligible, the manual workers, shopkeepers, merchants, and lesser decurions of the towns and the clerks of the civil service. The army was overwhelmingly pagan. The senate was pagan. So too in all probability was the bulk of the provincial and municipal aristocracy, and the majority of higher administration, drawn as they were from the army and the curial class. By making himself the champion of Christianity, Constantine can hardly have hoped to win for himself any useful support, and might reasonably have feared to provoke antagonism in many important quarters; and this is incidentally to my mind an important piece of circumstantial evidence in favour of the view that Constantine's conversion was not a calculated political move, but, as he himself consistently proclaimed in his public pronouncements, the fruit of a genuine if crude religious conviction that the Highest Divinity, who had chosen him as his servant, was a more potent giver of victory than the old gods.

The situation was not, however, as unfavourable as it appeared. For at the time when Constantine made his fateful decision Roman society was in a state of flux. The late Roman empire is often conceived as a rigid hierarchical society, in which every man was tied to the station in life to which he was born. The long series of laws on which this view is based seem to me to reveal a very different picture. They show that the imperial government was struggling to impose a rigid hereditary class system, but such legislation would not have been called for had not the familiar structure of society been shaken; and the constant re-enactment of the rules, and the periodical concessions made, show that the government was very imperfectly successful in checking the movements which it regarded as dangerous. There is much evidence which suggests that society was static in the second and early third centuries. The army was to an increasing degree recruited from the sons of soldiers and veterans. The peasants tilled the same farms, whether they were freeholders or tenants, from generation to generation. The decurions were a mainly hereditary class, where son succeeded father to the ancestral estates. The aristocracy of the empire, the senate, and the equestrian order, failed it is true to maintain its numbers and was constantly supplemented from below; but the rate of recruitment was slow, and the new members, who mainly came from the provincial aristocracy, were readily assimilated.

Under the impact of the prolonged crisis of the mid-third century this stable society was profoundly shaken. For a variety of reasons men of all classes became dissatisfied with their hereditary position in life, and the conditions of the time gave opportunities for change. The population had probably shrunk as a result of the wars, famines, and plagues of the years of anarchy, and at the same time the army was making increasing demands for men. The consequence was an acute shortage of manpower, which made itself particularly felt in the empire's major industry, agriculture. Landlords could not find enough tenants to cultivate their lands, and welcomed newcomers to their estates. As a result dissatisfied tenants found themselves able to throw up their farms and move elsewhere with the certainty that another landlord would offer them a home. This restlessness among the peasantry caused grave concern to the government, which saw the basis of its fiscal system imperilled. The poll-tax was based on the assumption that the peasants registered under each village or farm would remain there and in due course be succeeded by their sons. The land-tax too seemed to be threatened, since landlords everywhere complained that their estates had been abandoned by their cultivators. This would seem to be the situation which provoked the legislation tying the agricultural population to the land on which they were registered on the census.

The manpower shortage gave rise to a similar restlessness in other classes of society and provoked similar legislation where, as in the mining industry, the government felt that the interests of the state were threatened. Another disturbing factor was the vast expansion of the administrative services entailed by Diocletian's reorganization of the empire. More and more clerks were required in the growing government offices, and many sons of soldiers and veterans, instead of enlisting in the army as hitherto, preferred a more comfortable and lucrative career as officials; *curiales* of the humbler sort likewise flocked into the ministries. Once again the government, finding the intake of the army reduced and the city councils, on which the administration of the empire and the collection of the taxes ultimately depended, dangerously depleted, endeavoured to tie the sons of soldiers and decurions to their respective hereditary roles.

But the most revolutionary change brought about by Diocletian was the formation of the new imperial nobility of service which I have outlined earlier in this lecture. This change was of crucial importance for the future of Christianity. For it meant that Constantine and his successors did not have to face a firmly entrenched hereditary aristocracy hostile to their religious innovation, but were able to build up and mould a new nobility more subservient to their wishes.

The senate had, it is true, under the principate been powerless to resist a resolute and ruthless emperor. But an emperor could only impose his will by a reign of terror, and while emperors came and went, the senate remained. Through the generations the senatorial order preserved to a remarkable degree a corporate sense of its dignity, and a spirit of independence and even of opposition to the imperial office. The great aristocratic families regarded themselves as superior to jumped-up emperors, and their birth and wealth made them independent of imperial patronage. Such a body might be bullied into submission, but its sentiments could not be easily influenced.

The new nobility of service was a very different body. A heterogeneous collection of individuals, drawn from all ranks of society, it inevitably lacked any corporate sense. And since its members were dependent on imperial patronage for their advancement, it was as inevitably subservient to the emperor's will and took its tone from him. Constantine and his Christian successors were thus able to build up an aristocracy in sympathy with their religious policy.

In the first place they were in a position to show direct favour to Christians. They could choose their ministers and advisers with a free hand from all classes of society, and bestow rank and dignity on whomsoever they wished to favour. They certainly used this opportunity to promote Christians of low degree. Constantine himself, according to Eusebius, was lavish in bestowing codicils of equestrian rank, and even senatorial dignity, on the adherents of his religion. But such a policy had its limits. The number of qualified Christians was too few to fill the posts, and any systematic exclusion of pagans would have provoked dangerous discontent: it was not in fact until the early years of the fifth century that the imperial service was formally debarred to pagans. But it soon became obvious to the ambitious that their chances of promotion would be greatly enhanced if they adopted the emperor's religion, and Eusebius himself deplores that Constantine's open-handed favour to Christians resulted in a large crop of interested conversions.

But it would be a grave injustice to the many upper-class converts of the fourth century to assume that they were all hypocritical opportunists. A more potent cause of conversion than calculations of material gain was the fact that Christianity became respectable and indeed fashionable in high society; and this change of tone came about the more easily because high society was in a state of flux. The old senatorial aristocracy had a strong conservative tradition, and clung firmly to the old religion, even when it was on the wane, from a sense of *noblesse oblige*. They still had great social prestige, and to some extent set the tone of society in the West, but in the East their position was usurped by the new senate of Constantinople, and even in the West it was disputed by the new nobility which clustered around the *comitatus*. In the new aristocracy of service Christians were not perhaps at first very numerous, but enjoying exceptional imperial favour and achieving the highest honours, they set the tone of the whole. The lesser members tended to follow their lead, and the fashion spread in ever-widening circles through the lower ranks of the social order.

Christianity had made great progress during the first three centuries, but it still remained a minority sect: it was still largely confined to the middle and lower classes and had made little impression on the aristocracy. Within a few generations of the conversion of Constantine it had become the dominant religion of the empire. In this revolution the support given to Christianity by the imperial government was without doubt a major factor. But it is significant that the religious change coincided with a social change, which brought to the front men from the middle and lower classes.

PART 2

The Early Middle Ages
6th ꞏ 11th Centuries

Detail from "Psalm 150" of the Utrecht Psalter, showing a prototypical organ, c. 830 A.D.

The Early Middle Ages

In the sixth century, the western Roman Empire fell to the Germans, who replaced the Roman political system with independent kingdoms. These kingdoms expressed the political unity of tribal groups that had been brought into federations just before and during the migrations of the fifth century. In Gaul, it was the Franks; in Spain, the Visigoths; in Italy, the Ostrogoths; In North Africa, the Vandals. These major groups slowly absorbed smaller ones like the Burgundians, the Thuringians, and the Alemans.

After the kingdoms were established, the kings of the principal confederations consolidated their positions by assuming the mantle of Roman authority. Everywhere in Europe, the German kings sought and received confirmation of their new power from the Roman emperors in Constantinople. For their part, the emperors had nothing to lose by granting the kings Roman titles. It preserved the image of imperial power, even though its reality had been gone for decades, and it helped to maintain good relations between the eastern Roman Empire and the occupants of the old imperial territories in Europe.

The new society of barbarian Europe was a compound of the old provincial society of the Roman Empire and the tribal society of the German invaders. Aware of this compound society, the kings issued dual codes of law for their subjects. The Romans continued, therefore, to live under a simplified version of Roman law, while the Germans lived under their ancient laws. The amalgamation of the two communities took generations.

The first selection in Part 2 treats German tribal society in the period just before the migration into the Roman territories. E. A. Thompson uses a Christian work, the life of St. Sabas, to illuminate a dark corner of the fourth century, the society of the Visigoths. In the second selection, William Chaney looks at the Germans in the west, the Anglo-Saxon peoples who settled in England. Again, the sources are of Christian origin, but whereas the biography of St. Sabas focused on the society of the village, the Anglo-Saxon writings emphasize the position of the sacral kings. Both selections describe the process of Christianization among the Germans and therefore complement the article by A. H. M. Jones in Part 1.

The Germanic lords of Europe changed the countryside as well as the cities. Many old villages remained as they had been for generations, but the invaders carved new ones out of the European forest; in these, they introduced new agricultural techniques. During the early middle ages, a technical revolution occurred in European agriculture; as it spread, it changed the way of life of the great majority of the population, the peasants. In the third selection, Eileen Power recreates the world of a medieval peasant by telling the story of Bodo.

In the fourth selection, we turn from consideration of the majority to consideration of a small, but important, minority—the Jews. The Jews came to the towns of northern Europe in the ninth century and formed tightly knit, prosperous communities. The authorities recognized the value of these communities and both encouraged immigration of Jews and protected them. But the population found them alien and mysterious, and persecution was a common experience of the Jews. Robert Chazan's "The Jews in a Christian Society" reveals the experience of this unassimilated minority at the time when the towns had begun to grow into major centers of population and commerce.

The final selection, Joshua Prawer's "The World of the Crusaders," takes us to the Holy Land, where the European conquerors established a colonial society after the First Crusade (1096–1099). In fact, this colony was only the most famous of those built by Europeans during the eleventh century. Beginning in the middle of the century, northerners had pushed steadily to reconquer the Iberian peninsula from the Moors, the Islamic north Africans who had occupied it since 711. In Spain, the new conquerors organized their new territories as colonial extensions of the ancient Christian communities that had clung to the southern flank of the Pyrenees since the time of Charlemagne. The colonial state in the Near East had much the same character as those in Spain: It was a plantation of western society in an alien world, which influenced virtually every aspect of the colony's social life.

BIBLIOGRAPHY

On the Germans and Germanic society, see Malcolm Todd, *The Northern Barbarians, 100 B.C.–A.D. 300* (London, 1976); Lucien Musset, *The Germanic Invasions* (State College, Pa., 1975). E. A. Thompson brought his studies of Germanic society together in *The Early Germans* (Oxford, 1965) and *The Visigoths in the Time of Ulfilas* (Oxford, 1969). For contrast, see Samuel Dill, *Roman Society in the Last Century of the Western Empire* (London, 1898) and *Roman Society in Gaul in the Merovingian Age* (London, 1926). This last work covers the period of the kingdoms that succeeded to the power of Rome in Europe. For a contemporary view of this period, see Gregory of Tours, *The History of the Franks*, trans. by Lewis Thorpe (Harmondsworth, Eng., 1974). J. M. Wallace-Hadrill, *The Barbarian West, 400–1000* (London, 1952), provides a good modern survey.

Most studies of rural life focus on the late thirteenth century and afterward because it was only in that period that adequate documentation began to be preserved. For a sociological approach, see George C. Homans, *English Villages of the Thirteenth Century* (Cambridge, Mass., 1941). This work is built on the studies and methods of Marc Bloch, whose writings form one of the bases of modern social history. See Marc Bloch, *French Rural History*, trans. by Janet Sondheimer (Berkeley, 1966). Excellent modern studies are: J. A. Raftis, *Tenure and Mobility: Studies in the Social History of the Medieval Village* (Toronto, 1964); R. H. Hilton, *A Medieval Society: The West Midlands at the End of the Thirteenth Century* (London, 1966); and Georges Duby, *Rural Society and Country Life in the Medieval West*, trans. by Cynthia Postan (London, 1968), which covers the early as well as the late medieval period.

Robert Chazan draws much of his material from the Responsa of the medieval rabbis, and a large selection of these judicial decisions has been translated by Irving Agus in *Urban Civilization in Pre-Crusade Europe*, 2 vols. (New York, 1965). The most complete study of the medieval Jews is Salo W. Baron, *A Social and Religious History of the Jews*, 2nd ed., vols. 3–8 (New York, 1957–58). See also, Cecil Roth and I. H. Levine, eds., *The Dark Ages: Jews in Christian Europe 711–1096* (New Brunswick, N.J., 1966). The Jewish view of the crusades is represented in contemporary chronicles now published in English by Shlomo Eidelberg, trans. and ed., *The Jews and the Crusaders* (Madison, Wisc., 1977).

There are many books on the crusades. A good general history is Steven Runciman, *A History of the Crusades*, 3 vols. (Cambridge, Eng., 1951–54). See also the studies presented in Kenneth Setton and Marshall W. Baldwin, eds., *A History of the Crusades*, Vol. 1: *The First Hundred Years* (Philadelphia, 1955). On the crusaders' kingdoms, see Dana C. Munro, *The Kingdom of the Crusaders* (New York, 1935) and Joshua Prawer, *The Crusaders' Kingdom: European Colonialism in the Middle Ages* (New York, 1973). For studies of the colonial society in Spain, see Robert I. Burns, *Medieval Colonialism: Postcrusade Exploitation of Islamic Valencia* (Princeton, 1975) and *Islam under the Crusaders: Colonial Survival in the Thirteenth-Century Kingdom of Valencia* (Princeton, 1973).

German Tribal Society

E. A. THOMPSON

Most of the sources that purport to describe the society of the early Germans actually were written long after the primitive tribal life had been permanently altered by contact with the romanized population of the empire. In spite of this, scholars have constructed elaborate theories about the structure of the early German communities. Some of these theories are monuments to the creative imagination.

The earliest theory, published in 1768, pictured the Germans as free farmers living in communities whose institutions were the prototypes of the liberal, democratic institutions developed in the eighteenth and nineteenth centuries. The members of these communities inhabited *Marks*, territorial units encompassing many homesteads and named for their position on the *marches*, or frontiers, of the Roman Empire. In the yearly assemblies of these *Marks*, the free warrior peasants took care of common affairs and elected their chiefs. Here was the noble savage, and in fact the original presentation of this picture was explicitly influenced by Rousseau's speculations. In the nineteenth century, those who elaborated the theory changed it slightly by making property ownership in the *Marks* communistic rather than private. The free warrior peasant and the democratic political organization remained, however.

In the late nineteenth century, the great French historian Fustel de Coulanges attacked the *Mark* theory, pointing out that there was no evidence to support it. He argued that the word *marca* in the ancient Latin texts simply meant "boundaries," and that there was no such thing as a *Mark* or the community that was supposed to occupy it. Fustel's criticism was largely ignored, but it did force proponents of the *Mark* theory to change the name of their creation — a nonexistent *Mark* by any other name exists. Further work on the history of the Germanic communities has shown, however, that Fustel was correct. Early Germanic society was aristocratic, and the free warrior peasant did not exist. The elective chieftainries and democratic institutions were also figments.

In this selection, E. A. Thompson demonstrates the method used to reconstruct ancient German Society while he analyzes the position of Christians within that society. His source is an example of a common medieval literary genre, the biography of a saint. Saints' lives, a popular type of didactic literature during the Middle Ages, quickly became stylized and formularized. Many of the lives were written before the saint was canonized and were in fact products of the effort to get him or her accepted into the calendar of saints. Once the requirements for becoming a saint were established, the hagiographers made certain that the demands were met by their man or woman. Even if the work was written after canonization, it had to preserve the image of the saint and thus did not deviate from the same formularized tradition. As a result, Thompson must distinguish between glimpses of the real St. Sabas and his society and those elements of the story determined by the hagiographical tradition. Because many of the stories were written an appreciable time after the events occurred, there is the further problem of dealing with anachronisms and misconceptions introduced into the account.

A complete text of the *Passio S. Sabae* and of certain kindred documents was published by Delehaye more than forty years ago. These works give us priceless information about early Visigothic Christianity and especially, of course, about Sabas himself, who was martyred on 12 April 372. They are also invaluable for the study of the society which produced Ulfila and the Gothic Bible. The *Passio* does what the works of Caesar and Tacitus never do—it brings us for the first time into a Germanic village and enables us to see something of how the villagers managed their own affairs. Yet it has received strangely little attention either from students of Roman history or from students of early Germanic society. . . . Here it is proposed to glance at the *Passio* as a source for the social organization of the Visigoths in the days of Ulfila.

We know from our other sources that the Visigoths, whenever they went to war, elected an over-all military leader who is called in Latin *iudex* and in Greek *dikastes*. But the *iudex* seems to have had as little personal authority as Germanic chiefs had had in the days of Tacitus. He could "advise" and "urge" his followers to accept his point of view, but he could not impose his will upon them: he had no powers of coercion. Power, such as it was, rested with the *optimates*, as Ammianus calls them, or the *megistanes*, as they are termed in the *Passio*. These no doubt formed a sort of Council and (though the point is not directly attested) they may have been the chiefs of the φυκαί of whom Eunapius speaks. For Eunapius tells us that the Visigoths were organized in "tribes" under tribal leaders, and the word φυκαί is no doubt equivalent to the Latin *pagi*. At any rate, there were tribal chiefs, as we may call them, below the general military leader of the people as a whole. But the *Passio*, as we have said, deals in the main with humbler people than the chiefs and the optimates: it is primarily concerned with the village in which Sabas lived, though it is by no means silent about the relations between this village and the central authority.

It depicts a time of persecution when the loyalty of the villagers to the pagan gods is to be put to the test: by order of the megistanes the

From E. A. Thompson, "*The Passio S. Sabae* and Early Visigothic Society," *Historia* 4 (1955), pp. 331–38 villagers will be required to eat sacrificial meat in public. How this decision was conveyed to the villagers is unknown. But village affairs are discussed in the first instance by a village council; and this council has determined that the villagers among them who are Christian must be spared in spite of the order of the megistanes: the Christians in their midst shall merely be induced to eat unconsecrated meat rather than sacrificial meat so that a true test may be avoided and the persecutors cheated. This is the plan on which the council has decided, but it must be discussed by all the villagers assembled together before it can be put into practice. Sabas like the other villagers has the right to speak, and he comes forward on two separate occasions and uses his right boldly: he will not submit to any such subterfuge as the council had suggested—he will never deny his Christianity. Accordingly, the plan put forward by the council members has to be modified; and when a representative of the megistanes comes round to the village to see how the test is progressing, the village councillors tell him that in fact there is one Christian among them—Sabas himself.

The whole of this scene described in the third chapter of the *Passio* is a vivid representation of a clan society in action. There is no indication that Sabas' procedure in disagreeing with the council's decision was illegitimate or even unusual. He merely expressed freely an opinion which was unpopular. The scene does not quite prove that the decision of the villagers had to be unanimous before action could be taken, though this may have been the case. At any rate, there was no machinery for suppressing Sabas' opinion or for preventing him from making his views known to the visiting chief; and still less was there any means of compelling him to change his attitude and to fall in with the opinion of the majority. Nor was Sabas an isolated case. We learn from another source that in addition to Sabas other Christians were given an opportunity of coming forward and speaking bravely on behalf of the faith in their respective villages. A further point is also noteworthy. After his first speech refusing to eat the meat the village council compelled Sabas to leave the village for a while, but shortly afterwards permitted him to come back. Now this does not in itself mean that the freedom of the villagers was disappearing and that a man who expressed an unpopular opinion was liable to be penalized. Sabas, as we shall see, had offended against the gods of the community by refusing to share their meal; and an offence against the gods was an offence against the community itself. Sabas' temporary expulsion was due to this offence—his refusal to take part in the sacrificial meal of the villagers—and not to the unpopularity of his opinions as such or to his being a Christian. The fact that he was a Christian was known to the villagers throughout the proceedings and even before the proceedings began, and was not resented by them. Indeed, when the news reached the village that the persecution had been initiated the first thought of the village councillors was how they could save Sabas. The temporary expulsion, then, was not due to Sabas' Christianity but to his unwillingness even to make a show of joining in the sacrificial meal. To that extent the expulsion was unconnected with the persecution as such.

It is a pity that it was not to the author's purpose to tell us more about the sacrifice and the sacrificial meal, which evidently formed an integral part of Visigothic village life. In a clan society the communal eating and drinking were a symbol and a confirmation of mutual social obligations. The man who refused to eat the sacrificial meat with his fellows thereby dissociated himself from their religion and from their social duties and rights: he had made himself an outcast. That is why the public eating of sacrificial meat was regarded by the megistanes as a test for men suspected of having become Christian. On the other hand, it is noteworthy that when he was first expelled from his village Sabas was soon allowed to return. On the second occasion the villagers might not have expelled him at all if pressure had not been put upon them by the visiting chief; and even then the saint might well have been spared if the village councillors could have shown to the persecutor that Sabas was a man of some property (*v. infra*). But even so Sabas was not lynched: action was not taken on the spur of the moment without a hearing of the merits of the case. On the contrary, the case was heard, and the action was taken by a man who had some measure of recognized authority. True, Sabas wa not put to death by his fellow villagers: the men who killed him came from outside the village. Yet the villagers in the end did nothing to help him, but abandoned him to his fate. He had put himself outside their protection by his refusal to join th their sacrificial feast. Now the Presbyter Sansalas, who is also mentioned in the *Passio*, does not seem to have been a Visigoth, for he is thought to bear an Asian name; and he was presumably descended from the Asian prisoners who had been carried off by the Visigoths during their great raids on Asia Minor in the mid-third century. Accordingly, it is of great interest to notice that Sansalas was not requested, so far as we know, to partake of the sacrificial meal, and although he was tortured he was not put to death. He crime was less than that of the Visigothic tribesman Sabas. Sansalas' offence was that he was a Christian, and this in a man of Asian descent was an offence during the period of the persecution but it was not a capital offence. Sabas' crime was that he had offended against the gods of his people, and for this as a Visigoth he became an outcast and was put to death.

To return to the village council: we do not know how this was chosen or who composed it. We might perhaps guess that it consisted of elders who were noted for their long experience of affairs and for their wisdom or for their prowess as warriors or hunters. At any rate, the council's two known functions were, first, that it represented the village in meetings with a member of the confederate council, and, secondly, that it discussed the business of the village before bringing to to the general

assembly of the villagers. In this last point it resembles the council which
pre-considered the business that was to come before the general assembly *council*
of the warriors in the first century A.D. The "national" council, as it were,
which Tacitus describes in his *Germania* (xi. 1) is reproduced on a smaller
scale by the village council referred to in the *Passio*. Finally, it may be
observed that there is no mention of a village chief or headman, and if
one had been present at these proceedings the author of the *Passio* could
not well have avoided making some mention of him. The unnamed, per-
secuting "leader" (*archon*) of the *Passio* comes to Sabas' village from
outside and knows little or nothing about the villagers. He must be the
leader of some larger unit than the village, and I have little doubt that he
wa one of the "tribal" leaders like those referred to by Eunapius.

What light does the *Passio* throw on these tribal chiefs, as we have
called them? If the confederate chief possessed few coercive powers in
wartime, it is unlikely that the tribal chiefs occupied a stronger position in
times of peace. True, it would be easy to conclude from one or two sen-
tences in the *Passio* that the persecution of the Christians in Sabas' village
was initiated by "the persecutor" of "the leader," that is, by an unnamed
chieftain. But in fact what the *Passio* shows is that the chiefs were merely
responsible for seeing that the persecution was actually enforced. A
number of phrases in the *Passio* indicate clearly that the persecution was
initiated not by any ruler or chief but by the confederate council. Indeed,
in one passage the author explicitly states that Atharid acted "on the order
of the impious ones." The plural should be noted. It unquestionably
means the confederate council, the megistanes; and that the ultimate
responsibility for the persecution lay with the megistanes is shown again
and again by the language of the *Passio*. When the confederate council
decided to persecute the Christians, the tribal chiefs went round the villages to see how the council's instructions were being carried out; and
when a chief, as representative of the council, came to a village the
members of the village council would appear before him and would give
him the information which he required. This, at any rate, was the procedure in Sabas' village, and there seems to be no reason why we should
not generalize from it. But the tribal chiefs were merely the instruments
through which the council acted. In times of peace and indeed for the
most part in wartime also even the confederate chief is not known to have
had any power over the life, liberty, and property of the tribesmen except
in so far as he carried out the decisions of the council. What we should
greatly like to have is some information on the part which the village or at
any rate the village councillors were allowed to play in the election of a
tribal chief. But of this we know nothing. We cannot say whether the
humble villagers had any right at this date when it came to the choosing
of a tribal leader.

However that may be, it is certain that the old egalitarian system
which Tacitus had described long ago was disappearing among the fourth-

century Visigoths. Quantities of property had begun to accumulate in private hands c. 370, and political power was also tending to concentrate in private hands. This is strikingly illustrated in a vivid scene depicted in the *Passio.* When the unnamed tribal chief in the course of the persecution heard that Sabas was an unrepentant Christian, he had him summoned to his presence. He then turned to the members of the village council, who were present, and asked them whether Sabas owned any property. He was told that Sabas owned nothing more than the clothes on his back. Thereupon the chief considered the saint to be of no consequence and said, "Such a man can neither help not harm us," and ordered him to be driven out of the village. The mere fact that the author of the *Passio* turns aside to record this remark of the chief's would seem to suggest that the words were in his opinion significant and disturbing: in connection with these words he calls the chief *anomos* — he was no respecter of tribal custom. Clearly, at that date not only had private property associated itself in the chief's mind with social power but the poor man unlike the man of property could "neither help nor harm" with execution of the confederate council's resolutions. There were sharp divisions of wealth in Visigothic society in the days of Ulfila.

In fact, the Christians in Gothia in Ulfila's time seem in general to have been drawn from the humbler strata of society. The descendants of the Roman prisoners taken in the raids on Asia Minor in the third century will scarcely have been of much social influence among the Visigoths. The Christian presbyter and his associates who were used by Fritigern as intermediaries during his negotiations with Valens in 378 are explicitly said to have been humble persons. The Audian bishop Silvanus was presumably the descendant of Roman prisoners. True, he may have been a Visigoth who adopted this Roman name on his conversion; but to believe that is merely to multiply hypotheses, and in fact Epiphanius describes him not as a Goth but as being "from Gothia." It can scarcely be doubted that Ulfila himself, like Selenas after him, was also the offspring of a very humble family in Gothia, and not being a pure-blooded Visigoth he would not have been a member of any clan. His foreign descent would have rigorously excluded him from membership, unless he had been willing to undergo the pagan rites of initiation and adoption, which in a man of Ulfila's uncompromising Arianism can scarcely be considered as a possibility. It is true that three arguments have been put forward to show that Ulfila was a well-to-do and perhaps even noble Visigoth; but these arguments cannot stand. They are (i) that he was free to leave Gothia in 348 when the first persecution took place; but then it would follow that all those who were driven out or who fled in the persecutions were well-to-do, which was not the case; (ii) that he acted as ambassador to Constantius; but the Christian who acted as ambassador to Valens, as we have just seen, is known to have been of humble birth — these Christians were doubtless chosen as envoys because they might as

Christians carry more weight with the Romans than barbarian pagans could do; (iii) that Eusebius of Nicomedia would not have made him bishop if his position among his people had not been a distinguished one; but Eusebius' action only suggests that Ulfila's position was distinguished not among the Visigoths as a whole but among the Christians in Gothia — and his distinction was due not to his birth but to his learning. Finally, the one Visigothic Christian about whom detailed information has survived, Sabas, is explicitly stated to have owned no property whatever and to have been therefore of no political account. At all events, nothing in our evidence suggests that the tribal nobility had been seriously affected by Christianity in the decades preceding 372; and indeed the *Passio* gives us positive evidence to the contrary; for it was "the megistanes throughout Gothia" who had decided on the persecution in the first place.

Finally, the *Passio* makes it clear that the confederate council, the megistanes, were able to exert stronger pressure on the villages than the latter, we may suspect, would have submitted to in the days of Tacitus. The fact is that to some extent the persecution of the Christians in 369 – 72 was imposed on the villages from above, and it was the megistanes who specified the test of the public eating of the sacrificial meat without any consultation, so far as we know, with the rank and file of the Visigoths. Indeed, the council in Sabas' village was reduced to a subterfuge in its effort to avoid carrying out the orders of the megistanes: they proposed to allow Christians to eat unconsecrated meat instead of sacrificial meat "so that they might keep their own men unharmed, and deceive the persecutors." In the second wave of persecution the council was actually willing to declare without ado to the prosecutor that there was no Christian in their village. They were even prepared to make this declaration on oath, a fact which suggests that enthusiasm in the village for the decisions of the megistanes was not always unbounded. But once again the obstinacy of Sabas himself foiled their well-intentioned deceit; and they admitted with some reluctance that in fact there was one Christian among them. Thereupon the chief, who had come to the village to see how the persecution was progressing "ordered" Sabas to be driven out of the village. On the first occasion on which Sabas was expelled it was the village council who had ordered him to go. But on the occasion of the second expulsion the village council appears to have been give no voice in the matter: they simply received instructions from the tribal chief to drive Sabas out. In the final wave of persecution the henchmen of the tribal chief Atharid were able to beat and torture Sabas without any consultation with the rest of the villagers and without bringing any charge against him, though it may be significant that Sabas suffered thus when not actually present in his own village.

Clearly, political power has to some extent become concentrated in the hands of the optimates, and the village council is no longer in a position to assert its rights boldly on every issue that affects it. But individual

Visigoths were not afraid to disobey outright the most stringent orders of the tribal chief who represented the megistanes. At one stage in the torturing of Sabas the saint was tied hand and foot to two axles of a cart, and was thrown on his back on the ground to spend the night in this predicament. But when his guards fell asleep an old woman, who had stayed up all night to prepare meat for the members of her household, took pity on him and set him free. Had she not been willing to defy the confederate council the saint might well have finished his career there and then. Again, when his executioners had brought Sabas to the river Musaeus (Buzău) where they were to drown him they at first proposed to set him free: Atharid, they thought, would know nothing of it. And it was only when Sabas himself insisted that they should carry out their orders that they plunged him into the water. Finally, the whole course of events in Sabas' village shows that feelings for one's neighbour—or perhaps we should say kinsman—were stronger than respect for the orders of the optimates.

It is a curious picture. The persecution was enforced by the megistanes, whose reasons for doing so will be examined elsewhere. But the Visigoths at large, it seems, did not care very much whether one of their number ate the sacrificial meat or not—if he were willing to eat any meat, that would suffice. When no persecution was on foot Christian and pagan seem to have lived on friendly terms within the one village; and in times of persecution, if we may generalize from the behaviour of Sabas' fellow villagers, regard for one's neighbour was stronger than differences of religion among the rank and file of the Visigoths. Is it a coincidence that this picture of Visigothic life dates from the very eve of the general conversion of the people to Christianity? At any rate, the brotherly and sisterly intimacy of the Christians in Gothia is reflected in the diminutive names by which they addressed one another. As a German scholar has put it, the names of practically all the martyrs, in so far as they are Germanic, are "Kurznamen, Kosenamen, Beinamen, oder Spitznamen." But no "Kosenamen" are applied to chiefs like Winguric or Atharid or even the Christian Arimerius, who is known from a somewhat later period. The simplicity of these lowly Christians and their earnest truthfulness are reflected in the one document that they have left us, the *Passio*, which is in fact a letter from the Church in Gothia to the Church in Cappadocia. It is not the work of a Goth but of a Roman living in very close contact with the barbarians, and although it was scarcely written by the presbyter Sansalas himself, it may well be based on information supplied by him, for he had friends in the Roman Empire, had fled there when the persecution was at its height, and may well have returned there after Sabas' death to await the end of the storm. The vividness and innocence of the *Passio* reveal a community in which fanaticism was confined to the powerful, and humanity to the humble. Delehaye has justly described it as one of the pearls of ancient hagiography.

The Conversion of the Germans

WILLIAM CHANEY

By the middle of the sixth century, the Germans were masters of nearly all the western territory of the Roman empire. The society of the old western provinces was now a dual society; Roman provincials lived beside Germans, but the distinction, at least the social distinction, between the two populations lasted until the eighth century in many places. This durable social division stemmed not only from the attitude of the conquered population, but from the Germans, who in many places showed a desire to remain separate from the Romans. In Italy, for example, the Romanization of the royal family was one of the reasons for conflict among the Ostrogoths after the death of Theodoric the Great in 526. The Lombards, who came to Italy about 568, were for a long time dominated by men who wanted to preserve the ancient German customs and religion and, therefore, to resist Romanization.

The political and military success of the Germans, combined with their cultural conservatism, complicated the task of the Christian missionaries. From the late fifth century on, the Christian preachers had to convert both Romans and Germans if they were to succeed in establishing the new religion, and in many times and places the cultural conflict or the carefully tended distinction between the two populations made conversion difficult.

The establishment of the Germanic kingdoms, a process of settlement as well as of political action, enhanced the position and importance of the kings. Historians have long known that not all the Germanic tribes had leaders who could legitimately be called kings; consequently, they have concluded that the experience of migration and conquest, followed by the need to govern an alien population, created what we commonly call Germanic kingship. This view has now been modified by studies that show that the western German tribes had kings long before they invaded the Roman territories.

But these findings do not overturn the conclusion that the invasions had a great effect on the character of the western Germanic kings. Among the Anglo-Saxons, the Franks, the Visigoths, and other peoples (which were made up by the confederation of tribal groups), royal power was consolidated by a few, and sometimes by one, of the petty kings who had led the people into the promised land of the empire. The successful consolidators ruthlessly suppressed rivals and enhanced their power by gaining the support and taking on the trappings of the distant Roman government in Constantinople. The political tradition of the provinces, which were used to centralized government, helped to further the centralization of the German communities. The Roman population looked to the kings for protection and for law, and the kings provided legal codes for their new subjects. In fact, the earliest written law codes of the Germans were created as part of the effort of the German kings to govern a dual population, the Roman part of which expected law to be written.

We would call these military and legal functions of the kings secular functions, but neither the Roman nor the German population in the new kingdoms would have done so. For both, the political community and its leadership had a divine purpose and religious functions. In this selection, William Chaney looks at the western Germans, particularly at the Anglo-Saxons, and shows how the institution of sacral kingship became the basis for their conversion to Christianity. He also shows why the conversion was so impermanent during the first century of Christianization. The centrality of the kings, and their religious importance, made the success of the new religion depend on the commitment of the king and on the political fortunes of the often competitive members of the royal family.

Kingship is the Anglo-Saxon political institution *par excellence* and gives cohesion to the realms established by the invading tribes. In each kingdom the royal race—the *stirps regia*—which sprang from its founder provided the source from which the individual rulers were chosen, and beyond the earthly founder was the god who was the divine ancestor of almost every Anglo-Saxon royal house, Woden. The antiquity of the monarchic institution is reflected in the developed terminology for kingship, as in the twenty-six synonyms for "king" used by the *Beowulf* poet alone, and time itself was recorded according to the regnal years of these Woden-sprung monarchs. Their accessions and deaths are recorded in such histories as have survived, which are filled above all with the deeds of kings.

In spite of the paucity of sources, even in later traditions, for the age of migrations and the Anglo-Saxon settlement in the island, it is clear that the institution of kingship was a survival from pre-conquest Germanic custom and did not arise as rule peculiar to the insular development. Tacitus records it for the Teutonic tribes of the *Germania*, in which descent-chosen kings are found sharing power with war-chiefs. *Reges ex nobilitate, duces ex virtute sumunt* [the choose kings because of their nobility, war leaders on ability], he asserts. The "king or chief" (*rex vel princeps*) speaks first in the tribal assembly, but here he rules more "by right of advising" (*auctoritate suadendi*) than by any absolute right of command. Fines are paid in part to the king or state, and the king or chief participates in the priestly office of interpreting the most sacred auguries, the neighing of the white horses. Thus, far from an autocrat, the Teutonic king of the *Germania* exercises power which is honorific and priestly

From William Chaney, *The Cult of Kingship in Anglo-Saxon England* (Manchester: Manchester University Press, 1970), pp. 7–9, 11–12, 14–16, 156–61, 166–70, 172–73.

but neither unlimited nor arbitrary; kingship, however, is a firm part of this generalized portrait of Germanic society, and the Tacitean distinction between *reges* and *principes* seems to rest not so much on a fixed division between the two titles as on multiple rulership, with more than one prince, drawn from the *stirps regia*, ruling over a single tribe. Kingly government is general to early Germanic society, though two or more kings are sometimes found sharing rule over a single tribe. Even later, in Anglo-Saxon England, there are examples of multiple-rulership. Horsa and, after Horsa's death, Hengest's son Aesc shared the rule of Kent with Hengest, as Cerdic and his son Cynric were joint-kings over the West Saxons. Sigihere and Sebbe were later co-rulers in East Anglia, and five West Saxon kings were slain in a single battle by Edwin of Northumbria. . . .

The most fundamental concept in Germanic kingship is the indissolubility of its religious and political functions. The king is above all the intermediary between his people and the gods, the charismatic embodiment of the "luck" of the folk. The relation of the divine and the tribal is primarily one of action, of "doing," and to assure the favourable actions of the gods toward the tribe the king "does" his office as mediator between them, sacrificing for victory, for good crops and for peace, "making" the year. It is not that he is simply a priest; he is the leader of the folk and the guarantor of their *heil* who acts so that the gods may bless them. Thus, later distinctions between priestly and political functions are caught up into a union, a personal embodiment of the link with the divine on which the tribe's well-being depends. In a world in which the kingdoms of men depend upon the realm of the divine, the earthly king moves in a vital strand which binds them together. In a very real sense, then, the god is first of all the god of the king, whose role it is to assume this burden of favourable relationship with the deity, and only secondarily the god of the tribe, whose "luck" is mediated by that of the ruler. When the king's "luck" or charismatic power is maintained, the favour of the god rests with the tribe; when he has lost his "luck" and is impotent to secure the divine blessings, the people are justified, even obliged, to do the only thing possible, to replace him with another who can make the office more effective. . .

When the light of history and tradition falls on Germanic kingship of the age of migrations, the king is leader of the war-hosts but also the charismatic mediator with the divine, the sacral holder of the tribal "luck." Thus Germanic and Scandinavian history of the early Middle Ages knows no strong priesthood set apart from the secular rulers. The temples were private possessions, pagan parallels of the medieval *Eigenkirche* [private churches], and the head of the household was the temple's priest. The Germanic king himself offered sacrifices. Whether or not the *sacerdotes* [priests] of Tacitus are in reality only the *principes* in their magical and priestly role, by the time of the early migrations the chief of the *principes*—the king—has become the tribal high-priest, the "warden of the holy temple," as northern poetry calls him. Sacrificing for good crops and for victory in battle, he assured plenty among his people, but when the gods deserted him and his "luck" no longer flowed from him, he could be deposed or even killed in time of tribal disaster. So Ammianus Marcellinus records that Burgundian kings under whom crops or victory failed were deposed, and when bad harvests continued in Sweden under the Ynlingar King Domaldi, in spite of rich sacrifices by the ruler, he was killed. His descendant, King Olaf Tretelgia of Sweden, failed to make *blot*, neglecting the rites necessary for good crops, so that the latter failed; the Swedes, who "used always to reckon good or bad crops for or against their kings," burned the king in his house as an offering to Odin. Thus when the king maintained a proper relation with the gods, his realm was bathed in fullness, but when his "luck" left him, it was a sign that the gods themselves had deserted him; hence Odoacer, although an Arian Christian, when he was struck down by Theodoric the Ostrogoth in Ravenna, uttered his dying cry of despair at this withdrawal of the king's deity—"Where is God?"

The early Germanic king is, consequently, not a god and not all-powerful, but he is filled with a charismatic power on which his tribe depends for its well-being. This is the king's *mana*, "a force utterly distinct from mere physical power or strength, the possession of which assures success, good fortune, and the like to its possessor." This power permeates not the king alone but the entire "royal race," the whole kin from among whom the folk elect him, and its source is probably to be sought in the descent of this *stirps regia* from a god. The Woden-sprung monarchs of the Anglo-Saxons, like the god-descended royal houses of the Continent, contain within the clan the special virtue, the *mana* from on high, but hereditary as this power was, the office of kingship which embodied it might be filled by any member of the "divine race." "It was the virtue of their blood," as Fritz Kern writes, "that lifted the sons of Woden, the Astings, the Amals, and so on, out of the ranks of the folk, though without bestowing upon any individual prince a right to the throne independent of the popular will. The family's possession of the throne was as inviolable as the right of any individual prince to succeed to it was insecure." . . .

As Sir Frank Stenton has said, "throughout the country in which Augustine and his companions laboured, heathenism was still a living religion when it met the Christian challenge." The binding elements in that pagan faith, as has been observed, were the kin-group and the head of the tribe who bound the folk to the gods and the gods to the folk. The less, therefore, that a new religion attempted to isolate the converted from their group and to arouse a combined political-religious opposition, the less difficult would it be to effect a conversion to a new and more powerful God. When religious and political opposition were combined, as in King Olaf the Holy's attempted conversion of Norway, during the apostacy of Eadbald of Kent, or among the East Saxons under the sons of King Saberht, Christianity met formidable hostility; when there was little political opposition, on the other hand, the reception of the new faith was even undramatic in its lack of tension and high events. The crucial figure, consequently, in any conversion was the sacral king, the fact that in Anglo-Saxon England the paths of the new religion were made smooth was in every kingdom due to the role played by its ruler.

The story of the English Conversion opens in Kent with the arrival in Thanet of St. Augustine and about forty companions. The mission had left Rome probably early in A.D. 596 and landed early the next year in the realms of the *bretwalda* Aethelberht, the most powerful ruler in southern Britain. Its reception was not unfriendly. The king ordered it to be provided with *necessaria*, and after some days went himself into Thanet to hear the *nuntium optimum* which the Roman had claimed to bring. Since for at least nine years Christian services had been held in the royal capital, celebrated for Queen Bertha, the Christian daughter of the Merovingian King Charibert, by her chaplain, Bishop Liudhard, the *fama . . . Christianae religionis* had, as Bede says, come to the king before, and modern historians may have underestimated his knowledge of the faith. When Pope Gregory writes that "the news had reached him that the English people wished to become Christians," the possibility is at least open that Aethelberht himself or Bertha may have acted to instigate the mission. Certainly he acknowledged in terms of his own religion (*vetere usus augurio*) the possible power of Augustine's band, "for he would not permit them to come to him in any house, lest . . . if they practiced any magical arts they might deceive him by surprise, prevailing against him." Nonetheless, the Gospel impressed him as *nova . . . et incerta* [new and uncertain] so that, as he declared, he could not abandon the faith which he and his people had observed for so long. However, he not only welcomed Augustine with all courtesy and provided for his wants but gave permission for him to "win unto the faith of your religion with your preaching as many as you may." Some (*nonnulli*) were baptized before Aethelberht, but it was only after the royal conversion that many (*plures*) turned to Christianity, so that on Christmas, A.D. 597, Gregory reports in a letter to Patriarch Eulogius of Alexandria, more than ten thousand of the king's subjects were baptized.

The dependence of the Kentish mission on the royal role is seen with equal clarity after the death of the converted Aethelberht on February 24th, A.D. 616. His and Bertha's son, the new king Eadbald, was openly heathen and, following pagan practice, married his father's widow, the second and probably heathen wife of Aethelberht. When their king moved to the worship of the old gods, so did the superficially converted folk. The very life of the Christian mission was threatened when Augustine's successor, Laurentius, agreed with the fugitive bishops, Mellitus of London and Justin of Rochester, that "it were better for them all to return to their own country and there to serve the Lord with a free mind, than to abide without profit amongst barbarous men that were rebels of the faith. It was only the conversion and baptism of Eadbald and the strong royal support of the Church thereafter which brought his people once more into the Christian fold. His son and successor, King Eorcenberht, was the "first of the kings of the English who by his princely authority ordered that idols in his whole realm should be abandoned and destroyed," and with this visible sign of the king's allegiance to the new religion, we never hear of popular apostasy in Kent again.

The loose hegemony which the *bretwalda* Aethelberht exercised over the entire territory south of the Humber facilitated the advance of Christianity. Although none of the kings who acknowledged his overlordship was forced to change his religion when the king of Kent did, yet the latter's influence on these monarchs aided the adoption of the faith by them and consequently by their people. The first kingdom to be affected was that of the East Saxons, ruled by Saberht, the son of Aethelberht's sister, Ricula. When, in A.D. 604, Augustine consecrated his follower Mellitus as bishop to preach in Essex, not only were the king and, as Bede says, the *provincia* converted, but Aethelberht himself built the church of St. Paul in Saberht's capital city, London. Again, however, royal faith and popular faith moved together, for upon the death of the East Saxon monarch his three sons, still heathen, "gave free license to the people subject to them to worship idols"; so strong was the return to paganism that not only was Mellitus driven out, but when he returned and Eadbald had restored the faith in Kent, Essex remained true to its "idolatrous high priests."

It was not for almost half a century (A.D. 653) that a Christian mission entered Essex, when once again the baptism of its king preceded its conversion. The East Saxon king, Sigbert the Good, a friend and frequent visitor at the court of Oswiu of Northumbria, was persuaded in the North that "such could not be gods which had been made with men's hands." Following his baptism and return to Essex, the mission of Cedd was invited to his kingdom and there, since the cult-leader of the folk was now favourable to the mission, it was a success, and a "great church," increasing daily, was brought into existence. After the murder of Sigbert the Good, his successor, Swidhelm, son of Sexbald, was a Christian, having been baptized in East Anglia, and his subjects stayed firm in the faith of their monarch. However, when Sighere followed him to the throne, the great plague of 664 swept through the land, and the king himself, in old role as guardian of the health of his folk, restored the pagan temples and returned *cum sua parte populi* [with his part of the people] to the worship of idols, "as though they could thereby be protected from the mortal sickness." It was, thus, a national calamity such as paganism had called upon the king to cure, which caused King Sighere to offer *blot* to the offended gods, and "his part of the people" apostacized with him. Wulfhere of Mercia, overlord of Sighere, however, sent a mission under Bishop Jaruman to re-christianize the country, and it turned *populum et regem* together again to Christ. Essex remained firm thereafter, but the powerful role of the king in determining the religion of his people is obvious in the long history of the conversion. When Saberht was converted, so were the East Saxons; when his sons worshipped the old gods, their subjects followed their lead; when Sigbert turned to the new religion, the conversion was again successful; when the panic of the plague swept Essex, one king and his people alike reverted to the old gods; and, finally, both together returned to Christianity. The pagan Germanic notion that the gods are primarily the gods of the king, who mediates with them for his folk, is clearly witnessed in Anglo-Saxon England. . . .

Clearly, then, the history of the coming of Christianity displays the role of the English king as the converter of his people. In no kingdom did the conversion occur without royal support, and in none do we hear of the conversion of the folk without that of the monarch previously. Even in Mercia, it was only after Peada, who ruled as sub-king under his father [Penda], became a Christian and with the permission of the great pagan war-lord himself that the Gospel was preached; the major work of the mission was done nonetheless only after Penda's death. The tribal relation with the divine still was dependent on the king's relation with the divine, and the proper *blot* was primarily the ruler's affair. Consequently, the conversion of the *folc* stemmed from the conversion of the king to the more powerful deity, since it was the king's relationship with the gods which "saved" his people as much as did the gods themselves. When the king turned to Christ, it was done *cum sua gente* [with his people].

Further, in most of the kingdoms—Kent, Essex, East Anglia, Deira, and Bernicia—royal apostacy occurred, a fact which can best be explained by the long tradition of performing essential rites for the folk. In Deira and Bernicia the one-year rule of the apostate kings was so brief that we are told nothing of the popular reaction. However, when Redwald of East Anglia offered sacrifice to the former gods, it would certainly have had popular support for him to have done it in the face of his conversion. In Kent, King Eadbald led his people *ad priorem vomitum* [i.e., back to paganism], and in the realm of the East Saxons, Bede tells us, the apostate folk could not be recalled to faith in Christ even after Saberht's heathen sons had been killed in battle against the West Saxons. Converted again under Sigbert the Good, they apostacized once more when Sighere returned to his ancestral gods during the great plague of A.D. 664–665. Thus, as conversion of the subjects depends on that of the ruler, so also royal and popular apostasy are closely related.

In addition, as in the pagan North improper observance of the rituals was the cause of royal deposition and even king-slaying, so apostasy from the Christian faith was regarded as bringing about the loss of kingdom and on occasion the deletion from the line of Woden-sprung monarchs who had made the proper sacrifices. Thus, when Cenwalh succeeded his father, Cynegils of the West Saxons, Bede reports that he "refused to accept the faith and sacraments of the heavenly kingdom and not long after lost even the power over his earthly kingdom." When he was converted in East Anglia, however, he was restored to his realm. We have also noted that Osric of Deira and Eanfrid of Bernicia were removed from the king-lists because of their apostasy. However, when Eadbald of Kent apostacized after the death of his father Aethelberht, he was not stripped of his place in the line of monarchs, even though his subjects followed him, nor was Sighere of Essex. In both cases, however, they returned to the Christian faith. This cannot be said, though, of Redwald of East Anglia, who worshipped at two altars in one temple and who was nonetheless listed as a *bretwalda*. Thus, while the tribal culture was still strong enough after the Conversion to bring royal apostasy, both the old and the new religions related the fate of the kingdom to the cult of the king.

Christianity, however, even linked the destiny of king and kingdom not only with the worship of God but with obedience to his priesthood. Consequently, *pax et gaudium in populis et anni frugiferi victoriaeque in hostes* [peace and joy in the people and fruitful years and victories over enemies]—the traditional rewards to rulers for pagan *blot*—were given "by the aid of God" to King Egrith and Queen Aethelthryth, rulers of Deira and Bernicia, as long as they were obedient to Bishop Wilfrid; however, when the king was no longer at one with the bishop, his "luck" left him. Here, of course, unlike the old religion in which there was no powerful priesthood to be equated with the Divine Will and the *principes* themselves performed priestly functions, the possibility of division between two functions of the pagan Anglo-Saxon royal *persona mixta* appears. This division was to become crucial for the later concept of Christian kingship.

A final element in the royal role during the Conversion is the spiritual fatherhood of the Anglo-Saxon kings over pagan rulers whose submission to Christianity they had procured. The adoption of rulers by Roman emperors was, of course, not unknown, as in the adoption by the latter of Gothic kings through the symbolic handing over of weapons. The reception by a noble foster-father was, however, a feature of pagan baptism in the North, and it was most probably from this source that the Anglo-Saxon royal custom was derived. Thus Guthorm the Earl, for example, set the eldest son of King Harald Fair-Hair of Norway on his knee and became his foster-father. Thus spiritual relationship occurs as early as A.D. 635 in England, when the Christian Oswald of Northumbria received his future father-in-law, King Cynegil of the West Saxons, as his son upon the latter's conversion. When Cynegil's grandson, Cuthred, was baptized four years later, Bishop Birinus "received him for son," in a prelude to the later expansion of this custom of the adoption of rulers. Thus, in a letter of A.D. 798 to Pope Leo III concerning the see of Lichfield, King Cenwulf of Mercia, ruling those "who dwell at the end of the world," requests "that you will especially receive me as your son by adoption, just as I love you in the person of a father, and always honour you with obedience with all my strength. For it is meet that holy faith be kept among such great persons, and inviolate love be guarded." As pagan chieftains were received as foster-sons at the hands of other rulers, so Anglo-Saxon kings desired the prestige that would come from entering into this traditional spiritual sonship with the great chief of the new religion in far-off Rome. Such personal relationships "among great persons" were honourable and customary. Indicating the cautious reception of this apparently unfamiliar custom in Rome, however, Pope Leo does not even mention the matter in his reply to Cenwulf. He speaks of the problem of th see of Lichfield but confines his suggestions for a closer relationship to exhorting the Mercian monarch to continue Offa's annual payment of three hundred and sixty-five mancuses to Rome. . . .

The king's role in conversion in England is thus well established. The theological content of the old religion, as well as its integration into the social and political background of the Germanic tribes, helped cast the mould into which Christian doctrine was poured and affected the interpretation of the finished work. As the change was more palatable to the folk if the new God were worshipped in the temples of the old, as Gregory the Great realized, so Christianity was the more readily accepted if the tribes were able to follow the sacrificial king of the old religion into the new. The totality of life and worlds made impossible the later duality of Church and State, and the interweaving of cult and culture enhanced the sacral strand of kingship which knit together the tapestry of tribal life.

Peasant Life in the Middle Ages

EILEEN POWER

Medieval law placed the peasant and his family in formal subjection to his lord, and some lived the poor and restricted life that accords with this legal status. But most peasants considered their relationships with the aristocracy natural and advantageous. In the chaotic conditions of the early Middle Ages, it may have been much more important to the peasant that the land was tied to him than that he was tied to it. It was an age when farms needed protection both from marauders and from natural disasters. The lord provided military security and, in times of famine, could reduce the suffering of his villagers by buying grain and other foodstuffs in neighboring districts.

Beside the minor fluctuations of agrarian prosperity, there was a long-term improvement from the ninth to the thirteenth centuries. This growth in prosperity stemmed both from the advance of agricultural technology—an effective horse collar, the horseshoe, and the heavy, wheeled plow—and from the expansion of arable land. Especially from the tenth century on, after the end of the Viking invasions, lords and peasants put new lands into production. The reclamation of land provided the peasantry with a double reward. The productivity of the group as a whole increased, and the peasants were able to improve their status and living conditions by taking on the risks of increasing the arable.

Historians presume that the Romans kept records of the economic activity on their estates, but the practice seems to have declined sharply after the Germans assumed control of the western territories. In the late eighth century, Charlemagne ordered that his stewards make surveys of the royal estates and keep records of the income that could be expected from each. The great ecclesiastical corporations, which had accumulated large properties and which had the educated personnel necessary, also made surveys at this time, and we have a few of them still. These surveys reveal something about the peasant families that worked the estates and paid the rent and other fees that constituted the income from the property, but historians have had difficulty using the documents for a statistical analysis of the peasant community. In this selection, Eileen Power uses the surveys and other sources to create a composite picture of a ninth-century peasant, whom she calls Bodo.

This book is chiefly concerned with the kitchens of History, and the first which we shall visit is a country estate at the beginning of the ninth century. It so happens that we know a surprising amount about such an estate, partly because Charlemagne himself issued a set of orders instructing the Royal stewards how to manage his own lands, telling them everything it was necessary for them to know, down to the vegetables which they were to plant in the garden. But our chief source of knowledge is a wonderful estate book which Irminon, the Abbot of St Germain des Prés near Paris, drew up so that the abbey might know exactly what lands belonged to it and who lived on those lands, very much as William I drew up an estate book of his whole kingdom and called it *Domesday Book*. In this estate book is set down the name of every little estate (or *fisc* as it was called) belonging to the abbey, with a description of the land which was worked under its steward to its own profit, and the land which was held by tenants, and the names of those tenants and of their wives and of their children, and the exact services and rents, down to a plank and an egg, which they had to do for their land. We know today the name of almost every man, woman, and child who was living on those little *fiscs* in the time of Charlemagne, and a great deal about their daily lives.

Consider for a moment how the estate upon which they lived was organized. The lands of the Abbey of St. Germain were divided into a number of estates, called *fiscs*, each of a convenient size to be administered by a steward. On each of these *fiscs* the land was divided into seigniorial and tributary lands; the first administered by the monks through a steward or some other officer, and the second possessed by various tenants, who received and held them from the abbey. These tributary lands were divided into numbers of little farms, called manses, each occupied by one or more families. If you had paid a visit to the chief or seigniorial manse, which the monks kept in their own hands, you would have found a little house, with three or four rooms, probably built of stone, facing an inner court, and on one side of it you would have seen a special group of houses hedged round, where the women serfs belonging to the house lived and did their work; all round you would also have seen little wooden houses, where the household serfs lived, workrooms, a kitchen, a bakehouse, barns, stables, and other farm buildings, and round the whole a hedge carefully planted with trees, so as to make a kind of enclosure or court. Attached to this central manse was a considerable amount of land —ploughland, meadows, vineyards, orchards, and almost all the woods or forests on the estate. Clearly a great deal of labour would be needed to

From Eileen Power, *Medieval People* (London: Methuen, 1924), pp. 19–38 cultivate all these lands. Some of that labour was provided by servile workers who were attached to the chief manse and lived in the court. But these household serfs were not nearly enough to do all the work upon the monks' land, and far the greater part of it had to be done by services paid by the other land-owners on the estate.

Beside the seigniorial manse, there were a number of little dependent manses. These belonged to men and women who were in various stages of freedom, except for the fact that all had to do with the different classes, for in practice there was very little difference between them, and in a couple of centuries they were all merged into one common class of medieval villeins. The most important people were those called *coloni*, who were personally free (that is to say, counted as free men by the law), but bound to the soil, so that they could never leave their farms and were sold with the estate, if it were sold. Each of the dependent manses was held either by one family or by two or three families which clubbed together to do the work; it consisted of a house or houses, and farm buildings, like those of the chief manse, only poorer and made of wood, with ploughland and a meadow and perhaps a little piece of vineyard attached to it. In return for these holdings the owner or joint owners of every manse had to do work on the land of the chief manse for about three days in the week. The steward's chief business was to see that they did their work properly, and from every one he had the right to demand two kinds of labour. The first was *field work*; every year each man was bound to do a fixed amount of ploughing on the domain land (as it was called later on), and also to give what was called a *corvée*, that is to say, an unfixed amount of ploughing, which the steward could demand every week when it was needed; the distinction corresponds to the distinction between *week work* and *boon work* in the later Middle Ages. The second kind of labour which every owner of a farm had to do on the monks' land was called handwork, that is to say, he had to help repair buildings, or cut down trees, or gather fruit, or make ale, or carry loads—anything, in fact, which wanted doing and which the steward told him to do. It was by these services that the monks got their own seigniorial farm cultivated. On all the other days of the week these hard-worked tenants were free to cultivate their own little farms, and we may be sure that they put twice as much elbow grease into the business.

But their obligation did not end here, for not only had they to pay services, they also had to pay certain rents to the big house. There were no State taxes in those days, but every man had to pay an army due, which Charlemagne exacted from the abbey, and which the abbey exacted from its tenants; this took the form of an ox and a certain number of sheep, or the equivalent in money: 'He pays to the host two shillings of silver' comes first on every freeman's list of obligations. The farmers also had to pay in return for any special privileges granted to them by the monks; they had to carry a load of wood to the big house, in return for being allowed to gather firewood in the woods, which were jealously preserved for the use of the abbey; they had to pay some hogsheads of wine for the right to pasture their pigs in the same precious woods; every third year they had to give up one of their sheep for the right to graze upon the fields of the chief manse; they had to pay a sort of poll-tax of 4*d.* a head. In addition to these special rents every farmer had also to pay other rents in produce; every year he owed the big house three chickens and fifteen eggs and a large number of planks, to repair its buildings; often he had to give it a couple of pigs; sometimes corn, wine, honey, wax, soap, or oil. If the farmer were also an artisan and made things, he had to pay the produce of his craft; a smith would have to make lances for the abbey's contingent to the army, a carpenter had to make barrels and hoops and vine props, a wheelwright had to make a cart. Even the wives of the farmers were kept busy, if they happened to be serfs; for the servile women were obliged to spin cloth or to make a garment for the big house every year.

All those things were exacted and collected by the steward, whom they called *Villicus,* or *Major* (Mayor). He was a very hardworked man, and when one reads the seventy separate and particular injunctions which Charlemagne addressed to his stewards one cannot help feeling sorry for him. He had to get all the right services out of the tenants, and tell them what to do each week and see that they did it; he had to be careful that they brought the right number of eggs and pigs up to the house, and did not foist off warped or badly planed planks upon him. He had to look after the household serfs too, and set them to work. He had to see about storing, or selling, or sending off to the monastery the produce of the estate and of the tenants' rents; and every year he had to present a full and detailed account of his stewardship to the abbot. He had a manse of his own, with services and rents due from it, and Charlemagne exhorted his stewards to be prompt in their payments, so as to set a good example. Probably his official duties left him very little time to work on his own farm, and he would have to put in a man to work it for him, as Charlemagne bade his stewards do. Often, however, he had subordinate officials called *deans* under him, and sometimes the work of receiving and looking after the stores in the big house was done by a special cellarer.

That, in a few words, is the way in which the monks of St Germain and the other Frankish landowners of the time of Charlemagne managed their estates. Let us try, now, to look at those estates from a more human point of view and see what life was like to a farmer who lived upon them. The abbey possessed a little estate called Villaris, near Paris, in the place now occupied by the park of Saint Cloud. When we turn up the pages in the estate book dealing with Villaris, we find that there was a man called Bodo living there. He had a wife called Ermentrude and three children called Wido and Gerbert and Hildegard; and he owned a little farm of arable and meadow land, with a few vines. And we know very nearly as much about Bodo's work as we know about that of a smallholder in France today. Let us try and imagine a day in his life. On a fine spring morning towards the end of Charlemagne's reign Bodo gets up early, because it is his day to go and work on the monks' farm, and he does not dare to be late, for fear of the steward. To be sure, he has probably given the steward a present of eggs and vegetables the week before, to keep him in a good temper; but the monks will not allow their stewards to take big bribes (as is sometimes done on other estates), and Bodo knows that he will not be allowed to go late to work. It is his day to plough so he takes his big ox with him and little Wido to run by its side with a goad, and he joins his friends from some of the farms near by, who are going to work at the big house too. They all assemble, some with horses and oxen, some with mattocks and hoes and spades and axes and scythes, and go off in gangs to work upon the fields and meadows and woods of the seigniorial manse, according as the steward orders them. The manse next door to Bodo is held by a group of families: Frambert and Ermoin and Ragenold, with their wives and children. Bodo bids them good morning as he passes. Frambert is going to make a fence round the wood, to prevent the rabbits from coming out and eating the young crops; Ermoin has been told off to cart a great load of firewood up to the house; and Ragenold is mending a hole in the roof of a barn. Bodo goes whistling off in the cold with his oxen and his little boy; and it is no use to follow him farther, because he ploughs all day and eats his meal under a tree with the other ploughmen, and it is very monotonous.

Let us go back and see what Bodo's wife, Ermentrude, is doing. She is busy too; it is the day on which the chicken-rent is due—a fat pullet and five eggs in all. She leaves her second son, aged nine, to look after the baby Hildegard and calls on one of her neighbours, who has to go up to the big house too. The neighbour is a serf and she has to take the steward a piece of woollen cloth, which will be sent away to St. Germain to make a habit for a monk. Her husband is working all day in the lord's vineyards, for on this estate the serfs generally tend the vines, while the freemen do most of the ploughing. Ermentrude and the serf's wife go together up to the house. There all is busy. In the men's workshop are several clever workmen—a shoemaker, a carpenter, a blacksmith, and two two silversmiths; there are not more, because the best artisans on the estates of St Germain live by the walls of the abbey, so that they can work for the monks on the spot and save the labour of carriage. But there were always some craftsmen on every estate, either attached as serfs to the big house, or living on manses of their own, and good landowners tried to have as many clever craftsmen as possible. Charlemagne ordered his stewards each to have in his district 'good workmen, namely, blacksmiths, goldsmiths, silversmiths, shoemakers, turners, carpenters, swordmakers, fishermen, foilers, soapmakers, men who know how to make beer, cider, perry, and all other kinds of beverages, bakers to make pasty for our table, netmakers who know how to make nets for hunting, fishing, and fowling, and others too many to be named'. And some of these workmen are to be found working for the monks in the estate of Villaris.

But Ermentrude does not stop at the men's workshop. She finds the steward, bobs her curtsy to him, and gives up her fowl and eggs, and then she hurries off to the women's part of the house, to gossip with the serfs there. The Franks used at this time to keep the women of their household in a separate quarter, where they did the work which was considered suitable for women, very much as the Greeks of antiquity used to do. If a Frankish noble had lived at the big house, his wife would have looked after their work, but as no one lived in the stone house at Villaris, the steward had to oversee the women. Their quarter consisted of a little group of houses, with a workroom, the whole surrounded by a thick hedge with a strong bolted gate, like a harem, so that no one could come in without leave. Their workrooms were comfortable places, warmed by stoves, and there Ermentrude (who, being a woman, was allowed to go in) found about a dozen servile women spinning and dyeing cloth and sewing garments. Every week the harassed steward brought them the raw materials for their work and took away what they made. Charlemagne gives his stewards several instructions about the women attached to his manses, and we may be sure that the monks of St. Germain did the same on their model estates. 'For our women's work,' says Charlemagne, 'they are to give at the proper time the materials, that is linen, wool, woad, vermilion, madder, wool combs, teasels, soap, grease, vessels, and other objects which are necessary. And let our women's quarters be well looked after, furnished with houses and rooms with stoves and cellars, and let them be surrounded by a good hedge, and let the doors be strong, so that the women can do our work properly.' Ermentrude, however, has to hurry away after her gossip, and so must we. She goes back to her own farm and sets to work in the little vineyard; then after an hour or two goes back to get the children's meal and to spend the rest of the day in weaving warm woollen clothes for them. All her friends are either working in the fields on their husbands' farms or else looking after the poultry, or the vegetables, or sewing at home; for the women have to work just as hard as the men on a country farm. In Charlemagne's time (for instance) they did nearly all the sheep shearing. Then at last Bodo comes back for his supper, and as soon as the sun goes down they go to bed; for their hand-made candle gives only a flicker or light, and they both have to be up early in the morning. De Quincey once pointed out, in his inimitable manner, how the ancients everywhere went to bed, 'like good boys, from seven to nine o' clock'. 'Man went to bed early in those ages simply because his worthy mother earth could not afford him candles. She, good old lady . . . would certainly have shuddered to hear of any of her nations asking for candles. "Candles indeed!" she would have said; "who ever heard of such a thing? and with so much excellent daylight running to waste, as I have provided *gratis*! What will the wretches want next?"' Something of the same situation prevailed even in Bodo's time.

This, then, is how Bodo and Ermentrude usually passed their working day. But, it may be complained, this is all very well. We know about the estates on which these peasants lived and about the rents which they had to pay, and the services which they had to do. But how did they feel and think and amuse themselves when they were not working? Rents and services are only outside things; an estate book only describes routine. It would be idle to try to picture the life of a university from a study of its lecture list, and it is equally idle to try and describe the life of Bodo from the estate book of his masters. It is no good taking your meals in the kitchen if you never talk to the servants. This is true, and to arrive at Bodo's thoughts and feelings and holiday amusements we must bid good-bye to Abbot Irminon's estate book, and peer into some very dark corners indeed; for though by the aid of Chaucer and Langland and a few Court Rolls it is possible to know a great deal about the feelings of a peasant six centuries later, material is scarce in the ninth century, and it is all the more necessary to remember the secret of the invisible ink.

Bodo certainly *had* plenty of feelings, and very strong ones. When he got up in the frost on a cold morning to drive the plough over the abbot's acres, when his own were calling out for work, he often shivered and shook the rime from his beard, and wished that the big house and all its land were at the bottom of the sea (which, as a matter of fact, he had never seen and could not imagine). Or else he wished he were the abbot's huntsman, hunting in the forest; or a monk of St Germain, singing sweetly in the abbey church; or a merchant, taking bales of cloaks and girdles along the high road to Paris; anything, in fact, but a poor plough-man ploughing other people's land. An Anglo-Saxon writer has imagined a dialogue with him:

'Well, ploughman, how do you do your work?' 'Oh, sir, I work very hard. I go out in the dawning, driving the oxen to the field and I yoke them to the plough. Be the winter never so stark, I dare not stay at home for fear of my lord; but every day I must plough a full acre or more, after having yoked the oxen and fastened the share and coulter to the plough!' 'Have you any mate?' 'I have a boy, who drives the oxen with a goad, who is now hoarse from cold and shouting.' (Poor little Wido!) 'Well, well, it is very hard work?' 'Yes, indeed it is very hard work.'

Nevertheless, hard as the work was, Bodo sang lustily to cheer himself and Wido; for is it not related that once, when a clerk was singing the 'Allelulia' in the emperor's presence, Charles turned to one of the bishops, saying, 'My clerk is singing very well,' whereat the rude bishop replied, 'Any clown in our countryside drones as well as that to his oxen at their ploughing'? It is certain too that Bodo agreed with the names which the great Charles gave to the months of the year in his own Frankish tongue; for he called January 'Winter-month', February 'Mud-month', March 'Spring-month', April 'Easter-month', May 'Joy-month', June 'Plough-month', July 'Hay-month', August 'Harvest-month', September 'Wind-month', October 'Vintage-month', November 'Autumn-month', and December 'Holy-month'.

And Bodo was a superstitious creature. The Franks had been Christian now for many years, but Christian though they were, the peasants clung to old beliefs and superstitions. On the estates of the holy monks of St Germain you would have found the country people saying charms which were hoary with age, parts of the lay sung by the Frankish ploughman over his bewitched land long before he marched southwards into the Roman Empire, or parts of the spell which the bee-master performed when he swarmed his bees on the shores of the Baltic Sea. Christianity has coloured these charms, but it has not effaced their heathen origin; and because the tilling of the soil is the oldest and most unchanging of human occupations, old beliefs and superstitions cling to it and the old gods stalk up and down the brown furrows, when they have long vanished from houses and roads. So on Abbot Irminon's estates the peasant-farmers muttered charms over their sick cattle (and over their sick children too) and said incantations over the fields to make them fertile. If you had followed behind Bodo when he broke his first furrow you would have probably seen him take out of his jerkin a little cake, baked for him by Ermentrude out of different kinds of meal, and you would have seen him stoop and lay it under the furrow and sing:

> Earth, Earth, Earth! O Earth, our mother!
> May the All-Wielder, Ever-Lord grant thee
> Acres a-waxing, upwards a-growing,
> Pregnant with corn and plenteous in strength;
> Hosts of grain shafts and of glittering plants!
> Of broad barley the blossoms,
> And of white wheat ears waxing,
> Of the whole land the harvest. . . .

. . . .

> Acre, full-fed, bring forth fodder for men!
> Blossoming brightly, blessed become!
> And the God who wrought with earth grant us gift of growing
> That each of all the corns may come unto our need.

Then he would drive his plough through the acre.

The Church wisely did not interfere with these old rites. It taught Bodo to pray to the Ever-Lord instead of the Father Heaven, and to the Virgin Mary instead of to Mother Earth, and with these changes let the old spell he had learned from his ancestors serve him still. It taught him, for instance, to call on Christ and Mary in his charm for bees. When Ermentrude heard her bees swarming, she stood outside her cottage and said this little charm over them:

> Christ, there is a swarm of bees outside,
> Fly hither, my little cattle,
> In blest peace, in God's protection,
> Come home safe and sound.
> Sit down, sit down, bee,
> St Mary commanded thee.
> Thou shalt not have leave,
> Thou shalt not fly to the wood.
> Thou shalt not escape me,
> Nor go away from me.
> Sit very still,
> Wait God's will!

And if Bodo on his way home saw one of his bees caught in a brier bush, he immediately stood still and wished—as some people wish today when they go under a ladder. It was the Church, too, which taught Bodo to add 'So be it, Lord', to the end of his charm against pain. Now, his ancestors for generations behind him had believed that if you had a stitch in your side, or a bad pain anywhere, it came from a worm in the marrow of your bones, which was eating you up, and that the only way to get rid of that worm was to put a knife, or an arrowhead, or some other piece of metal to the sore place, and then wheedle the worm out on to the blade by saying a charm. And this was the charm which Bodo's heathen ancestors had always said and which Bodo went on saying when little Wido had a pain: 'Come out, worm, with nine little worms, out from the marrow into the bone, from the bone into the flesh, from the flesh into the skin, from the skin into this arrow.' And then (in obedience to the Church) he added 'So be it, Lord'. But sometimes it was not possible to read a Christian meaning into Bodo's doings. Sometimes he paid visits to some man who was thought to have a wizard's powers, or superstitiously reverenced some twisted tree, about which there hung old stories never quite forgotten. Then the Church was stern. When he went to confession the priest would ask him: 'Have you consulted magicians and enchanters, have you made vows to trees and fountains, have you drunk any magic philtre?' And he would have to confess what he did last time his cow was sick. But the Church was kind as well as stern. 'When serfs come to you,' we find one bishop telling his priests, 'you must not give them as many fasts to perform as rich men. Put upon them only half the penance.' The Church knew well enough that Bodo could not drive his plough all day upon an empty stomach. The hunting, drinking, feasting Frankish nobles could afford to lose a meal.

It was from this stern and yet kind Church that Bodo got his holidays. For the Church made the pious emperor decree that on Sundays and saints' days no servile or other works should be done. Charlemagne's son repeated his decree in 827. It runs thus:

> We ordain according to the law of God and to the command of our father of blessed memory in his edicts, that no servile works shall be done on Sundays, neither shall men perform their rustic labours, tending vines, ploughing fields, reaping corn and mowing hay, setting up hedges or fencing woods, cutting trees, or working in quarries or building houses; nor shall they work in the garden, not come to the law courts, nor follow the chase. But three carrying-services it is lawful to do on Sunday, to wit carrying for the army, carrying food, or carrying (if need be) the body of a lord to its grave. Item, women shall not do their textile works, nor cut out clothes, nor stitch them together with the needle, nor card wool, nor beat hemp, nor wash clothes in public, nor shear sheep: so that there may be rest on the Lord's day. But let them come together from all sides to Mass in the Church and praise God for all the good things He did for us on that day!

Unfortunately, however, Bodo and Ermentrude and their friends were not content to go quietly to church on saints' days and quietly home again. They used to spend their holidays in dancing and singing and buffoonery, as country folk have always done until our own gloomier, more self-conscious age. They were very merry and not at all refined, and the place they always chose for their dances was the churchyard; and unluckily the songs they sang as they danced in a ring were old pagan songs of their forefathers, left over from old Mayday festivities, which they could not forget, or ribald love-songs which the Church disliked. Over and over again we find the Church councils complaining that the peasants (and sometimes the priests too) were singing 'wicked songs with a chorus of dancing women,' or holding 'ballads and dancings and evil and wanton songs and such-like lures of the devil'; over and over again the bishops forbade these songs and dances; but in vain. In every country in Europe, right through the Middle Ages to the time of the Reformation, and after it, country folk continued to sing and dance in the churchyard. Two hundred years after Charlemagne's death there grew up the legend of the dancers of Kölbigk, who danced on Christmas Eve in the churchyard, in spite of the warning of the priest, and all got rooted to the spot for a year, till the Archbishop of Cologne released them. Some men say that they were not rooted standing to the spot, but that they had to go on dancing for the whole year; and that before they were released they had danced themselves waist-deep into the ground. People used to repeat the little Latin verse which they were singing:

> Equitabat Bovo per silvam frondosam
> Ducebat sibi Merswindem formosam.
> Quid stamus? Cur non imus?

> Through the leafy forest, Bovo went a-riding
> And his pretty Merswind trotted on beside him—
> Why are we standing still? Why can't we go away?

Another later story still is told about a priest in Worcestershire who was kept awake all night by the people dancing in his churchyard and singing a song with the refrain 'Sweetheart have pity', so that he could not get it out of his head, and the next morning at Mass, instead of saying 'Dominus vobiscum', he said 'Sweetheart have pity', and there was a dreadful scandal which got into a chronicle.

Sometimes our Bodo did not dance himself, but listened to the songs of wandering minstrels. The priests did not at all approve of these minstrels, who (they said) would certainly go to hell for singing profane secular songs, all about the great deeds of heathen heroes of the Frankish race, instead of Christian hymns. But Bodo loved them, and so did Bodo's betters; the Church councils had sometimes even to rebuke abbots and abbesses for listening to their songs. And the worst of it was that the great emperor himself, the good Charlemagne, loved them too. He would always listen to a minstrel, and his biographer, Einhard, tells us that 'He wrote out the barbarous and ancient songs, in which the acts of the kings and their wars were sung, and committed them to memory'; and one at least of those old sagas, which he liked men to write down, has been preserved on the cover of a Latin manuscript, where a monk scribbled it in his spare time. His son, Louis the Pious, was very different; he rejected the national poems, which he had learnt in his youth, and would not have them read or recited or taught; he would not allow minstrels to have justice in the law courts, and he forbade idle dances and songs and tales in public places on Sundays; but then he also dragged down his father's kingdom into disgrace and ruin. The minstrels repaid Charlemagne for his kindness to them. They gave him everlasting fame; for all through the Middle Ages the legend of Charlemagne grew, and he shares with our King Arthur the honour of being the hero of one of the greatest romance-cycles of the Middle Ages. Every different century clad him anew in its own dress and sang new lays about him. What the monkish chroniclers in their cells could never do for Charlemagne, these despised and accursed minstrels did for him: they gave him what is perhaps more desirable and more lasting than a place in history—they gave him a place in legend. It is not every emperor who rules in those realms of gold of which Keats spoke, as well as in the kingdoms of the world; and in the realms of gold Charlemagne reigns with King Arthur, and his peers joust with the Knights of the Round Table. Bodo, at any rate, benefited by Charles's love of minstrels, and it is probable that he heard in the lifetime of the emperor himself the first beginnings of those legends which afterwards clung to the name of Charlemagne. One can imagine him round-eyed in the churchyard, listening to fabulous stories of Charles's Iron March to Pavia, such as a gossiping old monk of St Gall afterwards wrote down in his chronicle.

It is likely enough that such legends were the nearest Bodo ever came to seeing the emperor, of whom even the poor serfs who never followed him to court or camp were proud. But Charles was a great traveller: like all the monarchs of the early Middle Ages he spent the time, when he was not warring, in trekking round his kingdom, staying at one of his estates, until he and his household had literally eaten their way through it, and then passing on to another. And sometimes he varied the procedure by paying a visit to the estates of his bishops or nobles, who entertained him royally. It may be that one day he came on a visit to Bodo's masters and stopped at the big house on his way to Paris, and then Bodo saw him plain; for Charlemagne would come riding along the road in his jerkin of otter skin, and his plain blue Cloak (Einhard tells us that he hated grand clothes and on ordinary days dressed like the common people); and after him would come his three sons and his bodyguard, and then his five daughters. Einhard has also told us that

> He had such care of the upbringing of his sons and daughters that he never dined without them when he was at home and never travelled without them. His sons rode along with him and his daughters followed in the rear. Some of his guards, chosen for this very purpose, watched the end of the line of march where his daughters travelled. They were very beautiful and

much beloved by their father, and, therefore, it is strange that he would give them in marriage to no one, either among his own people or of a foreign state. But up to his death he kept them all at home saying he could not forgo their society.

Then, with luck, Bodo, quaking at the knees, might even behold a portent new to his experience, the emperor's elephant. Haroun El Raschid, the great Sultan of the 'Arabian Nights' had sent it to Charles, and it accompanied him on all his progresses. Its name was 'Abu-Lubabah', which is an Arabic word and means 'the father of intelligence', and it died a hero's death on an expedition against the Danes in 810. It is certain that ever afterwards Ermentrude quelled little Gerbert, when he was naughty, with the threat, 'Abu-Lubabah will come with his long nose and carry you off.' But Wido, being aged eight and a bread-winner, professed to have felt no fear on being confronted with the elephant; but admitted when pressed, that he greatly preferred Haroun El Raschid's other present to the emperor, the friendly dog, who answered to the name of 'Becerillo'.

It would be a busy time for Bodo when all these great folk came, for everything would have to be cleaned before their arrival, the pastry cooks and sausage-makers summoned and a great feast prepared; and though the household serfs did most of the work, it is probable that he had to help. The gossipy old monk of St Gall has given us some amusing pictures of the excitement when Charles suddenly paid a visit to his subjects:

There was a certain bishopric which lay full in Charles's path when he journeyed, and which indeed he could hardly avoid: and the bishop of this place, always anxious to give satisfaction, put everything that he had at Charles's disposal. But once the Emperor came quite unexpectedly and the bishop in great anxiety had to fly hither and thither like a swallow, and had not only the palaces and houses but also the courts and squares swept and cleaned: and then tired and irritated, came to meet him. The most pious Charles noticed this, and after examining all the various details, he said to the bishop: 'My kind host, you always have everything splendidly cleaned for my arrival.' Then the bishop, as if divinely inspired, bowed his head and grasped the king's never-conquered right hand, and hiding his irritation, kissed it and said: 'It is but right, my lord, that, wherever you come, all things should be thoroughly cleansed.' Then Charles, of all kings the wisest, understanding the state of affairs said to him: 'If I empty I can also fill.' And he added: 'You may have that estate which lies close to your bishopric, and all your successors may have it until the end of time.' In the same journey, too, he came to a bishop who lived in a place through which he must needs pass. Now on that day, being the sixth day of the week, he was not willing to eat the flesh of beast or bird; and the bishop, being by reason of the nature of the place unable to procure fish upon the sudden ordered some excellent cheese, rich and creamy, to be placed before him. And the most self-restrained Charles, with the readiness which he showed everywhere and on all occasions, spared the blushes of the bishop and required no better fare; but taking up his knife cut off the skin, which he thought unsavoury and fell to on the white of the cheese. Thereupon the bishop, who was standing near like a servant, drew closer and said: 'Why do you do that, lord emperor? You are throwing away the very best part.' Then Charles, who deceived no one, and did not believe that anyone would deceive him, on the persuasion of the bishop put a piece of the skin in his mouth, and slowly ate it and swallowed it like butter. Then approving of the advice of the bishop, he said: 'Very true, my good host,' and he added: 'Be sure to send me every year to Aix two cartloads of just such cheeses.' And the bishop was alarmed at the impossibility of the task and, fearful of losing both his rank and his office, he rejoined: 'My lord, I can procure the cheeses, but I cannot tell which are of this quality and which of another. Much I fear lest I fall under your censure.' Then Charles, from whose penetration and skill nothing could escape, however new or strange it might be, spoke thus to the bishop, who from childhood had known such cheeses and yet could not test them: 'Cut them in two,' he said, 'then fasten together with a skewer those that you find to be of the right quality and keep them in your cellar for a time and then send them to me. The rest you may keep for yourself and your clergy and your family.' This was done for two years, and the king ordered the present of cheeses to be taken in without remark: then in the third year the bishop brought in person his laboriously collected cheeses. But the most just Charles pitied his labour and anxiety and added to the bishopric an excellent estate whence he and his successors might provide themselves with corn and wine.

We may feel sorry for the poor flustered bishop collecting his two cart-loads of cheeses; but it is possible that our real sympathy ought to go to Bodo, who probably had to pay an extra rent in cheeses to satisfy the emperor's taste, and got no excellent estate to recompense him.

A visit from the emperor, however, would be a rare event in his life, to be talked about for years and told to his grandchildren. But there was one other event, which happened annually, and which was certainly looked for with excitement by Bodo and his friends. For once a year the king's itinerant justices, the *Missi Dominici*, came round to hold their court and to see if the local counts had been doing justice. Two of them would come, a bishop and a count, and they would perhaps stay a night at the big house as guests of the abbot, and the next day they would go on to Paris, and there they would sit and do justice in the open square before the church and from all the district round great men and small, nobles and freemen and *coloni*, would bring their grievances and demand redress. Bodo would go too, if anyone had injured or robbed him, and would make his complaint to the judges. But if he were canny he would not go to them empty-handed, trusting to justice alone. Charlemagne was very strict, but unless the *missi* were exceptionally honest and pious they would not be averse to taking bribes. Theodulf, Bishop of Orleans, who was one of the Emperor's *missi*, has left us a most entertaining Latin poem, in which he describes the attempts of the clergy and laymen, who flocked to his court, to buy justice. . . .

Another treat Bodo had which happened once a year; for regularly on the ninth of October there began the great fair of St Denys, which went on for a whole month, outside the gates of Paris. Then for a week before the fair little booths and sheds sprang up, with open fronts in which the merchants could display their wares, and the Abbey of St Denys, which had the right to take a toll of all the merchants who came there to sell, saw to it that the fair was well enclosed with fences, and that all came in by the gates and paid their money, for wily merchants were sometimes known to burrow under fences or climb over them so as to avoid the toll. Then the streets of Paris were crowded with merchants bringing their goods, packed in carts and upon horses and oxen; and on the opening day all regular trade in Paris stopped for a month, and every Parisian shopkeeper was in a booth somewhere in the fair, exchanging the corn and wine and honey of the district for rarer goods from foreign parts. Bodo's abbey probably had a stall in the fair and sold some of those pieces of cloth woven by the serfs in the women's quarter, or cheeses and salted meat prepared on the estates, or wine paid in rent by Bodo and his fellow-farmers. Bodo would certainly take a holiday and go to the fair. In fact, the steward would probably have great difficulty in keeping his men at work during the month; Charlemagne had to give a special order to his stewards that they should 'be careful that our men do properly the work which it is lawful to exact from them, and that they not waste their time in running about to markets and fairs'. Bodo and Ermentrude and the three children, all attired in their best, did not consider it waste of time to go to the fair even twice or three times. They pretended that they wanted to buy salt to salt down their winter meat, or some vermilion dye to colour a frock for the baby. What they really wanted was to wander along the little rows of booths and look at all the strange things assembled there; for merchants came to St Denys to sell their rich goods from the distant East to Bodo's betters, and wealthy Frankish nobles bargained there for purple and silken robes with orange borders, stamped leather jerkins, peacock's feathers, and the scarlet plumage of flamingos (which they called 'phoenix skins'), scents and pearls and spices, almonds and raisins, and monkeys for their wives to play with. . . . Then there were always jugglers and tumblers, and men with performing bears, and minstrels to wheedle Bodo's few pence out of his pocket. And it would be a very tired and happy family that trundled home in the cart to bed. For it is not, after all, so dull in the kitchen, and when we have quite finished with the emperor, 'Charlemagne and all his peerage', it is really worth while to spend a few moments with Bodo in his little manse. History is largely made up of Bodos.

Jews in a Christian Society

ROBERT CHAZAN

Histories of European Jews have focused on their role in economic and intellectual life. On the one hand, historians have been concerned with estimating the importance of Jewish merchant and moneylending activities. On the other, they have traced the textual traditions of important philosophical, theological, and medical works that came to Europe through the Jewish communities of Sicily and Spain. Neither of these approaches has revealed much about the nature of the Jewish communities in Europe. Actually, there were two groups of European Jews in the Middle Ages; today they still form distinct communities. In the south, centered in Italy and Spain, Sephardic Jews were an integral part of the society, a bridge between the Moslem and Christian communities. Prior to their expulsion by Ferdinand and Isabella in 1492, the Spanish Jews had participated in one of the most interesting social amalgams in history. In medieval Spain three religious and national groups produced a brilliant civilization. This harmony between the Jews and their neighbors contrasted strikingly to he relations between Jew and Christian in northern Europe.

The Ashkenazic Jews of northern Europe (*Ashkenazim* is the medieval Hebrew word for "Germans") were segregated in religious communities that formed the nuclei of the ghettos of the modern era. The Ashkenazim seem to have originated from groups of Jews brought north from Italy in the ninth century by the Carolingian emperors. It was later reported that one of the most famous communities, that of Mainz in Germany, was created when Emperor Charles the Fat brought Rabbi Moses of Lucca to the north about 887. The Rabbi naturally brought his congregation with him, and the little community expanded rapidly. Charles may have brought the Jews north in order to establish a skilled commercial group in his kingdom. In the ninth through eleventh centuries, the kings generally protected the Jews because of their importance in commerce.

The records of these Jewish communities, principally the Responsa, decisions of the rabbis in law suits, show that in the first three centuries of Ashkenazic life the Jews were borrowers of money, not lenders. The surplus capital produced on the great estates was lent to the Jews for their commercial enterprises at a time when Christians had almost no use for such capital. For example, the surplus production of the Archbishopric of Narbonne, managed by Jews, was lent to other Jews for their business operations. It was only in the twelfth century, as a result of two movements, that the Jews began to lend money to Christians and to establish the economic pattern that eventually led to the stereotype of the Jewish moneylender. The first of these movements was the crusades; the crusaders needed considerable liquid capital for the long journey to the Holy Land and borrowed against the future income of their estates. The second was the emergence of a Christian merchant class that could use business capital and sometimes turned to the Jews to get it.

The Responsa also demonstrate that although the Jews were not popular among Christians, they clung together in the medieval cities not so much because the Christians forced them to as for religious reasons. Adherence to the Talmudic laws demanded a close-knit community that could support and regulate the provisioning of the restricted diet and maintain the religious service. In some parts of Europe, the communities described by the Responsa continued to exist into this century, though the great age of the Responsa came to an end with the First Crusade.

In this selection, Robert Chazan uses the Responsa and other, narrative, sources to describe the life of the northern Jews in the "golden age," from the ninth through eleventh centuries.

During the tenth and eleventh centuries northern France slowly rose from its torpor. Population increased, the economy developed, and cities grew. This progress contributed to—and benefited from—the establishment of more effective political units. The dukes and counts of northern France carved out for themselves ever larger territories and began to control their domains with increasing authority. The most powerful of these magnates, William of Normandy, was able, during the 1060's, to muster sufficient force to conquer for himself a kingdom across the English Channel. Unobtrusively the king of France, overshadowed often by his mighty vassals, was subduing the Île-de-France and bending it to his will, slowly laying the groundwork for the sudden expansion of royal power that materialized at the end of the twelfth century.

The revival of trade and of urban centers must have vitally affected the Jews of northern France; however, evidence from this period is sparse. Documentary records, generally meager for this early age, shed no light whatsoever on the role and position of the Jews. The only non-Jewish materials available are the random observations of churchmen, in some instances enlightening, in others misleading. Jewish sources likewise are slim, consisting of a few brief chronicles, a substantial number of rabbinic responsa, and commentaries on the classics of Biblical and Talmudic literature. While the paucity of evidence precludes a detailed reconstruction of Jewish history during this period, enough remains to sketch in outline the condition of northern French Jewry prior to the First Crusade.

From Robert Chazan, *Medieval Jewry in Northern France* (Baltimore: The Johns Hopkins University Press, 1973), pp. 9–29.

A precise geography of pre-Crusade northern French Jewry is impossible. There are, however, a number of locales for which Jewish settlement is attested: Auxerre, Blois, Châlons-sur-Marne, Le Mans, Orléans, Paris, Reims, Rouen, Sens, Troyes. These are major urban centers, all the seats of dioceses. Random evidence indicates Jewish presence in smaller towns as well. Thus, in the incident of 992, the villain, a convert from Judaism to Christianity, moved from Blois to Le Mans, visiting (and duping) a number of Jewish communities in western France along the way. Likewise the so-called Rashi ordinance, which dealt with taxation procedures in the Jewry of Troyes, reflects Jewish settlement in smaller towns. The ordinance was enacted by a major Jewish community surrounded by smaller satellites: "We the inhabitants of Troyes, along with the communities in its environs. . . ." By 1096 the Jews had begun to spread beyond the confines of the major cities of northern France.

Widespread insecurity had destroyed the centralized authority of the Carolingians and had brought to power the feudal barony of northern France. Endangered French society had reconstructed itself through a network of immediate personal ties; the unity embodied in Carolingian rule gave way to a host of localized principalities. The Jews, as perhaps the most exposed element in this society, had the deepest need for the protection that only these magnates could offer. They were thus cast into permanent dependence upon a plethora of seigneurs, ranging from king to petty noble.

It is difficult to trace the implications of this dependence in the pre-Crusade period. The political status of northern French Jewry was never specified in comprehensive charters, as was the case in Germany. It is only with the passage of time and the proliferation of records that a detailed picture of Jewish political circumstances emerges. In general it is obvious that even in this early period the political authorities were responsible for basic Jewish security. This included both protection of Jewish life and property and judicial jurisdiction over the Jews. In 992, when a serious charge was leveled at the Jews of Le Mans, the count not only constituted the court before which the Jews were to be tried; he in fact stipulated the procedure to be utilized. It is also possible that even at this early stage governmental support for the Jews included aid in Jewish business affairs. Detailed information on this comes only in the twelfth century, however.

Willingness to extend to the Jews protection and aid was contingent, of course, on significant advantage to be derived from these Jews. Governmental authorities anticipated two major benefits from Jewish presence: general stimulation of trade and urban life and, more tangible, the immediate profit to be realized from taxation. Tax records from the early period no longer exist, and information in the Jewish sources is fragmentary. There can be little doubt, however, that the flow of income from this taxation was the major factor in the protective stance taken by the barony of northern France.

The dangers inherent in this alliance with the ruling class were manifested early. While the authorities were relatively successful in protecting the Jews from others, there was no power that could effectively interpose itself between the Jews and their protectors. Only two incidents of any proportion mar the calm of Jewish life in northern France prior to 1096; in both cases it was rulers with unrestricted power over the Jews who were responsible for the persecutions.

The first crisis took place in 992 in the city of Le Mans. A convert from Judaism, one Sehok b. Esther, after earlier clashes with the Jews of Le Mans, deposited a waxen image in the synagogue ark and then unearthed it in the presence of the count of Maine, Hugh III, claiming that the Jews pierced the image regularly in hopes of destroying the count. In the face of adamant Jewish denials, Hugh of Maine ordered the Jews to be tried by combat with their accuser. The chronicle breaks off at this point, with the Jewish community seemingly on the brink of catastrophe. From the opening remarks of the communal letter which describes the incident, it is obvious that the community emerged unscathed. How this came about is unknown. Perfectly clear, however, is the danger stemming from the Jewish community's total reliance on the will of the governing authorities.

The second major incident was far more serious, both in scope and in consequences. According to a variety of extant sources, the years between 1007 and 1012 saw a series of edicts across northern Europe, posing to the Jews the alternatives of conversion to Christianity and expulsion or, on occasion, death. Most of the Jews seem to have chosen expulsion. In some cases, however, there was loss of life, the first instances of that readiness for martyrdom which became a significant characteristic of Ashkenazic Jewry. Although the factors in this persecution were of a religious nature, primarily a concern with the spread of heresy in northern Europe, the decision to convert or expel the Jews could only be made by those feudal lords who controlled Jewish fate—once more an important index of the potential dangers inhering in Jewish political status.

While the local lord exercised effective power over the Jews of his domain, there were other forces striving to make their influence felt. Chief among these was the Church. In some cases, churchmen were themselves feudal lords holding direct rights over Jews. Such overt control, however, was not so prominent in northern France as it was elsewhere. The normal channels of Church influence were twofold. The first was the Church's strong moral pressure on the barony. Clerics close to the feudal dignitaries would utilize this intimacy to further their views on the Jews. Thus, for example, in the 992 incident an anonymous churchman strongly bolstered the anti-Jewish animus by his inflammatory speech to the count of Maine. A more circuitous and less effective mode of influence was through the masses. This involved specifying the Jewish behavior which was unacceptable to the Church and threatening excommunication of those Christians having contact with recalcitrant Jews. According to Raoul Glaber, part of the early-eleventh-century program to eliminate Judaism entirely from sections of northern France was abetted by an episcopal decree outlawing all contact with Jews. The major problem with such boycotts was the difficulty of enforcement.

From the point of view of the Jews, ecclesiastical influence could be either beneficial or baneful. In the instance cited, the cleric of Le Mans much inflamed anti-Jewish passions. On the other hand, it was the awareness of potential Church protection that led a Jew of Rouen, Jacob b. Yekutiel, to deny the right of Richard II of Normandy forcibly to convert the Jews: "You lack the necessary jurisdiction over the Jews to force them from their faith or to harm them. This can only be done by the pope at Rome." The claim of Jacob was not a negation of the feudal rights of Richard over the Jews of Normandy; it was an assertion that the program undertaken ostensibly in the name of the Christian faith was in fact a perversion of Christian principles and had to be brought before the highest ecclesiastical officials for sanction or annulment. According to the Hebrew account, Jacob proceeded to Rome, pleaded his case, and secured a papal decree halting the program of forced conversion.

At this juncture the king exercised no special regalian rights over the Jews. He did, of course, possess normal baronial jurisdiction over the Jews of his own domain. Beyond this, he could on occasion exercise his prerogative as suzerain. It was on this basis that Robert the Pious intervened in the affairs of the county of Sens, deposing Count Raynaud on charges of Judaizing. In the incident of 1007–1012, the king exhibited strong moral leadership in the campaign of forced conversion. While the Hebrew chronicle emphasizes the king's central role in the affair, it also underscores the necessity of agreement by his vassals.

> Then the king and queen took counsel with his officers and his vassals throughout the limits of his kingdom. They charged: "There is one people dispersed throughout the various principalities which does not obey us. . . ." Then there was a perfect agreement betwen the king and his officers, and they concurred on this plan.

Thus the king could suggest action; its execution, however, depended on the consent and the support of the local authorities.

Yet another potential influence on the destiny of the Jews was the municipality and its burghers. In an early stage of development at this point, its lack of authority over the Jews was already manifest. For the Jews, this powerlessness was a boon. If to the princes the Jews promised economic advantage, to the burghers they offered primarily competition.

It was all to the Jews' advantage to be removed from the jurisdiction of the growing communes. Yet this removal added political animosity to the religious and economic antipathies already harbored by the townsmen towards the Jews.

During this early period, the populace at large does not appear as a major instigating force in anti-Jewish activity. This was, to be sure, an epoch of substantial violence, and the Jews felt this lawlessness on occasion. The chronicle of 992 mentions in passing economic competition between the renegade Seḥok and a member of the Jewish community. This rivalry led eventually to assassination of the Jew by hired killers from Blois. The responsa literature reflects the same instability. There is, for example, an interesting responsum dealing with Jewish merchants captured and held for ransom. More striking, however, is the frequency with which governmental oppressions such as those of 992 and 1007–1012 were accompanied by outbursts of popular antipathy. This is attested by the Hebrew chronicle for 992 and by a number of the sources for 1007–1012. The breakdown of official protection allowed the overt expression of that popular hatred normally suppressed by the authorities.

The Jews of northern France were by the eleventh century already supporting themselves primarily by commerce, and, as the century progressed, this led them increasingly into moneylending. The reliance on commerce and usury is reflected in a most interesting responsum from the early eleventh century. The community had "levied on every man and woman, while under the ban, a fixed amount per pound of value of his or her *money, merchandise*, and *other saleable possessions*"; trade and banking were obviously primary. Despite the ordinance's orientation towards taxation of merchandise and money, the community attempted to levy taxes on a local Jewess' vineyard, demanding a portion of the value of both the land and its produce. The terms in which the issue was debated are revealing:

> They [the community] claimed that vineyards were in the same category as the capital of a loan, while the harvested crop was equivalent to the interest. One derived no benefit from the vineyard itself, nor from the capital of the loan, during the first half year or year of its investment. Since they paid taxes from both the capital and the interest of their money investments, from their merchandise as well as from its profit, they held that L should do likewise. L, on her part, pointed out that a vineyard could not be compared to the capital of a loan, nor even to merchandise. . . . Thus they argued back and forth.

What is plainly assumed by both sides in the dispute is the centrality of wares and capital in communal taxation. The reply of R. Joseph Bon Fils agreed with the position that *only* merchandise, money, and the profits from both are taxable.

The economic reliance on commerce and moneylending emerges also from the famous ordinance of Rashi, dating from the end of the eleventh century.

> We, the inhabitants of Troyes, along with the communities in its environs, have ordained—under threat of excommunication—upon every man and woman living here that they be forbidden to remove themselves from the yoke of communal responsibility. . . . Each one shall give per pound that which is enjoined by the members of the community, as has been practiced since the very day of its founding. We have likewise received from our predecessors the practice of paying on all possessions, except household items, houses, vineyards, and fields.

A community which exempts "household items, houses, vineyards, and fields" from taxation is obviously heavily involved in mercantile pursuits.

Jewish commerce was probably largely local. As noted, evidence for settlement shows the Jews primarily in major urban centers. A number of responsa, however, indicate Jews traveling through northern France, trading at the fairs of this period. Insecurity made such travel hazardous on occasion; Jewish traders were seized and their goods confiscated. Sometimes the inherent dangers of commerce were magnified by involvement in shady dealings. An early-eleventh-century responsum deals with the legal complications arising from the disappearance and presumed death of an unscrupulous Jewish merchant. The questionable practices, which probably led to his violent demise, are described as follows:

> A was accustomed to travel to many places and to many towns situated within a day or two of his residence. He would sell to and buy from the overlords of these towns, his regular clientele. Whenever they were short of cash, he would sell to them on credit, against pledges of gold or silver, or exchange his merchandise for cattle (or horses) which they had robbed from their enemies. These cattle he would accept at a low price, bring them home and sell them for a much higher price. His activities aroused the anger and hatred of the plundered villagers, and of their feudal lords, who would say: "This Jew, by the very fact that he is always ready to buy looted goods, entices our enemies to attack and plunder us. . . ." Moreover, occasionally the overlords quarrelled with him on account of the pledges which A would eventually sell and because of the high interest he charged.

The normal hazards of eleventh-century trade were here much enhanced.

The same responsum reveals the very fluid transition which many Jews made from commerce to lending. When his customers lacked the necessary cash at hand to make their purchases, the Jewish merchant would extend credit. In fact, there is an indication of the mechanism utilized for safeguarding this investment. The debtors gained the necessary credit by depositing pledges, which were held as security for repayment of the obligation. In case of eventual nonpayment, these pledged objects could be sold. No litigation or third party was needed, and the creditor was amply protected from the moment that the loan was extended. Safeguarding loans through retention of a pledge is, of course, the simplest expedient available, and it was probably the most common method used during this period.

There are, nonetheless, fragmentary signs of more sophisticated arrangements. A responsum of Rashi deals with a dispute between a widow and her brother-in-law concerning gifts allegedly given to the widow and her deceased husband by his parents. Chief among these gifts was "the tithe collectible from a certain village, which tithe had been pledged with L and J [the parents] for a loan of seven rotl. L and J thus empowered R and A to collect the produce of that tithe and the principal of the loan in the event the original owner of the tithe should come to repay the loan and redeem his pledge." While this arrangement is also designated a pledge (mashkon), it is quite different from the pledges indicated earlier. The former were physical objects which were deposited at the time of the loan. When the debt was repaid, the pawn was returned; if the borrower defaulted, it would be kept or sold. In the case of the tithe, however, it was not a physical object that changed hands; it was a right. The difference in practical terms was twofold. First, there was constant revenue; the lender collected regular income, which was probably seen as the interest on the loan. More important, this was an arrangement that involved more than simply a creditor and a debtor; the implicit aid of a governmental agency was necessary. The creditor did not physically control the pledge; hence, should contention arise, he had to have the certainty of powerful support. Lending of the kind revealed in the responsum of Rashi is far more complex and generally more lucrative; it has as its result the further tightening of the crucial bond between Jew and baron. As Jews turned increasingly towards this kind of business operation, they began to depend on their overlords not only for physical protection but for buttressing their financial investments as well. Prior to the First Crusade this more complex method of lending may have remained rather uncommon. It was, however, destined to play an increasingly important role in Jewish economic life.

The aspect of pre-Crusade Jewish life that has attracted the most scholarly attention has been its communal organization. The Jewish communities of northern France were small, with a high level of internal cohesion and a broad range of activities. Yitzhak Baer has delineated three major functions in this community: the preservation of satisfactory relations with the ruling powers, the securing of internal discipline and order, and the establishment of necessary internal economic limitations and controls.

The alliance fashioned between the Jews and the barony was fueled by the tangible advantages realized by the feudal magnates. The most immediate expression of this was taxation. Collection of taxes was certainly one of the major functions assumed by the communal agencies. The responsum specifying those holdings open to taxation indicates that the purpose of the levy was "to collect the king's tax."

The methods for apportioning taxation were well-established and reflect the cohesiveness of the community. One method was that indicated in the above-noted responsum. This involved levying "on every man and woman, while under the ban, a fixed amount per pound of value of his or her money, merchandise, and other saleable possessions." This system depended for its effectiveness upon honest evaluation, by each member of the community, of his possessions. The likelihood of such honesty was enhanced by the religious sanctions mentioned and by the closeness of a small community, where the temptation to underevaluate would be tempered by the difficulty of concealing the truth. Occasionally, however, this arrangement broke down. R. Joseph Bon Fils was asked to resolve a complicated issue that began with the following circumstance:

> The people of T came to pay the king's tax. They complained against one another, saying: "You lightened your own burden and made mine heavier." Whereupon they selected trustees, the noble and great of the town, the experts of the land, from the community, and (agreed) to abide by their decision, for they dealt faithfully.

The role of the Jewish community organization as a liaison between the Jews and the ruling authorities was not exhausted by the collection of taxes. On occasion the organized community had to make representation before the authorities on matters affecting the security of the Jews. Thus, in 992, when faced with the danger of trial by combat, the Jewish community made vehement protestations before the count of Maine. They appealed to precedent, on the one hand, and offered substantial material inducements, on the other. While in this instance there was large-scale community response, in periods of crisis a prominent individual could take the initiative, thrusting himself to the fore as the community's spokesman. It was in this manner that Jacob b. Yekutiel ventured to step forth before the duke of Normandy and ultimately before the pope himself.

In a community desperately anxious to preserve its insulation from the local municipality within whose boundaries it lived and to achieve a measure of distance from even the more favorably-disposed feudal authorities, there was an absolute necessity for maintaining inner discipline. While the small size of the Jewish community contributed to cohesiveness, close living could on occasion produce sharp conflicts between members of the community. In the face of such conflict, the community marshaled its forces and ordained limitations on intracommunal strife. The community's goal in such cases was the preservation of peace within the community, without the intervention of outside powers.

The economic outlets available to the Jews were not extensive. For this reason the community had to exercise significant control in the area of economics also. The two major thrusts of communal limitation were the granting of exclusive commercial privileges and the restriction of the right to settle. The former usually involved business dealings with important secular lords of ecclesiastical institutions. From the slim evidence available, it seems that the arrangement was not everywhere operative and that, even where the prerogative of the community to give such privileges was recognized, the rights of exclusive trade were not widely granted. Restriction of settlement was directly related to the economic situation of the Jews. The small towns of northern France could absorb only so many Jewish traders and moneylenders. Overpopulation would simply force the available income of the community below the subsistence level. Again it must be noted, however, that the right of the community to declare a total or even a partial ban on new settlement was far from universally recognized.

To the three major functions of the Jewish community delineated by Baer at least a fourth must be added. The Jewish community of necessity had to supply certain essential religious and social services to its membership. The centrality of the synagogue in the Jewish community of this period is undisputed. It was far more than a center of worship, serving as an educational and general communal center as well. Details of Jewish schooling at the time are almost nonexistent. The literacy demanded by the business pursuits of the Jews and the already high level of cultural achievement indicate a successful educational system. Within the medieval municipality there were of course no "neutral" social welfare agencies; such facilities as did exist were Church institutions and, as such, closed to the Jews; thus the Jews had to provide for their own indigent, ill, and unfortunate. The needs of the local community were often augmented by the requirements of Jews whose business took them from town to town. In the case of the central figure in the Le Mans letter, as he proceeded through the Jewish communities of northwestern France, the Jews "supported him, as is their custom, in every town to which he came." Perhaps the most striking evidence of such concern is revealed in the following responsum:

Jews of Rheims, while on their way to the fair of Troyes, were attacked, plundered, and taken captive by "an adversary and an enemy." The charitable Jews of Troyes risked their own lives, (negotiated with the enemy,) and agreed to a redemption price of thirty pounds. The greater part of the ransom money was paid by the captives themselves; while in order to raise the remainder, the community of Troyes levied a tax of one *solidus* per pound on themselves, as well as on the neighboring communities of Sens and Auxerre, and on the Jews of Chalon-sur-Saône.

The locus of power in the Jewish community was the community membership itself. While the governing authorities benefited from the ability of the community to control its own affairs, particularly in the area of taxation, there was as yet no strong drive for more direct involvement in Jewish communal affairs or for more extensive exploitation of this useful and cohesive group. As noted, the community, for its part, was anxious to minimize outside interference.

The rhetoric of community enactments generally emphasized unanimous decision-making by the entire local Jewry: "The community of Troyes levied a tax . . ."; "the townspeople levied on every man and woman . . ."; "the community . . . heard about it and solemnly pronounced the ban. . . ." There was, in fact, even question as to the right of the majority to exercise its will over the minority.

At the same time, however, certain elements in the community did command special authority. Leadership was exercised by significant scholarly figures, such as Rashi, or by men of wealth and standing, such as Jacob b. Yekutiel. An interesting responsum indicates a more general tendency towards control by a segment of the community. In a conflict concerning the responsibility of individuals to accept the decisions fo the majority, the following question was asked:

> We are a small community. The humble members among us have always abided by the leadership of our eminent members, dutifully obeyed their decrees, and never protested against their ordinances. Now, when we are about to enact a decree, must we ask each individual member whether or not he is in agreement with it?

Even at this early point a leadership class does seem to have emerged, although it certainly lacked the direct governmental support and the recognized religious authority that would later develop.

With the community itself as the fundamental authority, it is in no way surprising to find power highly localized. The question of the right of one Jewish settlement to legislate for others was raised a number of times. In general a distinction was drawn between daily administrative affairs—where each community was autonomous—and principles of Jewish religious behavior—where coercion could be exerted. One of a number of expressions of this distinction is phrased in the following way:

> As to your question whether the inhabitants of one town are competent to enact decrees binding on the inhabitants of another town, and to coerce the latter inhabitants while they are in their own town, the following ruling seems proper to us: If the decree that they are enacting deals with the needs of their place, such as taxation, weights, measures, and wages—in all such matters the inhabitants of one town are not competent to legislate for the inhabitants of another town. Thus we quoted above the Talmudic ruling: "The townspeople are permitted," which means that only the people of the

town are competent to legislate in such matters but not outsiders. If, however, the inhabitants of a town transgressed a law of the Torah, committed a wrong, or decided a point of law or of ritual, not in accordance with the accepted usage—the inhabitants of another town might coerce them, and even pronounce the *herem* against them, in order to force them to mend their ways. In that case, the inhabitants of the former town may not say to the latter: "we are independent of you, we exercise authority among ourselves, as you do among yourselves." For all Israel is then enjoined to force them (to mend their ways); as we find in the case of the "rebellious sage," or "the condemned city,"that the Sanhedrin coerces them and judges them.

Extensive authority was exercised by outstanding scholarly figures, whose enactments were generally considered binding over a wide number of settlements. Thus, Rashi affirms that the important edict of R. Gershom of Mayence would certainly be applicable in all Jewish communities.

> Should it become established through the testimony of reliable witnesses who are recognized authorities on this restrictive ordinance of the great teacher (R. Gershom), that he enacted this ordinance with greater rigor and strictness than all other anathemas and restrictive measures customarily enacted in the last generations; that in this enactment he used the awesome term *shamta*; and that he solemnly prohibited to mention the disgrace (of temporary apostasy) not only to the culprits themselves who eventually returned to Judaism, but even to their descendants; and should it further become established that when A and his family were forewarned, the name of the great teacher (as author of the awesome ban) was mentioned to them—we cannot deal lightly with a ban of Rabbenu Gershom, since in our generation there is no scholar of his great eminence, capable to release a person from such a ban.

The sanctions at the disposal of the community were of course conditioned by the bases of its power. One possibility lay in the direction of the secular authority, but it was an avenue only sparingly utilized because of the danger inhering in such an approach. Thus, an early-eleventh-century Jewish community faced with the overt recalcitrance of two of its members and the support of a neighboring community for the rebels was "about to ask the king to order his constables to collect his tax directly from A and B. Upon further deliberation, however, they changed their minds and decided first to inquire whether their solemn decree was still valid, i.e., whether the cancellation thereof by the community of S was of any consequence." A turn to secular authorities was a step which most Jewish communities were reluctant to take.

Since the most tangible locus of power was the cohesive community itself, the ultimate weapon at the disposal of the Jews was the ban of excommunication. Given the importance of the Jewish community and its facilities to the individual Jew, the power of exclusion was a formidable one. The ostracized Jew was in a hazardous position politically, economically, socially, and religiously. At the same time, excommunication was not an infallible tool in the hands of the Jewish community. The realities of power within the community often limited the effectiveness of the ban. In one case, for example, "since the members of the community feared that B and his friends, living so near the synagogue, would remove the scrolls of the Law and other community articles, and that no one would be able to stop them from taking these articles, they transgressed the law on several occasions—all on B's instructions." Another limitation on the effectiveness of excommunication was the localization of Jewish authority already noted. Thus two Jews excommunicated in community T "went to S and related there the whole incident. The people of S took A and B into their homes, wined and dined them, transacted business with them, lifted from them the ban of community T, and gave them a written release of such ban." While the action of community S was judged illegal, in fact the localization of power did weaken the impact of any such ban.

The Jewish community of northern France thus emerges, from earliest times, as a remarkably cohesive and comprehensive organization. The isolation of the Jews forced them to create for themselves all sorts of agencies—political, economic, social, educational, and religious. The small size of the individual Jewish settlements precluded the independence of each of these agencies. What emerged then was a total Jewish community responsible for filling every one of the vital needs of its constituents. Therein lies the secret of the wide range of powers and the effectiveness of the Jewish community organization even at its early stage of development.

Perhaps the most persuasive index of the level of maturity reached by northern French Jewry prior to the First Crusade is its intellectual creativity. It seems reasonable to conclude that a community capable of producing extensive scholarly achievement like that of R. Solomon b. Isaac of Troyes (Rashi) must have been well-established and effectively organized. Rashi, already noted as an outstanding communal authority—one of the few whose eminence was broadly recognized—wrote copiously. His works, which quickly became classics in Ashkenazic circles, included primarily extensive commentaries on the Bible and the Talmud. While he was always revered as the beginning—and not the culmination—of a brilliant series of northern French scholars, his creations indicate that, by the last years of the eleventh century, northern French Jewry had come of age.

At the end of the eleventh century many of the creative forces that had been germinating steadily throughout western Europe burst forth into the passion, vision, and violence of the First Crusade. The Crusade was an expression of the new militance of Christendom against its external foes; it revealed also new potential for internal upheaval and disruption. While the goal of the pope and of the great barons was a military expedition against Islam, the feelings unleashed by the call to the Crusade could hardly be contained within the particular channels delineated by its instigators. Thus the First Crusade brought more than the conquest of Jerusalem; it left a path of death and destruction within Christendom itself.

The dispossessed who took up the chant "Deus lo volt" savagely vented pent-up furies upon many of their long-despised neighbors. Given the pervasive religiosity of medieval civilization and the distinctly religious hatreds that animated the Crusaders, it comes as no surprise that the prime object of the internal violence associated with the First Crusade was European Jewry.

France, particularly northern France, played a major role in the great drama of 1095–1099. It was in the French city of Clermont that Urban II issued his appeal; French barons were conspicuous in their leadership of the crusading forces; it was in the French countryside that Peter the Hermit began his preaching for a humble army of the pious to free the holy places from Moslem hands. Yet France, despite its prominence, was spared the upheavals that followed in the wake of Crusade preaching. France's eastern neighbors bore the brunt of the devastation that crusading fervor unleashed.

The relative calm with which France weathered the Crusade is reflected in the fate of her Jews. The same Jewish and Christian sources that are so copious in their description of Jewish sufferings in the Rhineland area say almost nothing of Jewish fate in France. Although arguments from silence are always suspect, it is difficult to believe that this set of Jewish and Christian chroniclers and editors would have been unaware of, or uninterested in recounting, extensive Jewish tragedy in nearby France. The Rhineland Jews who compiled the Hebrew chronicles knew the reactions of the French Jews to the organization of the Crusade, and they detailed Jewish persecution over a broad area. It is inconceivable that large-scale catastrophe in France could have gone unknown or unreported. Moreover, the longest of the Hebrew Crusade chronicles is embedded in a late-twelfth-century communal history of Spires Jewry, which includes a series of letters detailing the Blois catastrophe of 1171 and its aftermath. Th Spires editor would not have omitted information on Crusade tragedy in France had it been available.

There is satisfactory evidence for but one specific persecution of Jews within the area of northern France, an attack which took place in the Norman city of Rouen. The fullest description of this assault is given by Guibert of Nogent as a backdrop to his account of a monk of the monastery of Fly.

> At Rouen on a certain day, the people who had undertaken to go on that expedition [that is, the Crusade] under the badge of the Cross began to complain to one another, "After traversing great distances, we desire to attack the enemies of God in the East, although the Jews, of all races the worst foe of God, are before our eyes. That's doing our work backward." Saying this and seizing their weapons, they herded the Jews into a certain place of worship, rounding them up by either force or guile, and without distinction of sex or age put them to the sword. Those who accepted Christianity, however, escaped the impending slaughter.

The striking difference between the relative peace enjoyed by northern France and its Jews and the wholesale destruction, especially of Jewish life and property, further east can be accounted for in a number of ways. This difference is surely *not* a reflection of more benign French attitudes; as Norman Golb has argued, French Crusaders were deeply implicated in the wave of German atrocities associated with the First Crusade. In France, however, their antipathy was not translated into deed, partially because France was the very first area of organization. The problems of the undisciplined Crusader bands tended to multiply the further eastward they moved, the larger their numbers, and the slimmer their provisions. The initial rallying of these crusading groups in France and their speedy movement towards the East played a major role in the safety of French Jewry. A second factor was the protection afforded by the less pretentious, but more effective, French political authorities. While the emperor was the most exalted political dignitary of Europe, the base upon which his power rested was a shaky one. Thus, in town after town, the Jews found themselves separated from large and bloodthirsty mobs by the flimsy military and political power of the local bishop. Even the Hebrew chroniclers recognize that many of these bishops were sincere in their desire to protect their Jews; their failure resulted from a lack of the required force. In France, on the other hand, where the Capetian monarchy advanced none of the grandiose claims of the German empire, firm political power had been slowly crystallizing in a series of well-organized principalities. Within these principalities the count and his growing retinue of administrative officials exercised effective authority. It was this political stability also that aided in harnessing the violence of the Crusaders and in sparing the Jews.

Although the Jews of northern France suffered little during the tumultuous first months of the Crusade, they were hardly oblivious to the dangers. In fact they were far more aware of the impending threat than any of their fellow Jews, for it was in their land that the Crusade was called, that the first active preaching took place, and that the first crusading groups began to form. The same Hebrew chronicle that said nothing of overt persecution in France recorded faithfully the fears of the French Jews.

At the time when the Jewish communities in France heard [of the beginning of the Crusade] they were seized with fear and trembling. They then resorted to the devices of their predecessors. They wrote letters and sent messengers to the Rhineland communities, that these communities fast and seek mercy on their behalf from the God who dwells on high, so that they might be spared.

The Hebrew chronicles also reported the more immediate steps taken by French Jewry to avert the threatened catastrophe. This information is contained in the brief description of the passage of Peter the Hermit through Trèves.

When he came to Trèves—he and the multitude of men with him—to go forth on their pilgrimage to Jerusalem, he brought with him from France a letter from the Jews, indicating that, in all places where he would pass through Jewish communities, they should afford him provisions. He then would speak favorably on behalf of the Jews.

Given the lack of destructive violence against the Jews in northern France, we can readily understand the lack of a political aftermath parallel to that which took place in Germany. Guido Kisch has carefully chronicled the evolution in Germany of safeguards designed to protect the vulnerable Jewish communities. Jewish political status in France, however, underwent no significant development in the wake of the First Crusade. There had been, after all, no major calamity to arouse among the Jews themselves or among their baronial overlords a heightened sense of the urgent need for new protective devices.

Furthermore, French Jewry never viewed 1095–1096 as a watershed in its history, as did its German counterpart. While the works of Rashi represent an early high point of French Jewish religious creativity, his successors did not see themselves as mere compilers of his legacy; they considered their efforts a continuation, not a collection. When, much later on, the sense of a chain of giant figures emerges, this series runs from Rashi through R. Samson of Sens, from the late eleventh through the early thirteenth centuries. The years of the First Crusade are in no sense construed as a major dividing line. Interestingly enough, when in 1171 French Jewry suffered what it considered its first major catastrophe, the calamity at Blois, it very movingly expressed the feelings of horror evoked by the utterly senseless death of over thirty Jews. If ever one might expect French Jewish recollection of the First Crusade, this would surely be the point. Yet significantly there is no recall whatsoever of 1096. When old memories are summoned up, they are recollections of a much earlier period. Thus, according to Ephraim of Bonn, R. Jacob Tam ordained that the twentieth of Sivan, the day of the catastrophe itself, "is fit to be set as a fast day for all our people. Indeed the gravity of this fast will exceed that of the fast of Gedaliah b. Aḥikam, for this is a veritable

Day of Atonement." The fateful year of the First Crusade in no way dominated the subsequent consciousness of northern French Jewry.

Through the late tenth and on through the eleventh century, then, northern French Jewry continued to develop, benefiting from the general progress of western European civilization and making its own contribution to that progress. Already tightly allied with the powerful feudal barony, the Jews were involving themselves ever more heavily in the burgeoning urban commerce and had begun to develop viable institutions of self-government. By the end of the eleventh century, northern French Jewry was sufficiently mature to produce its first figure of renown, R. Solomon b. Isaac of Troyes. Relatively unscathed by the anti-Jewish outbreaks of the First Crusade, French Jewry proceeded into the twelfth century in a spirit of continued growth.

The World of the Crusaders

JOSHUA PRAWER

Popular histories of the crusades dwell on the formation of the crusading armies, the trek across Asia Minor to the Levant, and the revival of trade between East and West. They also indulge in endless discussions concerning the motives of the crusaders. This selection by Joshua Prawer treats an important aspect of the crusading movement that receives scant attention in most histories —the experiences and everyday lives of the Europeans who settled the new Latin principalities in Palestine and Syria. The First Crusade was successful not only in driving the Saracens out of Jerusalem, but also in establishing a feudal principality there to protect the recovered holy places. Many of those who went with the first army were landless knights who stayed in the Holy Land to carve out baronies for themselves. Their good fortune, as well as the continual need for reinforcements to keep the new state strong against Moslem counterattack, brought in a steady stream of European knights.

What was this society of immigrants and, eventually, of second- and third-generation Levantines like? The Arabs of the region considered the new arrivals barbarians—brutes whose ability to fight had to be respected, but whose culture was shockingly primitive. The Europeans born in the Levant may well have had the same reaction to newcomers, but they were cultural hybrids themselves. Their kingdom produced a feudal charter, the Assizes of Jerusalem, that shows a faithful adherence to the social and political ideal of Europe. Their life style, however, absorbed much from the arab aristocracy around them, with which they learned to live during the uneasy truces.

The noble and knight brought with them from Europe notions and ideals of the seigniorial life-style and transplanted them in the soil of the newly conquered state. Western Europe perpetuated itself under oriental skies. The French language, fashions and customs struck roots in the Levant, and soon a second and a third generation of the original conquerors and settlers had grown up in the country for whom "home" meant the Holy Land, whereas Europe—the "old home"—was a place of their ancestors' far-removed origin. This was a new breed of men and

From Joshua Prawer, *The World of the Crusaders* (New York: Quadrangle Books, 1972), pp. 83–92, 92–96, 99.

women nicknamed *Poulains*, which should probably be translated or understood in the sense of "kids." Their home life, family relations and tutors were all reflections of Europe and, more specifically, France. Yet their environment—the physical conditions of life, the daily meetings in street and bazaar—was the Levant. Thus a scion of a noble, or even a knightly, family underwent the same process of upbringing and education as his European counterpart. He was raised under the mantle of the same religion, instructed in the same tenets of faith, drew his intellectual attitudes and images from the same legends, pious tales, heroic romances and courtly poetry. A *France d'Outremer*, a "France overseas," was created.

Yet the Syrian-born Frank was not wholly European. Mixed marriages with Armenian and Byzantine ladies were a common occurrence in the upper strata of the Frankish nobility. It was thus considered quite "normal" that one's mother, grandmother or aunt was an oriental Christian. This was true not only for the nobility but even for the royal and princely Crusader houses. Such a marriage brought with it the oriental servants and attendants—whether Christian or Moslem—which abounded in every wealthy Frankish household. Members of the lower strata of Frankish society, whether simple knights or burgesses, often intermarried with oriental Christians on their own social level. A Crusader chronicler reflected upon the resultant state of affairs:

> . . . Consider, I pray, and reflect how in our time God has transferred the West into the East. For we who were Occidentals now have been made Orientals. He who was a Roman or a Frank is now a Galilean or Palestinian. One who was a citizen of Rheims or of Chartres now has been made a citizen of Tyre or Antioch. We have already forgotten the places of our birth; they have become unknown to many of us or, at least, are unmentioned. Some already possess homes and servants here which they have received through inheritance. Some have taken wives not merely of their own people but Syrians, or Armenians or even Saracens who have received the grace of baptism. Some have with them a father-in-law, or daughter-in-law, or son-in-law, or stepson or stepfather. Here, too, are grandchildren and great-grandchildren. One cultivates vines, another fields. Both use the speech and the idioms of different languages. These languages, now made common, become known to both races; and faith unites those whose forefathers were strangers.

Thus a young Frank, a *Poulain*, was accustomed from childhood to meeting and living with the Occident in the Orient. The house or citadel which he inhabited in the city was usually an oriental building which had belonged to a Moslem before the Crusader conquest and was very different from European buildings and fortifications. Timber, the most common building material in the West, was almost unknown in the Holy Land. Stone was the common building material used in both the cities and villages. It was usually quarried not far from the cities themselves, like the stone cut out of the slopes of Mount Carmel for Caesarea, those of Chastel Pèlerin dug out of the nearby ridge which blocked the eastward-moving dunes, or the lovely pink-coloured stone brought to Jerusalem from Anathot.

Two- and three-story stone houses were the normal type of habitat, but even five-story houses were not unknown. Their flat roofs, often dotted with potted palms or evergreen trees and shrubs, were a place to enjoy the cool breezes after the hot sun had set. Inside, the thick walls preserved warmth in the winter, when the temperature in places like Jerusalem and Safed, as well as in the mountains east of Acre, Tripoli and Antioch, descended to the freezing point. In the summer, the walls and narrow windows kept the rooms cool, even during the scorching days of the *hamsin*, the Levantine first-cousin of the *sirocco*. The ceilings were very high, and the slightly pointed arches added to the feeling of height in the atmosphere, for the narrow windows restricted the entrance of light as well as heat. The windows were not boarded up by planks or covered with parchment, but glistened with locally fabricated glass. Pure, transparent glass was rather rare, but green- or blue-tinted, semi-opaque glass enclosing air bubbles was used, unless one preferred stained glass.

The ground-floor facade of Eastern houses was usually a solid wall except for the entrance-way. The windows on the upper floors let in some light, but basically the house opened onto the inner courtyard, where the precious, life-giving well, stored rain water or, in some places, a pit connected to one of the ancient aqueducts was normally situated. In some courtyards, as we know from a description of a marvellous Crusader palace in Beirut, a fountain cooled the air and its water-jets fell back into a mosaic-paved pool.

In some houses the staircase was located outside the building, allowing access from the street to each floor. The houses of the wealthy often had a kind of out-building composed of canvas- or plank-covered arches to protect the entrance from sun and rain, like the elaborate awnings in our luxury hotels. The shafts of the arches had holes drilled into them so that horses could be tethered.

The interiors of the better-endowed houses were decorated with mosaics of exquisite Byzantine-Moslem craftsmanship. In addition, rugs, draperies or tapestries covered the walls. Mosaics were an integral part of interior decoration and often displayed geometric designs, flowers and animals. In wealthier households, the ceiling arches may have rested on sculpted consoles, or a display of archvaults and simple arches might have added to the decor. Furniture was far more elaborate than that found in Europe. At their best, tables and chairs and the legs and posts of beds were of wood carved in lace-like patterns of bas-reliefs or small sculptures of flowers or human or animal heads. The chairs often looked like a rounded letter x, their upper part serving as a seat with handles. Oblong, cylindrical cushions covered with silk or samite that ended off in tassels were added for comfort. Mother of pearl, which became the glory of Bethlehem's craftsmanship, may already have been used in furniture decoration, as it was in some of the mosaics. Each noble household or ecclesiastical institution had a box-like writing table with accompanying chair. The writing was done on the inclined top, whereas the ink-pots, colours, quills and other paraphernalia of the scriptorium were kept on the table's lower shelves.

Kitchen utensils and tableware varied with the strata of society. Cooking was done in large earthenware pots in open ovens. Those preserved in several Crusader sites are huge pits over which meat could have been broiled or pots suspended or the pit was covered by a special iron grid to hold the pots and pans. Spoons and knives were the basic table utensils, the first normally of wood, the latter of iron or steel. One often used his dagger as a table knife (these sometimes had ornate handles of ivory or carved wood and blades of the famous Indian steel), although metal utensils were often imported from Europe. In noble households the younger squires or pages served the meal; but when the family was receiving honoured guests, the younger sons of the family would sometimes perform this duty. The carved meat was transferred on slices of round bread, which served as plates and sauce-sponges, or the bread was placed on earthenware plates which were often glazed and decorated with designs. The most common glazed crockery was a basic dark colour covered with geometrical designs of brown, green and yellow glaze. Sometimes these decorations were Christian symbols—such as crosses, fish, tiaras, mitres—but heads of animals, legendary griffons and the like were also used. The most elaborate plates would have drawings of knights or riders on their mounts.

Metal plates and goblets were part of the decor of the house. Some were purely ornamental, such as large, copper-brimmed plates engraved with verses or even scenes from the Scriptures. These seem to have been imported from Europe; but such decorative or ceremonial crockery as that on which the Crusader king's meal was served in the Mosque of al-Aqsa after the coronation must have been of precious metal designed and engraved in Syria and Palestine. Metal cups and goblets were in common use. Some were inlaid, usually with silver, in the lovely patterns of the oriental arabesque. The Arabic inscriptions which praised Allah were no impediments to their use among Christians, though they might have been used for wine-drinking (which was certainly not what their artisan-creator intended). Whereas metal cups and goblets were also in common use in Europe, glassware was far more common in the Orient. Some examples of glasses painted with scenes and inscriptions, probably made in Tyre, display excellent form and exquisite decorations. One bears the heraldic sign of its owner, which must have been a common custom.

The oriental house and its interior decoration found their complement in the cuisine. Whatever gastronomical tradition had been imported
from Europe, it could hardly compete with the local menu. Not only was
oriental cuisine better adapted to the local climatic conditions, but the tan-
talizing spices and their use in meat, fish and sauces easily got the upper
hand in competition with the abundant but rather plain dishes known to
the Europeans. The oriental servants, like vendors in streets and bazaars,
had no difficulty introducing their specialities into both noble and lower
households. We even know about Crusader old-timers who boasted about
their Egyptian cuisine, as one would boast today of having a cook with a
cordon bleu.

Fashion and dresses also left their mark on Crusader society, but in
this sphere the Franks limited their adoption. The Frank was ready to
take advantage of the sumptuous textiles of the Near or Far East. Textiles which in Europe could have been found in royal and princely households only or occasionally among the ceremonial wardrobe of prelates
were within the range of people of even mediocre means in the Orient.
Silk, taffeta, brocade, cotton, wool and gossamer muslins were all worn by
the Franks and their ladies, but they resisted the adoption of oriental
style. One would wear oriental fabrics, but the cut of the dresses
remained European. A Frank never wore any oriental garb, at least not in
public. Sometimes he would wind a short shawl or mantle over his helmet as protection against the sun's strong rays; he might even use a white
cloak, as did the Orientals and members of the military orders. But his
vestments were basically European and changed with European fashions.
Articles of clothing which could not be found in the kingdom, like berets,
were imported from Europe. And the Franks' sense of ethnic identity
went so far that they prohibited non-Franks from wearing European-style
garments. This keeping to the *mores Francorum* was also expressed by the
resistance to the oriental custom of growing beards. Whereas the participants of the First Crusade were bearded, as was the custom in their home-
lands, when beards went out of fashion in Europe two generations later
(middle of the twelfth century), the Franks in the Holy Land followed
suit, and their clean-shaven faces and shoulder-length hair became as
much a clearly distinguishable mark of their identity as the object of
oriental disgust and ridicule.

Climate and environment had their influence in the realm of hygiene
and cosmetics. A nineteenth-century historian described medieval Europe
as a society which had forgone washing for a thousand years. This
description certainly did not apply to the Franks in the East. Soap was
produced locally and may even have been exported. The partiality of the
Poulains for baths earned them the charge of the vice of "luxury." The
austere Bernard of Clairvaux pointed out with pride that his protégés,
the Templars, had no use for baths! Fifty years later, James of Vitry,

the bishop of Acre, preached against this unholy institution which contaminated mores. He even hinted at some unsavoury goings on among the ladies of the Crusader upper class. The Genoese even allowed common bathing (albeit segregated by sex) in their *balneum* in Acre. Whatever the custom, Europeans who visited the kingdom returned to Europe with the impression that an effeminate society had succeeded the heroes of the First Crusade, who had since become legendary paragons of all chivalrous virtues. Today, one would probably describe such behaviour as subtlety, finesse or epicurean, but things looked different to the European newcomer. James of Vitry was rather vehement in his denunciation: "They were brought up in luxury, soft and effeminate, more used to baths than battles, addicted to unclean and riotous living, clad like women in soft robes." Beneath the heavy hand of the furious prelate, one detects a mode of life which a disgruntled contemporary observer would label as Levantine:

> They have so learned to disguise their meaning in cunning speeches, covered and bedecked with leaves, but no fruit, like barren willow-trees, that those who do not know them thoroughly by experience can scarcely understand their reservations and tricks of speech or avoid being deceived by them. They are suspicious and jealous of their wives, whom they lock up in close prison and guard in such strict and careful custody that even their brethren and nearest relatives can scarcely approach them; while they forbid them so utterly to attend churches, processions, the wholesome preaching of God's Word and other matters appertaining to their salvation, that they scarce suffer them to go to church once a year; howbeit some husbands allow their wives to go out to the bath three times a week, under strict guard.

As to crusader womenfolk:

> But the more strictly the *Pullani* lock up their wives, the more do they by a thousand arts and endless contrivances struggle and try to find their way out. They are wondrously and beyond belief learned in witchcraft and wickednesses innumerable, which they are taught by the Syrian women.

Despite almost chronic warfare, the amenities of the Holy Land made life less grim than it was under the grey, northern skies of Europe. Houses, dress, encounters in street or market-place, the gossip and politics in the baths recalled Hellenistic cities. The Frankish knight who grew up in such surroundings, despite his speech and dress, was not French but a Near Eastern Frank. One can hardly agree with the accusation of cowardice; they were good fighters. And while not always good diplomats, thirteenth-century Crusader nobles were born politicians who loved to have a finger in every political pie and conspiracy, like the Renaissance Italians in their city-states.

The Frankish noble seldom lived in the countryside. Even the few nobles who had castles as centres of seigniories would normally maintain a household in the city (usually in Jerusalem and in the thirteenth century in Acre or Tyre). Very few nobles lived in their manors. Basically they were a class of *rentiers* who collected the income from their rural estates and spent it in their urban residences. The countryside and its villages was a thing one lived off, supervised, but rarely inhabited. The squire-tenant or squire-serf relationship, typical in medieval Europe, was almost non-existent in the Orient. The steward or a similar official, often a scribe or *drugeman*, would supervise the village rents, though he seldom intervened in the work itself. The Crusader noble did not go into farming on his own, very seldom kept demesne land and was normally satisfied with the third or quarter of the village crops, which were usually well supplemented by income from urban taxation. As a matter of fact, a Crusader noble's visit to his rural possessions was rather exceptional. One went out to the countryside for hunting or fishing, but seldom for economic reasons. The amenities of country life, without its burdens, were supplied by the beautiful orchards, vineyards and olive groves which surrounded all the cities. Some nobles maintained a kind of cottage or similar structure in these "suburbs" where they passed the hot summer days and cooler evenings in the company of others of their class, sometimes even Moslem nobles. From here they would pursue the chase for fox or boar or hunt with falcons. A good part of time was spent in riding and military exercises. Crusader nobles, like their Moslem antagonists, vied with each other over the beauty of their horses. A considerable amount of money was spent acquiring horses and bedecking them with trappings of finery, expensive materials and precious metals. Pasture lands around the cities were also parade grounds to display horses and horsemanship. During periods of peace, even Moslems would participate in such exercises. The crowning glory of the mounted noble was, naturally, the tournament, a mock battle of nobles or of single champions. On such occasions the ladies appeared on city or castle battlements to participate in that most-cherished of medieval shows. Here the young squire or the experienced knight could achieve prize and renown for prowess and military skill. The horses, arms and armour of the loser, often of considerable value, became the property of the winner. Still, it seems that tournaments, which were often connected with festivities, were rarer in the Crusader East than in contemporary Europe. Perhaps in a war-ridden country mock battles were too close to everyday, grim reality to exercise the attraction that was so strong in Europe, despite ecclesiastical prohibitions.

The major part of a noble's or knight's time wa spent in his normal habitat, the city. A simple knight's time-table was regulated by duties of service in city garrison, manning the city's citadel, making the rounds of walls and towers or guarding the lord's palace. Higher nobility would spend a good deal of time in attendance on their overlord, often sitting in his court as councillors or judges. As councillors they would advise on matters put before them for deliberation; as judges they performed the feudal obligations judging their peers.

A short treatise entitled "On the Four Ages of Men," written by a mid-thirteenth-century Frank and describing occupations fitting to each age, gives the impression that the Franks in the East were a noble, church-going society. Unfortunately, this picture clashes too strongly with other sources—albeit of ecclesiastical origin—which give a very different version of the nobles' behaviour. Whatever the truth, whether or not one really attended daily mass, there is no doubt that a noble would participate in the great church festivities which, in a city like Jerusalem, were not only religiously moving, but offered a rich pageantry to participant and spectator.

For other amusements and social contacts, one would meet friends at home, at the bath or even in a tavern. Chess—the king's game—was known, but dice was the most popular entertainment, and one ran the risk of losing both fortune and soul. Meals and drinking—heavy drinking—were part and parcel of entertainment, and many a tavern or private house had its quota of Western-style prostitutes or Eastern-style dancing girls, sometimes slaves of an oriental *souteneur*. Prostitution, common in all medieval cities and most accentuated in ports, was quite extensive in a port city like Acre, where the pope had to warn clergy about renting houses to prostitutes. We have a vivid description of this city, recorded by James of Vitry, who was bishop of Acre for some time:

> Among the *Poulains* there is hardly one in a thousand who takes his marriage seriously. They do not regard fornication to be a deadly sin. From childhood they are pampered and wholly given to carnal pleasures, whereas they are not accustomed to hear God's word, which they lightly disregard. I found here foreigners who fled in despair from their native countries because of various horrible sins. These people, who have no fear of God, are corrupting the whole city by their nefarious deeds and pernicious examples.
>
> Almost every day and every night people are openly or secretly murdered. At night men strangle their wives if they dislike them; women, using the ancient art of poison and potion, kill their husbands so as to be able to marry other men. There are in the city vendors of toxins and poisons, so that nobody can have confidence in anyone, and a man's foes shall be they of his own household.
>
> And the city is full of brothels, and as the rent of the prostitutes is higher, not only laymen, but even clergymen, nay even monks, rent their houses all over the city to public harlots.

It is difficult to ascertain the degree of literacy among the Frankish nobility. It seems that the higher nobility was literate, and the rather few works written by them, as well as other testimonies, indicate that their level of literacy was equal to that of their European counterparts. We know of festivities where episodes from the Arthurian cycle, as well as the fabliaux popular in Europe were performed. But it is doubtful whether the same degree of literacy was common among the lower nobility. Likewise, we know very little about the nobility's intellectual interests. Very few seem to have been interested in the rich oriental heritage around them, and few mastered Arabic, the common language of the Orient and the key to its treasures. On the whole, this breed of Europeans in the East does not strike one as being bent on an intellectual adventure.

The general lack of intellectual interests is stressed by the fact that no scholarly or intellectual centre, no university or school was ever created in the Crusader colonies—and this in an age when all major European centres were dotted with colleges or universities. A man bent on acquiring a wider education went to Europe, as did the only historian of the kingdom, William, bishop of Tyre, a *Poulain*, who easily ranks among the greatest historians in the Middle Ages. This phenomenon in itself explains why the Crusader colonies never became bridges between the Orient and Occident, despite the fact that for two hundred years they were the outposts of Europe in the Eastern Mediterranean. . . .

If Frankish nobility could usually trace their origin to a noble house in their European homeland—though not to the famous houses of Christendom—the burgesses, despite their title, were hardly descendants of European burghers or city dwellers. The lower strata of Frankish population were predominantly of peasant stock, villeins and serfs. They had left Europe either with one of the crusades or as part of a wave of migration. And it was these strata of society which made up the majority of the Frankish population. The transition from their basically rural life-style to the mastery of urban occupations was not an easy one. The native craftsmen, oriental Christians or Moslems, could offer far superior products which were better adapted to local needs and certainly more elegant than anything usually produced in the manorial worksheds of Europe. The burgesses, however, had the advantage of being able to produce goods according to European tastes and create fashions more easily acceptable to the new settlers. They also enjoyed the fact that the new immigrants preferred their own kin; but this advantage quickly disappeared—as it always does—in the face of the competitive prices of local talent.

It was these strata of immigrants which made up the new society's middle class of craftsmen and merchants, occupations which were seldom distinct. They filled the demand for tailors, shoemakers, goldsmiths, carpenters, smiths, millers, cooks, bakers, confectioners, and candle-makers. In the ports and anchorage places, the new profession of catering, to assure ships provisions for the three-week voyage to Europe, developed. And other new occupations appeared, like the muleteers and camel-drivers; porters of water; spice, incense and perfume vendors; and, naturally, guides, suppliers of holy relics, and publicans. The latter were notorious throughout Christendom. Pilgrim and immigrant alike constantly complained of being cheated. Some taverns which served as hostelries in the ports and in centres of pilgrimage were often also bawdy houses. It was here that prostitution and dice games flourished to the outrage of those who were bent on penitence and spirituality.

On another plane, the burgesses filled the ranks of the kingdom's lower officialdom, whether in the city or in the lordship's rural administration. Some acquired enough Arabic to serve as dragomans; others, more literate, filled the office of scribes or petition-writers. We can visualise them squatting near the lord's or bishop's dwellings, with their portable tables, ink-pots, quills and strips of parchment, penning (for remuneration) the humble requests of the simple people. Then there were the administrative tasks proper. Both lordly and ecclesiastical institutions needed stewards to run their estates and their revenues, assure provisions for their households and to supervise their servants. At the gates of cities and entrances to the ports, a swarm of scribes, customs and tax collectors performed these duties in the din of haggling and recriminations.

The Crusader burgesses in the triple bazaars of Jerusalem or the *souks* of Antioch, Tripoli and Acre rented their nooks, stalls and benches from the city lord or an ecclesiastical institution. Here they sold their wares, the agricultural yield of their gardens and orchards or products purchased in the countryside to be resold to the city dwellers. Another typical burgess occupation was that of the money-changer. It was often connected with lending money and was the nearest the Frankish burgess ever came to the realm of high finance. Serious activities in high finance were beyond his reach because historical circumstances during the earliest period of conquest made the field a *de facto* monopoly of the Italian (later also Provençal and Catalan) merchants.

Beginning with the First Crusade, but especially during the following first decade of the kingdom, when the crusaders were fighting the Moslem powers from Cilicia to the Red Sea, the fleets of Venice, Pisa and Genoa —the great European emporia—were instrumental in the conquest of the maritime cities of Syria, Lebanon and the Holy Land. The Italians, whose participation in the Crusades was motiviated by a mixture of religious ideals and material calculations, asked to be remunerated for their services. The pious declaration that they sailed to the East to fight the Holy Was and in the service of Christianity did not prevent them from assuring themselves a share in the conquest—not only the immediate, tangible booty (which was not negligible), but more permanent gains in the form of streets or quarters in the cities, exemptions from tax and customs and privileges of immunity and autonomy in ruling their nationals and managing their possessions. Thus every major Frankish city in the Levant—and with the exception of Jerusalem, all of them were maritime cities—had at least one, but usually several streets or quarters which belonged to the various Italian communes. The Italians were the third distinctive class among the Franks (along with the nobles and burgesses), and their presence added to the variety of nations and to the Babel of languages.

The Italian settlements were not created immediately after the conquest. Few merchants settled during the early years of the kingdom, but the administrative nucleus sent from the Italian metropolis to safeguard its rights and privileges was a permanent fixture even then. It represented a foothold, but its future depended on the ability to use possessions in Antioch, Tyre or Acre as a basis for business. Realities never matched their expectations because even the great Crusader cities were not centres of production, or at least could not compare with Constantinople or Alexandria. Neither were they outlets for a rich hinterland. Consequently, European commerce could not forgo direct contacts with such Moslem or Byzantine centres. Nonetheless, the privileged position of the communes in the Crusader establishments counter-balances the obvious economic handicaps. For example, the customs exemptions enjoyed by the communes made the Crusader centres an ideal depot for merchandise imported from the Moslem hinterland—like medieval free ports on the Mediterranean. With the growing volume of trade and more daring penetration of the Moslem hinterland, Italian merchants who had used the Crusader ports only as way-stations began to prolong their stay in the Levant, and fairly sizeable Italian-merchant settlements were founded in all the major ports of the Crusader establishments in the East.

The communes, as such settlements were called, were a strange world—sort of colonies within colonies. A minority surrounded by a French-speaking majority, the Italians used and abused the "foreign language," as did every one else, in their contacts with their fellow Franks. But inside their quarters, in the precincts of the "*fondaco*," one was transported to beloved Italy. Once Byzantine or Moslem merchandise was acquired, business was often transacted between the Italian merchants themselves. Here each spoke his peculiar dialect of Venetian, Tuscan or Ligurian. Notaries wrote Latin, or sometimes thirteenth-century French, but thought in Italian. The Italians had all the conditions to preserve their identity. The commune overlord was not only of the quarter but also proprietor of all real estate within it. Large and often resplendent buildings—once the lodgings of a Moslem, Byzantine or Turkish governor or official—or houses which belonged to the Moslem merchant aristocracy of the city became *palazzi* in the Italian inventories and were taken over by the commune's administration. Buildings too large to serve any practical needs were divided into *camerae* (rooms rented for limited periods) and *magazini* (rooms to store merchandise). They often stood empty for the greater part of the year, but filled to overflowing when a *stola* (fleet of ships) arrived from Europe at around Easter time.

The main street or square of the quarter became the market-place, and the houses which surrounded it usually contained ships, stalls and magazines where the oriental merchandise waiting to be exported to Europe or imported European merchandise waiting for buyers were deposited. The merchants lodged in the upper floors. Taverns and hostelries catering to the Italian palate were to be found everywhere. In addition, *banci* (benches) were set up by money-changers and vendors of perishable foodstuffs. Besides shops and magazines, a market-place and usually a vaulted bazaar, each quarter had its bakeries, ovens and baths. Some Italian banking families even saw fit to open subsidiaries in the Crusader cities, and big business, still being family business, sent members of the trading class to Palestine.

The center of the quarter was the *palazzo* of the commune, which housed its administration. It housed the *vicomte* or consul, the governor sent from the mother-city. Supported by a council, he represented the commune's interest vis-á-vis the city's lord, ruler or king and was responsible for the management of the commune's possessions and privileges in the city. The notaries attached to him would draft agreements betwen merchants and marriage contracts; the jurors would sit in judgement or arbitration in cases regarding their own nationals, but in some cases they would also judge other inhabitants of the quarter. Crimes punishable by death, such as homicide or rape, were sometimes excepted from this system, and the guardians of peace—beadles or sergeants—would arrest the accused and turn him over to the seigniorial authorities. There was always some bickering in such cases as the Italians were naturally reluctant to hand over one of their own to external jurisdiction. The law of the communal courts was not that of the kingdom but that of the Italian mother-city. The proceedings were held in the merchants' native language, the procedure was familiar from homeland and the judgement was made by their peers. The head of the commune had his contingent of scribes and sergeants. The first were responsible for the inventory of the commune's property and for collecting rents, which were duly registered in "*quaterna*" (account books) and guarded in the community chest. The town crier and sergeants announced the ordinances of the commune's council and supervised their execution. Time and again ordinances prohibiting prostitution and gambling were issued, but in such communities of travelling salesmen, they were of doubtful effect. . . .

The degree to which the settlers of Italian origin mixed with the local Franks is rather difficult to ascertain. We know of Italians who looked for brides in Europe, but marriages with the local Frankish population were common. A Frankish family may well have seen it as advantageous to marry off their daughters to the Italian and Provençal merchants. Such a union was not considered a *mésalliance*, and it normally meant a step up on the social and economic ladder. The story of the wealthy merchant from Pisa who married a member of the Frankish aristocracy in Tripoli must have made the rounds of oriental *souks*. To receive the permission to marry the young lady, the merchant paid to the maiden's noble warden her weight in gold! A hundred and twenty or so pounds of pure gold could weigh down many barriers.

Some other families entered Frankish life not through marriage but through feudal positions. A Genoese family like the Embriaci, to whom the commune rented its property in the city of Gebal, severed its links with the mother-city and became part and parcel of the Frankish aristocracy. That they continued to favour their compatriots in the city, however, was to be expected. On a lower level, Italian families entered the Frankish *bourgeoisie* through marriage, which we know from documentation of the legal bickering over whether the marriage contract should follow local or Italian custom. Whatever the degree of assimilation through marriage, the Italians remained a power unto themselves, maintaining the customs, language and institution of the Rialto or Porto Vecchio in the Holy Land.

PART 3

The Peak of Medieval Civilization
12th - 13th Centuries

Godfrey of Boulogne and his knights, c. 1100.

The Peak of Medieval Civilization

The eleventh century was a turning point in the history of Europe. For the first time in more than a millennium, Europe was not attacked by outside invaders, and its social and political life was not disrupted by massive migrations. European monarchs now began the long process of consolidating their power, and the Church succeeded in establishing its independence from secular powers. In the same period, the various elements of medieval society reached a mature stage of development, marked by stability and increasing institutional consistency throughout Europe.

This century of change was followed by one of cultural rebirth, the so-called twelfth-century renaissance. Scholastic philosophy, Gothic architecture, the revival of jurisprudence and medical studies—all are products of twelfth-century society and were carried over into the thirteenth. Medieval civilization flowered in this period. The selections that follow reveal the character of the institutions and social conditions that underlay this flowering.

The selection by Sidney Painter recounts the youth of one of the most famous knights of the period. The knightly class dominated the aristocratic society, which historians have traditionally called "feudal" because of land tenure on which it was based. In this society, aristocrats held landed estates, called fiefs (feudum or feodum in Latin), in return for services. Fief-holders also owed loyalty to the lord from whom they held their estates. But by the twelfth century, the aristocracy had been expanded by the addition of armed retainers—trained soldiers who depended for their livelihoods on the great landholders. These soldiers were the knights, new members of the noble class. Whatever differences— and they could be vast—existed between the great baron and the landless knight, both belonged to the order of knighthood, and they shared a common code of behavior and a common system of values. William Marshal, the subject of Painter's piece, pursued his successful career in the second half of the twelfth century, the golden age of the knight.

The next selection, by John Burke, describes the physical and social context of knighthood—the castle. The building of fortified houses, surrounded by earthen walls and wooden pallisades, had a long history in Europe, but from the twelfth century on, the greater lords reconstructed their family seats as stone castles. This movement resulted from the consolidation of political and economic power and from the development and spread of techniques for construction in stone. The castles became centers of administrative and political power and the sites of aristocratic courts, where knights, educated clerics, and artisans gathered. The households of the great barons became centers of power and civilization, and, in many instances, the mistress rather than the master ran its affairs.

Reflection on the character and function of medieval households, even of peasant households, should dispel the often-held view that women of the period spent nearly all their time in childbearing and child-rearing. In the upper classes, women rarely nursed their children; nursemaids and tutors raised them. But the mother still dominated the consciousness of children, and, in the third selection, Mary Martin McLauglin examines the relationship between mother and child. Such a study relies perforce on the accounts of a few educated churchmen who reflected on their early lives, and we must therefore treat its results with care. But it was the reflections of men like Peter Damien (c. 1007–1072) that established the standards and ideas of child-rearing, and it is worth studying their sentiments.

During the eleventh century, reformers gained control of the central ecclesiastical institutions, the papacy and bishoprics, and transformed them. The reformers wanted to create a clerical hierarchy that would be a moral elite able to carry out the mission of the Church. They pursued a program to eradicate illiteracy and concubinage among the clergy.

The new leadership eventually concluded that the root of the evils they found in the Church was secular interference in ecclesiastical affairs. Parish priests, bishops, and other churchmen were appointed by laymen who had little concern for the care of souls. The reformers significantly reduced secular influence, creating a respectable ecclesiastical hierarchy in which the conscientious bishop was a common rather than a rare personage.

But the enthusiasm for reform was not confined to the clerical elite. It also stirred the piety of the laity. During the eleventh century already, laymen, encouraged by the preaching of the reformers, came forward to accuse churchmen of sins and crimes. The laity wanted to participate in the work of reform. This participation was but a sign of a rising tide of popular piety that took many forms. From the late eleventh century on, ecclesiastical leaders became increasingly concerned about popular heresies, many of which were anti-clerical and therefore undermined the authority of the Church. The Franciscan and Dominican orders were founded to combat heresy and to provide the people with instruction in the true faith. Naturally, the members of these orders, and others like them, became interested in the state of religion among the people. In the fourth selection, Alexander Murray uses a manual for Dominican preachers to examine popular religion in the thirteenth century.

The population that heard the preaching of Dominicans and Franciscans was superstitious and fearful of foreigners. In the final selection, Malcolm Barber recounts a incident that shows what effect such fear and ignorance could have. Scholars have discovered that the population of Europe was subjected to plagues and famines from the late thirteenth century and was declining long before the Black Death struck in 1348. The bad harvests, the constant threat of war, the endemic disease all made the populace susceptible to rumor and to mob action. In 1321, the people of France went into a paroxysm of fear when it was rumored that the Lepers and Jews, supported by the Caliph of Granada in Spain, planned to poison the wells and seize the country.

BIBLIOGRAPHY

For an introduction to the institutions of feudalism, see F. L. Ganshof, *Feudalism* (New York, 1961). Richard Barber's *The Knight and Chivalry* (New York, 1974) and Georges Duby's *The Chivalrous Society*, trans. by Cynthia Postan (London, 1977) provide good surveys of the cultural milieu of the knights. The classic work on feudal society is Marc Bloch, *Feudal Society*, trans. L. A. Manyon, 2 vols. (Chicago, 1961); see especially Parts IV, VI, and VIII. Lynn White, Jr., argues that the feudal system developed because the Franks introduced new military technology, particularly the horseshoe and the stirrup. See his *Medieval Technology and Social Change* (Oxford, 1962).

A remarkable amount of literature about women was published in the 1890s, perhaps stimulated by the women's suffrage movement. See, for example, A. R. Cleveland, *Woman Under English Law from Anglo-Saxon times to the Present* (London, 1896) and M. A. R. de Maulde la Clavière, *The Women of the Renaissance: a Study of Feminism* (London, 1900). Eileen Power, whose account of the peasant Bodo was printed in Part 2, wrote a fine article on women in C. G. Crump and E. F. Jacobs, eds., *The Legacy of the Middle Ages* (Oxford, 1926). Her characterizations of medieval women have now been collected in *Medieval Women* (Cambridge, Eng., 1975). Margaret Labarge gives a full account of the role of baron's wife in *A Baronial Household of the Thirteenth Century* (London, 1965). See also the articles in Susan M. Stuard, ed., *Women in Medieval Society* (Philadelphia, 1976) and in R. T. Morewedge, ed., *The Role of Women in the Middle Ages* (Albany, N.Y., 1975).

In recent years, historians have given increasing attention to popular religion and to heretical sects, as the two articles reprinted here indicate. For example, Alexander Murray contributed a companion piece to the article reprinted here, "Piety amd Impiety in Thirteenth-Century Italy," to G. J. Cuming and Derek Baker, eds., *Popular Belief and Practice* (*Studies in Church History* VIII: Cambridge, Eng., 1972) pp. 83-106. See also the articles printed in James Obelkevich, ed., *Religion and the People, 800–1700* (Chapel Hill, N.C., 1979). For an attempt to understand the nature of heresy in the Middle Ages, see Jeffrey B. Russell, *Dissent and Reform in the Early Middle Ages* (Berkeley, 1965); Gordon Leff, *Heresy in the Later Middle Ages: The Relation of Heterodoxy to Dissent c. 1250-c. 1450*, 2 vols. (Manchester, Eng., 1967); Robert E. Lerner, *The Heresy of the Free Spirit in the Later Middle Ages* (Berkeley, 1972). W. L. Wakefield and A. P. Evans, eds., *Heresies of the High Middle Ages* (New York, 1969) contains a substantial collection of translated sources. For recent work, see Walter L. Wakefield, *Heresy, Crusade and Inquisition in Southern France, 1100–1250* (Berkeley, 1974) and Richard Kieckhefer, *Repression of Heresy in Medieval Germany* (Philadelphia, 1979).

The Training of a Knight

SIDNEY PAINTER

The knight in shining armor is mostly a figment created by medieval romance writers, refurbished and given new impetus by nineteenth-century authors. The real knight lived a life not so far removed in its material aspects from that of prosperous contemporary peasants. He was almost constantly on the move, living the hard life of a traveler and engaging in tournaments or real campaigns. The rules governing his life, so embellished by the romance poets, were largely responses to the demands of his existence and served to make its hardships bearable. Most of the rules evolved out of the conditions of feudal warfare; they regulated the treatment of prisoners taken in combat and the relations between the ranks in the feudal army. In the constant round of fighting, one week's victor might be next week's victim, and the economics of knightly life dictated a refined treatment of captured knights. A dead knight was not worth very much, but a live one might ransom himself at a considerable price. If a knight was one of the majority in his class who did not possess any landed estate and therefore had no stable income, collecting ransoms constitituted a livelihood. Other aspects of the chivalric code, as the rules were called, were aimed at preserving the social and political structure of feudalism, although these too were related to military activities. The feudal system depended on the loyalty of vassals to their liege lords, and this loyalty was the cohesive element of the feudal army. Loyalty was won and kept by open-handedness, so generosity too was a knightly virtue.

It is important to study the training of a knight in order to understand the character of the class. In this selection, we observe the early training of William Marshal, a man who achieved the idea of knighthood according to the writings of his time. He was born about 1146 in England, the fourth son of a petty baron, John, who was marshal for King Henry I. The marshal was originally in charge of the royal stables and the provisioning of the household, but by John's day these duties had been delegated to others, and the marshal was a hereditary post in the king's entourage. William, as a younger son, had little chance of inheriting his father's position, but he was trained as a knight anyway, since he could make his way in the world as a feudal soldier. As it turned out, his talent won him one of the premier places in the feudal hierarchy of England.

There were several stages in the life of a successful knight. In his early youth, he was taught to ride and perhaps given the rudiments of his education in chivalry. But his real training began around the age of thirteen, when he was sent to a relative's or lord's household as a squire. There he learned to handle a knight's weapons and to be part of a feudal army. He also learned the details of the life style he was expected to adopt. After the squire became a knight, he began an often long period of itinerancy, traveling from tournament to tournament and joining in real campaigns when the opportunity arose. Sometimes knights errant, as such men were called, joined the entourage of great lords or kings and became part of their "team" in the tournaments. William became a member of Prince Henry of England's (son of Henry II) entourage and quickly rose to a preeminent position within it. In William's time, the tournaments were not the controlled combats of the later Middle Ages so often described in popular literature. They were virtual free-for-alls in which knights teamed up and fought as armies. One of these mêlées is described in this selection.

For the knight who did not inherit a position within the feudal hierarchy, the period of errancy often lasted until he was past forty. At this point, if he was lucky, he would marry into the hierarchy. William achieved this goal in 1190 when Richard I of England (son and successor of Henry II) permitted him to marry the heiress of the great earldom of Pembroke. The marriage made William one of the first lords of England, and when Richard's successor, John, died in 1216, William became one of the regents of the realm. He himself died in 1219.

William's career demonstrates that there was mobility within the feudal ranks during the twelfth century. He was clearly the outstanding example of the possibilities that existed, but many others had similar if not so illustrious careers. In the later Middle Ages, the possibility of rising in the ranks became increasingly restricted as the feudal elite found its position challenged by the kings on one side and by the burghers on the other. In its heyday, the knightly class exhibited vitality and adaptability. Once it was forced to take a defensive stance, it became rigid and regressive in its social, economic, and political attitudes.

W illiam Marshal was the fourth son of John fitz Gilbert and the second of those born to the castellan of Marlborough by the sister of Earl Patrick of Salisbury. Our knowledge of William's youth is confined to a few brief glimpses through the fog of time—scenes which made so vivid an impression on his mind that he could recount them years later to his squire and biographer, John d'Erley. The earliest of these recollections concerned a comparatively unimportant incident in the contest between Stephen and Matilda. In the year 1152 King Stephen at the head of a strong force suddenly swooped down on John Marshal's castle of Newbury at a time when it was inadequately garrisoned and poorly stocked with provisions. The constable, a man both brave and loyal, indignantly refused the King's demand for the immediate surrender of the fortress. When the garrison successfully repulsed an attempt to take the place by storm, Stephen prepared for a regular siege and swore that he would not leave until he had captured the castle and hanged its defenders. The constable, realizing that his lack of provisions made an extended resistance

From Sidney Painter, *William Marshal* (Baltimore: The Johns Hopkins University Press, 1933), pp. 13–29.

impossible, asked for and obtained a day's truce so that he might make known his plight to his lord, John Marshal. This was the customary procedure for a castellan who found himself in a hopeless position. Once granted a truce, he would inform his master that unless he were relieved by a certain day, he would be forced to surrender. If no assistance appeared within the specified time, the commander could surrender the castle without failing in his duty to his lord. The besieging force was usually willing to grant a truce in the hope of obtaining the castle without long, wearisome, and expensive siege operations. When John Marshal learned of the predicament of his garrison of Newbury, he was sadly perplexed. As he could not muster enough men to drive off Stephen's army, his only hope of saving his fortress lay in a resort to strategy. John asked Stephen to extend the truce while he sought aid from the Countess Matilda in whose name he held the castle. The king did not trust his turbulent marshal, but he finally agreed to give the garrison of Newbury a further respite if John would surrender one of his sons as a guarantee that he would observe the terms of the truce. John was to use the days of grace to communicate with Matilda—the hostage would be his pledge that he would not reinforce or provision the castle. Acceding to Stephen's demand, John gave the king his son William as a hostage. Then he promptly sent into Newbury a strong force of knights, serjeants, and archers with a plentiful supply of provisions. Newbury was prepared to withstand a siege—the cunning of John Marshal had saved his castle.

His father's clever stratagem left William in an extremely precarious position. By the customs of the time his life was forfeited by his father's breach of faith. Stephen's entourage urged him to hang William at once, but the king was unwilling to execute the child without giving his father a chance to have him by surrendering Newbury. But John Marshal, having four sons and a fruitful wife, considered the youngest of his sons of far less value than a strong castle. He cheerfully told the king's messenger that he cared little if William were hanged, for he had the anvils and hammers with which to forge still better sons. When he received this brutal reply, Stephen ordered his men to lead William to a convenient tree. Fearing that John planned a rescue, the king himself escorted the executioners with a strong force. William, who was only five or six years old, had no idea what this solemn parade portended. When he saw William, earl of Arundel, twirling a most enticing javelin, he asked him for the weapon. This reminder of William's youth and innocence was too much for King Stephen's resolution, and, taking the boy in his arms, he carried him back to the camp. A little later some of the royalists had the ingenious idea of throwing William over the castle walls from a siege engine, but Stephen vetoed that scheme as well. He had decided to spare his young prisoner.

For some two months William was the guest of King Stephen while the royal army lay before Newbury. One day as the king sat in a tent strewn with varicolored flowers William wandered about picking plantains. When the boy had gathered a fair number, he asked the king to play "knights" with him. Each of them would take a "knight" or plantain, and strike it against the one held by the other. The victory would go to the player who with his knight struck off the clump of leaves that represented the head of his opponent's champion. When Stephen readily agreed to play, William gave him a bunch of plantains and asked him to decide who should strike first. The amiable king gave William the first blow with the result that the royal champion lost his head. The boy was vastly pleased with his victory. While Stephen, king of England, was playing at knights with the young son of his rebellious marshal, a servitor whom Lady Sibile had sent to see how her son fared glanced into the tent. As war and enemies meant nothing to William, he loudly welcomed the familiar face. The man, utterly terrified, fled so hastily that the pursuit ordered by the king was fruitless.

The story of William and King Stephen is, no doubt, merely reminiscence recounted years later with the embellishments usual in such tales, but it bears all the ear-marks of veracity. It serves to confirm the statements of the chroniclers as to Stephen's character—that he was a man of gentle nature, far too mild to rule the barons of England. Furthermore the incidents of the tale are essentially probable. It was quite customary to give young children as hostages to guarantee an agreement and equally so to make them suffer for their parents' bad faith. When Eustace de Breteuil, the husband of a natural daughter of Henry I, put out the eyes of the son of one of his vassals, the king allowed the enraged father to mutilate in the same way Eustace's daughter whom Henry held as a hostage for his son-in-law's good behavior. Again in the year 1211 when Maelgwyn ap Rees, prince of South Wales, raided the marches, Robert de Vieuxpont hanged the prince's seven-year-old son who was in his hands as a pledge that Maelgwyn would keep the peace. The fact that Earl William of Arundel is known to have taken part in the siege of Newbury and might well have twirled his javelin before the fascinated William tends to confirm this story still further. Hence one can accept as essentially true this pleasant and very human picture of a dark age and an unfortunate king.

When peace was finally concluded between Stephen and Henry Plantagenet, William was returned to his parents who, according the *History*, had been very unquiet about him. While John Marshal had probably counted to some extent on Stephen's notorious mildness, he had had plenty of justification for any fears he may have felt for his son's safety. Meanwhile the boy was growing rapidly. Within a few years the Marshal family would be forced to consider his future. If the romances of the time are to be believed, it was customary for a baron of any importance to entrust his sons' education to some friendly lord. John Marshal decided to send William to his cousin, William, lord of Tancarville and hereditary chamberlain of Normandy. The chamberlain was a powerful baron with a great castle on the lower Seine and ninety-four knights to follow his banner. Being himself a well known knight and a frequenter of tourneys, he was well fitted to supervise the military education of his young kinsman and to give him a good start on his chivalric career. When he was about thirteen years old, William started for Tancarville attended by a valet, or companion of gentle birth, and a servant. The fourth son of a minor English baron was setting forth to seek his fortune.

For eight years William served as a squire to the chamberlain of Tancarville. During this time his principal duty was to learn the trade of arms. The squire's body was hardened and his skill in the use of weapons developed by frequent and strenuous military exercises. While the chain mail of the twelfth century was far lighter and less cumbersome than the plate armor of later times, the mere wearing of it required considerable physical strength. To be able, as every squire must, to leap fully armed into the saddle without touching the stirrup, was a feat which must have required long and rigorous training. The effective use of the weapons of a knight—the spear, sword, and shield—was a highly intricate science which a squire was forced to master if he wished to excel in his chosen profession. In addition a knight should know how to care for his equipment. A squire spent long hours tending his master's horses and cleaning, polishing, and testing his arms and armor. William's success in battle and tourney will show how thoroughly he mastered these fundamentals of his profession. But while it was essential that a knight be brave and skillful in the use of his weapons, other quite different qualities were also expected of him. God and Woman, the church and the troubadour cult of Courtly Love, were beginning to soften and polish the manners of the feudal aristocracy. For a long time the church had demanded that a knight be pious, now ladies were insisting that he be courteous. If a squire hoped to be acceptable to such devotees of the new movement as Eleanor of Aquitaine and her daughter, Marie of Champagne, he must learn some more gentle art than that of smiting mighty blows. If he could not write songs, he could at least learn to sing them. Finally the professional creators and distributors of the literature which embodied these new ideas, the trouvères and the jongleurs, were formulating another knightly virtue—generosity. Their existence depended on the liberality of their patrons, and they did not fail to extol the generous and heap scorn on the penurious. Every time the squire confessed to a priest, he was instructed in the church's conception of the perfect knight. As he sat in the great hall of the castle while some trouvère or jongleur told of Tristan and Iseult or of Lancelot and Guenevere, he was imbued with the doctrines of romantic chivalry. The squire himself might be expected to while away the leisure hours of his lady and her damsels with one of the gentle songs of the troubadours. Possibly William owed his love for singing which remained with him to his death to the advanced taste of the lady of Tancarville.

By the spring of 1167 William was approaching his twenty-first year. As a squire he seems to have given little promise of future greatness. He gained a reputation for drinking, eating, and sleeping, but for little else. His companions, who were jealous of the favor shown him by the chamberlain, made fun of his appetite, but he was so gentle and debonnaire that he always kept silent and pretended not to hear the remarks. A hearty, healthy, good natured, and rather stupid youth was young William. The author of the *History* furnishes a personal description which probably belongs to this period of William's life. "His body was so well formed that if it had been fashioned by a sculptor, it would not have had such beautiful limbs. I saw them and remember them well. He had very beautiful feet and hands, but all these were minor details in the ensemble of his body. If anyone looked at him carefully, he seemed so well and straightly made that if one judged honestly, one would be forced to say that he had the best formed body in the world. He had brown hair. His face even more than his body resembled that of a man of high enough rank to be the Emperor of Rome. He had as long legs and as good a stature as a gentleman could. Whoever fashioned him was master." Is this a purely conventional portrait or a true one of William Marshal as he reached man's estate?

In a military society, be it that of the early Germans or the feudal aristocracy, the youth comes of age when he is accepted as a full-fledged warrior. Every squire burned to end his apprenticeship by receiving the insignia of knighthood. The squire followed his master to battles and tournaments, cared for his horse and armor, nursed him if he were wounded, and often guarded his prisoners, but he himself could not take an active part in the combat. Being simply an attendant, the squire had no opportunity to win renown. As eight years was, at least according to the testimony of contemporary romances, a rather long time to remain a squire, William must have been extremely impatient for the day when he would be admitted into the chivalric order. He longed for the time when the approach of a promising war or a great tourney would move the chamberlain to dub him a knight and give him a chance to show his worth.

The occasion for which William had hoped came in the summer of 1167. King Henry II was at war with his suzerain Louis VII of France. While Louis himself occupied Henry's attention by ravaging the Norman Vexin, the French king's allies, the counts of Flanders, Boulogne, and Ponthieu, invaded the county of Eu. Count John of Eu, unable to hold his own against the invaders, was forced to retire to Neufchatel-en-Bray, then called Drincourt. There he encountered a force of knights which Henry had sent to his assistance under the command of the constable of Normandy and the lord of Tancarville. The chamberlain decided that this was an auspicious time for knighting William. A goodly array of Norman barons was at hand to lend dignity to the occasion, and the future seemed to promise an opportunity for the young knight to prove his valor. William's induction into the order of chivalry was attended by little of the ceremony usually associated with the dubbing of a knight. Dressed in a new mantle, the young man stood before the chamberlain, who girt him with a sword, the principal emblem of knighthood, and gave him the ceremonial blow.

William had not long to wait for an opportunity to prove himself worthy of his new dignity. As Drincourt lay on the northern bank of the river Bethune at the southern extremity of the county of Eu, it was directly in the path of the army which had been ravaging that district. Count John of Eu and the constable of Normandy had no desire to await the advance of the enemy. On the morning following William's knighting they left Drincourt by the road which led south toward Rouen. Before they had gone very far, they were overtaken by a messenger with the news that the counts of Flanders, Boulogne, and Ponthieu, and the lord of St. Valery were marching on Drincourt at the head of a strong force of knights and serjeants. As the two barons halted their party to consider what they should do, they saw the chamberlain followed by twenty-eight knights of his household riding toward them from the direction of Drincourt. As soon as he was within speaking distance, the chamberlain addressed the constable, "Sire, it will be a great disgrace if we permit them to burn this town." "You speak truly, chamberlain," replied the constable, "and since it is your idea, do you go to its defence." When they saw that they could hope for no assistance from either the count of Eu or the constable, the chamberlain and his knights rode back toward Drincourt. Between them and the town ran the river Bethune. When they reached the bridge which spanned this stream, they found it occupied by a party of knights under the command of William de Mandeville, earl of Essex, who, lacking sufficient men to dispute the enemy's entrance into the town, had retired to hold the passage of the Bethune. The chamberlain hurried to join Earl William, and William Marshal, anxious to show his mettle, spurred forward at his leader's side. The chamberlain turned to the enthusiastic novice, "William, drop back; be not so impatient; let these knights pass." William, who considered himself most decidedly a knight, fell back, abashed. He let three others go ahead of him and then dashed forward again until he was in the front rank.

The combined forces of the chamberlain and the earl of Essex rode into Drincourt to meet the enemy who were entering the town from the northeast. The two parties met at full gallop with a thunderous shock.

William's lance was broken, but drawing his sword, he rushed into the midst of the enemy. So fiercely did the Normans fight that they drove the French out of the town as far as the bridge over the moat on the road to Eu. There the enemy was reinforced, and the Normans were pressed back through Drincourt to the bridge over the Bethune. Once more the Normans charged, and once more they drove the French before them. Just as their victory seemed certain, Count Matthew of Boulogne came up with a fresh division. Four times the enemy beat their way into the town, and each time the Normans drove them out again. Once as William turned back from a charge, a Flemish serjeant caught him by the shoulder with an iron hook. Although he was dragged from his horse in the midst of hostile foot-soldiers, he managed to disengage the hook and cut his way out, but his horse was killed. Meanwhile the good people of Drincourt had been watching from their windows the fierce battle being waged up and down the streets of the town. Hastily arming themselves, the burghers rushed to the aid of the Norman knights, and the enemy was completely routed.

That night the lord of Tancarville held a great feast to celebrate the victory. The burghers of Drincourt were loud in their praises of the chamberlain and his knights. While the constable and the count of Eu had deserted the town, the chamberlain and his household had saved it from burning and pillage. As the revelers discussed the incidents of the battle, someone remarked that William had fought to save the town rather than to take prisoners who could pay him rich ransoms. With this in mind the earl of Essex addressed the young knight—"Marshal, give me a gift, a crupper or an old horse collar." "But I have never possessed one in all my life." "Marshal, what are you saying? Assuredly you had forty or sixty today." The hardened warrior was gently reminding the novice that war was a business as well as a path to fame.

The war was soon brought to an end by a truce between King Henry and Louis of France. As their services were no longer needed, the chamberlain and his entourage returned to Tancarville, Since no true knight would willingly rest peacefully in a castle, the lord of Tancarville gave his followers leave to seek adventure where they pleased. William now found himself in a most embarrassing position, for he had lost his war horse at Drincourt, and the cost of a new one was far beyond his resources. While he still had his palfrey, this light animal could not be expected to carry him in full armor through the shocks of a battle or tourney. The chamberlain, who normally would have seen to it that William as a member of his household was properly equipped, felt that the young man should be taught to take advantage of his opportunities to capture horses in battle and hence showed little sympathy for his predicament: By selling the rich mantle which he had worn when he was dubbed a knight, William obtained twenty-two sous Angevin with which he purchased a baggage horse to carry his armor, but while this arrangement allowed him to travel in comfort, it would not enable him to take part in a tourney. One day word came to Tancarville that a great tournament was to be held near Le Mans in which the knights of Anjou, Maine, Poitou, and Brittany would oppose those of France, England, and Normandy. The chamberlain and his court received the news with joy and prepared to take part in the sport, but William, who could not go without a horse, was very sorrowful. The chamberlain, however, decided that his young cousin had had enough of a lesson in knightly economy and promised to furnish him with a mount. After a night spent in making ready their arms and armor, the knights gathered in the castle court while their lord distributed the war horses. William received a splendid one, strong and fast. He never forgot the lesson taught him by the chamberlain and William de Mandeville. Never again did he neglect to capture good horses when he had the opportunity.

On the appointed day a fair sized company assembled to take part in the tournament. King William of Scotland was present with a numerous suite while the chamberlain himself took the field at the head of forty knights. This tourney was not to be one of those mild affairs in which everything was arranged beforehand even to the price of the ransoms, but a contest in which the vanquished would lose all they possessed. After the knights had armed in the refuges provided at each end of the field, the two parties advanced toward one another in serried, orderly ranks. William wasted no time in getting about the business of the day. Attacking Philip de Valognes, a knight of King William's household, he seized his horse by the rein and forced him out of the mêlée. Then after taking Philip's pledge that he would pay his ransom, William returned to the combat and captured two more knights. By his success in this tourney William not only demonstrated his prowess, but rehabilitated his finances as well. Each of the captured knights was forced to surrender all his equipment. William gained war horses, palfreys, arms, and armor for his own use, roncins for his servants, and sumpter horses for his baggage. His first tournament had been highly profitable.

This success sharpened William's appetite for knightly sports. When word came to Tancarville of another tourney to be held in Maine, he asked the chamberlain, who had decided to stay at home, to allow him to attend. He arrived at the appointed place just as the last of the contestants were arming in their refuges, and leaping from his palfrey hastened to put on his armor and mount his charger. In the first onslaught the young knight handled his lance so skillfully that he was able to unhorse one of his opponents, but before he could complete the capture of the fallen knight he was attacked by five others. Although by drawing his sword and smiting lusty blows on every side William managed to beat off his enemies, he received a stroke on his helmet which turned it around on his head so that he could no longer breathe through the holes provided for that purpose. While he was standing in the refuge repairing this damage, two well known knights rode past, Bon Abbé le Rouge and John de Subligni. "Sir John," said the first, "who is that knight who is so capable with his weapons?" "That is William Marshal," replied the other. "There is no man more true. The device on his shield shows that he hails from Tancarville." "Surely," said Bon Abbé, "the band which he leads should be the gainer in valor and hardiness." Much pleased by these words of praise, William put on his helmet again and reentered the contest. So well did he bear himself that he was awarded the prize of the tourney—a splendid war horse from Lombardy.

William now felt that he was well started on his chivalric career. He had achieved the dignity of knighthood and had shown his prowess in the combat at Drincourt and in two tournaments. It was high time that he visited England to parade his accomplishments before his admiring family. John fitz Gilbert had died in 1165 while William was still a squire at Tancarville. Of his two sons by his first wife the elder had outlived him but a year, the younger had predeceased him. Hence John, the eldest son by Sibile of Salisbury, had inherited the family lands and the office of marshal. When William sought the chamberlain's permission to go to England, the lord of Tancarville feared that his young cousin, being the heir presumptive to the family lands, might be tempted to settle down at home. He gave him leave to go, but urged him to return as soon as possible. While England was a good enough country for a man of mean spirit who had no desire to seek adventure, those who loved the life of a knight-errant and the excitement of the tourney should stay in Normandy and Brittany where such pastimes were appreciated. If one were to acquire the prizes of battle, one must live in a land of tourneys. England seemed to the chamberlain to be an orderly, dull, spiritless country. Carried across the channel by a fair wind, William traversed Sussex and Hampshire on his way to his Wiltshire home. At Salisbury he found his uncle, Earl Patrick, who received him joyfully as a gallant young knight and his own sister's son.

William's vacation in England was destined to be a short one. In December 1167 Earl Patrick was summoned to the continent to aid the king in suppressing a revolt of the nobles of Poitou led by the counts of La Marche and Angoulême and the house of Lusignan. Being in all probability heartily tired of his quiet life in England, William was only too willing to follow his uncle to Poitou. King Henry captured the castle of Lusignan, garrisoned it, and then turned north to keep an appointment with Louis VII in the Norman marches near Mantes. His wife, Eleanor, who was by right of her birth duchess of Aquitaine and countess of Poitou, stayed at Lusignan with Earl Patrick. Their position was far from comfortable. Of all the restless nobility of Poitou none were more turbulent than the five de Lusignan brothers, and none played so great a part in the history of their day. Two of the brothers, Hugh and Ralph, became respectively counts of La Marche and Eu, while Guy and Aimery, expelled from Poitou for their perpetual rebellions, both attained the throne of Jerusalem. Such a family was unlikely to stand by quietly while an enemy held their ancestral castle, even if that enemy was their liege lord. One day near Eastertide as the queen and Earl Patrick were riding outside the castle, they were suddenly confronted by a strong force under the command of Geoffrey and Guy de Lusignan. Although Patrick and his men were unarmed, the earl was unwilling to flee. Sending Eleanor to shelter in the castle, he called for his war horse and ordered his followers to prepare for battle. Unfortunately the de Lusignans were not sufficiently chivalrous to wait while their foes armed. Just as Earl Patrick was mounting his charger, a Poitevin knight killed him with a single blow at his unprotected back. Meanwhile William had donned his hauberk, but had not had time to put on his helmet. When he saw his uncle fall, he jumped on his horse and charged the enemy, sword in hand. The first man he met was cut down at a single stroke, but before he could satisfy his thirst for vengeance on the slayers of his uncle, a well directed thrust killed his horse. When he had freed himself from the saddle, William placed his back against a hedge to fight it out on foot as the loss of his horse made flight impossible. For some time he managed to hold his own by cutting down the chargers of his opponents, but at last a knight crossed the hedge, came up behind, and leaning over the barrier, thrust his sword into the young man's thigh. Disabled, William was easily made prisoner.

His captors mounted him on a mare and set off. No one paid any attention to William's wound, for, according to the *History*, they wanted him to suffer as much as possible so that he might be the more anxious to ransom himself. William took the cords which bound his braies and tied up his wound as best he could. Dreading the king's vengeance, the rebel band kept to the wooded country and made its halts in secluded spots. Henry Plantagenet was not a monarch who would permit the slayers of his lieutenant to go unpunished. One night while they were resting at the castle of one of their partisans, a lady noticed the wounded prisoner. She cut the center out of a loaf of bread, filled the hole with flaxen bandages, and sent the loaf to William. Her kindness enabled him to dress his wound properly. Another evening William's captors amused themselves by casting a great stone. William joined in the game and defeated all the others, but the exertion reopened his wound, and as he was forced to ride night and day with little rest, he grew better very slowly. Finally Queen Eleanor came to his aid. She gave hostages to his captors to guarantee that his ransom would be paid, and he was delivered to her. To recompense him for his sufferings, she gave him money, horses, arms, and rich vestments.

The Poitevin campaign had a far-reaching effect on William's life. In it lay the origins of his intense hatred for the house of Lusignan and his close personal relationship with the Plantagenet family. To understand his bitter feud with the Lusignans one must realize that the killing of Earl Patrick, which seems to us a normal act of war, was in William's sight a dastardly crime. The author of the *History* calls the earl's slayer felon and assassin. Not only did he strike down an unarmed man, an unknightly act in itself, but he slew the lieutenant of his feudal suzerain. The first of these offenses probably did not trouble William greatly. Some years later when Richard Plantagenet was in rebellion against his father, William came on that prince when he was unarmed and slew his horse. William afterward insisted that it would have been no crime had he slain Richard himself. To attack an unarmed man was at worst merely a breach of knightly courtesy. But for a rebel to kill the representative of his suzerain was the most serious of feudal crimes—treason. William held Geoffrey de Lusignan responsible for his uncle's death. Whether he simply blamed Geoffrey as the leader of the party and responsible for his men or whether he believed him the actual slayer is not clear. Geoffrey himself denied his guilt, and one chronicler places the blame on his brother, Guy. One is inclined to believe that the two de Lusignan brothers were in command of the party, but had no intention of killing Earl Patrick. Some careless or over-enthusiastic subordinate struck down the earl whom the leaders were simply hoping to capture. This view is confirmed by the care exercised by the rebels to take William alive when, as he was fighting without his helmet, he could have been killed easily. But, rightly or wrongly, William never forgave the house of Lusignan.

The same brief combat which made William the mortal enemy of the de Lusignans brought him to the attention of Queen Eleanor, the ideal patroness for a young knight. The richest heiress of Europe by reason of the great duchy of Aquitaine which she had inherited from her father, Eleanor had at an early age married Louis VII of France. Divorced from him, she had promptly given her hand to Henry Plantagenet. As ruler of more than half of the homeland of the troubadours, as patroness of such artists as Bernard de Ventadour, and the mother of the countesses of Champagne and Blois whose courts were centers of romantic literature, Eleanor was the high priestess of the cult of courtly love. Unfortunately little is known of William's relations with this great lady. One cannot say whether she became interested in him because of his fondness for singing and his knightly courtesy, or simply because he had undergone hardships in her service. But whatever its origin, her favor was an invaluable asset. Normandy and England were full of brave young knights, but there were few who could say that they had suffered wounds and imprisonment in the service of Queen Eleanor and had been ransomed and reequipped by her.

When William Marshal left Poitou in the autumn of 1168, he may well have considered with satisfaction the accomplishments of his twenty-two years. While he had followed what the contemporary romances tell us was the usual course of a young man's education, he had done so with rare success. At the age of thirteen he had left home to seek his fortune in the service of William of Tancarville. At the chamberlain's court he had served his apprenticeship in the trade of arms and from his hand he had received the boon of knighthood. In the combat at Drincourt and in at least two tourneys he had shown himself a brave and capable warrior. The campaign in Poitou had not only given him a taste of the hardships of a soldier's life, but had gained him the favor of Eleanor of Aquitaine. William could with justice believe that he was on the high road to fame and fortune.

Life in a Medieval Castle

JOHN BURKE

The houses and households of the leading families were the centers of government and culture in the Middle Ages. Even for the kings, the great hall of their residence was the place where decisions and judgments were made, in the presence of their friends and supporters, who were the great men of the realm. Medieval lawyers were slow to distinguish between the person and the office of a ruler, and the populace could never make sense of such a distinction. Consequently, our notion that the public and private functions of officials are separate and that the business of state ought not to be carried out in the homes of public officers would have been incomprehensible to medieval people. The house was the place where all the business of living was done.

The great families only slowly replaced their substantial houses of wood with the grand stone castles that we associate with medieval aristocracy. In the early Middle Ages, the aristocratic establishment usually consisted of a strong wooden house, surrounded by an earthen wall with a wooden palisade. In times of trouble, the peasants of the local village, who were usually subject to the lord of the house, could take refuge in this enclosure, and they would help to defend it.

Stone construction was very expensive and required skilled labor and considerable experience with the structural characteristics of the material. People with these skills were rare. Only in the eleventh century did the greatest lords began to build stone fortifications. Among the leaders of this new construction was the Duke of Normandy, who built a series of stone towers (keeps) in England in order to fortify strategic points after his conquest of Britain in 1066. The White Tower, in the Tower of London, is one of these buildings.

By the late twelfth century, most of the greatest barons had at least one stone castle, usually the home that the family considered its principal seat. Here, the household of the lord lived most of the time and, here, his records were kept and his servants carried out his managerial and governmental functions. The culture of the aristocracy—the songs and romance literature, the games and pastimes, the new methods of management—developed in the castle. The way of life in the castle was the model for those who would hardly ever even enter one. In this selection, John Burke describes that way of life.

Through many generations the great hall was the centre of all castle life, shared by the lord and the majority of his household. Here the business of the estate was largely transacted, here men, women and children slept, and here they ate together. 'It is not seemly,' decreed a medieval book on etiquette, 'that a lord should eat alone.'

Waking in the morning, the lord and his lady would find themselves in their bed at one end of the hall, usually at the back of the dais, curtained off from the rest. Or perhaps they were among the pioneers of what later became customary: a small private chamber partitioned off from the main body of the hall or even recessed into the wall of the keep, with wainscoting and some painted panelling to distinguish it from the whitewashed walls elsewhere. If the hall was of the two-storey variety, family bedrooms could be set behind the gallery, and from his solar above the dais the lord was in a position to study activities in the great space below.

Lesser members of his household slept on benches along the walls, upon straw-filled palliasses, or simply on a carpet of rushes and herbs on the floor, pulling cloaks or rugs about them. Since, in spite of regular shifting and replacing, these rushes were all too likely to be impregnated with the grease and spillage from the food consumed in the hall, and with the droppings of favourite dogs and falcons who were present at mealtimes, such a couch must have been none too salubrious. Even in the lord's private recess, carpets were a rarity until well into the thirteenth century, and other luxuries were equally scarce. Tapestries gradually made their appearance, combining pleasant decoration with the need to combat draughts. Early halls had an open fire in the middle of the floor; and even when fireplaces were built into the walls, proper chimneys were unknown until the late thirteenth century, so that the primitive flues driven through the walls combined with draughts from the unglazed windows to swirl a great deal of smoke about, soon discoloring the whitewash.

The household rose early. The first duty was attendance at mass in the chapel—a small chamber in most early castles, before it became fashionable to sponsor more and more elaborate chapels as prestige symbols. When larger buildings could safely be built within the confines of a reasonably secure bailey, many included a crypt in which generations of the family would be buried. It was rare, though, in Norman times to find anything quite as ambitious as the domestic chapel within the keep at Castle Rising in Norfolk.

Mass was said by the lord's chaplain, or—from the word 'chancel' —chancellor. He would also say grace before meals, and attend to his master's personal and official correspondence.

From John Burke, *Life in the Castle in Medieval England* (Totowa, N.J.: Rowman and Littlefield, 1978), pp. 33–52.

The first meal of the day was spartan for most: usually a hunk of bread and a pot of ale before work commenced, though the baron himself might have white wheaten bread and a slice of cold meat, perhaps even a glass of wine. While his servants went about their duties, the baron and his steward would then settle down to administrative matters in the hall. Tenants arrived with rents or respectful complaints, submitting local disputes for judgment. There might be ticklish matters of inheritance to settle, or deaths or marriages to discuss. When a knightly sub-tenant died and the son wished to take over, the lord could claim a fee which might be as much as the first year's income from the relevant holdings. He might also wish to suggest a suitable match for the dead man's widow; or, if the heir was still a minor, could act as guardian and work out what extra profits this would entitle him to from the estate. If his own son were to be knighted, he expected contributions towards expenses from his vassals. If his daughter married, a wedding donation was imperative.

There were two complementary divisions in the household: one military, the other administrative. The military included knights in the magnate's service, stabling their horses in the bailey under the care of a stable marshal, and the numerous squires, men-at-arms, castle watchmen, archers and crossbowmen, and sub-tenants doing a spell of service as sentries along the battlements. Smiths and carpenters maintained the more advanced engines of war; farriers attended to the horses. Not all of these would be simultaneously or permanently on the premises, save in some royal castles built specifically to defend strategic points and keep constant watch over the more unsettled parts of the realm. Rather than keep expensive standing garrisons, it was more usual practice to call on men to fulfil their feudal duties only when an emergency loomed.

At the head of the other section was the steward or major-domo. Originally his responsibilities took in both the domestic routine and the management of his master's rural estates, but in the case of a baron whose power and possessions were growing it became common to subdivide these functions. One steward or seneschal took over indoor matters, the other went out of doors.

The domestic staff lived in a hierarchy as clearly marked out as that of their overlord's feudal obligations. Close to the steward, and sometimes combining the steward's duties with his own, was the chamberlain, responsible for the whole organisation supplying the great chamber, or hall. There was an usher on duty at the door of the hall. The cook worked in a team which was to survive in similar form through many centuries into Victorian days, and even beyond. There was a pantler, or officer in charge of the pantry, taking his name from the French *pain*, or bread; the butler (bottler) supervising the buttery where drink was kept in butts or bottles; and a butcher, baker and—quite literally—candlestick maker. There were maids, skivvies, and stable lads. And with seamstresses and laundresses at his command there was the highly esteemed keeper of the wardrobe.

In the baronial court, often entrusted with its entire supervision in the absence of his lord, the estates [sic] seneschal would sit with the chaplain or his clerk beside him to take notes and prepare documents. He kept full accounts of the manors within the baronial domain and their output in food, timber, service or taxes, and toured them several times a year. According to a thirteenth-century treatise on *Husbandrie*, a qualified seneschal

> should have lands of demesne measures, should know by the perch of the country how many acres in each field for sowing (wheat, rye, barley, oats, peas, beans and dredge), ploughing (each plough should plough 9 score acres—60 for winter seed, for spring seed and in fallow), also how many acres to be ploughed by boon custom and how many by the desmesne [sic] ploughs; reaping (how many acres by boon and custom and how many for money), meadows and pastures (how much hay is needed, how much stock can be kept on pastures and on common). Also how stock is kept and improved. Fines imposed if loss or damage due to want of guard. No under or over stocking of manors. If lord needs money for debts, Seneschal should see from which manor he can have money at greatest advantage and smallest loss.

The 'boon' mentioned in this passage refers to the donation of free service at special times required from a tenant or villein by his lord.

When the morning's business had been transacted in the hall, the main meal of the day was forthcoming, at what may seem to us the disconcertingly early hour of ten or eleven o'clock. Trestle tables were set up and laid with silver for the lord and his lady on their dais, earthenware vessels and horn or wooden implements for the others. While his retainers sat on the benches which some of them had used for sleeping the night before, the lord and lady might use chairs—imposing but heavy, and through most of the Norman period lacking such comforts as upholstery.

The chaplain said grace. The food was brought in. Because of the difficulty of disposing of smoke and smells, a great deal of cooking was almost certainly done out in the open when weather permitted. Kitchens might be incorporated in buildings against one of the bailey walls, or on the lower floor of the keep with ovens and fireplaces set in the walls, but either way the food was unlikely to arrive very hot at the table after traversing the draughty courtyards or being carried up spiral stone staircases.

The estate and its tenants supplied many ingredients for the various dishes, but in addition there were imported luxuries such as wine and the spices essential to disguise the flavour of bad and rancid meat, fish or soups. With no means of preserving meat other than by salting it down, the practice wherever possible was to eat an animal within a day or so of its being slaughtered; but salting was essential to ensure supplies throughout the winter, since the efficacy of root crops as winter feed had not yet been discovered, or to keep the inmates from starvation during a siege.

There was no lack of variety in foodstuffs. Beef, mutton, pork and bacon were as familiar then as now, though not so plentiful for the man in the street—or in the fields. Much of it had to be stewed rather than grilled or roasted since it came from tough animals ranging more energetically and fed a less calculated balanced diet than ours. Some of the rest was powdered or minced into a paste with milk, herbs and breadcrumbs, not unlike a modern rissole. Birds such as starlings, pigeons and gulls were more acceptable on the table then, along with peacocks and herons, and larks' tongue pie was a great delicacy. Of course there was a great deal of game in castles near the preciously preserved hunting forests: venison was roasted or, like other viands, ground to paste by pestle and mortar.

Most of the fruits and vegetables of our own day were available, apart from potatoes and tomatoes—onions, peas, beans, cabbages, leeks, apples and pears among them—though in some quarters they were looked down on as peasants' fare. Herbs and a number of vegetables could be grown in a kitchen garden within the castle precincts. A typical salad would include parsley, sage, garlic, leeks, borage, mint, fennel, purslayne, rosemary and rue, dressed with oil, salt and vinegar or with verjuice—the acid juice of crab apples, also used as a liquor for cooking meat.

Butter and cheese were brought in from the estate or sometimes made on the premises, often from ewes' or goats' milk. The miller ground flour for delivery in sacks to the castle baker. Anything lacking in the immediate vicinity was purchased from merchants who could guarantee seasonal supplies of herring, fruit, spices, and delicacies such as wine, figs and raisins.

At table a thick slice of bread was commonly put in the bottom of a bowl, and then soup or stew poured over it, or a paste of minced meat spread on it. More solid pieces of meat, carved from a joint or bird roasted on the spit, would customarily be served on to the silver plate of the lord or the flat wooden platters of his retainers, and eaten with the fingers. Here again, a slice of bread might if wished be set on the platter as a foundation—a sort of primitive open sandwich—or a slice of stale bread from the previous day could itself serve as platter.

Wine from the barrel was poured into jugs and served at the top table, while the lower orders contented themselves with ale brewed by the resident ale-wife. In this at least they were at one with the folk of field and village: even the humblest cottagers brewed their own ale or cider in those days.

A couple of recipes which have been handed down to us may or may not whet the twentieth-century appetite:

LAMPREYS IN GALYTYNE—Take lamprey and skin him with vinegre and salt. Skald him in water. Slytte him and take the guttes out at the end. Kepe the bloode. Put ye lamprey on a spytt. Rost him and keep the greece. Grinde raysons and mix them with vinegre and crusts of bread. Add thereto powder gynger and ye bloode and ye greece. Boyl ye sauce and salte it.

AN ENTRAYLE—Take a sheepis stomache. Take pullets roasted and hew them to pieces. Then take pork, cheese, and spicery, and put it in a mortar and grynde it all fyne. Then take uppe the egges hard boyld, and put it in the stomache with salte, and boyle it till it be enough, and serve it forthe.

During Lent the Church forbade the eating of meat, and in those days the Church's dictates rang more formidably than now. Many castles, like the monasteries, had their own fishponds, or used the moat for this auxiliary purpose. Local rivers might supplement the diet. But local supplies were rarely enough to last through the fasting period, and vast consignments of salted herring had to be transported from the coast. This trade was of the greatest significance for the fishing ports through which it was channelled. In return for guaranteed supplies, calculated as sternly as scutage and tithe and the boon work and feudal service owed by those who lived and worked inland, the fishermen were exempted from many of the obligations which weighed on those who tilled the soil. So many concessions had been made to the East Anglian and south-east coast communities by the time of Richard II, including freedom from appropriation of their boats for national service or official voyages, that many farm lads left the oppressions of the land and moved out to farm the sea.

Salt, so important for the preservation of fish and meat, made those who worked the mines and saltpans people of some consequence, able to do profitable deals with the owners of great estates. One thirteenth-century document prepared on behalf of the Earl of Chester by his clerk records such a contract:

Know that I have given and granted and by this present charter of mine have confirmed to Thomas of Croxton for his homage and service half a salthouse of the fee of Ralph Brereton which Gilbert, chaplain of Middlewich, gave me, as well as all the land which Erneis the chaplain held between the estate of William Brun and the brook which runs close to the earl's bakehouse.

One notes the usual feudal requirement of 'homage and service'.

At the end of dinner, whether the main course had been meat, fowl, or good red herring, the chaplain's almoner would collect such bones and scraps as had not been tossed to the dogs, and bread left soaking in the bottom of soup bowls. It was his duty to visit the poor and distribute these scraps, and also

> to receive discarded horses, clothing, money and other gifts, bestowed on alms, and to distribute them faithfully. He ought also by frequent exhorta-tions to spur the king to liberal almsgiving, especially on saints' days, and to implore him not to bestow his robes . . . upon players, flatterers, fawners, talebearers or minstrels, but to command them to be used to augment his almsgiving.

Assuming that the lord of the castle was today spared any such exhortation from his almoner, and that there was no further pressing busi-ness to attend to, his mind might well turn to the prospect of an afternoon's hunting. The best days of all were those when there were no administrative duties to be performed and he could set out in the early morning for a whole day in the forest, with a picnic meal to be served during a lull in the chase. Today his treasured falcon had probably been sitting hooded on the back of his chair throughout the meal, and now it was high time to exercise him—or her, for the male tiercel was far less aggressive and less favoured than the female falcon.

To a nobleman, hawking was perhaps the dearest of all aspects of the chase. Deer and wild boar might be pursued avidly through the forests, with the more adventurous ladies accompanying the hunt; but the skilled falconer was the aristocrat of huntsmen, and the falcon more precious than any hunting dog. Animals on the ground could be cornered or worn out before the kill. Birds were more enticingly elusive. There were as yet no guns to massacre them in mid-air, and they could swiftly wing their way out of arrow range. Winged predators had to be trained to swoop on them and bring them down. Training was arduous both for the hawk and hawker, and when it was completed the birds were looked after with the greatest devotion in the castle mews.

William I, said to have 'loved the tall deer as if he had been their father', preserved them for his own sport. Anyone who without royal per-mission killed a hart or a hind was blinded. Peasants who in Saxon times had supplied themselves with kindling and small game from the woods had been banned from certain areas set aside for royal diversion, but now in Norman times found themselves deprived of almost all such facilities in growing expanses of forest and open country. Feudal forest law permitted the wholesale demolition of villages and hamlets with game reserves set aside for exclusive royal or baronial use. Verderers' courts enforced the harshest penalties on a hungry man who touched as much as a rabbit. Poachers were hanged or mutilated, and anyone who raised the mildest protest against the verderers was liable to be deprived of all his posses-sions. The only concessions were to warreners who helped keep down hares, badgers, foxes, and other animals thought to be harmful to the more highly valued game. Even so-called 'free warren' was a perk for the lord or minor gentry rather than the needy peasant, being yet another of those things which could be won from the king in return for payment or service. It has more than once been pointed out that the adjective 'free' in any medieval transaction generally meant the freedom of one member of the community to oppress others.

On return from the chase the lord might take a bath. Water was poured into a wooden tub in his bedchamber or curtained recess, and he sat in it upon a stool. The soap used would have been made on the premises from meat fat, wood ash and soda, unless he was prepared to import expensive soap from Mediterranean countries, made with an olive oil base and perfumed with herbs.

Shaving must have been an uncomfortable operation with knife blades which, by our standards, were surely jagged and liable to rasp the skin.

As to our usual adjunct to the bathroom, the privy or garderobe, this was set into an outer wall or even built out over a shaft which might end in a ditch, in the moat, or, ideally, in running water. Sometimes a number of latrines on different floors fed into such a shaft, the deposits being cleaned out at intervals by some unfortunate serf. In hot weather or after the visit of a king's or fellow nobleman's retinue, or during a siege, the smell within the castle must have been a sore trial. Sanitation in even the most exalted households left much to be desired. Henry III once objected so strongly to the stench in the Tower of London that before returning to it from his travels he adjured the constable:

> Since the privy in the chamber of our wardrobe at London is situated in an undue and improper place, wherefore it smells badly, we command you on the faith and love by which you are bounden to us that you in no wise omit to cause another privy chamber to be made . . . even though it should cost a hundred pounds.

After completing his ablutions, and as twilight fell, the lord presided over his ménage at supper. This was a less substantial meal than dinner unless there were a special feast with visitors to be impressed and diverted.

In his absence during the afternoon his wife and other ladies of the castle had perhaps worked on their embroidery, gossiped and told tales or riddles, thereafter joining the children when the tutor had released them. Children and adults shared much the same romps and pastimes, including 'hoodman blind' and other variations on blind-man's-bluff, skipping and dancing games, and various simple dice games. The more skilled devoted themselves to chess or forms of billiards and backgammon. After supper they might continue in the same mood with the lord joining them or, if he was exhausted by the business and outdoor exercise of his day, retiring to a chamber where some of the ladies might wait on him, flirt with him, and perhaps play music. In the hall other musicians were perhaps tuning up —strolling players to entertain the household and accompany an hour or so of dancing.

With darkness settled down outside, the interior was lit by candles made from wax or animal fat rendered down and then solidified, set on iron-spiked candlesticks or in wall brackets which also held torches of resinous wood or rushlights made from dipping twisted strands of rush into grease or tallow. A portable lantern with its candle shielded by translucent slices of horn was used when negotiating draughty passages or staircases.

When it was time to call an end to the evening, the captain of the guard would ensure that the sentries were properly posted and alert, and the lord and lady retired to their room, said their prayers, hung up their clothes . . . and so to bed.

In such chill surroundings it was usual to dress warmly rather than stylishly. Men wore thick cloth or woollen stockings, sometimes simply extensions of a sort of combination under-garment, covered with tunics or cloaks reaching almost to the ground. In moments of relaxation a noble might don a fine woollen or linen tunic with sleeves narrowing to the wrist, and over this a shorter sleeveless tunic belted at the waist. His lady's long-sleeved tunic, girdled at the waist and perhaps with a gold, silver or jewelled clasp, might sport sleeves wider from shoulder to forearm; and as time went on a number of extravagances appeared in the sleeves, sprouting long hangings from the wrist or elbow. Women's trim headgear—a white veil in the twelfth century, a folded wimple held in place by a stiff cap in the thirteenth—blossomed through the fourteenth century into the awe-inspiring extravagances of the fifteenth. As living conditions grew less austere, so clothing became less austere and more mannered, lighter to wear and easier to cut and shape into imaginative designs. Head-dresses (by no stretch of the language could they be called hats) rose into lofty gilded cones which must have presented problems when the wearer passed under a low lintel, or aped a bishop's mitre with constructions of velvet, brocade, embroidery, golden threads and precious stones. Men, too, indulged increasingly in coxcomb flamboyance: tight-waisted tunics, fur collars and cuffs, and, for indoor wear, long leather shoes which remind one of the much derided 'winkle-pickers' of the mid-twentieth century. Sexual suggestiveness, romantic and flirtatious display, have combined into many patterns, postures and colours throughout the centuries; but the basic drama has remained much the same, even if the relative roles of hero and heroine are no longer as ill balanced as they once were.

In the Middle Ages a girl might be betrothed at the age of nine or ten and married well before her fourteenth birthday. Many parents pressed for early marriage in order to avoid possible depredations to their estates if the father, or both of them, should die before the child came of age. Yet another of the Crown's sources of feudal income was the guardianship of orphaned minors, which could be sold or leased out at profit to some other lord; and, as we have seen, local magnates had a financial interest in local widows and juvenile heirs.

When ordering the compilation of records of royal dues throughout the land, Henry II did not omit to order the inclusion of widows and heirs under such wardship in case there might be some tax outstanding or some profitable investment overlooked. Even ladies of the greatest consequence found it hard to avoid the dictates of their guardian, especially when the king was nominally that guardian. Richard I, greedy as ever to subsidise one of his foreign expeditions, decided to collect the fee due to him on the marriage of the Earl of Essex's widow, and commanded her to marry a man he had picked out for her. She desired no such marriage; but the king made it clear that if she refused he would confiscate all her possessions, so in the end she had to submit.

Marriages of convenience were the rule rather than the exception. Desirable liaisons were encouraged by sending daughters of the family away to the castles of other noble families for their education. Failing a deliberate plan of this kind, the girls were sometimes tucked away and educated in a convent until a suitable bridegroom was found. If none was forthcoming or if they found their true vocation in the convent itself, they often remained there.

Unmarried, the young woman was her father's chattel. Once married, no matter how great the dowry she took with her, she became her husband's chattel. He could use her property and her body as it pleased him, and could strike her not merely with impunity but with the tacit approval of friends and relations if he felt she needed chastisement or encouragement. In time of outrageous wrong the lady might appeal to influential kinsfolk for help against him, but it was rare for this to happen.

It was the wife's duty to take good care of the household and even to familiarise herself with the duties of the seneschal, no matter how trusted he might be, so that, though supposedly of inferior sex, she should be able to stand in for her lord, since of so many women it could be said that 'often they dwell at home without their husbands, who are at court or in divers lands'. Divers lands indeed: many were called upon to accompany their king on Crusade, or even to go in his place; others served in repetitive dynastic wars in France and Normandy; some were often abroad slyly negotiating favours for themselves and their estates with would-be usurpers whose cause it might prove prudent to espouse.

In spite of her legal disabilities the lady could not, then, afford to be forever meek and downtrodden. Matilda had proved a formidable claimant to the throne in Stephen's time, and even those without royal blood in their veins often proved as knowledgeable and courageous as their menfolk. They were often better read and with wider interests, in spite of being shut away for so much of the time while their husbands roved the outside world.

A striking example of a woman's victory on behalf of her husband and his property is that of the wife of Sir John de Pelham, constable of Pevensey castle in the time of Richard II. John had decided to support the cause of the exiled Henry Bolingbroke, and in his absence on campaign the king's supporters moved in to seize Pevensey. During the siege the châtelaine wrote 'To my trew Lorde':

> My dere Lord, I recommande me to your hie Lordeschipp wyth hert & body, & all my pore myght; and wyth all this I think zow, as my dere Lorde, derest & best yloved of all erthlyche Lordes; I say for me, and thanke yhow, my dere Lord, with all thys that I say before, off your comfortable lettre that ze send me from Pownefraite that com to me on Mary Magdaleyn day; ffor by my trowth I was never so gladd as when I herd by your lettre that ye warr stronge ynogh, wyth the grace off God, for to kepe you fro the malyce of your ennemys. . . . And my dere Lord iff it lyk zow for to know off my ffare, I am here by layd in manner off a sege, with the counté of Sussex, Sudray, & a great parcyll off Kente, so that I ne may noght out nor none vitayles gette me, bot wt myche hard. Wharfore my dere iff it lyk zow, by the awyse off zowr wyse counsell, for to sett remedye off the salvation off yhower Castell, and wtstand the malyce off thes schires forsayde. And also that ye be fullyche enformed off these grett malce wyrkers in these schyres whych yt haffes so dispytffully wrogth to zow, and to zowr castell, to yhowr men, and to zour tenants, ffore this cuntree have yai wastede, for a gret whyle. Farewele my dere Lorde; the Holy Trinyté zow kepe fro zour ennemys, and son send me gud tythings off yhow.
>
> Ywrten at Pevensay in the castell on Saynt Jacobe day last past,
>
> By yhowr awnn pore
> J. PELHAM

The lady Pelham seems, however, to have been far from poor in spirit. It was not just the defence of the castle which was noteworthy, but the penning of the letter itself. So far as can be ascertained this is the first letter written in her own hand by a lady of rank in the English language rather than in the courtly French or Latin one would have expected.

John de Pelham was rewarded by the new king, Henry IV, with the constableship of Pevensey and the estates of the 'Honour of the Eagle' not merely for his own lifetime but as a legacy for all his male descendants., Male descendants, of course: a poor acknowledgement of the part played by the lady in the matter. One suspects that once the master was home the mistress of the castle ceased to have any say in its destinies and was expected to revert to the role of a gracefully feminine, loving, subservient wife. She must dress to please her husband, attend to his creature comforts, and tempt him with such perfumes and makeup as were available and allowable: much frowned on by the Church, the commonest makeup was a fine white flour used to lighten the complexion and, in all probability, cover the blemishes of commonplace illnesses and unbalanced diet.

In his absence, as in his presence, it was in order for her to listen to the songs of troubadours and verbose poems of courtly love—the medieval equivalent of the romantic novel and women's magazine serials —and to joke archly about them with her lord. But although a woman might dabble with sentimental fantasies, and even have male acquaintances dancing attendance on her and pouring out conventional flowery phrases, it was all play-acting—and had best remain so. A man's adultery while away, or at home with castle wenches and those in his fields and villages, was winked at; but a lady's adultery was a criminal blot on the escutcheon.

Mother and Child

MARY MARTIN MCLAUGHLIN

Historians have assumed that medieval women were no better off than their Roman counterparts, described by Sarah B. Pomeroy in Part 1 of this volume, and they have devoted little space to women in histories of the Middle Ages. Some scholars have suggested that, as an escape from the restrictions and drudgery of their lives, noble women patronized the literary genre of courtly love romances which was created by *jongleurs* (minstrels) of the twelfth century. During the long absences of their husbands, who were often occupied with the rounds of tournaments and wars, it is said that women listened to these singers, who naturally catered to the dreams of their patronesses. But while the romances do place women in an unaccustomed position of importance, they also focus on men and their exploits, and they were popular with men as well as with women. Moreover, recent research has indicated that the wives of barons did not conform to the stereotype presented by the romances.

Women of the peasant class undoubtedly worked hard alongside their husbands, and although there were differences in the work done by each of the sexes, those differences were dictated more by the demands of the job than by socially defined sex roles. An assessment of the position of upper-class women is difficult. In the eleventh and twelfth centuries—about the same time that the romance literature came into being—aristocratic women emerged from the shadows and began to play an active role in politics. Agnes of Poitiers (c. 1024–77), wife of Henry III of Germany, was an active queen who was regent of her kingdom for almost ten years after the death of her husband in 1056. Countess Mathilda of Tuscany (1048–1115) governed one of Italy's most populous and richest provinces for more than four decades and held the difficult middle ground between the papacy and the German empire during the Investiture Contest. Another Mathilda (1102–67), daughter of the English king Henry I (1100–35), waged a long civil war in England on behalf of her son Henry II. Henry II's succession to the largest domain in Europe was largely the result of the persistence and abilities of his mother. Henry's wife Eleanor of Aquitaine (1122–1204) was, perhaps, the most famous of these politically important women.

But political activity was not, of course, the normal occupation of medieval women—as it was not the normal occupation of medieval men. Women spent the bulk of their time running the household, and obviously the role of a woman as wife depended on the kind of household she presided over—noble, bourgeois, or peasant. It is not so obvious that a woman's role as mother also depended on her class. Aristocratic families used wet nurses and often sent young children to be raised in the household of a higher lord. Charlemagne's household became a kind of boarding school for the children of his greatest subjects. William Marshal, the subject of an earlier selection, was sent to his cousin's house at about thirteen years of age. Legal sources reveal that aristocratic children were often betrothed very young; the young couple, to be married when they reached thirteen or fourteen, was sometimes raised in the house of the boy's parents. Urban middle-class families also used wet nurses, but their children were raised at home until they entered apprenticeships. The apprentices, who were of course all male, lived with the families of their masters. Girls were simply raised at home.

Finally, peasant families shared the characteristics of poor families everywhere and in nearly every age. The children were not given out to wet nurses unless the mother had difficulty producing milk or died in childbirth—and then the nurse was likely to be a neighbor or relative in the same village. Peasant children lived at home until adulthood, and they became part of the family's work force early in life. In addition, the differences in work between the sexes were less extreme in this class than in the upper classes, so that the training of male and female children differed less than it did higher up the social scale.

These very general remarks rest on tidbits of information gleaned from chronicles, rare treatises on household affairs, and legal records. How can we get a closer view of childhood and child-rearing in the Middle Ages? In this selection, Mary Martin McLaughlin uses another source, the reminiscences of some eleventh- and twelfth-century men, to discover their childhood experiences and to delve into the relationship between mother and child.

"In her despair, his mother wholly rejected her baby, weaning him before he had hardly begun to nurse, and refusing to hold or touch him with her own hands."

John of Lodi, *Life of St. Peter Damian*, late eleventh century

"Yet thou knowest, Almighty One, with what purity and holiness in obedience to Thee she raised me, how greatly she provided me with the care of nurses in infancy and of masters and teachers in boyhood, with no lack even of fine clothes for my little body, so that I seemed to equal the sons of kings and counts in indulgence."

Guibert of Nogent, *Memoirs*, 1115

Some Introductory Reflections on Two Eleventh-Century Childhoods

For the period from which these voices speak, as for all but the most recent times, the realities of early life must remain a largely hidden world,

From Mary Martin McLaughlin, "Survivors and Surrogates: Children and Parents from the Ninth to the Thirteenth Centuries," *The History of Childhood*, ed. L. deMause (New York: Psychohistory Press, 1974), pp. 101–41.

accessible to us only partially and indirectly, through the recollections, portrayals and fantasies of those who were no longer children. Among such fragile if indispensable witnesses, the two works just quoted have for our period and purposes a singular importance. Offering us the fullest, the most intimate and revealing accounts of infancy and childhood in Western society during the time-span of this study, they lead us most directly into the virtually uncharted hinterland of childhood during these distant centuries. To suggest that much of this terrain is still unexplored is by no means to undervalue the contributions of modern scholarship in many areas that impinge upon it. Studies concerned with the family and its changing structure, with medieval demography, law and education, with the history of medicine and especially pediatrics, with religious movements and cultural transformations, as well as essays on the "idea" and the "cult" of childhood: all of these and many others help us in some measure to recreate both the immediate and the social settings of children's lives in the remoter past. Still in its own infancy, however, is the effort to approach more closely the psychic realities of the experiences of childhood, the modes of rearing and the relations of parents and children, with all of their profound implications for the development of both individuals and societies. Whatever may be the verdict on the various hypotheses advanced in this volume, the discovery of childhood in these and in other centuries must inevitably, like all such novel ventures, pose fresh and formidable questions that will leave almost no field of history uninvaded. . . .

The man whose childhood John of Lodi describes was, indeed, no ordinary person. For Peter Damian, who was born in the early eleventh century, perhaps in 1007, in the Italian city of Ravenna, to respectable but evidently far from prosperous parents, was destined to become one of the great spiritual reformers of his age and one of its most notable saints. An eloquent preacher and zealous ascetic, head of a congregation of hermits dedicated to the contemplative life, a powerful opponent of abuses and in later life a cardinal-bishop of the Roman Church, he played a major part in the most important ecclesiastical movements of the century. He also wrote copiously and sometimes brilliantly on many subjects; but his writings, though variously self-revealing, contain little that is directly autobiographical. For our most substantial and sequential knowledge of his life, in both its earlier and its later phases, we must turn to John of Lodi, a devoted disciple of Peter Damian's last years, who wrote at the request of his fellow-monks of Fonte Avellana a biography that was, like other such works, intended above all to demonstrate the sanctity of its hero.

No doubt John's story of Peter Damian's early life reflected also his own ideas and fantasies of childhood and it is perhaps this concern, as well as the immediacy of his sources and his intense devotion to his subject, that explains the vividness, empathy and apparent veracity in which this biography markedly transcends the conventions of the medieval saint's life. Strikingly absent from it are the visions, dreams and portents that commonly attended the births of saintly children and the glorification of their parentage that was also a tradition of this genre. In keeping with its principles, however, John did wish to stress those experiences which formed and tested the heroic virtues of his subject, and so, perhaps, he did not hesitate to record a childhood of almost unrelieved misery and deprivation. Peter's adversities began, in fact, at the very moment of his birth, to a mother "worn out by child-bearing," into a family already so numerous and so impoverished that when this son was born, an adolescent brother bitterly reproached their mother for having added yet another child to an overcrowded household, to the "throng of heirs" competing for a meagre inheritance.

Enraged by this attack, the mother fell into what John of Lodi describes as "a violent fit of feminine malice" (in which we may perceive the symptoms of postpartum depression), wringing her hands and declaring that she was utterly wretched and unworthy to live any longer. In her despair, she wholly rejected her baby, refusing to nurse him and "to hold or touch him with her own hands." Cast away "before he had learned to live," disinherited from the maternal breast that was his only possession, this tiny creature began to grow dark with hunger and cold, and so weak that he could hardly cry; "only the barest whisper came from his scarcely palpitating little chest." At this point, when the baby seemed about to perish from maternal neglect, he was rescued through the intervention of a certain priest's wife, or concubine, who had been a domestic servant in his father's family and who had perhaps assisted at the child's birth. Clearly hers was also an important role in the symmetry as well as the sensibility of John's story, for she is the "good" foil of the "bad" mother in a pairing that is later balanced by the contrast between Peter's "good" and "bad" brothers. Appalled by the inhuman harshness of his mother, this compassionate woman vehemently reproached her, asking how a Christian mother could behave as no lioness or tigress would do. If these mothers faithfully nurse their cubs, she cried, how could human mothers reject children formed in the image of God and shaped in their own wombs? Clinching her argument with the stern warning that to continue in this way would be to risk being judged guilty of filicide, the priest's wife contrived to soften the mother's heart and restore the dying child to life.

To set an example of proper maternal solicitude, in whose details John of Lodi took evident pleasure, she freed the baby's withered limbs from their swaddling bands, warmed the naked little body at the fire and cured the rash or scabies that covered it by rubbing it lavishly with oil. Then, he exclaimed, "you would have seen the tender little limbs, wrapped in poultices soaked in melted fat, begin to grow rosy as their vital heat returned, and the beauty of infancy flower again." So, we are told, the compassion of a "sinful little woman" snatched a desperate child from the jaws of death and saved his mother from "the dreadful sin of infanticide." Indeed, restored to that maternal self and feeling which "an alien savagery had driven out," Peter's mother from that time on showed unstinting diligence and love in the nursing of her baby, who flourished under this care until he was weaned.

Shortly after this, however, when he was still a very young child, Peter was prematurely orphaned by the death of both of his parents. Left to the care of his family, he was, unhappily, adopted by the very brother, probably the eldest, who had been so angered by his birth and who, with a wife equally harsh and cruel, now treated the little boy, according to his biographer, in a savage and "stepmotherly" fashion. Fed grudgingly with slops fit only for pigs, he was forced to go about barefoot, clad in rags, a "battered child," frequently kicked and beaten. Subjected to this brutality for some years, compelled to live "like a slave," he was eventually turned out to become a swineherd. From this period of Peter's boyhood only one episode, which John considered highly significant, is reported at length. One day the miserable boy chanced to find a gold coin and, delighted by this unexpected wealth, he reflected for a long time on what he might buy with it. After long inner debate, he was at last divinely inspired to renounce his dreams of transitory pleasure and to give up his cherished coin to a priest for a Mass to be offered for his father's soul. If to his biographer this renunciation of the ephemeral for the eternal seemed to presage his later sanctity, to us it may seem not without meaning that only his father and not his rejecting mother was included in this generous offering.

Concluding his tale of childhood misery on a happier note, John reports that when Peter was perhaps twelve years old, he was delivered from his tormentors and placed in the care of another brother, as kind as the first was cruel, who lavished on the boy so much affection that "it seemed to exceed a father's love." It was to this brother, Damian, who later became an archpriest of Ravenna, that Peter owed the education that made possible his career first as a secular teacher and then as a distinguished churchman. To this brother, whose name he adopted, Peter remained deeply devoted in later life, as he was to a nephew, also called Damian, for whose education he in turn provided, and to the sisters of whom his biographer says nothing. To this last attachment Peter himself testified in a fashion that adds suggestively to our knowledge of his childhood and the lasting effect of his sufferings in it. In a letter written when he was perhaps sixty, he described an earlier visit to the deathbed of a beloved sister, who had been "like a mother" to him; as he crosses the threshold of the family house for the first time since his youth, he declared, such a "cloud of timidity" hung over his eyes that he could see almost nothing of the household during the time he spent there.

Although John of Lodi failed to mention this affectionate sister and her role, perhaps because her presence would have disturbed the symmetry of his story, its essential truth is supported by Peter's own revelation of the enduring anxieties aroused by this visit to the home of his childhood and the painful memories associated with it.

Unlike Peter Damian, Guibert of Nogent was neither particularly influential nor, if we may judge by his account of himself, very saintly. Born a half-century or so after Peter, in Clermont-en-Beauvaisis in northern France, into a noble family of only local importance, he was destined from the first for the monastic life, which he entered at the age of twelve or thirteen. Much later, he became the abbot of a small monastery, Nogent-sous-Coucy, and also, though his role on the larger scene was never more than modest, an acute observer, recorder and critic of his turbulent society. No less fascinated by himself than by the world in which he moved, he distinguished himself most strikingly from all but a few of his contemporaries by telling his own story in his *Monodiae* of "songs for one voice," a somewhat miscellaneous collection of memoirs which has been described, with some exaggeration, as "the first comprehensive autobiography of the middle ages." Although these memoirs are by no means so encompassing autobiographically as we might wish, there is no work of these centuries that gives us so immediate a sense of what at least one medieval child and childhood might have been like. Indeed, his intense, perhaps obsessive, concern with his early life reveals to us not only the young Guibert in his strangely isolated and rigorously disciplined childhood, but the child living still in the man of fifty. Remarkable as his memoirs are in their portrayal of the dramas of his world, and the wealth of insights they offer into the details of its life, the true singularity of his work lies in its major theme and inspiration, that passionate attachment to his mother which remained the central and apparently the only emotionally significant relationship of his existence.

Dominating all that is most personal in his story, this possessive and somewhat ambivalent devotion is first clearly disclosed in Guibert's uncommonly precise account of the shared dangers and deliverance of his birth. For, like Peter Damian's, Guibert's early hold on life had been extremely tenuous and his entrance into the world even more dramatic, in circumstances of great peril to both mother and child. In reporting them he took, in fact, considerable retrospective pleasure, dwelling at length on his mother's prolonged and painful labor and the dangers that led his father, in hope of a safe delivery, to promise him to the monastic life even before he had been born. When at last he appeared, "a weak little being, almost an abortion," and was on that same day, Holy Saturday, brought to the baptismal font, he was, as he was often told jokingly in later years, tossed from hand to hand by "a certain woman," probably the midwife, who exclaimed: "Look at this thing! Do you think such a child can live . . . ?" After his lively picture of this important occasion, Guibert tells us disappointingly little of his very early childhood. The youngest child in a family that included at least two brothers, whom he barely mentions throughout his memoirs and for whom he apparently felt little affection, at the age of about eight months he lost his father, at a time when he had, he says, scarcely begun to cherish his rattle. After his father's death, which Guibert later saw as a stroke of good fortune, his mother remained a widow, devoting herself to the rearing of this, in his view at least, her favorite child, "truest to me," he insists, "of all that she bore."

What sort of woman was this whom her son regarded throughout his life as his "sole personal possession among all the goods I had in the world"? In his portrayal of her, "beautiful, yet chaste, modest, steeped in the fear of the Lord," we glimpse faintly the influences of another childhood, formative perhaps for both mother and son. And we see more clearly the effects of the marriage of which he was the offspring. For terrified from her earliest years by fears of sin and sudden death, she had been given in marriage to Guibert's father, himself a mere youth, when she was still a child, "hardly of marriageable age." Probably because of their youthful ignorance and inhibitions rather than through the "bewitchments" to which Guibert attributed their failure, his parents' marriage remained unconsummated for several years. During this time the impotent young husband and his still virginal wife were subjected to heavy and humiliating pressures from their families and neighbors, until at last the "bewitchment was broken," probably, as their son suggests, by his father's successful liaison with another woman. Thereafter his mother submitted, though clearly not eagerly, to those wifely duties for which, according to Guibert, she had little taste. Still a young and handsome woman when her husband died, she resisted with formidable determination the self-interested efforts of his kinsmen to persuade her to remarry so that they might gain control of her children and property. Continuing for the rest of her life in what was to her and to many other women in this period the highly desirable state of widowhood, she showed herself the conventionally dutiful, efficient, extraordinarily pious, in some ways generous but, it seems emotionally inhibited woman whose image emerges from Guibert's recollections. Illiterate but practically gifted, burdened with all of the responsibilities of governing a noble household, she was evidently assiduous in her concern for the physical and spiritual welfare of her son, providing him, he says, with nurses in his infancy, dressing him in fine clothes and, when she had leisure from her household cares, teaching him how and for what to pray. From his earliest years Guibert appears to have been powerfully influenced by his mother's piety and sense of sin, and particularly by her uncommonly rigid standards of sexual purity and control. He was also strongly affected by her concern for his education, for as soon as this child who was destined for the monastic life had begun to learn his letters, at the age of four or five, she procured the services of a teacher who became his private tutor for at least six years, living in the household and giving his full attention to his pupil, whom he worked very hard and whose every waking moment he supervised.

Between his mother and his tutor, who "guarded him as a parent not as a master," Guibert was evidently brought up with excessive, indeed, repressive care, kept, he says, from ordinary games, never allowed to leave his master's company or to eat anywhere but at home, or to accept gifts from anyone without his leave. "While others of my age wandered everywhere at will and were unchecked in the indulgence of such inclinations as were natural at their age," says Guibert, "I, hedged in by constant restraints and dressed in my clerical garb, would sit and look at the troops of players like a beast awaiting sacrifice." Rarely permitted a holiday, he was constantly driven to study by an assiduous but poorly educated teacher who tried to compensate for his own deficiencies with scoldings and frequent beatings. Persuading himself, at least retrospectively, of the genuine concern, the "harsh love," underlying this rough treatment, and himself returning this love, mingled with a certain contempt, Guibert was also pleasurably aware of the rivalry for his affections between his master and his mother, who was grieved and distressed, according to her son, when she saw the evidence of excessive beating. On one occasion when, he says, "she threw off my inner garment and saw my little arms blackened and the skin of my back everywhere puffed up with the cuts from the twigs," she was "grieved to the heart" and protested bitterly, "weeping with sorrow," that he should never become a cleric or "any more suffer so much to get an education." Yet when she offered to give him the arms and equipment of a knight, when he had reached the age for them, Guibert proudly refused, insisting that "if I had to die on the spot, I would not give up studying my lessons and becoming a clerk."

Different as their childhoods were in many ways, Guibert evidently shared with Peter Damian not only heavy physical punishment but also the experience, or the feeling, of maternal rejection, although Guibert's came at a much later time, when in fact, he was past twelve and his mother, in her growing obsession with her own spiritual welfare, decided to withdraw from the world and undertake the life of a recluse. Regarding this decision as desertion, Guibert thought of her in putting her salvation before his wellbeing as, for all her devotion to him, a "cruel and unnatural mother."

> She knew that I should be utterly an orphan with no one at all on whom to depend, for great as was my wealth of kinsfolk and connection, yet there was no one to give me the loving care a little child needs at such an age; though I did not lack for the necessities of food and clothing, I often

suffered from the loss of that careful provision for the helplessness of tender years that only a woman can provide. . . . Although she knew that I would be condemned to such neglect, yet Thy love and fear, O God, hardened her heart . . . the tenderest in all the world, that it might not be tender to her own soul's harm.

Clearly, as this passage suggests, what is extraordinary in Guibert's reminiscences of his childhood is his capacity to convey not only its significant details but the intense, if ambivalent, emotions that were persistently evoked by his profound attachment to his mother. Living constantly, it seems, under the scrutiny of her critical and demanding eye—for even in her retirement she continued to supervise his life and to show her anxiety about him—he never ceased to feel the sense of guilt she had apparently instilled and to long for the love and approval that were, perhaps, never fully given. Throughout his recollections he shows himself as always, essentially, the jealously possessive and dependent child to whose self-concern we owe what is certainly our fullest and most intimate account of the relationship of a medieval mother and son. . . .

To Live or to Die: The Dramas of Birth and Survival

Racked by pains long endured and her tortures increasing as her hour drew near, when she thought I had at last in natural course come to birth, instead I was returned within the womb. By this time my father, friends and kinsfolk were crushed with dismal sorrowing for both of us, for while the child was hastening the death of the mother; and she her child's in denying him deliverance, all had reason for compassion.

Guibert of Nogent, *Memoirs*

If Guibert gives us some sense of the emotional atmosphere surrounding childbirth, he also provides as realistic a description of this occasion as we are likely to find in any but the medical writings of this period. The reason for the lack of direct description is simple; the authors of most such works, being men, were rarely, if ever, present at the actual occasion of birth, which was customarily attended only by women. Until the appearance of popular, vernacular treatises fairly late in our period, moreover, the obstetrical and pediatric knowledge available in medical works of this period, can hardly have affected more than a very small minority of mothers and children. This knowledge appears in any case to have been an amalgam of theoretical learning with the customary and empirical practices which were the stock in trade of the midwives or "sages femmes" who commonly supervised labor and childbirth, and we have almost no trustworthy evidence regarding their training. It was the midwife, Bartholomew of England writes in the early thirteenth century, who knew how to soften the uterus with unguents and fomentations so that the child might be delivered with less difficulty and pain. It was she who received the infant from the womb, severed and tied the umbilical cord at a length of four fingers, washed or bathed the baby, rubbed it with salt and sometimes crushed rose leaves or honey "to comfort its limbs ad free them of mucus," and with her finger rubbed the palate and gums with honey to clean the insides of the mouth and to stimulate the infant's appetite. Bartholomew strongly recommended the frequent bathing of newborns, as well as anointing with oil of myrtle or rose and the massaging of all their limbs, especially those of boys, which should be more strenuously exercised. He also provided a rationale for what was in most regions of Europe the apparently universal practice of swaddling the limbs of newborn and young infants; this should be done, he says, not only to prevent the deformities likely to occur because of the "fluidity" and "flexibility" of infantile limbs, but also to ensure that "natural heat might be restored to the interior of the body" and aid in the digestion of food, which was further encouraged, he thought, by the gentle rocking of infants in their cradles. . . .

Once having made the hazardous passage from the womb, the infant's survival depended upon one thing above all else: its access to breast milk of good quality. In these centuries this meant, for all but the small minority of the noble and prosperous who could afford wet-nurses, the mother's milk. For all classes the mother who nursed her own children reflected the ideal maternal image. Celebrated in contemporary representations of the *Virgo lactans,* the nursing Mother of Christ, and in the poignant Eve nursing her child portrayed on the bronze doors at Hildesheim, and later at Verona, this essential maternal function was emphasized and extolled in literary and didactic works of various kinds. Praising it on both scientific and emotional grounds, Bartholomew of England explained that "while the foetus exists in the womb it is nourished on blood, but at birth nature sends that blood to the breasts to be changed into milk." Its own mother's milk, therefore, was better for the newborn child than another's. Anticipating modern views on the subject, he stressed also the emotional bonds thereby strengthened; "for the mother loves her own child most tenderly, embraces and kisses it, nurses and cares for it most solicitously." Repeating these themes, another thirteenth century writer stressed also the idea that as every plant draws its strength from its roots, and maternal milk best shapes the child's nature, that mother does ill who cuts her child off from these fostering sources.

If the nursing mother represented the ideal of these centuries, she was also to a very large extent the reality; for the vast majority of children, except in cases of dire necessity, must have been dependent on their mother's milk. But it also seems clear that among women of the noble classes—again, it must be emphasized, a small but highly visible minority—the practice of resorting to wet-nurses became increasingly common. What has been called perhaps over-enthusiastically the "nursing revolution" of this period may thus have made some contribution to a growing population, since the use of wet-nurses is thought to have shortened the interval between pregnancies and, in general, to have encouraged the production of more children. The practice of wet-nursing was, in fact, fairly common throughout this time; in the mid-eleventh century, for example, Guibert's mother provided nurses both for her own son and for the child whom she adopted in expiation of her husband's sins. As this case and many others show, however, the infant was not ordinarily, so far as I have been able to discover, sent out to nurse, after the fashion of later centuries; the wet-nurse was, rather, brought into the household to the child. That the use of wet-nurses in general was resisted in some noble circles is suggested by the story, intended as exemplary, of the Blessed Ida of Boulogne, which in its most inflated version describes how violently this saintly and devoted mother of three sons, who had never permitted them to be nursed by anyone but herself, reacted to the flouting of her wishes in this matter. . . .

But there is more to the care of babies than nursing, and here again what evidence we have points largely to the habits and practices of the noble class and to the prominent role of the nurse. By the early thirteenth century, in a work of "popular science," she was assigned the functions doubtless performed by the mother in households farther down the social scale. Assuming the maternal role in nursing the baby, she also rejoiced with the child when he was happy and sympathized with his sorrows; she bathed, cleaned and changed him when he was soiled; she chewed the meat in her own mouth for the toothless child and fed him with her finger. Hers was the hand that rocked his cradle and hers the voice that soothed him with lullabies; it was she who begin teaching him to speak, "lisping and repeating the same words." She was, it seems, something more like a "nanny" than a wet-nurse and by this time such nurses in some noble households remained with their charges throughout their childhood years.

Whether or not it was rocked by a nurse, one accoutrement of infant life assumed a growing importance during these centuries, and this is the cradle. Although our earliest pictorial representations of the rocking-cradle date from the thirteenth century, the cradle in simpler forms must certainly have been in use very much earlier; there was, for example, a deep basket-like cradle, easily portable, in which the baby was held in place by bands, and there are many literary references to cradles of one kind or another, among them the silver cradle that figures in the life of St. Elizabeth of Hungary. But if this object might be something of a "status-symbol," its use could also be regarded as a matter of life and death, as is clear from numerous injunctions of ecclesiastical authorities directed at keeping children out of the parental bed and thus avoiding the danger of "overlaying" and suffocation. In a series of such exhortations extending through the thirteenth century the English bishops strongly urged that children be kept in cradles at least until the age of three. Quite apart from its other implications, which will be more fully considered elsewhere, this legislation is suggestive regarding the sleeping arrangements of many parents and children in this period.

Babies who spent their days playing and sleeping and their nights demanding the attention of their mothers or nurses were doubtless no less trying, if less comprehensible, in this period than in later times, and the difficulties of soothing them might even encourage thoughts of demonic possession. But there are also clear signs, especially from the twelfth century onwards, of tenderness towards infants and small children, interest in the stages of their development, awareness of their need for love, and active responsiveness to that "beauty of infancy" which John of Lodi had earlier portrayed. Hildegard of Bingen, for example, explains at length, in terms favorable to the dignity of the species, why human infants are so slow to walk, compared with animals, and why they must crawl or creep on hands and feet before they walk. Several poets show us, though without noting its age at this momentous advance, the child taking its first steps, holding on to benches and stools, or standing by a table, being tempted by pieces of bread held just out of its reach; another writer pictures a child playing "peek-a-boo," covering its eyes and thinking no one sees it. There is also Caesarius of Heisterbach's story of the affectionate nun to whom Jesus appeared as a child of three, "just beginning to talk," and, regarding speech, Salimbene's well-known tale of the babies in Frederick II's experiment, who all died when cut off from human speech, "because they could not live without the petting and the joyful faces and loving words of their foster mothers, or without those "swaddling songs" which a woman sings to put a child to sleep and without which "it sleeps badly and has no rest.". . .

After birth and baptism, the best milk, the most careful nursing and, after weaning, sufficient food might, as we have seen, markedly improve the chances of survival and thus explain why, as David Herlihy puts it, "those blessed with the goods of this earth were also blessed (or burdened) with children; in contrast, the deprived, the heavily burdened, the poor left comparatively few heirs." If this is true, it is probably not because the poor produced fewer children, but because they could not support them. For they were most directly and constantly at the mercy of the chronic cycles of famine, malnutrition, disease and death, and their children were by far the most common victims of the parental negligence and despair, of the abandonment, exposure and even infanticide, which must be counted among major threats to young life in this period.

If all of these practices were related to the pressures, material and psychological, of a society living often at the limits of subsistence, they are related most specifically to the problem of population, or "family," control in a time when the means of limiting births were totally inadequate, if not, for practical purposes, virtually non-existent. That there were attempts at such control through contraception and abortion is evident from the records condemning these practices, as well as in works recommending the means by which they might be achieved. That they were largely ineffective is demonstrated by the incidence of other practices to which the records of this period also bear substantial testimony. The problem of infanticide in Western society during this period has only very recently become the subject of the serious investigation which will doubtless increase our knowledge of what, insofar as it was a secret sin, or crime, must in large measure lie beyond our closest scrutiny. As the case of Peter Damian's mother suggests, simple failure or refusal to nourish may well have been the most common form of infanticide. There is, in any case, considerable evidence, especially from the earlier medieval centuries, that wherever selective or neglective factors were at work, they were likely to work to the disadvantage of girls, who were not highly valued in a predominantly military and agricultural society, and even more drastically to the disadvantage not only of the illegitimate but of the physically deformed and mentally retarded, of those children who were regarded as "changelings," the works of another powerful enemy of children, the Devil. . . .

The Exiles: Perspectives on the Experience of Childhood in the Eleventh and Twelfth Centuries

Although Guibert of Nogent's relationship with his mother may seem in its intensity, as well as in the fullness of its portrayal, very much a special case, her qualities appear with significant frequency in other maternal portraits drawn or sketched in our sources. Like her, the noble mothers of these centuries are commonly depicted as the efficient administrators of their often extensive households, prudent yet generous and charitable to the poor, distinguished for their piety and their devotion to the physical and spiritual welfare of their children. All of these virtues, and others, were impressively displayed, according to his biographer, by the mother of St. Bernard of Clairvaux, who combined "gentleness with firmness" in the rearing of her seven children, six boys and one girl, all of whom ultimately entered the monastic life. "As soon as a child was born to her," we are told, "Aleth would offer it to the Lord with her own hands," and it was for this reason that, unlike many mothers of her class, she refused to allow her children to be nursed by anyone else, "for it almost seemed as though the babes were fed with the qualities of their mother's goodness as they drew the milk from her breast." By contrast with Guibert's mother, she offered her children, when they were older, only plain and simple fare, "never allowing them to acquire the taste and habit for elaborate ad delicate dishes." As in her case and many others, an active concern for the education of their children was another prominent feature of the maternal portraits of our sources: the saintly Queen Margaret of Scotland, for example, was famous for having taught her children herself, as was Countess Ida of Boulogne, who had received some training in letters.

If we look for the realities behind this doubtless idealized image, Guibert's more penetrating observations concerning his mother's background and experience offer us some clues to the preparation of such women as these for the arduous responsibilities of marriage and motherhood. Illiterate, as he tells us, she had evidently received little or no education as a child, and this lack of concern for the education of daughters, unless they were destined for the monastic life, was probably more common among noble families in the eleventh century and before than it was thereafter. But even in this earlier period, a number of royal and noble ladies had learned at least enough Latin to read the Psalter, and a few of them were considerably further advanced in their learning. By the twelfth century the level of literacy was probably higher among women of the nobility than it was among their husbands and brothers, unless these last were monks or clerics. Illuminated Gospel books and Psalters were often prized possessions of such ladies, and their texts and illustrations were, it seems, a major channel through which the newer currents of piety circulated. We may assume, therefore, that the religious devotion of our mothers and their early instruction of their children had a growing basis in reality. Some of them may, in fact, have made use of the alphabet cards and similar teaching games and devices to which Peter Damian, among others, refers.

Whatever the extent of their education, early marriage was the destiny of those girls who did not enter the religious life, and in either case the choice was rarely theirs to make; the decision almost always lay with their parents, for whom practical considerations and advantages commonly outweighed the desires ad feelings of their children. An unusual and illuminating instance of successful resistance to parental authority is the story of Christina of Markyate, a famous English recluse of the twelfth century, whose biographer paints a picture of contemporary parents much less favorable and perhaps more realistic than that offered by many of our sources. Although this girl had early shown marked signs of her spiritual vocation, conversing with God in her bed as a little child, and had later vowed herself to virginity, the determination of her rich and worldly parents to force her into a desirable marriage led to a long and often violent struggle in which she was finally victorious. In explaining why they were ready to stop at nothing, from bribes and threats to beating and imprisonment, to gain their end, her biographer makes it clear that, though she was "very dear" to them, they regarded her essentially as a valuable property and "feared losing her and all they could hope to gain through her."

Most parents were evidently more successful than Christina's in arranging the futures of their children and most girls were, like Guibert's mother, married off by their fathers to husbands not of their own choosing and often, as in her case, at an age when they were barely nubile, if not still children. According to canon law, the minimum ages at marriage were twelve for girls and fourteen for boys, and many, it seems, were married or at least betrothed below these ages, although a growing ecclesiastical opposition to child-marriage may have had some effect as a deterrent. So also, apparently, did the emphasis of canon lawyers on consent and "marital affection" as important, if not essential, elements in a valid marriage and even more perhaps, in the long run, an increasingly powerful effort to exalt the sanctity and sacramental character of Christian marriage. We need not assume that all marriages were as miserable as that of Guibert's parents seems to have been to suspect that, in the setting of feudal society, conjugal affection was more often a happy accident than a natural condition and that his mother's sexual and emotional inhibitions may have been shared by many women who came as frightened children to marriages in which physical brutality and rejection were evidently far from uncommon. Whatever the realities may have been, in theory and in law the husband's power and authority were supreme. Even in what his biographer regarded as the "model marriage" of St. Bernard's parents, not their mutual affection but his mother's submissiveness is emphasized; "in so far as a woman can and may who is submissive to her husband's authority and who does not even have rights over her own body, she anticipated her husband's every wish." That marriage was quite widely regarded by women of this period as a state to be endured rather than enjoyed is strongly suggested by the readiness, often the determination, of many of them, once widowed, to remain in that admirable condition, and by the alacrity with which many also, like Guibert's mother, turned to the consolations and securities of the religious life. . . .

Whatever the virtues and deficiencies of actual mothers may have been, there can be little doubt that, as in Guibert's case, maternal example and maternal values were dominant in the lives and ideals of those children of whose experience we have some knowledge. When Bernard of Clairvaux, for instance, was still living the life of a carefree and worldly youth, "the memory of his holy mother was always in his mind, so that he seemed to see her coming to him, reproaching and upbraiding him that she had not brought him up with such love and care that he could adopt this empty kind of existence." If by the standards of their time the success of these mothers was judged by the spiritual distinction of their children, we may consider remarkable, too, in view of contemporary prospects, the numbers of sons and daughters they succeeded in rearing to maturity. What is still more impressive, however, is the enduring devotion that some of them seem to have inspired. To this there is in the literature of this period no more eloquent testimony, not even Guibert's, than Peter the Venerable's epistolary portrait of his dead mother, in whose lovingly depicted life and character—she was not only saintly, compassionate and incessantly anxious for her children but "always happy and gay"—are reflected every facet of the contemporary maternal ideal.

By contrast with this emphasis on the maternal figure and her influence, fathers and their relations with their children assume a more modest and sometimes ambiguous place in our sources. If the father was not virtually absent from the child's early life, as he frequently was in a military and expansionist society, he is often depicted as the worldlier, less admirable figure, drawing the child away from his religious vocation, or more rarely, displaying the outright hostility that drove Anselm to renounce his patrimony and his native land and to find, at length, a more satisfactory father in Lanfranc at Bec. Among the records examined here, only briefly in Abelard's *Story of Calamities* and more fully in the life of St. Hugh of Lincoln is the early relationship of a father and son portrayed sympathetically and even in the latter there are distinct overtones of deprivation. For, "deprived of a mother's care" by her death, Hugh was barely eight years old when he and his father together entered a community of canons regular. As he himself later reported, in "talking confidentially" with his companions: "Truly, I never tasted the joys of this world. I never knew or learnt how to play." When Hugh was "learning to read," his father divided his patrimony by lot among his children, and gave the portion that fell to this youngest son to the community which he then entered by his father's choice. They evidently remained closely associated in their life there, and as his father grew old, Hugh devoted himself almost entirely to his care. According to this biographer, "he often used to relate with great pleasure how for the rest of his father's life, he used to lead him and carry him about, dress and undress him, wash him, dry him and make his bed, and, when he grew feebler and weaker, prepare his food and even feed him."

Although nearly all of the children with whom we are here concerned found their way eventually, like Hugh, into some form of the religious life, they did not all enter it so early or so involuntarily or by the same route. St. Anselm, for example, was perhaps twenty-seven when he became a monk at Bec, and Peter Damian was also in his twenties at the time of his conversion, as was Bernard of Clairvaux when he renounced the pleasures of the knightly life and eventually persuaded all of his brothers to do the same. Intended for a secular career, like many boys of whose childhood we know nothing, Ailred of Rievaulx, a priest's son, had served in his boyhood at the Scottish court before his conversion to the monastic life. But others, like Guibert, were much younger, often destined for this life from the outset and entering it as "oblates," children offered to monasteries by their parents, usually at an early age. It was such children as these who faced most acutely the separation and the exile poignantly recalled by Orderic Vitalis when as an old man he wrote . . . :

> And I, a mere boy, did not presume to oppose my father's wishes, but obeyed him in all things, for he promised me for his part that if I became a monk I should taste of the joys of Heaven with the Innocents after my death. . . . And so, a boy of ten, I crossed the English channel and came into Normandy as an exile, unknown to all, knowing no one.

When Orderic entered his Norman monastery in the late eleventh century, the practice of oblation was already on the wane, and its sharp decline during the next fifty years is yet another symptom of the transformations of this time. But for at least two centuries and perhaps longer, the offering of noble children by their parents had been a major, indeed, probably the principal means of monastic recruitment, and its history and the motives that inspired it are most revealing of the attitudes of parents as well as the experience of children during this period. Few aspects of this experience are, as Dom Knowles observes, more repellent to modern sensibility than the rearing of children "from infancy in the cloister, without home life, or the free society of other boys and girls, and without entry into many wide areas of innocent life." To us this custom may seem, in fact, the most distressing instance of child-rearing practices which, though diverse and variable over this long period, frequently involved, at least among the noble classes, the early separation of children from their parents and siblings. . . .

Entrusted to the care of masters, one of whom was to remain between every two boys wherever they went, they were always to sit apart from one another "in such a way as to prevent any physical contact, never making signs or speaking to anyone or rising from their places without the master's permission." In their relations with each other and with other monks they were not to hand anything to anyone or receive anything from anyone except the abbot, prior or masters and no one but these was ever to "make a sign to them or smile to them." None of the other monks was to enter their school or speak to them anywhere without the permission of the abbot or prior. In the dormitories, their beds were to be separated by those of their masters and often one of these was to keep watch throughout the night by the light of candles or lanterns; no child was ever to visit the lavatory or the latrine unaccompanied by a master.

Since, as at least one custumal put it, "children everywhere need custody with discipline," the children were not only beaten in their school and elsewhere, but in their own chapter, as the older monks were.

Plainly intended, among other things, to prevent sexual activities among the children and the development of dangerous intimacies with their elders, this rigorous watchfulness reflected, and no doubt enhanced, fears that were evidently well founded. Testimony to the facts and fantasies of sexual temptations of every variety abounds in the monastic sources of this period, which also invite serious reflection on the impact of this environment on young minds exposed to no other experience. The omnipresence of the Devil and his minions, the lurid visions and nightmares that might haunt their overcharged imaginations, are vividly described by Guibert of Nogent, among many others, and with perhaps greater penetration by his older contemporary, Otloh of Saint-Emmeram. Seeking self-understanding through the recording of his temptations, dreams and hallucinations, this extraordinary monk discloses with particular clarity how deeply he had been affected by the experiences of his childhood and youth and especially by his fear of beating, which fostered his own later belief in the moderate discipline of the young, with words rather than blows.

But no criticism of the abuses affecting children in monasteries is more revealing and significant than St. Anselm's admonition to a certain abbot who had complained to him of his difficulties in controlling the obstreperous boys in his charge, declaring that "we never give over beating them day and night, and they only get worse and worse." Even the barest summary of Anselm's remarkable answer may convey the import of an argument that not only underscores the weaknesses of a system, but offers an impressively positive statement of a new and more sympathetic approach to the rearing of children. Pointing to the destructive effects of the use of force and "injudicious oppression" upon the personalities of their young victims, Anselm declared that "feeling no love or pity, goodwill or tenderness in your attitude towards them, they have in future no faith in your goodness but believe that all your actions proceed from hatred and malice against them; they have been brought up in no true charity towards anyone, so they regard everyone with suspicion and jealousy." Then he demanded urging his benighted colleague to greater empathy, "Are they not human? Are they not flesh and blood like you? Would you like to have been treated as you treat them, and to have become what they are now?" Finally stressing, as did Peter Damian and others, the importance of firm but gentle molding and shaping in the rearing of the young, he insisted that they must have "the encouragement and help of fatherly sympathy and gentleness" and that teaching and discipline should be adapted to the temperaments and capacities of individuals. . . .

Concern for the physical care and training of young children becomes more articulate and specific in a growing number of didactic works of the thirteenth century; such treatises, displaying often also some sense of the needs of children at different stages of development, point to ways in which, with increasing literacy among laymen, more favorable values ad attitudes, as well as useful pediatric information, may have become more widely diffused, at least among the more prosperous classes. Despite the obvious limitations of these writings as mirrors of childhood realities, their popularity suggests a felt need for works offering guidance for parents, and while some of them reflect the clerical perspectives which have dominated this study, in others, more novel, parental views are directly stated.

Representing the churchman's approach, Bartholomew of England provides, in one of the earliest and most influential of popular encyclopedias, a precise description of the physical constitution, emotional qualities and habits of children, and conveys as well a now more articulate sense of early childhood as a carefree and playful stage of life. Little boys (*pueri*), he tells us, echoing a common though by no means universal opinion, are so called because of their "purity," since at this age the insufficient development of their organs makes then incapable of sexual activity and they are not ashamed of their nakedness. Despite their innocence, however, they are capable of guile and deceit, and so in need of discipline ad teaching. Painting what will seem to many a fairly lifelike picture of small boys, he describes them as "living without thought or care, loving only to play, fearing no danger more than being beaten with a rod, always hungry and hence always disposed to various infirmities from being overfed, wanting everything they see, quick to laughter and as quick to tears, resisting their mothers' efforts to wash and comb them, and no sooner clean but dirty again." Little girls, in Bartholomew's hardly original view, are better disciplined, more careful, more modest and timid, and more graceful; because of the likeness of sex they are also, he thought, dearer to their mothers than boys.

Strongly urging the careful education of girls in reading and writing, Vincent of Beauvais maintained that these pursuits would keep them busy and thus distracted from "harmful and idle thoughts." They should, in his view, be trained in the "womanly arts" as well as in letters, and both boys and girls should be carefully instructed in the duties and responsibilities of marriage. As a theorist of education and an adviser in the rearing of the young, this most zealous of medieval encyclopedists was not particularly original, but he drew on traditional and contemporary learning in the development of ideas that display a genuine concern for the actual needs and capacities of children at different stages of early life. Like his contemporary, Master Aldobrandino of Siena, Vincent repeats with slight variations the Soranian precepts concerning the physical care of children, ideas now readily accessible in learned circles. In a suggested regime for the young child, he provides for frequent baths, at least two daily, careful feeding and ample playtime; to similar recommendations Aldobrandino adds the advice that the child should be given what he asks for and relieved of what displeases him. When at six the child begins school, he should be taught slowly and without forcing, being allowed plenty of time for sleep and for diversion. With others among his fellow-clerics, Vincent of Beauvais advocates a moderation in instruction and discipline in which we may perceive the significant assimilation and diffusion of ideas expressed by St. Anselm and his contemporaries a century and a half earlier. Teaching without beating is the ideal commonly stated, although Vincent suggests that in the matter of discipline distinctions should be made between those children for whom physical coercion is unnecessary and disastrous and others whose temperaments seem to require it; even in this case discipline should never be sudden and unpremeditated but should spring from motives of love and foresight rather than a mistaken sense of kindness. It is poetically summed up, around 1200, by Walther von der Vogelweide:

> "Children won't do what they ought
> If you beat them with a rod.
> Children thrive, children grow
> When taught by words, and not a blow. . . .
> Evil words, words unkind
> Will do harm to a child's mind."

In some ways less enlightened are several works representing a paternal view of child-rearing, which may in their stress on the importance of discipline and correction provide a closer reflection of the actual practice of parents. For the elderly Philip of Novara, the infant and small child possess three great gifts: he loves and recognizes the person who nurses him, he expresses pleasure and affection for those who play with him, and he inspires a natural love and sympathy in those who rear him. Like the great Jewish philosopher, Moses Maimonides, in the preceding century, this father believed that parental love increases as children grow older, but he cautioned strongly against the excessive and indulgent display of affection, which may encourage children to be bolder in their naughtiness. They should not be permitted to do everything they wish, but should be firmly corrected while they are young, first with words, then if necessary, by beating, and as a last resort by "imprisonment." Parents and their surrogates should, he advised, be especially watchful for early signs of tendencies to such vices as theft, violence and blasphemy which may lead the child to a bad end. . . .

Some Concluding Reflections

If a central issue of this history, abstractly viewed, has been the enduring conflict between destructive or rejecting and fostering attitudes, this issue was stated with extraordinary, almost prophetic clarity in John of Lodi's story of Peter Damian's early years. Throughout our period and beyond, it is true, the power of destructive forces may seem little diminished. Certainly, the fundamental menace of infant and maternal mortality continued, apparently unabated; here there was to be little substantial progress before the early years of our own century. The neglect, exploitation and abandonment of children continued also, but these practices were now more widely and consciously opposed and in efforts at control or suppression, however immeasurable their effects, may be discerned clear signs of the awakening consciences and sensibilities of this time. The idea of the child as the possession and property of its parents continued to dominate parental attitudes and actions in these, as in earlier and later centuries. But the dangers inherent in this conception had achieved wider recognition and the salutary intervention of external authorities had made some modest advances. The proprietary notion had also been joined by more favorable conceptions, by a sense of the child as a being in its own right, as a nature of "potential greatness," and by a sense of childhood as a distinctive and formative stage of life. That churchmen should have been pre-eminently active in the diffusion of more humane attitudes and ideas is, given the character of medieval society, hardly surprising. Nor is the fact that attempts to translate law and precept into practice were in this sphere, as in many others, faltering and often ineffective. The fostering role of churchmen as pastors and preachers, reformers and surrogates, has been noted in this study, but it deserves more coherent and critical attention, in the setting of contemporary spiritual and religious movements, than it could be given here.

Clearly, as the cases of Anselm and Hugh of Lincoln suggest, in many matters affecting the lives of children the example ad influence of a few great figures may have counted for a good deal, not least in giving powerful expression to the new impulses and currents of feeling whose growing strength is displayed in numerous works of this period, among them the two with which we began. In Guibert of Nogent's recollections of his early life, a new awareness is written large; and if he offers us our fullest insight into the realities of childhood during these centuries, he also draws us most deeply into that world of ambivalence and wishful thinking which encompasses the relations of parents and children, introducing us to what appear to have been, in both fact and fantasy, certain dominant experiences of many children in this time. Among the many great changes that emerged during the century and more spanned by the lifetimes of Peter Damian and Guibert, none was more profound than the slow transformation in modes of consciousness and expression with which the relationships and experiences of childhood were inextricably bound up. Tenderness, compassion, the capacity to comprehend the needs and emotions of others: these are fragile and late-maturing plants of feeling and they flowered slowly in the hard and sometimes violent lives of this period, especially in the lives of parents who were themselves often literally, as well as emotionally, little more than children. Yet it is in this realm of feeling that the most deeply rooted and fruitful developments of our centuries are likely to be found.

Religion of the People
in the Thirteenth-Century

ALEXANDER MURRAY

The Church of the Middle Ages grew slowly during the first millennium of Christian Europe. In the first century, the Apostles and their assistants spread out through the Roman empire establishing Christian communities in its great cities. At the end of the third century, the bishops emerged as the successors of the Apostles and as the rulers of the Christian communities. These leaders patterned their government of the Church on the imperial system established by the Roman emperor Diocletian (284–305). The diocese and its bishop became the basic unit of ecclesiastical organization. From the reign of Constantine on, the great decisions concerning the life of the Church—the definition of its faith and the establishment of its discipline—were made in general councils of bishops.

In the early Church, each bishop had a *familia*, a group of helpers whose functions were gradually differentiated to form the clerical orders of the Church and who administered the diocese under the bishop's direction. The *familia* lived with the bishop in the city, but as the Church made progress in converting the population of the countryside, the *familia* divided into two groups. One group continued to help the bishop in the diocesan administration, while the other spent an increasing amount of its time in the outlying areas, preaching and ministering to the peasants.

This episcopal system was very successful. In many respects the medieval Church was made up of a patchwork of independent dioceses, each administered by a clergy with strong ties to the local population. But there were centralizing as well as decentralizing elements in the ecclesiastical institutions. The unity of doctrine and liturgical practice, which was so important to the Church, was matched by a need for uniformity in the structure of the clergy and in the law governing its behavior. This need for uniformity required that a central institution be developed to maintain it against the centrifugal forces of localism.

In the first two centuries after the Roman imperial household became Christian, ecumenical councils, summoned by the emperor, provided the means for maintaining the unity of the Church. As legislative bodies, the councils succeeded well in stating the unified creed and the general principles of ecclesiastical organization and practice. But they could not ensure that the conciliar statements would be put into effect. For this purpose, the Church needed central administrative and judicial authority, and in respect of this need, the bishops in Rome, Constantinople, Alexandria, Jerusalem, and Antioch—all of which claimed to have succeeded to the authority of one or more of the original Apostles—jostled for primacy. The success of Rome in this contest resulted both in the division of authority between the bishops of the dioceses and the pope and in the split between the eastern and western Churches.

These developments took centuries. In the eleventh century, when a party of reform gained control of the papacy, papal power really began to dominate the Church. The period starting in the eleventh century was also one of population growth and urbanization in Europe. The size of the clergy grew to meet the needs of the increasing population, but by the late twelfth century the Church could hardly keep pace with those needs, and heresy became a major problem throughout western Christendom.

The foundation and development of the orders of friars, the Franciscans and the Dominicans, was one of the results of these changes in the population. St. Francis and St. Dominic sought to combat heresy by sending preachers out among the people, and it soon became clear that it was in the urban centers that these preachers would flourish and do the most good. The new religious orders operated under the direct authority of the papacy; they undermined the independent authority of the bishops and of their clergy—and consequently had a significant effect on the constitutional history of the Church. However, for us, they are most interesting because they had to cope with the popular religion of their time. The mendicants, as the friars were called, preached to the masses. To do so, they needed to know their audience. In the following selection, Alexander Murray reveals the religious character of that audience, using a manual that a leading thirteenth-century Dominican wrote for his preaching brethren.

B_y 1277 the Dominican order probably counted some 5,000–10,000 members. The training of young preachers could not be left to mere word of mouth. Handbooks *De arte predicandi* were accordingly written; and some of them still feature among the remnants of convent libraries. From the thirteenth-century phase of the literature, it happens that one of these survivals recommends itself to us particularly. Its recommendation is a simple one: it was designed specifically for 'out-of-season' preaching. Free from the rhetoric and other accidents of the ordinary public sermon, its business is to tell us directly, as if in the classroom, about the religious and moral vagaries of the layfolk young Dominicans had to preach to.

The least inaccessible printed edition of this work, or part of it, gives it the title: *'De modo prompte cudendi sermones'*: 'How to Sew a Sermon Together Quickly.' The title has no greater authority than any of the various others that appear in earlier versions, except that it is appropriate, and has gained more currency than the others among specialists who have noticed the work. The compilation as a whole, including the unprinted

From Alexander Murray, "Religion among the Poor in thirteenth-Century France: The Testimony of Humbert of Romans," *Traditio* Vol. 30 (1974), pp. 287–90, 292–96, 298–306, 317–23.

parts, was presented in four books. Their order is not the same in all versions, so it would be confusing to number them. All consist of sketches for sermons. The sketches are presented obliquely, as to a pupil preacher, with imperative and gerundive: 'remember to say this,' or 'that should be noted.' What distinguishes each book is that it categorises sermons in its own way. One does it by feasts ('For a patron saint'; 'Mary Magdalene or Similar'; 'The Dedication of a Church,' etc); another by 'times' ('Any Day'; 'Any Sunday'; 'Palm Sunday'). In practice these classification systems overlap, and doubtless this was one reason why neither the author nor subsequent copyists seem to have felt much enthusiasm for these two books. Both together add up to fewer pages than either of the others separately, and they were left out of five of the seven known manuscripts, and out of all printed versions. The remaining two books are, by contrast, self-confident, as to both plan and scale. One arranges its sermon sketches according to the various conditions and professions of men and women ('To Cistercians'; 'To Rich Women in Towns'; 'To Young Girls,' etc); the other, by places and events which invite sermons ('Elections'; 'Fairs'; 'Embarkations'). Each of these two books runs to a hundred chapters, and takes some eighty pages of manuscript. It was mainly these two books which earned the work a certain modest celebrity in preaching circles during the late-Middle Ages. And when the age of printing came, the two long books enjoyed a total of three editions, the last being in Lyons in 1677, as part of volume twenty-five of the *Maxima bibliotheca veterum patrum*.

The work's author—whose identity was once for a brief moment in doubt, but is no longer—was the Dominican, Humbert de Romans. The second part of that name derives from a small town or village in the Rhône valley where Humbert was born about 1200. According to his early Dominican biographer, he qualified in arts and canon law in Paris University, and then, in his early twenties, took what was then the eccentric course for a well-born young man (which he was) of joining the new preachers' order, still in its first flush of evangelical fervour. Like some other seemingly eccentric youths, Humbert soon floated up into dizzy prominence. He was head of his convent in Lyons in 1237, and of the central Italian province of Dominicans from 1238 to 1240. He may even have been mooted for pope, during the vacancy eventually filled by Innocent IV in 1243. Instead of that, he became—just as the Dominicans were coming to the height of their influence—head of the order, in 1254. Humbert's direct importance for us nevertheless does not lie in all these dignities. It lies in what he did when he had put them aside. After some thirty years of office-holding, he said goodbye to public life in 1263 (apparently on grounds of ill-health), and spent his last fourteen years— from then until 1277—writing his tracts and homilies on divers topics of churchmen's concern: councils, reform, the crusade and, not least, the teaching of preachers.

Humbert's Sermon Book—as I shall call it—belongs to this last period. If it was written all at once, as seems likely, it dates from between 1270 and 1274. So its writer cannot be accused of inexperience. One reason why he might have been ill in his sixties was that leading Dominicans often had to travel literally thousands of miles annually, mostly on foot: Humbert had visited London, Barcelona, Naples, and the city we call Budapest, as well, of course, as many places between, and including a full five years in Italy. How much further even than all this Humbert's horizons went is shown by his crusading and missionary interests, and his promotion of schools to teach preachers Greek, Hebrew, and Arabic. These were nevertheless vague horizons (as is apparent when he writes on Saracens). For all his physical and mental wanderings, the centre of Humbert's experience remained France. Paris and Lyons between them, with adjacent areas, account for a known forty years of his life, and probably more unknown ones. His Latin appears to have a southeastern dialect of French behind it. On the rare occasions when the Sermon Book specifies national practices, it is German or Italian practices it specifies, as if its readers did not belong to those nations. The manuscript tradition shows, certainly, that the work had an appeal outside France, notably in Germany. But that was when all things French were spreading there anyway. . . .

Towns, meanwhile, were even more socially mobile and complex than the countryside. Late thirteenth-century France possessed over 500 officially recognised 'towns.' Only a few were giants comparable with modern cities: Paris at their head, with a population in 1300 perhaps over 100,000. Yet more than a score (Humbert's Lyons one of them) would each have had a population well into the thousands. In all there were big gaps between rich and poor: bigger, probably, the bigger the town was. A shifting patriciate would own most non-church property. (In the bourg of Toulouse in 1335, as we happen to know, 7½ per cent of the population owned about 60 per cent of the town's real estate.) Below this summit stretched three graded hierarchies, often interjoining: of traders, professionals, and artisans (i.e. tailors, carpenters, etc.). The poor, by any standards, began towards the base of all three hierarchies. The bulky base of the hierarchies, especially the small traders and artisans, would have made a significant proportion of that urban mass which, while not abounding in wealth, usually had a roof and food—or let their rulers know about it. Artisans are known to have made up a third of Paris' taxable population in about 1290.

We know that fact, and others about those three hierarchies, through tax-returns; and all classes in tax returns had a certain amount of property.

Their title to be called 'poor' was weakened in that particular. But below them were as many again, perhaps two or three times as many, with too little property to tax. Many of these were dependents, or servants in richer men's households. The biggest single group was probably wage-earners. A recent study of Paris wage-earners allows us to picture their life, and hence gauge for ourselves how miserable or otherwise it was, about 1300. Despite variations in conditions and wages—the highest about three times the lowest—an average worker's day can be reconstructed: to work at dawn ('when a Paris penny can be distinguished from a Tours penny'), stop for a lunch-hour at nine and a dinner-hour at one (both meals taken at the master's table), home at dusk. A lucky wage-earner would sleep in his own house or room, a less lucky one in a garret, quite possibly shared, at the top of a three- or four-storied house. The burden of their nine- to fourteen-hour day was relieved by many holidays. What with half-days and a month for the harvest in August these brought the average working-week down to about four and a half days.

One feature Humbert de Romans himself adds to this portrait of wage-earners (he says it of small traders too) is that many of them spent too much of their earnings in pubs, especially on holidays. So, he says, they both stay poor, and take nothing home to their wives and children. While these wage-earners were certainly 'poor,' therefore, at least by literary usage, and though the life of many was arduous, even dangerous, we must balk the temptation to equate them as such with the indigent. Humbert gives more than one hint in the other direction. A man with a paid job in town may well have been (as in some modern underdeveloped countries) more envied than pitied by his acquaintances. Only the bottom boundary of this class would live near the hunger-line, and need other income—from thieving or beggary—to survive. This bottom boundary covered single women, whose wages we know to have fluctuated at about half the men's level: a plight which was unquestionably one cause of the prostitution we shall be meeting later on.

Who the other dwellers on the hunger-line were, i.e. *pauperes* in the narrowest sense, can be roughly learned from a list of them made in mid-century. The list was designed to settle a dispute about who did and did not deserve to benefit from the period's decentralised social welfare system. It lays down who may beg. The working class is represented by— besides the person paid below subsistence level—the unwillingly unemployed, and apprentices until they have learned a trade. Some more illustrious beggars are there: [the] decayed gentleman; and persons writing or reading, or even fighting, for expressly Christian purposes. More familiar, however, than any of these able-bodied beggars, were the sick and old. The wretched condition of the former, when without private means, is a topic on which Humbert is eloquent when he speaks of hospitals, and of lepers in leper-houses;—the job of nursing whom is so little recommended by its natural pleasantness, he says, that among many thousands of people, only the smallest handful will be found prepared to take the job on. As for poor old age, one of Humbert's best-informed contemporaries called it a condition 'bitterer than winter with all its cold,' and named it as a not infrequent cause of premature death.

In the country, the poorer peasantry; in towns, small shopkeepers, artisans and wage-earners. These were the poor, in the largest sense, of late-thirteenth-century France. At the bottom edge of these classes and below them were persons poor by a narrower standard: a medley of men and women kept alive only by lawbreaking or charity. What, now, can Humbert tell us of religion, or lack of it, among all these 'poor'?

Like all medieval divines, Humbert drew his first social division along a line more important to him than any economic distinctions. The basic split (occasion, in some people's eyes, of an ageless class struggle) was that, not between rich and poor, but between clergy and laity. Our business is with the laity. Lower clergy and monastic *conversi*, certainly, were often from poor families, and only in the church for a living (a motive Humbert makes a charge against them). Some clergy, too, stood in sharp financial need, not least the self-induced need of the mendicants: Humbert himself would have eaten, travelled and slept for most of his life much like a manual worker. Clergy, nevertheless, however poor their origin or present condition, remained a special case, both economically and religiously. So they will be left out. . . .

For all that a thirteenth-century peasant or labourer was illiterate, and lived—as some academics (not Dominicans) pointed out with a shudder—a life not far removed from that of animals, the Christian doctrine Humbert had learned in Paris unfalteringly declared every man's dignity as a rational being. Men were not merely to obey the commandments of Scripture, but to appreciate and act according to the natural law of which their reason told them. Christianity, said Humbert—who was not much more meticulous than other Christians of his time when writing about non-Christian religions—was peculiar among world religious in that it demanded the avoidance of sin not only in act, but in thought. All this applied to every Christian, rich and poor; and indeed some of it applied to all human beings.

That the ordinary Christian was rational did not, however, entail stiff demands on his intellect. His mind taught him the difference between good and evil, goods of the body and of the soul, of Creator and creation: that was common to all men. As a Christian he should 'know the nature of Christ.' But this last obligation was to be understood at its simplest level. The layman should not 'scrutinise the secrets of the faith . . . but adhere to them implicitly.' It was the clergy's job to do any scrutinizing there was to be, and all the layman had to do was show proper respect for the clergy, and content himself with their teaching. In terms of actual homework, what the simple layman had to know by heart was a trio of simple prayer-formulas: the 'Our Father,' the 'Hail Mary,' and the Creed. This trio appears so often both in Humbert's book, and in various records of instruction designed for the illiterate during the late Middle Ages, that it can be accepted as the basic ingredient in the church's recipe for them.

The poor layman's obligation as to observance was similarly simple. He must be baptised. It was desirable, too, that he should be able, in an emergency, to baptize other people: the formula for doing so was made simple specially so that everyone could learn it. (There were no limits to who could baptize: young or old, man or woman, good or wicked). The reforming council of 1215, held at a time when Humbert was just starting at university, had laid down that all laymen should make a confession to a priest, and take communion once per year. Humbert was content to repeat this modest requirement, though he pointed out that it was a minimum. As for other kinds of church attendance, laymen were enjoined to attend church on Sundays and Feast Days. They should also, every day, say the three prayer-formulas a certain number of times.

In morals, finally, the layman was urged to—in this order—acquire a wife and stay faithful to her; bring up his children virtuously; do charitable acts towards his neighbour; and give alms according to his means:—even the poor man should share his little generously. Man was by nature —our scholastic repeated—a kindly animal, and Christians, who worshipped a God of mercy, should look for occasions of doing merciful acts.

These, in theory, were the obligations of every Christian—as to knowledge, observance, and moral conduct. They were to apply universally. They come together in one place, where we can watch them, as it were, incarnate. Humbert cites the ideal self-portrait (from a current miracle-story) of the Christian peasant:

> I am a peasant, and live by my own labour. By God's grace, I have never know woman except my wife. I have kept myself from harming my neighbour, and I have never let my oxen stray over someone else's field without first putting bits in their mouths to prevent them from eating what other people have sown. Each morning, before I go to work, I call in at the church to pray; and on my homeward journey I call in again, to thank God for all that has happened to me that day.

That guileless boast can summarise for us Humbert's religious ideal for the poor man. Happy those peasants—he adds—who lead such a life!

The question is, how many did?—among thirteenth-century peasants and their urban brethren? In practice, all three aspects of the church's demands, in knowledge, observance and morals, met with widely varying degrees of acceptance. It is Humbert who says so, and the evidence he gives can appropriately be reviewed under each of the three heads in turn.

The whole idea of sending out poorly-dressed preachers into the streets was to teach people who would otherwise be ignorant. The very existence of our sermon book is therefore evidence for some ignorance up to the time of its composition. It is scarcely astonishing, then, that many people Humbert recommends to his pupil-preachers as likely audiences he recommends on these precise grounds. Some popular ignorance touched one or other particular article of faith. Persons who think baptism can be performed with wine, or another liquid, says Humbert, are to be enlightened. Again, the faithful are not to imagine that the Eucharist is a mere figure of Christ's body: it would not be spoken of with such awe in the New Testament if it were only that. These erring faithful—who are merely simple, and to be distinguished from heretics (whose similar view has a graver origin)—must be taught the proper doctrine. Yet popular ignorance went deeper than such *technicalia*. It could touch Christian doctrine *en bloc*. The chronically sick, for instance, Humbert described as ill-placed to attend functions where they might learn something, and thus 'a very large number of such people are very simple, since they rarely hear God spoken of.' But it was not just the sick. Of wage-labourers, Humbert says: 'many of this sort are profoundly ignorant of matters, pertaining to their salvation.' The same went for 'the poor' in general, who 'know little of what pertains to their salvation.'

One reason why these 'poor' knew little of their salvation was that they rarely came to church: *raro veniunt ad Ecclesiam.* What *raro* meant for Humbert is hard to gauge. The statutory one communion per year, as he and most of his colleagues agreed, was a somewhat desperate minimum, due to the 'perversity' of the age, and out of keeping with the practice of the early church. Yet even the statutory minimum was something: *inter alia* a chance for preachers to catch spiritual fish. We hear Humbert advising disciples to take the chance, at a general communion, or a baptism. He speaks here of *magna multitudo*, or *multi*: so some of the people, we must allow, must have come to church for some of the time. But that it was not enough people, for enough of the time, is clear from the exceptions Humbert speaks of. He only twice uses the word 'never' in this connection: about servants who follow wicked masters 'in never coming to church,' and about lepers, who 'never come to sermons with others.' 'Rare' attendance, by contrast, was a prevalent failing. In notes showing how to preach at the dedication of a church, Humbert puts this first among the abuses 'which many people are guilty of towards churches. For there are some who, though bound by the church's mandates to attend church at certain times, nevertheless extremely rarely come there, either at those times or otherwise.' (The same superlative, *rarissime*, is even applied to clergy; 'there are some clergy who extremely rarely come to church'). Specific jobs are occasionally mentioned, besides 'the poor' generally. Women servants in the households of the rich 'can rarely go to church, and hear the church's instruction.' This applies generally to rich men's households: 'this type of household, because of various occupations, is rarely accustomed to convene at church, except perhaps at the great feasts, and then it is only for morning mass.' In the country, peasants were to be urged, among other things, to 'come to their church at the proper times,' as if they sometimes did not. But the accusation was more emphatic among some townsmen. The violation of feast-days by work—a charge made against both traders and labourers—might not necessarily entail non-attendance at church. But Humbert makes this consequence explicit in respect of weekly local markets. When a market is held on a feast day, 'wretched men, leaving aside divine service, leaving aside the sermon, and sometimes neglecting to hear the church's mandates, frequently defy the church's ban by attending such markets.'

But suppose people did come to church. Even then, much of the world's dirt, neglect, and noisy sacrilege was to be found transferred there. The dirt was literal. In two sermon sketches Humbert refers, obliquely, to churches whose pastors fail to clean God's house properly: pigs, dogs, and such animals wander around in them, leaving a corresponding mess. But the more serious pollution was human. Some people made an effort at church attendance, but not enough, or of the wrong sort. Among those who made not enough were attenders who 'leave so quickly that they scarcely wait for the end of mass.' Others attended physically, but 'carry nothing away with them but words,' saying 'the spoken office was good' or 'the sermon was good'; and so on. 'Such people are like those who climb laden fruit-trees, and fetch down nothing but leaves.' A form of misplaced effort equally recognisable to modern readers was to be found, in country churches, in the idiosyncratic pieties of peasant women.

> Some are so undevout to God's word that when they are in a church where a sermon is being preached, now they talk, now they say their prayers, now they stay kneeling in front of images, now they cross themselves with holy water. They can scarcely be prevailed on to come towards the preacher and leave their usual spots.

The indignation of a graduate from the big city, finding his wise words ignored, will be easily understood.

But the graduate had far worse than conservative peasant women to deal with. Ordinary conduct in a full church was often such that the devout had little chance of concentration. 'Some people while in church simply indulge in empty chatter. . . . Some do worse, by making a tumult, so that others are prevented from hearing the office or saying their prayers. . . . Others again sometimes do business transactions there, or other secular work. . . . And some desecrate the church by using physical violence there.' Doing business in church may, perhaps, have been just one more sign of that mixing of holy and secular which the Middle Ages are famous for. But tumults were another matter. The worst occasion for them, paradoxically, was that of the vigils for some saints' days. There was a practice, for which Humbert was at most lukewarm, that parishioners stayed up at night before the feast. Things had come a long way from the early church, he said, when such vigils were piously kept. Now, some people

> spend all night in noise, stopping others from concentrating on God. Instead of speaking themselves to God, in prayer, they pass the night gossiping to each other, not only about vain subjects, but about evil and indecent ones. They should be listening carefully to godly matters, but instead sing frivolous, wordly songs.

Humbert more than once suggests, too, that indecency often went beyond the sphere of mere talking and singing. 'Some people, on some vigils, when they gather at a church, make a practice of spending their time in all sorts of singing and dancing, and sometimes in sins. They are like Saracens,' adds Humbert—who may have seen Frederick II's Saracen soldiers in Italy, and whose low view of Saracen morals was one fairly widely shared in the West—'who spend their fast-days in lust, drunkenness, and all that sort of wickedness.'

Attendance at church, and behaving properly there, naturally played a big part in the unsophisticated layman's religion. But they were not all of it. Times, for one thing, as well as places, were set apart for God. Apart from what you might do or not do in church on a holy day, there were plenty of other ways you could violate it. Feast days were an ideal, widely agreed to in practice for physical and psychological reasons, as holidays (Humbert himself gives as the first reason for their institution 'the relief of human infirmity: since if working men did not rest sometimes their life would be intolerable'). But from an ecclesiastical point of view the days were nearly as much loss as gain. It was not just that those labourers and merchants sometimes went on working, or even that markets were sometimes deliberately arranged for feast days. Work, or some kinds of work, at least had the merit of keeping people from mischief. The real trouble came with leisure, and what was done with it. 'Some indulge in games and pleasures, and all that sort of amusement, on these holy days. These turn God's feast into a feast of the world. . . . Others go in for excessive eating and drinking, and other such things belonging to carnal pleasure. . . . Others still, and this is worse, sin more on these days than at other times. . . . The devil exults in such people' The only parties to gain by the proliferation of saints' days, Humbert once confessed, were innkeepers and prostitutes.

Apart from his respect for sacred places and times there were private observances the layman was expected to maintain. If our Paris-trained Dominican had more interest in psychology than some thirteenth-century churchmen, he was nevertheless, like them, still mainly interested in the more tangible of these observances. While he only briefly touches on persons who 'rarely pray during the day' (in a sermon-sketch for 'any day'), he is eloquent on the neglect of penance or fasting. As for penance, and apart from the case of sinners who neither know nor care about their sin and so never bother with penance, there are many others who are

> terrified of penance, because of the penalties involved, like baring their bodies, giving back other people's property, leaving off their sin, accepting the customary penalty, and such like. So they do not dare to come to penance. . . . Many, again, having begun doing penance, get bored with it, because they find it unpalatable . . . and many leave off a penance they have begun.

It was the same with fasting. Humbert's remarks on fast-breaking, like those on neglect of penance, make no class distinctions. A reference to 'gluttons who so often break fasts, stuffing themselves with wines and fine foods' might be thought to have no place in a study of the poor. But the very absence of distinctions in Humbert should warn us, for our part, against seeing any. (Wine was no luxury in thirteenth-century France— though it would have been in England.) Much of what Humbert says could in fact apply to anyone above the hunger line, who put himself among those 'who scorn to keep the prescribed fasts, taking food now here, now there, now fruit, now something else.'. . .

The poor were given a simple religion to understand, and to practise, both in observance and morals. Some of them came up to expectation, some fell short: often a long way short. Can we speak, then, of the offenders as having been 'irreligious'? The description certainly cannot apply to the poor as a class, either in town or country. Humbert himself, despite all I have quoted—one-sidedly—states in his chapter on 'The Popular Crowd in Cities' that, for all its gullibility and fickleness, the crowd is peculiarly devout and zealous for Christ. They 'are more devoted to God's word, so that the seed of the word does not so easily perish in them.' The crowd has what Humbert calls the *facultas fidei*: in the Gospel, it characteristically believed Jesus more easily than its social superiors did. All this is said of the crowd specifically in cities. Since in another chapter Humbert says cities are *more* sinful than other places, his general impression of the peasantry is unlikely to have been any worse.

All this popular devoutness left room nevertheless for considerable reservations. Certain practices, one feels on reading Humbert's account, had a momentum of their own which the sophisticated Dominican would not have started if he had had the choice: like those vigils for saints, and peasant women's attachment to images. Humbert in one place mentions devotions performed in the name of the Holy Spirit—confraternities formed for it, theories devised about it, special celebrations, and offices sung for it—which often, he says, lack any actual inspiration from the Spirit. His views on pilgrimages, too, are ambivalent. Pilgrimages offered great advantages. But they could also be occasions for sin: more sin, sometimes, than a participant committed in all the rest of the year put together. These reservations were not only Humbert's. Tension between the mendicant orders and some popular devout practices is in evidence about this time from other parts of Europe.

Pseudo-devotion, empty of spirit, nevertheless touched only the periphery of Humbert's misgivings about popular religion. There were worse things: in particular, misbelief. I do not refer now to any formal heresy: heresy has had its historians, and Humbert refers to heresy remarkably little, in fact, for a contemporary of the Albigensian crusade. Among the poor it was another kind of misbelief that most troubled him. He speaks of it as the first among faults found commonly in peasant women. 'They are normally much prone to sortilege,' he says; 'they practise it either on their own behalf, or for some other reason: for their children when they are sick; or for their animals, so that wolves do not catch them, and so on. . . . Some use this kind of divination for personal profit. . . . Some are so obstinate, nay even incorrigible, that they simply cannot be stopped, either by excommunications, or by any other kind of threat.'

In the next century the heat of this particular battle would be raised, on both sides, and send a sour incense through the air of early modern Europe. In Humbert's day the battle against witchcraft was less intense. One reason is that this battle was no more than one aspect of an attempt by reformers, founded on what they had learned in Paris and other universities, to rationalise Christian practice in general. Old women's spells were only one of an array of dubious practices, many of them still ill-distinguished from Christian orthodoxy. Trial by ordeal, which Humbert refers to as a thing of the past, had only formally been knocked on the head by the council of 1215, and we know that practices akin to it were still much alive. Humbert himself tells us that the use of divination at criminal trials was still practised by 'many of the less faithful.' For his own part, too, our author evinces a trace of that equivocal view of the occult which has long perplexed students of medieval writers: he calmly points out, for instance, that necromancy (the conjuring of the dead) has at least this one virtue among its many evils, that it helps prove man's corporeal immortality.

Divination and its divers ugly sisters appear from one angle as a kind of alternative religion to Christianity, feeble and unsystematic as that religion might be. From another, they may be said—if such a short cut through the realms of M. Lévi-Strauss is allowable—to have represented a materialism in belief, parallel to the practical materialisms already spoken of. Humbert more than once refers to materialistic declensions from right belief; in the undertaking of pilgrimages, for instance, from curiosity to see physical things, or in devotions to the holy spirit which *lack* the Holy Spirit. In trouble, Humbert says in another place, some people turn, not to God, but to things that money will buy: such as 'to doctors in illness, to lawyers in dispute, or to soldiers in war, all of which can be had for money.' All such resort to material things, rather than to God, had some conceptual affinities with witchcraft; and in fact Humbert mentions reliers on money and reliers on magic in the same paragraph.

Like bad morals, all this bad belief was a derogation from Christian precept. So we cannot be surprised to find, corresponding with these positive vagaries, some negative areas in people's Christian belief. Negative attitudes to church authority are already a familiar feature of late medieval church history. Humbert occasionally has something to say about them. He speaks of contempt for excommunication, by people who continue going to church in spite of it, or—these are 'innumerable'—who have social intercourse with excommunicates. He refers once, indirectly, to reluctance to pay tithes; and, more directly, to people who blame the poor state of church government on bad bishops. Humbert adds a dimension to his picture of anticlericalism by entering it himself, as peacemaker—deftly telling critics on the one hand they might attend more profitably to their own sins, while bidding church authorities, for their part, keep their house in order, and be extra strict with delinquent clergy, punishing them publicly.

Beyond any mere anticlericalism, or neglect of the church's authority, there are occasional signs of more deeply dissentient attitudes to religion. A strict judge might read these signs already in blasphemy, which French sources tell us was fairly endemic among the common people, especially (apparently) in the hilly southeast. Humbert speaks of the embittered blasphemies of some of the less contented poor, and of lepers, who curse God for their condition. The chronic, needless imprecations of traders at weekly markets are exemplified *verbatim*. ('By God,' says one, 'I will not give so much for it!' 'By God,' rejoins the other, 'I'll not let you have it for less.' 'By God,' the first returns, 'it is not worth so much!' By God, it *is* worth so much.' So they go on.') 'Swear not at all,' the puritan enjoins.

The psychological relationship of blasphemy to religion is a subtle one, and not necessarily negative. It need not be discussed now. For there are in fact less equivocal signs of negative attitudes to religion in Humbert's milieu. Some reveal mere indifference. Certain people, we learn, 'caught up in worldly ambitions, scarcely ever during the day lift their thoughts towards God.' Death, we might think—in view of all those horrible deaths people died in the Middle Ages, and the preoccupation of some schools of art with the subject—might have brought such people to their senses. But apparently it did not. 'Some people, although they think occasionally of death, nevertheless envisage it as a long way away. So they stay unprepared, in that they fail to accumulate good works and, worse, expose themselves to evil, all because they hope to be able to repent, secretly promising themselves a long life. A study of the Old Testament shows, says Humbert, that the 120-year life-expectation of the patriarchs was forfeited by mankind after the Flood, because of sin. Modern men cannot hope to live so long, Humbert feels it necessary to insist—even where nature is left to work alone. (In the light of certain orthodoxies about the shortness of medieval life expectation, we may accuse Humbert of understating his case here. But contemporary Florentine evidence suggests that not a few people in preachers' audiences there —which excluded babies, it should be remembered—did actually expect, rightly or wrongly, to live to 60 or even 80.) Elsewhere, Humbert draws attention to the likelihood of accidents. He does so with the same urgency: since some men and women 'fail to reflect what a small number or people, during their life, escape the world's dangers.' The very people you would expect to have thought most of human frailty often ignored it. Many seafarers, says Humbert, though their lives could scarcely be in greater peril, often behaved as if the opposite were the case. This, he argues, 'is either because they despair of their salvation, or because they hold their souls of no account, having received them in vain.' The same recklessness was to be found among some lepers in leper houses. In Humbert's eyes they seemed to be saying, crazily, to God: '"You have taken away my body from me. I will take my soul from you."'

Some people seemed indifferent, then, to God and death. But Christian doctrine could also be repudiated in a more technical sense. The repudiation might be merely implied. Some wretches, Humbert says, 'turn away their ears' when Christ is spoken of. There are 'many,' similarly, who 'do little or nothing for the Gospel. For they do not rise in church when it is read, or take off their headdress, sign themselves, or kiss the stone, or wood, or earth, or anything like that. For they seem not to believe the Gospel, when they are neither enticed by its promises, nor deterred by its threats.' Others, again, 'are actually . . . ashamed of what the Gospel commands.'

Yet behind all such mere implications there are hints, too, of a more express dissent. Humbert speaks once or twice against *infideles,* in the present tense, in a manner suggesting he means Westerners, not Saracens. The actual content of such disbelief is also hinted at. A key doctrine, distinguishing believers from unbelievers, was that of human immortality, and more particularly that of the body's resurrection. Observers of the

Italian scene in Humbert's time report that some people denied these doctrines (observing, for instance, that 'man dies like an ox'), and as often as not expressly coupled their denial with one of God's existence. Humbert, too, for his part, refers to the denial of immortality. While he calls it a doctrine of the ancients, he still takes the trouble to rebut it at length, in the present tense, as if it were a living issue. 'This error,' he writes, 'is the worst of all errors. It destroys almost all the articles of faith, and gives men occasion to expose themselves to all evil, and lose hold of all good.' In another passage Humbert employs the same tense about *infideles* who 'are very unhappy when their beloved ones die. This is because they do not believe they will live after this life. The faithful, he insists, 'should not behave thus.'

This evidence for unbelief, while far from negligible in itself, nevertheless has one shortcoming for our present purpose. It does not refer explicitly to the poor. None of it comes in the part of Humbert's work divided by social categories, nor is any hint given of the culprits' social position. Humbert's allusion elsewhere to the relative ease the poor found in believing what they were told, and the absence of express unbelief in the fairly detailed lists of their religious vagaries, forbid our seeing unbelief as a special peculiarity of the lower classes.

Fear and Prejudice in Medieval Society

MALCOLM BARBER

In the Middle Ages, communities were well-defined, and people were constantly conscious of belonging to them. The village communities were defined by their territories, by the genealogies of their leading families, and by their relationships to the local lords. The cities, while they grew rapidly from the eleventh century on, maintained a communal coherence by developing central municipal government and by building walls. Within these localities, parishes and other religious institutions united people in long-standing associations. On the grand scale, the kingdoms and the Church provided the medieval population with communality—in one case, focused on the monarchy, in the other, on the creed.

The feeling of belonging to a community and the importance of the feeling were enhanced by Christian ideas about what would happen in the last days of the world, when Christ came again. Before the end, there would be a great battle between the followers of Christ and the followers of the Antichrist, which would cleanse the Church—the body of Christ as it was often called—of the false Christians in preparation for the second coming of Christ. The power of these ideas was demonstrated when the crusades began in 1095. Among the uneducated classes, the call for war against the Saracens in the east looked like the heralding of the end of the world. In order for the new world to dawn, all had to be baptized or killed, and the religious fervor led to pogroms against Jews in many northern European cities. Similar events occurred in connection with nearly every crusade afterward.

For their part, the Jews did not try to assimilate into the Christian population. Their religious practices, as well as their beliefs, isolated them from Christians. The communal nature of their prayer, their dietary laws, and the way they celebrated the Sabbath all separated them from their neighbors. Thus, the Jews became the quintessential outsiders within Christendom.

But they were not the only ones alienated from society. By positive steps, the authorities segregated the lepers, who suffered from a disease which progressively disfigured them. These people were forced to live apart and to wear distinctive dress with bells attached, so others would know when they were coming and could get away. The lepers lived in colonies, which were endowed as charitable institutions. Since the disease progressed slowly, they formed stable communities, connected to, but separate from the normal society. The general populace looked upon the Jews and lepers with fear and loathing. The Jews were prosperous and resisted conversion and assimilation. The lepers bore the mark of impurity, and people had strong prejudices against them. These feelings caused many minor incidents during the Middle Ages, but in 1321 they created a panic during which the authorities and the mobs killed a great many Jews and lepers. In the following article, Malcolm Barber tells the story of that panic and, while doing so, reveals much about the popular prejudices of the period.

'In 1321', says Bernard Gui, Inquisitor at Toulouse between 1307 and 1324, 'there was detected and prevented an evil plan of the lepers against the healthy persons in the kingdom of France. Indeed, plotting against the safety of the people, these persons, unhealthy in body and insane in mind, had arranged to infect the waters of the rivers and fountains and wells everywhere, by placing poison and infected matter in them and by mixing (into the water) prepared powders, so that healthy men drinking from them or using the water thus infected, would become lepers, or die, or almost die, and thus the numbers of the lepers would be increased and the healthy decreased. And what seems incredible to say, they aspired to the lordship of towns and castles, and had already divided among themselves the lordship of places, and given themselves the name of potentate, count or baron in various lands, if what they planned should come about.' In this way, Bernard Gui begins his description of the hysteria which gripped a large part of France during the spring and summer of 1321 and which swelled into a tide of panic which engulfed the king and the court as well. For a short period, it was seen as the ultimate threat to the faith as conceived by the orthodox: a plan of subversive elements, both inside and outside society, to overthrow the whole structure of Christendom.

In June 1321, King Philip V was staying at Poitiers, where he intended to hold an assembly of representatives of the towns of southern and central France. According to the anonymous monk who continued the chronicle of Guillaume de Nangis, it was there that, about the time of the Feast of St. John the Baptist (24 June), rumour reached him that many lepers in Upper Aquitaine had been arrested and burned to death because they had confessed to infecting the fountains and wells with poison, with the purpose of either killing or making leprous all the Christians of France and Germany. A French historian, G. Lavergne, has shown from a study of local archives that the lepers in and around Périgueux had been accused of this plot in the spring of 1321, and, on 16 April, a systematic arrest of the lepers of the neighbourhood had been ordered by the mayor of Périgueux. By May, many had been tortured into confession and condemned to death by burning. The news may

From Malcom Barber, "Lepers, Jews and Moslems: The Plot to Overthrow Christendom in 1321," *History* Vol. 66 (1966), pp. 1–17.

therefore have been brought to the king by the representatives of Périgueux who had been sent to attend the meeting of the towns at Poitiers
on 14 June.

The chroniclers, Jean de Saint-Victor and the Nangis continuator
report that 'about this time', further details arrived from another source:
that of the lord of Parthenay (just to the west of Poitiers), who is conveniently not named. 'It is said', relates the continuator of Nangis with
the customary caveat, that this lord sent the king a sealed letter containing
the confession of an important leper who had been captured in his lands.
The letter broadened the implications of the plot considerably, for the
leper had confessed that he had been led to take part in the poisoning by
'a certain rich Jew', who had given him the poisonous potions together
with 10 *livres*, promising a large amount of money if he would corrupt the
other lepers. The Jew had told him that the potion consisted of a mixture
of human blood and urine, three unnamed herbs, and a consecrated host,
all of which were mixed into a powder, placed in bags, tied with a weight,
and thrown into the wells and fountains. The Nangis continuator claimed
that he himself had seen at Poitiers the potions made by a certain female
leper, which were intended for the town, but which she had thrown away
in a panic, still in their bag, as she feared capture. 'There was found in
the bag the head of a snake, the feet of a toad and hairs as of a woman,
having been mixed with a certain black and fetid liquid, so it was not only
horrible to feel, but also to see.' The strength of the poison was revealed
when this bag was thrown on a fire, for the contents would not burn.

Philip V, himself a man of deeply superstitious nature, seems to
have been prepared to believe the reports and, on 21 June, issued an ordinance from Poitiers to his *baillis* to effect a general arrest of the lepers.
The ordinance states that 'public knowledge and the course of experience'
have shown that the lepers have attempted to kill Christians by throwing
poisonous potions into the waters, not only in France, but 'in all kingdoms subject to the faith of Christ'. For this reason the king had caused
them to be arrested and some had confessed and been burnt for the
crime. However, others remained unpunished, so, with the advice of his
council, the king had decided upon the following measures: (i) lepers who
have confessed or who confess in the future are to be burnt alive; (ii) if
they will not confess 'spontaneously' then torture should be applied 'so
that the truth can be extracted'; (iii) female lepers should be treated in
the same way, except those who were pregnant, who should be
imprisoned until their infants are of sufficient age 'to live and feed
without their help,' and then these women should be burnt; (iv) lepers
who confess nothing, those who will be born in the future, and leper
youths, both male and female, who were less than 14 years old, should be
imprisoned in their places of origin; (v) lepers who have reached their
majority, which was 14 years of age, and who confessed in the way set out

above, were to be burnt. According to the ordinance, the crime of the lepers was one of *lèse-majesté* and therefore all the goods of the lepers 'should be placed and held in our hand'. The imprisoned lepers should be provided for from there, as should the brothers and sisters who had taken care of them and who had lived from the revenues of the leper property. The ordinance stressed that the nature of the crime meant that the administration of justice in this case appertained to the royal power only and not to any temporal lords.

However, unlike the arrest of the Templars in October 1307, which had been instituted by Philip IV and kept secret until a predetermined day, many lords had already executed lepers and confiscated their goods. The provisions of the ordinance notwithstanding, therefore, Philip V was unable to take advantage of the situation and reserve the goods entirely for himself. Although the *baillis* acted upon the royal orders, the king nevertheless found it politic to issue another ordinance on 16 August. This declared that, at the request of several prelates, barons, nobles, communities and others who said that from ancient times they possessed the right to administer the *léproseries* and to appoint their governors, he had restored the goods which he had seized, without prejudice to his own rights and without creating any new right. The king had already been forced to acknowledge local rights over *léproseries* in particular cases. In Narbonne the *sénéchal* had taken over the goods of the lepers in the king's name, but the *consuls* of Carcassonne had protested that they had been accustomed to administer the goods for pious ends, a protest accepted by the king who, on 4 August, ordered the *sénéchal* to release the goods. The king found it equally difficult to control local action against the lepers themselves. The Bishop of Albi and his justiciars, for instance, were among those who had taken the law into their own hands and arrested the lepers. Some had been condemned to death while the rest were imprisoned. Since the king had said that the crime was one of *lèse-majesté*, he had levied a fine on the bishop. However, by 18 August, he had been obliged to remit the fine and to order his *sénéchaux* at Carcassonne and Toulouse to accept the episcopal jurisdiction over the lepers' case on the grounds that there was some doubt whether the crime could be regarded as *lèse-majesté*. In a matter such as this, he said, which required immediate action, the delays caused while it was being resolved would be too great.

Local authorities were perhaps themselves carried along by popular fervour. According to the anonymous continuator of the chronicle of Rouen, the lepers were burnt 'more by the people than by secular justice'. Bernard Gui confirms this. 'In many places, in detestation of the horrible act, the lepers, both men and women, were shut up in their homes with all their things, (and) fire having been applied, they were burnt by the people without any judgement.' Flanders seems to have been an exception for, according to the *Genealogia Comitum Flandriae*, although they were arrested, they were afterwards freed, which 'displeased not a few people'.

The extent of popular involvement in the affair is shown by the pogrom against the Jews which accompanied the attacks upon the lepers. The royal ordinances make no mention of the involvement of the Jews, but their part in the well-poisoning was nevertheless readily believed, both by the chroniclers and by the populace. The anonymous *Chronique Parisienne*, for instance, asserts that 'this devilry was done by the encouragement and the incitement of the Jews'. According to the Nangis continuator, 'the Jews in some parts were burnt indiscriminately and especially in Aquitaine'. They seem to have received little protection from the authorities. At the royal castle of Chinon in the *bailliage* of Tours, for instance, the continuator of Nangis reports that 160 Jews were burnt to death in a large pit. Many women, widowed by the executions, were said to have thrown their own sons onto the fire to prevent them being baptized 'by the Christians and the nobles present there'. It seems unlikely that this could have taken place without the connivance of the *bailli* of Tours. Indeed, the chroniclers claim that attacks also took place against the Jews in Paris from which the king gained direct financial benefit. Those found guilty were burnt, while others were condemned to perpetual exile. Some of the richest were kept until their debts were known, and their incomes and goods were absorbed into the royal fisc. The king was said to have had 150,000 *livres* from them.

The chroniclers have one more dramatic example of the fate of the Jews. At Vitry 40 Jews held in the royal prison, despairing of survival, decided to commit suicide. Their most aged and venerable member was chosen to cut their throats, a task which he was not prepared to perform without the assistance of a younger man. The two men did as the community wished, but when they were the only ones left, they were faced with the problem of who should kill the other. At length the old man prevailed in his wish to be killed first, and the younger man was left the sole survivor. However, instead of killing himself, he took whatever could be found from the bodies in the way of gold and silver, made a rope from clothes and climbed down from the tower in which they had been imprisoned. Unfortunately, the rope was shorter than he needed and this fact, together with the weight of the gold and silver, caused him to fall and break his leg, thus making his recapture possible. He, too, was then executed. Lehugeur, in his study of the reign of Philip V, believes this to be merely a fable, 'for the edification of the reader', and he is probably correct to be sceptical, since the story of the mass suicide among Jews in the face of adversity was well-established by 1321. Moreover, certain details, such as the possession of gold and silver by the imprisoned Jews, strike a false note. Nevertheless, because of the extent of popular fury not only in 1321, but also in the rising of the Pastoureaux of the previous year, the possibility of some further outrage at Vitry cannot be discounted.

Local jurisdictional claims and mob action therefore considerably diminished the control which the king sought through his ordinance of 21 June; nevertheless, he had ordered a general arrest and interrogation of the lepers. A number of depositions must undoubtedly have been produced by this action and, indeed, a royal order of 8 February 1322 commands that the *baillis* of Tours, Chaumont and Vitry send to *Parlement* 'the confessions of the lepers and the Jews' relating to the poisoning of the waters and other crimes. Such depositions have not apparently survived, but they may well have been extensive, for the affair was widely known throughout France. Contemporary references to it occur in the provinces of Flanders, Vermandois, Anjou, Touraine and Aquitaine, and in the specific towns of Paris, Amiens, Rouen, Caen, Avranches and Coutances in the north, Chaumont, Vitry and Mâcon in the east, Tours, Ouches, Limoges, Poitiers and Périgueux in the centre, and Toulouse, Carcassonne, Albi, Narbonne, Pamiers and Lyons in the south. However, the diligence of Jacques Fournier, Bishop of Pamiers between 1318 and 1325, makes it possible to examine a deposition of the kind which might have been produced by royal inquiries. The contents of this document suggest that it was through this and other depositions that tortured lepers greatly broadened the implications of the conspiracy to include not only lepers and Jews but also outside Moslem powers as well. The chroniclers, writing after the event, were then able to incorporate this additional strand within their narratives.

Guillaume Agasse, head of the leper colony at Estang in Pamiers, appeared before Marc Rivel, Fournier's deputy, on 2 June 1321, nearly three weeks before Philip V issued orders for the general arrest. In the story told by Agasse, two lepers for Estang, Guillaume Normand and Fertand Espanol, as long ago as the previous Feast of St. Catherine (25 November 1320) had gone to Toulouse to seek some poisons, staying overnight on the way back with a leper called Gaulaube, commander of the house of Auterive. On their return to Estang, they told the witness that they had done good work, for they had brought poisons which would be put into the waters of Pamiers and which would make everybody into lepers. They then proceeded to poison the water of the fountain of Tourong, among other water-sources in Pamiers. Gaulaube at Auterive had been given poisons for the same purpose, while Etienne de Valès, a leper in Cahors, had poisoned the waters there too. At Estang the witness claimed that when the bank of the ditch of a local spring was opened up, he had seen a great ball of dung sunk into it, and that he had also seen, about a year ago, a certain leper coming away from that place. When asked if he had tried to prevent the poisoning, he replied that, on the contrary, it pleased him.

Guillaume Agasse appeared again on 9 June before Bernard Fassier, the official of Pamiers, and this time implicated himself more directly. In May 1320, a certain youth, whom he did not know, brought him some letters in which the preceptor of the lepers of Porte Arnaud Bernard of Toulouse asked him to come at once on the following Sunday to his house 'to conduct and order certain things which would result to his advantage and honour'. He set out, stopping overnight at the leper colony in Saverdun, where he discovered that Raimond, the commander of that house, had received a similar letter, and so, the next morning, they travelled to Toulouse together. On the Saturday night, they stayed at the house at Toulouse 'with many other lepers, ministers and preceptors'. On Sunday, 11 May 1320, about 40 lepers assembled in the main hall (*aula*) of the house and were addressed by the commander: 'You see and hear how other healthy Christians hold us who are ill in shame and disrespect, and how they throw us from their meetings and gatherings and that they hold us in derision and censure and disrespect.' Because of this, it was decided that all healthy Christians in the world should be poisoned so that they too became lepers, and then the present lepers would take 'their administration and governance'. 'And to obtain and cause this, the preceptor said and announced that it had been decided and ordained among the leaders that they would have the King of Granada in their aid and defence, which king . . . had already announced to other leaders of the *malades* that he was prepared to give his advice, help and aid in the matter. . . .' The plot would be achieved by placing powders in the waters, and to this end 'with the advice of doctors' many powders had been made, a portion of which each of those present would receive in a leather bag. The meeting broke up on the Tuesday, the witness and Raimond de Saverdun returning to their respective houses each with a full bag of powder. About a month after, Guillaume Agasse, 'wishing to keep the oath which he had sworn at Toulouse', carefully distributed the powder in various fountains and wells in Pamiers, finally throwing what he had left into the River Ariège. Agasse knew that the commanders of the houses of Saverdun, Mazères, Unzent and Pujols had been present at the assembly at Toulouse, but had not recognized any of the others. They had done it because they had been promised the lordship of the various places where they lived. He repeated his story about the journey made to Toulouse by Guillaume Normand and Fertand Espanol, but this time confessed that he had helped Guillaume Normand place a bag of poison in the local fountain of Rive, which they had pegged down among the stones and tiles.

Guillaume Agasse made a third appearance on 6 July, before Jacques Fournier himself, stating that he had been tortured on the day that he had made his first confession, but not since. He still maintained, however, that his confessions were true. He then repeated his story of 9 June concerning the delivering of the letters and the journey to Toulouse, but appreciably enlarged his account of what had happened there. This time the number present had risen to 50 or 60 and he specified that they came from the Toulousain, the Quercy, the Limousin, and from Gascony and the Agenais. The commander of the house of Porte Arnaud Bernard was named as Jourdain, and he made them all swear an oath 'on a certain book' from the chapel of the house not to reveal anything that occurred there, and to agree to do all the things which they were ordered to do. The assembly itself took place in the main hall of the house and there 'on one side next to the door stood a certain man, tall and black, wearing a sword, having a helmet on his head, as it seemed, (and) holding a halberd in his hands.' When one of the lepers asked what this man was doing there, Jourdain replied, that he was there 'on account of those things which they ought to do there', adding that there were many others in the house who would come if it was necessary. Jourdain then explained that the plot to poison the Christians was supported by 'the King of Granada and the Sultan of Babylon', who, in return for obedience to their orders, promised the leper commanders 'great riches and honours' and the lordship of the places where they lived. The messenger from the two rulers was the commander of the leper house of Bordeaux. The Moslem rulers demanded that the lepers 'deny the faith of Christ and his Law', and that they should receive the poison which the kings had ordered to be made. This was a mixture of the powdered remains of a consecrated host, 'which the Christians call the body of Christ', and a concoction made from snakes, toads, lizards and bats, together with human excrement. If any of the commanders resisted these orders, then the man with the halberd would at once decapitate him.

When the lepers present had denied Christ, Jourdain told them that in the near future there would be another chapter-meeting in which all the leper commanders of the Christian world would be present, where they would meet the King of Granada and the Sultan of Babylon. There, the commanders would again deny Christ and 'spit on the cross of Christ and upon his body, and also that the body of the Lord and his cross should be trampled underfoot'. This had been promised by the commander of Bordeaux and without this denial the two Moslem rulers 'would not come to them nor confide in them'. All the commanders present promised to do all this when the King and the Sultan came and to obey their orders. Indeed, there were said to be present at the time representatives of the two kings, who would report what had happened. Jourdain told them that these things 'were done to the end that the Sultan of Babylon and the King of Granada would be lords of the whole land, which was now held by the Christians, the Christians having been killed or made lepers'.

Jourdain and another commander, whom Guillaume Agasse thought was the commander of Bordeaux, then briefly left the room before returning with the deadly powders. Jourdain carried a large pot and the commander a large basin, which were placed in their midst. Jourdain told them that the pot contained the powdered host, and then proceeded to mix this with the powder in the basin, before distributing a portion contained in the leather bag to each of the commanders present. Guillaume Agasse received about half a pound. This was the powder which would infect the waters; care should be taken to put it in linen bags held under the water by a stone so that the poison did not dissipate too quickly, and should have the maximum effect. This was the end of the assembly and that day they ate together before returning to their homes. Ten or twelve days later (*i.e.* 24 or 26 May), he began to put poison in the wells and fountains of Pamiers and into the Ariège, as he had explained before.

Finally, at the end of his deposition, Guillaume Agasse denied that the evidence which he had given against his fellow lepers, Guillaume Normand and Fertand Espanol, was true. It was he who had done these things and it was he who had remained for three months in the belief that the Christian faith was of no value. He had told no one nor given any poison to other lepers to place in the waters. He had also given false testimony against Raimond de Saverdun (who had already been burnt to death) and Pierre de Mazères. He confessed this 'without any torture applied or threatened to him, freely and spontaneously, wishing to save his soul and repentant that he had committed the aforesaid'. A year later, on 5 July 1322, Guillaume Agasse abjured his crime and received sentence of perpetual prison from Jacques Fournier. Bernard Gui was among those present.

Between Agasse's second and third depositions, two further pieces of evidence appeared which apparently lent support to stories such as those told by him involving Moslem powers in the plot. These are two letters allegedly written by the Moslem kings of Granada and Tunis, which suggest that they were actively providing financial support for the plot and indeed sending actual poison. The letter of the King of Granada is addressed to Sanson, son of Helias the Jew, and speaks of a plot already in being in which the king had provided money for the Jews, so that they could persuade the lepers to distribute poison in the cisterns, wells and fountains, poison sent by the king himself. One hundred and fifteen lepers had taken an oath that they would participate. The king was sending a special poison to be put into the water drunk by Philip V. No effort was to be spared to gain success. The letter of the King of Tunis is addressed generally 'to his brethren and their children' and promises them sufficient money for their expenses. If they should wish to send their children to him he would guard them like his heart. The agreement between the king, the Jews and the lepers had been made the previous Easter. An oath was sworn which involved 75 Jews and lepers. The letters are in French, having been translated from Arabic by Pierre d'Aura, a physician. The date given is 2 July. Unlike Agasse's deposition, however, they do not seem to have emanated from Languedoc, but from Mâcon, since Francon d'Avinières, the royal *bailli* of Mâcon, Pierre

Maiorelli, a royal clerk, and two clerics, Bartholomew de Go, an archdeacon, and Guiot de l'Aubépin, a canon of Mâcon, together with 4 royal notaries and Pierre de Leugny, a leading citizen of the commune of Mâcon and keeper of its seal, attested their presence. The letters give no indication of the location of the originals or of how and where they entered France, but there seems little likelihood that they are genuine. Their content strongly suggests that whoever created them based his information upon confessions extorted from lepers similar to that made by Guillaume Agasse, following the ordinance of 21 June.

Some of the chroniclers also believed in Moslem perfidy. The Nangis continuator claimed it was generally said that the King of Granada, wishing to take revenge for his defeats at the hands of the Christians, especially by Peter, uncle of the King of Castile, had plotted this evil in concert with the lepers. He had promised the Jews 'an infinite amount of money' if they would carry it out, but they refused to do so themselves because, 'as they said, they were suspect to the Christians'. The Jews, however, were 'susceptible to evil' and, instead, arranged for the actual poisoning to be done by the lepers, 'who continually mix with the Christians'. The leaders of the lepers convoked four general councils, attended by representatives from all except for two English *léproseries,* and persuaded them that if everyone in the world became a leper then they would no longer be despised. As a further incentive, the offices of power were divided among the lepers in anticipation of their future victory. The Nangis continuator knew of a leper burnt at Tours who had called himself the Abbot of Marmoutier. Not all chroniclers, however, mention the Moslem connexion. The author of the *Chronique Parisienne* is apparently unaware of this dimension to the conspiracy, while Bernard Gui, who knew of the content of confessions such as that of Guillaume Agasse, nevertheless omits the accusation against the King of Granada, which suggests a certain scepticism on his part about this aspect of the affair.

Just like the Pastoureaux of the previous year, the disturbances seem to have spent themselves within a few months. The following summer, on 31 July 1322, at Paris, Charles IV issued an ordinance which permanently imprisoned the lepers within walls, their subsistence to be provided from their goods. In parishes where no proper endowments existed, the lepers were to be maintained at parish expense. Bernard Gui records this decision with approval, for although he believed in the existence of a plot, he clearly deplored action without due legal process as had characterized the pogroms of 1321. 'At length more mature advice and consultation having been taken, the rest, all and individually, who had remained alive and were not found guilty, circumspectly providing for the future, were enclosed in places from which they could never come out, but wither away and languish in perpetuity, so that they would not do harm or multiply, men being completely separated from women.' As for the Jews, the accusations seem to have provided yet another excuse for monarchical financial extortion and, in 1322, for another 'expulsion in perpetuity'.

The delusion that a conspiracy between the lepers, the Jews and the Moors actually existed in 1321 is a revealing instance of medieval mental attitudes under the strains created by the economic and social problems of the fourteenth century. Neither singly nor in combination did the elements in the supposed plot present any threat to society nor, as the anonymous chronicler of Tours admitted, did any Christian die or suffer ill from the poisoning of the water-supplies, yet the accusations were widely believed through the whole spectrum of the social order from the king downwards. They were believed because the nature of the accusations accorded with the contemporary mental climate during a period of stress in which a scapegoat for society's ills seems to have been sought. The prosecutions of the previous twenty years had accustomed people to expect to find anti-social conspirators, ready to overturn society by whatever means came to hand. Most shocking of these plotters had been the Templars who, during their trial between 1307 and 1312, had confessed to the denial of Christ, spitting, trampling and urinating on a crucifix, the worship of monstrous idols, the encouragement of sodomy, and the abuse of the sacraments, especially by the omission of the words of consecration during the mass. These had been perpetrated in secret chapters and reception ceremonies which excluded outsiders. Other signs of stress had been present for some years. The famines between 1315 and 1317 in northern Europe had clearly been more prolonged and more serious in their impact than the frequent local shortages which were inseparable from the medieval agrarian system. However, local disasters also occurred, for in some regions affected by the leper conspiracy such events are recorded under the same year. In Flanders, for instance, extensive flooding from the sea is reported, destroying houses and drowning men and animals, while at the opposite end of the kingdom, at Lyons, there was a shortage of fruit, a lack of sun, famine and disease. At Tours, the chronicler was more cosmic in his observations. 'In this year, on the Feast of the Consecration of the Body of Christ (18 June), the halo (*radius*) of the sun was red in colour for the whole day, as if it were blood.' This is not, however, to argue that there is a direct causal connexion between the famines of 1315–17 and the accusations against the lepers, or indeed to imply that the chroniclers make any link between the leper conspiracy and the natural and supernatural phenomena which they report, beyond the close juxtaposition of the events. It is rather to suggest that the existence of the widespread belief in such a plot is itself evidence of a society under stress and should be added to other such indications noted by historians.

These are, however, generalizations. Two specific questions arise from this affair: why did these particular groups become scapegoats and why were these particular allegations made? The Jews were of course the traditional victims of medieval prejudice, especially during the crusading era. They had suffered severely the previous year when the Pastoureaux or Shepherds' Crusade, frustrated in the attempt to reach Outremer, turned its fury upon the Jews more conveniently near at hand than the Moslems. The shepherds' movement had begun in the spring of 1320. Initially, they had concentrated upon Paris, but having failed to rouse the king to begin his long-awaited crusade, set off towards Languedoc. Here, during the summer, they attacked the Jews wherever they could find them: towns specifically named include Saintes, Verdun, Grenade, Castelsarrasin, Toulouse, Cahors, Lézat, Albi, Auch, Rabastens and Gaillac. Royal enquiries after the event stress the excesses committed against the Jews in the *sénéchaussées* of Toulouse, Périgord and Carcassonne. Property was plundered, documentary evidence of debts burnt and whole communities of Jews massacred or forcibly baptized, usually with the complicity of the local inhabitants. The return of the Jews in 1315 after the expulsion of 1306 and the energetic pursuit of their debts by royal agents had made a major contribution to the diversion of these would-be crusaders against the Jews. Quite possibly, increased small-scale debts owed to the Jews incurred during the hardships of 1315–17 underlay some of the animosity. However, although the Pastoureaux had been crushed by royal military force, the fundamental reasons for anti-Semitism in medieval society—religious, cultural and economic—had been left untouched.

The association of the Jews with the lepers is more difficult to identify. It may have been the revival of an old prejudice which finds its written origins as long ago as the third century B.C., in which the Jews were chased out of Egypt as impure and leprous, a story which thereafter established itself in the mentality of the ancient Mediterranean world, or it may stem from a contrary idea based on the belief that the Jews rarely contracted leprosy, and could therefore have plotted with the lepers without fear of infection. Henri de Mondeville, physician to Philip the Fair and Louis X, listed as one of the causes of leprosy, sexual intercourse during menstruation, but explained that since Jews rarely have sexual intercourse during this time, few Jews are lepers.

The lepers themselves were new victims, but their circumstances made them vulnerable. Like the Jews, they formed distinctive and definable communities, and they could be recognized by their dress and sometimes by their disfigurement. The Church had contributed to their separation from society by applying the Levitical precepts of ritual defilement to leprosy, so that they were, in theory, to be regarded as unclean people to be kept apart from the rest of the community. A standard church service laid down detailed regulations for the separation of lepers and their conduct in relation to the rest of the community, and some of these are reiterated in the rules of leper-houses. Ecclesiastical regulations, however, may simply have been formalizing an existing separation created by local communities rather than making new conditions. Canon 23 of the Third Lateran Council of 1179 established separate churches and cemeteries for lepers, but the reasoning behind the canon was that lepers had not been able to live with the healthy and attend their churches and therefore no proper religious provision was being made for them.

Perhaps most pertinent to the question of popular attitudes towards leprosy is the fact that it was the community which usually had to decide if a person had contracted the disease, for medical advice was frequently unavailable. Leprosy, therefore, gained an accusatory aspect not dissimilar to heresy or witchcraft. Fear of infection, or simply repulsion at the appearance of those in the more advanced stages of the disease, must have powerfully reinforced the Church's precepts. The Nangis continuator portrays the leper leaders at their four great assemblies describing themselves and their fellow lepers as 'the most vile and abject persons among the Christians', while the king demanded, in the ordinance of 18 August 1321, that the land be cleansed of the 'putridity' of the 'fetid lepers'. Popular stories expressed this instinctive repulsion. The story from the *Gesta Romanorum*, for instance, 'On the Evils of Leprosy', which must have had wide circulation in oral versions even though the stories were not collected together and written down until *c.* 1340, taken literally, perpetuates the idea that leprosy could be sexually transmitted and this was in itself a means of ridding oneself of the disease and passing it on to another. At the same time, the moral interpretation of the story takes leprosy as a synonym for wickedness and describes the Fall as a process by which 'man was spiritually made a leper'. Even the Cathars, themselves outcasts and fugitives by 1321, viewed the lepers as the lowest among humanity. Guillaume Bélibaste, the last of the Cathar *perfecti*, is reported as describing the arrest of Christ in the following way: 'And on these words the pharisees and their servants with them, sons of the devil, came, and they took him, and all the injuries and opprobrium which they could bring to him, the pharisees and ministers brought to the Son of God, to such an extent that a certain leper spat at him in the face. . . .' Contemporary medical opinion did nothing to dispel this popular image. Henri de Mondeville apparently believed that the physical deterioration was accompanied by a disintegration of the leper's character, presumably because of a growing imbalance in the bodily humours. When the blood of a leper is washed through a cloth, he said, black stains will remain, which are the evil elements. Perhaps this is what the chronicler Jean de Saint-Victor meant when he presents the Jews as saying that the lepers would consent to the plot, 'having been easily debased (*dejecti*) by them (i.e. the Jews)'. Until this time, however, the lepers were less likely objects of antagonism than the Jews, since they were at least co-religionists and were seen as worthwhile objects of charity during the fashion for the endowment of hospitals in the twelfth and thirteenth centuries. Indeed, while both Biblical precepts and popular fears continued to influence the treatment of lepers throughout the High Middle Ages, the harsher effects of these attitudes had been mitigated by the greatly increased provision of leper hospitals. Ironically, in the long term, this contributed to the lepers' vulnerability, for it helped to make them an identifiable minority, collected in a distinct place, just like the Jews.

The second question which arises concerns the nature of the allegations. The essence of the allegations centres upon the magical use of poison which would either kill or make leprous. The ingredients of the poison have no apparent relationship to the alleged effects in the sense that they are not herbal or chemical poisons. The preference for a magical form of poison is further evidence of the panic which gripped society for, despite limited scientific knowledge, it is clear that more specific methods of poisoning, without the use of magic, were known even at a popular level. To take another contemporary example from the depositions of the Cathars: when the group of exiles in Catalonia centred upon Guillaume Bélibaste wished to poison a suspected traitress, an attempt was first made with 'a herb called *vulaire*' placed in her food, and when this failed they tried to purchase *realgar* or red arsenic from the local apothecary for the same purpose, making the excuse that they wanted it to cure ailments among their animals. The necessity for making an excuse does itself suggest that the poisonous properties of the substance were well-known. The lepers' plot therefore was essentially based on magic in the sense that it is defined by Professor Thorndike: 'Magic appears . . . as a way of looking at the world which is reflected in a human art or group of arts employing varied materials in varied rites, often fantastic, to work a great variety of marvelous results, which offer man a release from his physical, social and intellectual limitations. . . . The *sine qua non* seems to be a human operator, materials, rites, and an aim that borders on the impossible, either in itself or in relation to the apparently inadequate means employed.'

The poison itself was a mixture, although the proportions of the elements included are not given and were indeed regarded as unknowable. According to the reported letter of the lord of Parthenay it included human blood and urine, three unnamed herbs and a consecrated host; in the continuator of Nangis it is made up of a head of a snake, the feet of a toad and the hairs of a woman, all of which was mixed with a black and fetid liquid; and Guillaume Agasse claimed that it contained the powdered remains of a consecrated host mixed with a concoction made from snakes, toads, lizards and bats together with human excrement. However, despite the irrelevance of the constituents to leprosy, they did at least have harmful associations. The reptiles named were those thought to be born in corruption or earth, like worms, rather than from seed, and they were believed in themselves to be poisonous. The popular view of these creatures was expressed by Guillaume Bélibaste, even though the Cathar outlook on the created world differed radically from that of the orthodox.

He explained that Cathar *perfecti* could not kill anything that had blood, whether it walked on the ground or flew in the air, except for a group which he called 'impure', which included mice, snakes, toads, frogs and lizards. Human waste, which might be seen by some as the poisonous part of the elements being expelled from the body, was the corruption in which the 'impure' beings flourished and therefore associated with them, while the desecrated host linked the whole mixture with anti-Christian and heretical groups such as the Jews, who had been frequently accused of desecrating the host during the thirteenth century.

Finally, in the most detailed account of how the plot was supposedly organized—that of Guillaume Agasse—the 'heretical' element emerges most markedly, which is not surprising in view of the inquisitorial nature of the hearing. In Agasse's deposition there are secret chapters, an oath sworn to preserve secrecy, the denial of Christ, spitting and trampling on the cross, and a sinister armed man or devil figure. Agasse's confession suggests not only that both he and his inquisitors had been directly influenced by the accusations made against the Templars in their recent trial, but also that their ideas could still pass muster as a means of establishing who were the enemies of society.

The attacks upon the lepers and the Jews were symptoms of pressures with which society could not cope. The previous year they had taken the form of a pseudo-crusade; in 1321 they expressed themselves as a belief in a phantom plot to overturn society. The need to protect society from enemies both external and internal had been a fundamental tenet of the twelfth and thirteenth centuries. But, despite massive efforts, it seemed that the threats remained, for the Mameluks had pushed the Christians into the sea in 1291, and the inquisitors continued to insist upon eternal vigilance against the enemy within. Even the idea that Moslem agents were sometimes sent to poison the Christian population had already had some currency, for Matthew Paris alleged that there had been found in the baggage of one of the leaders of the Pastoureaux movement of 1251 a large sum of money, some documents in Arabic and Chaldean and various poisonous powders. The documents were found to be letters from the Sultan, exhorting the leader to act in return for a promise of a great reward. Apparently, it was intended that innumerable Christians would be handed over to the Sultan. In 1321 this idea caught the imagination of a large section of the French population, although then the agents took the form of the lepers and the Jews. It can be seen as a prelude to the much more widespread pogroms which accompanied the Black Death, and perhaps helps to explain the nature of the society which was struck by the plague and therefore society's view of the causes of that disaster.

PART 4

The Late Middle Ages
14th - 15th Centuries

Leaf from an Italian Book of Hours, "The Month of January, House of Aquarius," Padua.

The Late Middle Ages

Many studies of social life in premodern Europe focus on the fourteenth and fifteenth centuries, for two main reasons. First, during the late thirteenth and early fourteenth centuries, record-keeping by governmental and private institutions became a standard practice. Studies of rural society, which are so dependent on records of landholding, naturally focus on this record-rich period. Studies of cities follow the same rule, and even legal history assumes a new dimension when it concerns itself with the period of the Yearbooks—reports of cases brought before the royal court in England, which were first circulated in 1292.

Second, war and pestilence profoundly disrupted the society of this period. The Hundred Years' War, originating in sporadic conflicts between England and France in the early fourteenth century, created a new nationalism in those countries and caused destruction on a scale that could not fail to affect the character of both rural and urban communities. The Black Death, recurrent in Europe from about 1348 to the end of the fourteenth century, drastically reduced the population of all social groups and created instability throughout the society. The selections in Part 4 reflect both the record-keeping proclivities of fourteenth- and fifteenth-century institutions and the effect of war and plague on those institutions.

In the late middle ages, the European world was tied together by roads and rivers, and many Europeans spent time abroad. The main purposes of travel were study at one of the major scholastic centers, business at the papal court or at one of the royal courts, and pilgrimage to holy shrines. By the late twelfth century, Paris and Bologna had become the principal centers for advanced studies in the liberal arts and in theology, law, and medicine; students from all over Europe came to these cities in steadily increasing numbers throughout the middle ages. The papal court remained mostly at Rome, except during the summer when it escaped the heat by going to the mountains, but the royal courts travelled incessantly around their kingdoms; travel was a common and frequent experience of all who had business with the governments of Europe.

But the most common reason for travel was pilgrimage, and the most common travelers were pilgrims. These travelers created a market for an extensive network of inns and for ship owners who ran tours to the Holy Land. They also created a literature about travel. By the middle of the twelfth century, there was a guidebook to Rome and its wonders, including the colliseum, which was described as if it were the world's first domed arena. There were also travel accounts which served as manuals for the prospective pilgrim. From this literature, Jonathan Sumption draws an account of medieval land and sea travel.

The Black Death did not strike all communities equally, but the common view is that it killed between a third and a half of the population of Europe. In this part, we look at one of the results of this disaster, the rise of mass movements of protest; in the next part, we look at another, the development of institutions of public health.

In "The Peasants in Revolt," R. H. Hilton considers the causes and the character of movements of social protest in the late fourteenth and the fifteenth centuries. The wars, famines, and outbreaks of plague during this period caused shortages of labor and of goods, and the authorities tried to control the injured and erratic economy by issuing repressive legislation. The combination of this repression with the miseries caused by nature gave rise to the unrest that was expressed violently in the series of mass movements that occurred throughout Europe.

BIBLIOGRAPHY

On the peasant rebellions and other late medieval mass movements, see the book from which the selection "The Peasants in Revolt" comes, R. H. Hilton, *Bond Men Made Free: Medieval Peasant Movements and the English Rising of 1381* (London, 1973). See also Wallace K. Ferguson, *Europe in Transition, 1300–1520* (Boston, 1962), and Michel Mollat and Philippe Wolff, *The Popular Revolutions of the Late Middle Ages* (London, 1972). On specific rebellions, see Charles Oman, *The Great Revolt of 1381* (Oxford, 1906); Eileen Power, "The Effects of the Black Death on Rural Organization in England," *History*, Vol. 3 (1918), pp. 109–16; Steven Runciman, *The Sicilian Vespers* (Cambridge, Eng., 1958); and Howard Kaminsky, *A History of the Hussite Revolution* (Berkeley, 1967).

For a general history of war in medieval Europe, see the classic book by Charles Oman, *A History of the Art of War in the Middle Ages* (London, 1924). See also John Beeler, *Warfare in Feudal Europe, 730–1200* (Ithaca, N.Y., 1971); R. C. Smail, *Crusading Warfare (1097–1193) A Contribution to Medieval Military History* (Cambridge, Eng., 1956); Sidney Toy, *A History of Fortification from 3000 B.C. to A.D. 1700* (New York, 1955). On medieval weaponry, see Claude Blair, *European Armour, circa 1066 to circa 1700* (New York, 1959), and R. Ewart Oakeshott, *The Archaeology of Weapons: Arms and Armour from Prehistory to the Age of Chivalry* (London, 1960). For a general history of the Hundred Years' War, see Eduard Perroy, *The Hundred Years' War* (London, 1957). See also H. J. Hewitt, *The Organization of War under Edward III* (Manchester, Eng., 1966), where traditional ideas about the limited destructiveness of medieval armies and strategy are put to rest. For a general introduction to the character of medieval warriors, see A. Vesey B. Norman, *The Medieval Soldier* (New York, 1971).

The study of medieval cities has flourished in recent decades. See David Herlihy, *Medieval and Renaissance Pistoia* (New Haven, 1967); and Robert Brentano, *Rome Before Avignon* (New York, 1974). Christopher Brooke and Gillian Keir, *London 800–1216: The Shaping of a City* (Berkeley and Los Angeles, 1975). On the planning and founding of towns in the Middle Ages, see M. W. Beresford, *New Towns of the Middle Ages* (London, 1967), and F. Haverfield, *Ancient Town Planning* (Oxford, 1913). For an introduction to the urban populations, see, Fritz Rörig, *The Medieval Town* (Berkeley, 1967).

On the history of education in general, see Henri Marrou, *A History of Education in Antiquity* (New York, 1956); Stanley Bonner, *Education in Ancient Rome* (Berkeley, 1977); M. L. W. Laistner, *Thought and Letters in Western Europe A.D. 500 to 900* (Ithaca, N.Y., 1957, 1966); Pierre Riché, *Education and Culture in the Barbarian West: Sixth Through Eighth Centuries*, trans. J. J. Contreni (Columbia, S.C., 1976). For background material on the schools of the twelfth century, see the classic work of Charles Homer Haskins, *The Renaissance of the Twelfth Century* (Cambridge, Mass., 1927) and the essays in a volume that commemorates the fiftieth anniversary of Haskins's work, *Renaissance and Renewal in the Twelfth Century*, ed. by R. L. Benson and G. Constable (Cambridge, Mass., 1982). On the universities, the basic work is H. Rashdall, *The Universities of Europe in the Middle Ages*, ed. F. M. Powicke and A. B. Emden, 3 vols., rev. ed. (Oxford, 1936). Two good short introductions are Charles Homer Haskins, *The Rise of the Universities* (New York, 1923) and Lowrie J. Daly, *The Medieval University, 1200–1400* (New York, 1961). On the internal organization of the universities, see Pearl Kibre, *The Nations in the Mediaeval Universities* (Cambridge, Mass., 1948). On later developments, see Gordon Leff, *Paris and Oxford Universities in the Thirteenth and Fourteenth Centuries* (New York, 1968).

There is a study of ships of the late Middle Ages in M. E. Mallett, *The Florentine Galleys in the Fifteenth Century* (Oxford, 1967). Mallett includes a ship's log from the period in his book. See also E. L. Guilford, *Travel and Travellers in the Middle Ages* (New York, 1924). On pilgrimages, see A. Kendall, *Medieval Pilgrims* (London, 1970). See also Robert S. Lopez, "The Evolution of Land Transport in the Middle Ages," *Past and Present*, Vol. 19 (1956), pp. 17–29. Irving Agus, in *Urban Civilization in Pre-Crusade Europe* (New York, 1965), includes an entire section on travel. His material focuses on the activities of the Jews in the period from the ninth to the eleventh centuries, when political conditions made travel difficult and dangerous.

Pilgrimage and Medieval Travel

JONATHAN SUMPTION

Beginning in late imperial times, pilgrims traveled to shrines throughout Europe. The churches of St. Martin at Tours and of Santiago de Compostella in northwestern Spain were two of the most popular destinations, and the latter became particularly important after the beginning of the reconquest of Spain in the eleventh century. Pilgrimage to Jerusalem and the holy places in its vicinity also became popular in the eleventh century, and the establishment of the Latin kingdom of Jerusalem in 1099 facilitated the movement of pilgrims to that region.

In early times, pilgrims were probably the most numerous travelers in Europe—along with some of the Jewish merchants whose activities Robert Chazan described in "Jews in a Christian Society." By the later Middle Ages, commercial travelers were by far the most important group, although the number of pilgrims had also increased dramatically. The pilgrims followed the trade routes and in fact became an important part of the traffic going through the great Italian commercial centers. The seriousness with which city fathers regarded the pilgrim trade is indicated by the steps taken by the Venetian doges. They created elaborate regulations to govern sea captains who transported pilgrims to the Holy Land, and who even seem to have offered "packaged tours." The pilgrims have left many accounts of their journeys across Europe and the Mediterranean; these travel diaries are the principal source of our knowledge of the conditions of transport and travel during the medieval and early modern periods. In the following selection, Jonathan Sumption uses these accounts to create a picture of pilgrimage and of travel on land and sea during this long period.

Preparations

'He that be a pilgrim,' declared the London preacher Richard Alkerton in 1406, 'oweth first to pay his debts, afterwards to set his house in governance, and afterwards to array himself and take leave of his neighbours, and so go forth.'

His first act, if he was a man of substance, was to make his will. Pilgrims enjoyed the special privilege of disposing of their property by will, a

From Jonathan Sumption, *Pilgrimage* (Totowa, N.J.: Rowman & Littlefield, 1975), pp. 168–70, 171–74, 175–83, 184–87, 188–90, 192–96.

privilege which, until the late middle ages, was accorded to very few. As well as naming his heirs, the will would deal with such matters as the administration of his property in his absence and the length of time which was to elapse before he should be presumed dead. In Normandy local custom required every landowner to make a will which would automatically be executed if he did not announce his return within a year and a day. Some pilgrims also made private agreements with their wives as to how long they should leave before remarrying. The Church did what it could to ensure that the terms of a pilgrim's will were respected. In Spain, for instance, it made his companions responsible for looking after his personal effects. Failing companions, the local clergy were expected to keep them for a year and a day and, if they remained unclaimed, to sell them and apply the money to endowing masses for the repose of the dead pilgrim's soul.

In his absence, a pilgrim's property was immune from all civil claims in a court of law. The service which he owed to his feudal lord was usually suspended during the pilgrimage, and in northern France, according to Beaumanoir, pilgrims were exempt from the obligation to take part in family vendettas. In effect, there was no legal remedy to be had against a bona fide pilgrim, so long as he returned home to face his adversaries within a reasonable time. Illegal remedies were *a fortiori* forbidden, and those who had recourse to them faced both civil and ecclesiastical sanctions. In the bull *Quantum Praedecessores* of December 1145, Eugenius III proclaimed that the wife and children, goods and chattels of every pilgrim or crusader were 'placed under the protection of the Holy See and of all the prelates of the Church of God. By our apostolic authority we absolutely forbid anyone to disturb them until their return or death.' Before the first crusade this principle had probably been honoured chiefly in the breach. But effective protection was essential if crusaders were to be recruited for the defence of the Holy Land, and by the end of the twelfth century, flagrant violations of a pilgrim's rights never failed to arouse indignant protest. The invasion of Normandy by Philip Augustus of France while Richard Coeur-de-Lion was in the Holy Land was bitterly criticized, and some of Philip's own vassals refused to follow him. When, at the beginning of the thirteenth century, it seemed that the entire Angevin empire in France must shortly fall into the hands of the French king, loyal vassals of John were afraid that Philip would seize their lands. Some of them regarded a pilgrim's privileges as the best guarantee of the rights of their heirs. This, at any rate, was the reason given by Archambert de Monluc when he joined the fourth crusade, appointing as trustees of his property a formidable list of ecclesiastical personages.

Although few pilgrims went to the extremes recommended by the preacher of the sermon *Veneranda Dies*, most of them made some concession to the principle that a pilgrimage should be accomplished in poverty. Rich pilgrims often made generous donations to the poor before leaving.

The cartularies of monasteries, from the eleventh century onwards, are full of deeds recording the gifts made by departing pilgrims and crusaders. A donor could have the best of both worlds by making his gift conditional on his not returning alive. Then, when he returned home, he could demand the usufruct of his property for the rest of his life, after which it would become the unencumbered possession of the Church. When Aimeric II, count of Fézensac, gave some windmills to the canons of Auch in 1088 as he was about to leave for the Holy Land, he insisted that 'if I come back alive from Jerusalem, I can have them back until my death.' If the knight never returned, the monks were often required to give a pension to his widow and sometimes even to his children. In fact, even if no such conditions were explicitly mentioned, they were almost certainly implied by both parties. When Leteric de Chatillon died in Palestine in 1100, the monks of La Charité allowed his widow half the revenues of his estates, although no such arrangement is found in the deed whereby Leteric had made the monks his heirs. Hughes de Lurcy, on returning from the Holy Land in the 1080s, claimed back his lands from the monks, promising to leave it [sic] to them on his death. Pilgrims probably adopted this roundabout procedure in order to ensure that their lands were safe in their absence. Some of them may also have borrowed the cost of the journey from the monks and left the lands with them as a pledge.

The true pilgrim, urged the preacher of the sermon *Venerenda* [sic] *Dies*, ought before his departure to make amends to all those whom he has offended, and to ask the permission of his wife, his parish priest, and anyone else to whom he owed obligations. The most important of these, for a layman, was his feudal lord, whose consent would be necessary if the pilgrim wished to nominate his heir or safeguard the position of his wife. Even the kings of France, Louis VII in 1146 and Philip Augustus in 1190, sought formal permission to leave with the crusade from St. Denis, whose vassals they recognized themselves to be. A cleric was required to ask the permission of his superior before making a pilgrimage, and until the fourteenth century this obligation was enforced with vigour. The German annalist Lambert of Hersfeld recalled how he had set out for Jerusalem in 1058, immediately after his ordination, without asking his abbot:

'I was afraid that since I had set out without his blessing, I might have given him offence. If he had died in my absence I would have remained forever unreconciled to him and would thus have committed a terrible sin in the eyes of God. But God's favour was with me, . . . for I returned in safety, confessed my sin, and was received with kindness. I felt as if I had just escaped alive from the fires of Hell.'

He was, in fact, only just in time, for the abbot became feverish that very evening and died a week later. . . .

When his enemies had been placated and his creditors satisfied, the pilgrim sought out his parish priest or, occasionally, his bishop, and received a formal blessing. Texts of these blessings for travellers survive from the early eighth century, though they did not pass into general use until the eleventh. Blessing ceremonies reflected the growing feeling among pilgrims that they belonged to an 'order' of the Church, distinguished from other men by a uniform and by a solemn ritual of initiation. Mass departures to the Holy land or Santiago were marked by public ceremonies in the cathedrals. But most pilgrims received their blessing privately from their parish priest, or else from a monk whose sanctity they respected. The hermit St. Godric of Finchale was said to have performed the ceremony regularly. Joinville, in 1248, sought out the Cistercian abbot of Cheminon on account of his saintly reputation, and then, after receiving his blessing, made his way on foot without shoes or coat to the embarkation point of the crusade at Marseilles.

Pilgrims' Dress

Once initiated into the 'order' of pilgrims, he signified his attachment to a new way of life by wearing a uniform, as distinctive in its own way as the tonsure of a priest. 'When the debts be thus paid and the meine is thus set in governance', continued Richard Alkerton in 1406, 'the pilgrim shall array himself. And then he oweth first to make himself be marked with a cross, as men be wont to do that shall pass to the Holy Land. . . . Afterwards the pilgrim shall have a staff, a sclavein, and a scrip.' The staff, a tough wooden stick with a metal toe, was the most distinctive as well as the most useful part of the pilgrim's attire. The 'sclavein' was a long, coarse tunic. The scrip was a soft pouch, usually made of leather, strapped to the pilgrim's waist; in it he kept his food, mess-cans, and money. Such was the attire of every serious pilgrim after the end of the eleventh century. Much later, probably in the middle of the thirteenth century, pilgrims began to wear a great broad-brimmed hat, turned up at the front, and attached at the back to a long scarf which was wound round the body as far as the waist.

The origin of this curious garb is not at all clear. The staff and pouch were used by the migrant monks of Egypt in the fourth century, but they were obvious and sensible accessories for any traveller on foot, not only for pilgrims and not only in the middle ages. The tunic, on the other hand, whose practical usefulness is not as readily apparent, seems to make its first appearance at the beginning of the twelfth century. Canute, setting out for Rome in 1027, 'took up his scrip and staff as did all his companions', but there is no mention of the tunic. St. Anselm, in 1097, 'took his scrip and staff like a pilgrim', but again, no tunic. Orderic

Vitalis, writing in about 1135, said that he could remember a time when pilgrims were indistinguishable from other travellers, except by their unshaven faces. Indeed it is probably about this time that the normal clothing of the traveller took on a sudden rigidity and became peculiarly the garb of the spiritual traveller.

This was almost certainly due to the fact that at the end of the eleventh century the Church began to bless the pilgrim's clothes and sanctify them as the uniform of his order. A special order of ceremony for pilgrims, as opposed to ordinary travellers, was now coming into existence. This usually took the form of blessing the pilgrim's pouch and mantle and presenting him with his staff from the altar. The ceremony has its origin in the blessing conferred on knights departing with the first crusade, and it is referred to in 1099 as a 'novel rite'. Behind the 'novel rite' is the pronounced tendency of the Church in the eleventh and twelfth centuries to stimulate lay piety by assigning to laymen certain defined spiritual functions. Those who fulfilled these functions were clothed with a special, almost ecclesiastical, status; they enjoyed spiritual privileges and ultimately secular ones as well. Hence the religious ceremony which now almost invariably accompanied the dubbing of a knight. Indeed, the ritual presentation of the pilgrim's staff bears a striking resemblance both to the dubbing of a knight and to the ordination of a priest. To the more austere pilgrim, the act of putting on his travelling clothes might have the same significance as taking the monastic habit. One such pilgrim was Rayner Pisani, an Italian merchant who experienced a sudden conversion during a business visit to Tyre in about 1140. Rayner took his pilgrim's tunic under his arm to the Golgotha chapel in Jerusalem and, in full view of an astonished crowd, removed all his old clothes and gave them to beggars. He then placed his tunic on the altar and asked the priest serving the chapel to invest him with it. This the priest did, and Rayner passed the remaining twenty years of his life as a hermit in Palestine.

In the course of time the Church invested the pilgrim's uniform with a rich and elaborate symbolism. Already in c. 1125 the author of the sermon *Veneranda Dies* is found explaining that the pilgrim's pouch is the symbol of almsgiving, because it is too small to hold much money and the pilgrim who wears it must therefore depend on charity. The pilgrim's staff is used for driving off wolves and dogs, who symbolize the snares of the Devil; the staff is the pilgrim's third leg, and three is the number of the Trinity; the staff therefore stands for the conflict of the Holy Trinity with the forces of evil, etc. This kind of imagery became very popular in the fourteenth and fifteenth centuries and it provided the theme for most of the sermons delivered to congregations of pilgrims before their departure. To Franco Sacchetti, the pilgrim's tunic stood for the humanity of Christ. The staff recalled the wood of the Cross in which lay the pilgrim's hope of salvation.   Perhaps the most involved as well as the most popular of these allegories was the work of Thomas of London, a Dominican who taught in France and who wrote, in c. 1430, an *Instructorium Peregrinorum*. Here the staff, pouch, and tunic stand for faith, hope and charity, respectively, for reasons which are pursued as far as scholastic subtlety will permit. These arid academic exercises make dull reading today, but at the close of the middle ages they were much enjoyed.

On his way home, the pilgrim usually wore a badge or token showing where he had been. The best known and probably the earliest of these souvenirs was the palm of Jericho which pilgrims customarily brought back from Jerusalem. It is the origin of the English word 'palmer'. Like so many of the rituals associated with the pilgrimage to the Holy land, this seems to have had its origin in the eleventh century. The palms, which were collected in the plain between Jericho and the Jordan, were regarded as a symbol of regeneration, of the victory of faith over sin. Peter Damian refers to the picking of palm leaves as 'customary' in c. 1050, and the soldiers of the first crusade all travelled *en masse* to the Jordan in July 1099 to baptize themselves in the river and collect their palms. William of Tyre, writing in c. 1180, remarks that the palm of Jericho was 'the formal sign that the pilgrim's vow has been fulfilled'. And so it remained throughout the middle ages, though later generations did not have to travel as far as the Jordan for their palms. After the twelfth century palm-vendors carried on a thriving trade in the market of the 'Rue des Herbes' in Jerusalem and stalls piled high with palms could be seen beneath the walls of the Tower of David. . . .

Travel Overland

A long journey in the middle ages was not a thing to be lightly undertaken. The great sanctuaries were separated by hundreds of miles of unmade, ill-marked roads, many of them running through unpopulated tracts of Europe infested with bandits. 'O Lord, heavenly father', ran a blessing commonly conferred on pilgrims in the twelfth century, 'let the angels watch over thy servants N.N. that they may reach their destination in safety, . . . that no enemy may attack them on the road, nor evil overcome them. Protect them from the perils of fast rivers, thieves, or wild beasts.' The outbreak of a war could interrupt the flow of pilgrims to an important sanctuary or even choke it altogether. Thus the disordered state of central Italy brought about the serious decline of the Roman pilgrimage in the tenth century and again in the thirteenth. The Hundred Years War ruined the abbey of St.-Gilles and many other shrines of southern France, and significantly affected the prosperity of Santiago itself. In the fifteenth century a sudden Arab or Turkish descent on Rhodes might prevent all travel to the Holy Land for a year.

The condition of the roads was the first obstacle. Europe relied, throughout the middle ages, on the network of roads bequeathed to it by the Roman empire. This network was far from comprehensive, but new roads did appear from time to time in response to changing needs. Thus the Roman road from Lyon to the south-west was diverted in the eleventh century through the hard granite mountains of the Ségalas to take it past the abbey of Conques; when the pilgrimage to Conques was forgotten, in the fourteenth century travellers returned to the old road. In France, the roads were never allowed to fall into complete disrepair, as they were in parts of England. Nevertheless travel was not easy and even an experienced rider could not expect to cover more than thirty miles in a day. The seigneur de Caumont, who rode from Caumont to Santiago in 1418, was reduced to six miles a day in the Pyrenees and the Asturias, but he was capable of doing twenty-seven miles when the terrain was good.

The manor was responsible for the upkeep of the roads, but too often it had few resources and little enthusiasm for the work. Important roads, particularly if they were used by pilgrims, were frequently maintained by volunteers. For the maintenance of roads was regarded as a work of charity equivalent, for example, to alms-giving. Bridge-building was particularly meritorious, 'a service to posterity and therefore pleasing to God', declares a charter of 1031 concerning the construction of a bridge over the Loire at Tours. French hermits in northern Spain were active road-builders at the time when the great road to Santiago was being rebuilt by the Castilian kings. Their names are preserved in the *Guide for Pilgrims to Santiago*, 'and may their souls and those of their companions rest in everlasting peace.' The bridge over the river Miño at Puerto Marin was rebuilt after a civil war by Peter the Pilgrim. St. Domingo 'de la Calzada', another French immigrant, founded a celebrated hospice on the site of his hut by the river Oja, and spanned the stream with a wooden bridge; he built the first cobbled road across the marshy expanse between Nájera and Redecilla. Several mediaeval roads and bridges still survive in Spain and southern France, built under the impulsion of the pilgrimage to Santiago. At St.-Chély d'Aubrac and St.-Michel Pied-de-Port the old track, its stones worn or displaced, can still be followed for a few hundred yards. The fine stone bridges which span the river at Orthez and Oloron in Gascony date from the fourteenth century and replaced older, wooden ones. At Puente la Reina one can still see the great five-arched bridge where the two roads from southern France to Santiago came together.

The *Guide for Pilgrims to Santiago* catalogues the full range of catastrophes which could overcome the traveller on the roads in the twelfth century. It is both a historical guide and a route-book, offering its readers information about towns and hospices, a few useful words of the Basque language, an architectural description of Santiago cathedral, and precise directions on how to get there. The pilgrim is warned that the eight-mile ascent of the Port de Cize, the principal pass over the Pyrenees, is a steep climb; that in Galicia there are thick forests and few towns; that mosquitoes infest the marshy plain south of Bordeaux where the traveller who strays from the road can sink up to his knees in mud. Some of the rivers are impassable. Several pilgrims had been drowned at Sorde, where travellers and their horses were ferried across the river on hollowed-out tree trunks. Other rivers were undrinkable, like the salt stream at Lorca, where the author of the *Guide* found two Basques earning their living by skinning the horses who had died after drinking from it. Pilgrims were in theory exempt from the payment of tolls, but nevertheless the *Guide* reports that the local lords exacted payment from every traveller in the Béarn. At the foot of the Port de Cize, pilgrims were searched and beaten with sticks if they could not pay the toll. The author demanded immediate action by the bishop and the king of Aragon, but it was more than half a century before the extortionist suffered retribution at the hands of Richard Coeur-de-Lion.

The supply of food and fodder is a constantly recurring theme in the *Guide*, and an important one at a time when it dictated the beginning and end of the travelling season much more effectively than the weather. There was no fodder to be had in the Landes south of Bordeaux, and the horseman was well-advised to bring three days' supply with him. There were parts of the route where the pilgrim would find it hard to buy a good meal for himself, even in summer. The food and wine were excellent in Gascony but dreadful in the Basque country. Fish caught in the river Ebro were disgusting, even poisonous. In general, concludes the *Guide*, Spanish meat should be avoided by those who are unused to it, 'and if any one can eat their fish without feeling sick, then he must have a stronger constitution than most of us.'

Against wild animals, bad roads, and natural catastrophes, the traveller had no protection. But, in theory, he enjoyed a measure of protection against man-made hazards. Every criminal code imposed special penalties on those who molested travellers, and synods of bishops regularly threatened them with the severest ecclesiastical censures. In 1096 a steward of the king of France was excommunicated for seizing a vassal of his on the road to Vézelay during Lent. 'But you should know', the archbishop of Lyon pointed out, 'that all those who travel to the shrines of the saints are protected against attack at all times, and not only in Lent. Those who disturb their journey will suffer the harshest penalties of the Church, so that the fear of God may remain for ever in their eyes.' From 1303 onwards, molesters of pilgrims were included in the annual bull *In Coena Domini*, in which the pope solemnly anathematized an ever-lengthening list of obnoxious persons. But although it is true that pilgrims were marginally safer from attack than other travellers, they can never have felt secure. In the eleventh century the Tuscan nobleman Gerard of Galeria supported himself in part by attacking rich pilgrims on the roads north of Rome. King Harold's brother Tostig was one of his victims. The French robber-baron Thomas de Marle owed much of his notoriety to his practice of holding pilgrims to ransom and mutilating them if the ransom was not paid. He terrorized the roads of northern France for many years before Louis VI mounted a military expedition against him in 1128. From the constant complaints of the ecclesiastical authorities, it is clear that Thomas had many imitators. We are better informed, however, of the bandits of the fourteenth and fifteenth centuries, most of whom were never brought to justice. The Roman Jubilee of 1350 brought considerable prosperity to one Berthold von Eberstein, who descended daily on the long processions of pilgrims winding through the Rhine valley. The German *routier* Werner von Urslinger was another bandit who enriched himself in 1350. His hunting-ground was Tuscany, where several of the main routes to Rome met. Jacopo Gabrielli, the papal rector of the Patrimony, was allowed 14,000 florins to raise mercenaries against him, the cost to be defrayed from the offerings at the Roman basilicas. The banditry of the later middle ages is remarkable for its international quality. The roads of northern Italy were infested with German robbers. On the roads which crossed northern Spain to Santiago, many of the bandits seem to have been Englishmen. In 1318 the provost of Estella spent several weeks in pursuit of one John of London, who had robbed pilgrims as they slept in a local hospice. In the following year a number of English bandits were captured at Pamplona. It was the same in the middle east. After the disappearance, in 1187, of the crusading kingdom of Jerusalem, the hills of Palestine were terrorized by brigands from every western nation, Englishmen, Frenchmen, and Germans, common criminals and former knights Templar, living side by side with Arabs for whom brigandage had been a way of life for centuries.

To the depredations of professional robber bands were added those of innkeepers and villagers, who found the constant stream of pilgrims passing their doors a temptation too great to resist. The inhabitants of the coastal villages of southern Normandy repeatedly waylaid pilgrims bound for Mont-St.-Michel. Those of northern Italy were said, in 1049, to be murdering Norman pilgrims 'daily'. Rather later, the villages of Navarre and the Basque country took to preying on pilgrims passing on the roads to Santiago; at the border towns of Sorde and Lespéron this was even described as 'customary'. Lawlessness on this scale was a familiar problem whenever the rise of a great sanctuary drew its seasonal flux of pilgrims onto the roads. The anarchic state of Italy in 1350 encouraged whole villages to seize and despoil pilgrims travelling to the Roman Jubilee. Peter, bishop of Rodez, and his companion were ambushed outside the village of Sant' Adriano in Sabina and were saved only the the timely arrival of Napoleone Orsini. The Romans themselves were reported to be mounting expeditions to rob pilgrims on the roads north of the city. One observer believed that half the pilgrims who set out for Rome in 1350 were robbed or killed on the way.

Innkeepers, never the most popular of men, were blamed for many thefts and murders. The most celebrated of all the miracles of St. James told of a man wrongly hanged for stealing money from the pockets of some wealthy German pilgrims as they slept in an inn at Toulouse. The true culprit, it transpired, was the innkeeper, 'wherefore it is clear that pilgrims should take great care before staying at an inn lest a similar fraud be perpetrated on them.' German pilgrims were notoriously the victims of these frauds, probably because they travelled in a somewhat more showy style than others. Tales of gruesome murders of pilgrims in lonely inns were commonplace. In the forest of Châtenay, near Mâcon, there lived, at the beginning of the eleventh century, an innkeeper who used to accommodate travellers at night and murder them as they slept. According to Radulph Glaber, an investigation by the authorities revealed eighty-eight bodies hidden in his hut.

No one doubted that the journey to Jerusalem was by far the most dangerous that a pilgrim could undertake. Every hazard which a mediaeval traveller could encounter is exemplified in the experiences of those who walked three thousand miles or endured six weeks in a tiny, unstable boat, in order to visit the Holy Places.

At the beginning of the eleventh century the conversion of Hungary and the revival of Byzantium had brought most of the overland route to Jerusalem under nominal Christian rule. Latin pilgrims learned how nominal that rule was in 1053, when the Irish pilgrim, Colman, was battered to death at Stockerau outside Vienna, after an angry mob had taken him for a government spy. Although travellers now passed the frontier of the Byzantine empire at Belgrade, behind that frontier lay tracts of untamed territory which never recognized Byzantine rule. Lietbert, bishop of Cambrai, found Christian slaves being sold here in the summer of 1054. The valley of the Danube was so insecure in 1053 that travellers were being turned back by border guards at Belgrade. Pilgrims passed the southern extremity of the Byzantine empire at the coastal town of Lattakieh in northern Syria. Here again, they encountered a deeply hostile and suspicious population. Gerald of Saumur was battered to death by Syrian peasants in 1021, while others, like Anselm of Ardres, fell into the hands of Moslem fanatics and were lucky to escape by renouncing their faith....

The eleventh century had been the heyday of the overland route to the Holy Land, but the growing instability of eastern Europe sharply reduced its popularity in the twelfth. Wealthy pilgrims with large escorts might fight their way through the Balkans as Henry the Lion, duke of Saxony, did 'cum magna gloria' in 1172. But for most men, a pilgrimage to the Holy Land involved a long and expensive journey by sea. After the final disappearance of the crusading states at the end of the thirteenth century, there is scarcely a single case on record of an overland pilgrimage to Jerusalem.

Travel by Sea

A voyage by sea in the middle ages was an uncomfortable experience. Pilgrims were crowded like grains of corn into small, unstable boats where, for six weeks or more, they endured stale food and water, boredom, disease, and intense discomfort.

> *Men may leve alle games*
> *That saylen to seynt James,*

sang an Englishman of the fifteenth century with bitter memories of a voyage to Santiago. The seamen shouted at him and rushed to and fro, continually ordering him out of their way. The bark swayed and tossed, so violently that he did not feel like eating and could not hold a tankard to his lips. The poorest pilgrims, stowed in the most uncomfortable part of the ship, slept next to the bilge-pump, and had to make do with bread and salt and water.

The well-to-do pilgrim could mitigate the discomfort of the journey by paying a little more for his passage. Two types of ship were available at Venice. There were large, oared galleys which were safe, comfortable, and expensive; and small ships for the use of the poor, which were crammed to overflowing. Sebald Rieter, the opulent merchant of Nurnberg, paid sixty-seven ducats for his fare to the Holy Land in 1479 and shared the ship with only sixty-three other passengers. On the other hand an anonymous German pilgrim who travelled in the cheap ship paid only thirty ducats. The Florentine, Lionardo Frescobaldi, took the expensive ship to Alexandria in 1384 and watched the cheap one foundering in the first storm with two hundred pilgrims on board. When the demand for places fell, both rich and poor would share the same ship but occupied different parts of it. 'Chose yow a place in the sayd gallery in the overest stage', advised William Wey, 'for in the lowst under hyt is ryght smoulderyng hote and stynkyng.' When Hans von Mergenthal sailed to the Holy Places in 1476, the place allotted to poor pilgrims was so narrow that it was impossible to turn over in one's sleep. Sleepers were bitten by insects and trampled over by large rats. The animals penned up on the deck to be slaughtered for food broke out from time to time and trod on the sleeping bodies. When the sea was rough, passengers could not stand upright for fear of being struck by swinging booms and ropes.

Pilgrims were advised to bring mattresses and warm clothes with them. Frescobaldi, Gucci, and Sigoli, the three Italians who travelled together in 1384, brought several mattresses, a large number of shirts, a barrel of Malmsey wine, a Bible in several volumes, a copy of the *Moralia* of St. Gregory, a silver cup, 'and other delicate things'. Santo Brasca, who did the journey in 1480, recommended a long thick coat, and also suggested some provisions which every pilgrim would need to supplement the ship's meagre diet: a good supply of Lombard cheese, sausages, salted meat, white biscuits, sugar loaves, and sweetmeats. He should also bring some strong spices for curing indigestion and sea-sickness, 'and above all a great quantity of fruit syrup, for this is what keeps a man alive in hot climates.' William Wey agreed that the prudent pilgrim should arm himself with laxatives, restoratives, ginger, flour, figs, pepper, saffron, cloves, and other 'confections and comfortaciouns': it was essential to have half a dozen chickens in a cage 'for ye schal have need of them many tymes.' All travellers were agreed on the appalling quality of ship's food. 'Sum tymes', declared William Wey, 'ye schal have swych feble bred, wyne, and stynkyng water, that ye schal be ful fayne to eate of yowre owne.'

The manner in which the food was served was not calculated to stimulate the appetite. At the sound of a trumpet the passengers separated into two groups, those whose fare included food, and those who were seeing to their own wants. Members of the first group then scrambled for a place at one of three small tables in the poop. After dinner another trumpet signalled for the diners to retire, while their place was taken by the ship's officers and crew. Their food was even more frugal than that of the pilgrims, but it was served with great pomp on silver dishes, and their wine was tasted before it was offered to them. The galley was a scene of unending chaos. 'Three or four hot-tempered cooks struggle with the food in a narrow passage lined with pots and pans and provisions, while a fire crackles away in the middle. Sounds of angry shouting issue forth from the room while, outside, crowds of passengers shout each other down in the effort to order special meals from the cooks.'

After hunger and sleeplessness, boredom was the principal problem of the passengers. 'Unless a man knows how to occupy himself, he will find the hours very long and tedious', Felix Faber observed. Saxons and Flemings, 'and other men of low class', usually passed the days drinking. Others played dice or cards. Chess was very common. Communal singing went on in the background all the time. A small group of contemplative pilgrims gathered in a corner to read or pray. Others slept day and night. Many wrote travel diaries. A number of pilgrims, Faber remarked with contempt, amused themselves by running up and down the rigging, jumping up and down on the spot, or weight-lifting. 'But most people simply sit about looking on blankly, passing their eyes from one group to another, and thence to the open sea.' During Faber's first pilgrimage, in 1480, the news of Turkish naval activity in the eastern Mediterranean caused the passengers to agree on measures of moral reform which would preserve them from capture. All games were forbidden, together with quarrels, oaths, and blasphemies. Disputes between the French and the

Germans were to cease, and the bishop of Orléans promised to give up gambling. Extra litanies were added to the daily service.

Sermons were the only organized recreation. The company who travelled with canon Casola in 1494 were fortunate enough to have amongst them one Francesco Tivulzio, 'a holy friar with a wonderful library in his head'. Whenever the ship was becalmed, he would rise and deliver an elaborate and learned sermon, many hours in length. On the eve of the feast of St. John, he delivered a sermon on the merits of that saint in nine parts which lasted from 5 p.m. to sunset, and promised to deliver the rest of it on the following day. While waiting for permission to disembark at Joppa, the pilgrims listened to another sermon from friar Tivulzio on the allegorical significance of sailing ships, followed, a few hours later, by 'a beautiful sermon on trade'. Such discourses, however, were not always received in rapturous silence. On Faber's first pilgrimage his preaching was repeatedly interrupted by inane laughter, after which he refused to utter again. On his second pilgrimage the company was more polite, and he favoured them with regular sermons. Even so, a number of noblemen disliked his preaching, which Faber attributed to the fact that they practised the vices that he castigated, 'and truth ever begets hatred.'

The tedious serenity of a long sea voyage was occasionally disturbed by the appearance of pirates. The law of the sea required all passengers to assist in defending the ship, and although pilgrims were exempt from this obligation on account of their religious calling, they usually fought as hard as any. In 1408, a Venetian galley returning from the Holy Land was attacked by a Turkish pirate in the gulf of Satalia. The captain was found to have no cross-bows on board, and it was only after the pilgrims had beaten off their assailants in fierce hand-to-hand fighting that the ship escaped capture. In consequence, the Venetian senate enacted that a proper supply of bows, arrows, and lances was to be carried on every pilgrim-ship. . . .

The fact that pilgrims continued to visit the Holy land in large numbers, in spite of the obstacles in their way, was largely due to the enterprise of the Venetians. The ship-owners of Venice provided the earliest all-inclusive package tours. Galleys licensed by the republic left for Joppa every year as soon as possible after Ascension Day and returned in the autumn. When the demand for passages was high, two fleets sailed from Venice, one in March and one in September. The fare included food and board throughout the journey as well as in the Holy Land itself; the ship-owner, who was generally the master as well, paid all tolls and taxes, and met the cost of donkeys and pack-horses, guided tours of Jerusalem, and special expeditions to the Jordan. The popularity of these tours was entirely due to the high reputation of Venetian ship-owners. The stiff regulations of the serene republic enforced on them standards of safety and commercial morality which were uncommon in other ports. The anonymous English pilgrim of 1345 was advised by the inhabitants of Brindisi that it was unsafe to travel in any ship but a Venetian one. If he entrusted his life to a Sicilian or a Catalan master 'he would undoubtedly enjoy eternal rest at the bottom of the sea.' The ship-owners of Genoa and Pisa were suspected of selling their passengers into slavery at Arab ports. Francesco da Suriano gave four reasons for sailing from Venice in the latter half of the fifteenth century. It was so busy that a traveller never had to wait more than a few days before a ship sailed for his destination; the port was safe from pirates; the Venetian navy patrolled much of the route; and Venetian sailors were 'the finest travelling companions in Christendom'. He might have added that the Venetian currency was among the most stable in the west, and it was the only one which passed for legal tender in Arab territories. 'And so', counselled Santo Brasca, 'travel via Venice, for it is the most convenient embarkation point in the world.'

The Venetian republic began to license and regulate the traffic of pilgrims at the beginning of the thirteenth century. The maritime statutes of 1229 laid down the maximum number of pilgrims which one ship could carry and the date of sailing. At that time there were two fleets per year. The first, which reached the Holy Land in time for Easter, was to return not later than 8th May, while the second was to leave Joppa before 8th November. Further regulations, in 1255, enjoined officers of the republic throughout the eastern Mediterranean to inspect every pilgrim ship calling at their ports and to impose heavy fines if they were overloaded. Mariners were required to swear an oath not to steal more than five shillings from the passengers. The rights and duties of the pilgrim were set out in a lengthy contract, which was signed by both parties. Some of these contracts have survived. The contract between Jan Aerts and the shipowner Agostino Contarini, signed in April 1484, is in every way typical. It permits the pilgrim to go ashore whenever the ship is in port, and to visit Mount Sinai instead of returning with the ship, in which case Contarini will refund ten ducats of his fare. Contarini undertakes not to take on too many passengers or too few crewmen and not to appropriate the pilgrim's chattels if he dies during the journey; he promises to supply enough arms for twenty-five men in case of attack, and to accompany his passengers wherever they go in Jerusalem. The passengers may elect two of their number to oversee him. But there were no standard forms of contract, and pilgrims occasionally insisted on a special term. A contract dating from 1440 provides for a four-day stop at Nicosia, in Cyprus. William Wey advised English pilgrims to insist on a clause forbidding the owner to call at Famagusta on account of its unhealthy air. Once signed, the contract was lodged with a magistrate in Venice who would hear any disputes that arose. In 1497, for example, pilgrims protested that the space allotted to them was too small; port officials boarded the ship and resolved that each passenger should have one and a half feet of deck on which to sleep. On another occasion, pilgrims complained on their return to Venice that they had been manhandled and ill-fed and that their sleeping-quarters had been filled with cargo. Some of them had refused to return with the ship and had instead taken a passage from Beyrut in a Genoese vessel. The rest returned to Venice in an exceedingly hostile mood and, as they included a number of 'great lords', the Senate hastily sequestered the vessel and ordered the owners to refund the fares. . . .

Strange Customs and Foreign Languages

It would be pleasant to learn that pilgrims returned from their travels with minds broadened by the experience of strange people and unfamiliar customs. But it would be the reverse of the truth. Such exchange of ideas as had occurred in the 'dark ages' of the west did not survive the onset of an age of mass-pilgrimage. All too often, those who lived on the pilgrimage roads regarded pilgrims as fair game to be plundered at will. The pilgrims in turn had little incentive to understand their hosts, and viewed them with that uncomprehending contempt which uneducated people commonly accord to foreigners. The impressions of French pilgrims in Spain are a case in point. So loathsome a race as the Basques, thought the author of the *Guide for Pilgrims to Santiago*, could only have originated in Scotland. After describing their national dress, he goes on to comment on their food and language in the following terms:

> 'Not only are they badly dressed, but they eat and drink in the most disgusting way. The entire household, including servants, eat out of the same pot and drink from the same cup. Far from using spoons, they eat with their hands, slobbering over the food like any dog or pig. To hear them speaking, you would think they were a pack of hounds barking, for their language is absolutely barbarous. They call God *Urcia*; bread is *orgui* and wine *ardum*, while meat is referred to as *aragui* and fish *araign*. . . . They are in fact a most uncouth race whose customs are quite different from those of any other people. They have dark, evil, ugly faces. They are debauched, perverse, treacherous and disloyal, corrupt and sensual drunkards. They are like fierce savages, dishonest and untrustworthy, impious, common, cruel and quarrelsome people, brought uyp in vice and iniquity, totally devoid of human feeling. . . . They will kill you for a penny. Men and women alike warm themselves by the fire, revealing those parts which are better hidden. They fornicate unceasingly, and not only with humans. . . . That is why they are held in contempt by all decent folk.'

In the *Chanson de Roland* the Basques appear in an extremely sinister light, and the influence of this celebrated poem may well be responsible for the contempt which many pilgrims expressed for them. But this alone will not explain the venom of the *Guide*, which entertains a remarkably similar opinion of the Gascons, characterizing their way of life as impious, immoral, and 'in every way detestable'.

If a Poitevin could write thus of the Gascons, he was unlikely to feel closer in spirit to the Greeks and oriental Christians, let alone to the Arabs. Throughout this period, relations with the Greeks were marked by a bitterness which can only be understood in the light of the tortuous relations of Byzantium with the crusaders. Most Latin Christians despised the Greeks as effeminate schismatics and believed with immovable conviction that they had betrayed the twelfth-century crusades. A guide-book written at the end of the century refers to them characteristically as 'cunning men who do not bear arms and who err from the true faith. . . . They also use leaven bread in the Eucharist and do other strange things. They even have an alphabet of their own.' This mood of suspicion was aggravated by the widespread belief that the Byzantine authorities deliberately obstructed pilgrims passing through Constantinople. The emperor Alexius Comnenus was once described by an eminently sane Latin writer as 'that great oppressor of pilgrims to Jerusalem who hinders their progress by guile or by force.' Indeed, it never struck western pilgrims that their habit of helping themselves to whatever they required, and of insulting and attacking local people, might arouse justifiable resentment on the part of their hosts. The importance which Greeks attached to their own traditions was regarded by some Latin pilgrims as nothing less than a calculated insult. Jacques de Vitry denounced them as 'foul schismatics moved by sinful pride', and then went on to consider the Jacobite and Armenian Christians, 'barbarous nations who differ from both Greeks and Latins . . . and use a peculiar language understood only by the learned.'

Language was indeed the principal barrier. Few mediaeval men, however cultivated they were, understood more than a few words of any language but their own or Latin. Travelling through regions such as eastern Europe or Egypt, where pilgrims were rare and Latin unknown, was a difficult and dangerous undertaking. Lietbert, bishop of Cambrai, who passed through the Danube valley on the way to Jerusalem in 1054, listed 'the strange and foreign language of the Huns' amongst the perils which he had encountered, together with mountains, swamps, and impenetrable forests. During the twelfth century, French was the language of Jerusalem, and this is said to have made difficulties for the Germans. At any rate, one of the reasons given for the foundation of the German hospice in Jerusalem was that 'in such a place Germans might talk in a language they can understand.' In Venice the authorities were constantly embarrassed by the activities of sharp traders or shipowners who took advantage of foreigners bound for the Holy Land. 'It is well-known that many scandalous mistakes have been made of late, on account of the great number of pilgrims boarding ships at Venice', the senate noted in 1398; 'for the said pilgrims are of divers tongues . . . and unless a remedy is found, still greater scandals will follow.'

It is worth following the Burgundian pilgrim Bertrandon de la Brocquière in his efforts to learn a few words of Turkish. Bertrandon visited the Holy Land in 1432–3, but he avoided the Venetian package tour because he wished to spy out the land at leisure, with a view to planning a crusade. In Damascus he made the acquaintance of a Turk who spoke Arabic, Hebrew, Turkish, and Greek. Bertrandon spoke none of these languages, but he had a working knowledge of Italian, and the Turk found a Jew who knew a little Italian and some Turkish. The Jew compiled a list of everything that Bertrandon would require on his journey, in parallel columns of Turkish and Italian. In the first day after leaving Damascus, Bertrandon had occasion to ask a group of peasants for some fodder for his horse. He consulted his piece of paper and made his request, but there was no reaction. He showed the paper to the leading peasant, who began to roar with laughter. The group then gave him an impromptu lesson in Turkish, picking up various articles and pronouncing their names very carefully several times. 'And when I left them I knew how to ask in Turkish for almost everything I wanted.'

Italian was the only European language known to a significant number of Arabs. Pilgrims who visited Mount Sinai via Egypt could usually find an Italian-speaking interpreter at Alexandria or Cairo, but this was an expensive luxury of which few travellers availed themselves. In 1384 Lionardo Frescobaldi's party spent more than forty-nine ducats on interpreters between Alexandria and Damascus. In addition, one of their interpreters stole eight ducats from them, and another was in league with a group of Bedouin bandits. More than a hundred ducats was spent on bribing the personal interpreters of various Arab officials to present their requests for safe-conducts in a favourable way.

Phrase-books, then as now, were the simplest way to overcome the language difficulty. As early as the ninth century, we find a phrase-book entitled *Old High-German Conversations (Altdeutsche Gespräche)* being used by Franks travelling in Germany. It consists of orders to servants, requests for information, and demands for hospitality such as 'I want a drink':

'Erro, e guille trenchen; id est, ego volo bibere.'

A number of early phrase books of Greek and Hebrew survive, most of which were clearly intended for the use of pilgrims to the Holy land. The abbey of Mont-St.-Michel had, in the eleventh century, a Greek phrasebook containing useful demands like

'Da mihi panem: DOS ME PSOMI.' ['Give me bread.']

An interesting manual for crusaders, dating from the twelfth century, includes such tactful requests as 'What is the news about the Greek emperor? What is he doing? He is being kind to the Franks. What good things does he give them? Much money and weapons.' During the period of mass-pilgrimages in the late middle ages, an immense number of phrase-books was available, some of them very comprehensive. The library of Charles V of France contained a manual for pilgrims entitled *How to ask in Arabic for the necessities of life*. Another French-Arabic phrase-book, preserved in the Swiss abbey of St.-Gall, has a long section on how to ask one's way in a strange town.

Some pilgrims found oriental alphabets a source of limitless fascination. *Mandeville's Travels*, that strange mixture of fact and fantasy, sets out the Greek, Hebrew, Arabic, and Persian alphabets, though they contain many mistakes and the Hebrew one is incomprehensible. Johann Schiltberger appended to the account of his travels the *Pater Noster* in Armenian and Turkish. But the most proficient linguist amongst the pilgrims of the fifteenth century was certainly Arnold von Harff, a wealthy young nobleman of Cologne who, between 1496 and 1499, travelled through Italy, Syria, Egypt, Arabia, Ethiopia, Nubia, Palestine, Turkey, and Spain. He was a worldly pilgrim of the type mocked in the *Canterbury Tales* and the *Quinze Joies de Mariage*, but he took a genuine interest in the people of each country and particularly in their languages. Von Harff collected alphabets. His memoirs contain many oriental alphabets (some of them are undecipherable), as well as useful phrases in nine different languages, Croatian, Albanian, Greek, Arabic, Hebrew, Turkish, Hungarian, Basque, and Breton. He was a cultivated man, a gallant knight and an aristocrat whose range of phrases was broader than that of most conventional pilgrims. Thus, 'Wash my shirt for me—I do not understand —Will you sell me that?—How much is this?—Madam shall I marry you?—Madam shall I sleep with you?—Good woman, I am already in your bed.'

But Arnold von Harff was scarcely typical even of his own worldly age. He was an acute observer who was interested in such diverse matters as wild animals in the Nile valley, and the Mamluk system of government. He doubted the authenticity of the body of St. James at Santiago, and openly disputed the claims of several Roman relics. He considered the Turks closer to the spirit of Christianity than the Spanish. A more faithful reflection of the mentality of pilgrims is found in the account of the Arab way of life in the travel diary of one of Frescobaldi's companions, which begins, 'now let me tell you of their bestial habits.'

The Peasants in Revolt

R. H. HILTON

France in 1251 and 1358, Sicily in 1282, Flanders in 1255, 1267, 1275, 1280, and 1302, and England in 1381—all experienced violent lower-class rebellions. But these are only the major uprisings; there were many others. In 1251, Louis IX of France, on a crusade in Egypt and recently defeated at Cairo, sent home a call for help. All over France, peasants rose to form a huge army that would bring succor to the king, but within a short time segments of this army forgot their mission and went rampaging through manors and cities. Under Louis' mother, Blanche of Castille, the royal government had at first supported the peasant army, but when Blanche and her counselors recognized the anarchic character of the movement, they acted in concert with city authorities and feudal lords to put a bloody end to it. In 1358, after twenty years of war with England and several plague epidemics, the peasants of France again rose in revolt. The immediate cause of the uprising was an order that the hard-pressed peasants must help rebuild the castles and manor houses of the rich in preparation for further fighting. The rising was incredibly vicious and bloody on both sides.

In Flanders the rebellions were mostly urban, since that area was, and still is, one of the most densely populated regions in Europe. The weavers and other lower-class groups in the cities rose against the patriciate, which had allied itself with the hated French king. The worst of these uprisings was the Matins of Bruges, which took place on May 17, 1302. When the town's church bells sounded matins, the first prayer service of the day at 2 A.M., the population rose to slaughter the French garrison and officials. Under the leadership of the count of Flanders, an army of weavers and workers devastated a French army sent to put down the rebellion. All the rebellions of Flanders were tied up with the political competition between the count and the French king. During the Hundred Years' War, the count sided with the English and further deepened the political divisions.

The Sicilian Vespers was also a popular uprising with political overtones. The people rose to drive out the French conquerors of the island, leaving the way open to Spanish intervention. But politics and social grievances were inextricably mixed up in the rebellion, and hundreds of French citizens, including women and children, lost their lives. Castles and other buildings occupied by the ruling class were also destroyed.

Perhaps the most famous insurrection, however, was the Peasants' Rebellion of 1381 in England. There had been unrest among the lower classes of the country for years following the plague (1348–1349). The drastic population decrease caused a severe labor shortage and led to a general disruption of the economy. Workers demanded higher wages, peasants left their farms to seek higher-paying jobs in the cities. The nobility, whose income depended on the rents received from peasant farmers, and the merchants, whose profits were being squeezed, took action against this movement in the Statutes of Laborers, which fixed wages and prohibited migration from the farms. That these provisions were not effective is shown by the complaints brought out in the parliaments of the period.

Why was late medieval society so prone to these upheavals? Was there some characteristic or set of characteristics that permeated all European society and would explain these events? In this selection, R. H. Hilton gives an overview of the movements, their causes, and their programs.

The best known of the late medieval peasant rebellions are: the revolt in maritime Flanders 1323–1327; the Jacquerie in the Paris region in 1358; the Tuchin movement in central France, from the 1360s to the end of the fourteenth century; the English rising of 1381; and the wars of the *remensas* in Catalonia during the 1460s and the 1480s. This is not an exhaustive list. Other specifically peasant movements on a smaller scale included the strike of the vineyard workers of the Auxerrois in the 1390s; and, more difficult to evaluate, movements involving peasants, in which the peasants might have formed the majority of participants, but which aimed at goals other than theirs or theirs specifically. The peasants might be full participants, or they might be being used by others for their own purposes.

The Taborite movement in Bohemia (the militant wing of the national Hussite movement against German and papal domination) was clearly to a considerable degree a peasant one in its composition and there were millenarian elements in its religious outlook, but it was led by gentry and clerics and there was a considerable artisan element. It hardly aimed, then, to fulfil specifically peasant demands. Peasants also participated in the risings in various parts of England in 1450, of which the most important was that in Kent led by Jack Cade, but their motivation was to such a degree political, and even dynastic, that there is some doubt as to whether they can be designated as peasant movements. In some ways they more resemble the provincial risings in parts of England in the 1530s which were directed against real or imagined oppression by the government, and to a considerable extent led by the local gentry.

What then are the problems posed by peasant movements, and particularly by the large-scale movements of the later middle ages? We should remember the basic tensions in a society where peasants were the majority of the basic producers, but the course of each movement must be

From R. H. Hilton, *Bond Men Made Free* (New York: Viking Press, 1973), pp. 112–25, 130–34.

investigated separately. And although a mere narrative history of events will not in itself throw much light on the fundamentals of the movements, such a narrative history must be established in order to discover the existence (or otherwise) of a common pattern in the sequence of events. Emerging, too, from an examination of the sequence of events must come some notion of the organization of the movements, and of the degree to which they either arose spontaneously, or were carefully planned by groups or individual organizers. This brings us to the vital question of the social and intellectual origins of the leaders of the movements—a problem which once answered necessarily involves the allied problems of the social composition of the participating masses. These considerations will lead us to the problem of the ideas guiding the various elements involved; this is by no means the same problem as that of the immediate or long-term goals, which also need scrutiny.

Finally some assessment of the historical consequences must be undertaken, not simply in terms of success or failure in the realization of explicitly stated goals, but also in terms of such changes of direction in the history of society which peasant movements may effect. An examination of the major European movements in terms of the problems thus classified could in turn be used to look afresh at the history of the English rising of 1381—one of the most interesting and significant as well as the best documented of all medieval peasant rebellions.

It is, of course, insufficient to prove that peasants and landowners had incompatible interests in the division of the social product, and that peasants therefore had a propensity to withhold rents and services and come into juridical or even political conflict with their lords. The fact is that the traditional social relationships between peasant and lord in varying forms persisted in different parts of Europe, probably from the bronze age until the eighteenth or nineteenth century. Something more than the natural antagonism between an exploiting and exploited class must therefore have precipitated movements which often seemed to the participants on both sides a break in the "natural order" of things; this phrase gives us a clue to the outbreak of many of the more serious movements.

Peasants, even more than their lords, tended to cling to custom, even when, without knowing it, they were constantly seeking to mould custom to suit their own interests. Günther Franz, in his history of the peasants' war in Germany at the beginning of the sixteenth century, noticed that (at any rate to begin with) rebellious peasants saw themselves as defending "the old law." And so it was innovation by the lords which (in peasant eyes) seemed to justify their own renunciation of their humble role in the social hierarchy. It was the imposition of the indemnity tax by the King of France to be collected by the officials of the Count of Flanders (who should have been their protector) which pushed the self-

assertive, unservile peasants and artisans in the maritime districts of
Flanders into rebellion; it was the requisitions for the victualling of the
castles of the nobility in the region of Paris, done at the expense of the
peasants in the surrounding villages, which provoked the Jacquerie in
1358; it was the insolent taxation imposed by the king's lieutenant, the
Duke of Berry, on his subjects in central France, when he was unable to
protect them from the English and their hired *routiers*, which began the
equally serious, though less well-known, Jacquerie of the Tuchins; and it
was the extra demands by the lords of Catalonia for the so-called *malos
usos*, or "evil customs," which precipitated the long war of the *remensas*,
the servile peasants.

In none of these cases can it be supposed that the breach of customary expectations was the only cause of the outbreak. There were
important, indeed essential, predisposing factors. The resistance to the
collection of the indemnity tax in Flanders in 1323 was not a sudden decision on the part of a normally passive population. This population was
composed for the most part of descendants of free settlers in the coastal
districts. Many of them were quite poor, although their leaders were
among the richest of the peasants of the district, as is shown in the
enumeration of the lands and goods of the dead after the defeat of the rising in 1327 at the battle of Cassel. Many of the peasants were involved in
the textile trade, which was already spreading from town to country.
Their obligations to their lords were mainly acquitted in money rent, and
they were of free status, and made up a strong quasi-communal element
in the organization of local government. Although presided over by the
Count of Flanders' bailiff (usually a noble), the local courts were composed of jurors, *keuriers* or *échevins*, many of whom were peasants. And
when the revolt reached fever pitch at the beginning of 1325, the peasants
took over the existing organization and put their own captains in place of
the count's bailiffs. Above all, there had existed since the beginning of
the century a strong sentiment of hostility to the French-speaking nobility
and their patrician allies among the great merchants of the towns. They
had, for these reasons, supported the Count of Flanders so long as he
resisted his suzerain, the King of France. No doubt they remembered the
battle of Courtrai in 1302, when peasants and weavers defeated the
mounted knights of France, but in spite of which they had had imposed
upon them by the count's capitulation at Athis (1304) the first heavy
indemnity payment to the French crown.

The general conditions in the area to the north, north-east and south
of Paris, in the spring of 1358, were even more likely than those in maritime Flanders to enable any extra oppression to spark off a rebellion. For
a year, the hired soldiers of the French and English, now under truce, had
been living off the countryside, and the peasants could no longer distinguish between their "own" and the enemy's supporters. The situation

was further complicated by the entry into the game of Charles, King of Navarre, a possible pretender to the French throne, whose troops were as likely to be fighting for the English or for themselves, as for the Regent of France, the king being in prison in England. Furthermore, from March 1358, there had been civil war between the regent and his supporters, on the one hand, and a reforming party, on the other, led by Etienne Marcel, provost of the merchants of Paris.

The nobility was discredited, and unable to perform its traditional function of defending the other orders. Its landed income was insufficient, for rents were low; and the price of grain was low, while wages and other costs were high. Many of the male members of the nobility had to be ransomed. Hence, the nobles and their men-at-arms in the castles of the Île de France, were as likely to pillage and slay the local peasants as were the bands led by such foreign captains as the Englishman James Pipe, lieutenant of the King of Navarre, who was operating south of Paris. While the traditional explanation of the Jacquerie as a revolt against misery contains an element of truth, it is insufficient. Included in the rebellious area were prosperous villages, especially north of Paris, where exasperation at taxation and requisition, and disillusion with the collapse of the traditional social order, were combined with the economic grievances of the normally well-to-do cereal farmers who were unable to get a good price for their product. At the same time, the impoverished and badly harassed area to the south-west of the city—precisely where one would expect an explosion of pure misery—was virtually untouched by the rebellion.

A combination of pillaging by bands of soldiers, and heavy, even illegal, taxation was also responsible for the further and very different Jacquerie in the France of the Hundred Years' War—the counter-brigandage of the Tuchins. If the Jacquerie of 1358 in Paris gives the appearance (even if illusory) of being a short, sharp and elemental protest against miserable conditions, the Tuchins are the prototype of a very different form of poor people's protest, one which we have come to recognize as "social banditry." We find here no rising en masse of an outraged peasant population, but a cunning adoption by the mountain population of Auvergne, both the suburban artisans of towns like St Flour and the peasants of the district, of the pillaging habits of their erstwhile oppressors. From the early 1360s until the middle of the 1380s, the Tuchins troubled the authorities, while the Jacques around Paris were crushed after only two weeks by the noble companies under the command of the King of Navarre. All the same, the immediate causes were the same for both Jacqeries—the pillage of the military companies, and government taxation.

One of the most sustained of peasant wars was that of the Catalan remensas, or servile peasants, in the fifteenth century. Catalonia, compared with most other parts of Spain, was heavily seigneuralized, and the majority of peasants were unfree. Apart from the various rents and services which they owed to their lords, they were particularly restricted in their freedom of movement, and these restrictions had been strengthened from the thirteenth century—the lords' response to emigration southwards to colonize the newly conquered lands and to the growing cities. After the Black Death, there was a further seigneurial reaction, prompted by the fall in landed revenues, when extra rents in kind were demanded, and boon services were made compulsory.

All those peasants who were already forbidden to leave their holdings except on payment of a heavy redemption, the *remensas*, were now reckoned automatically liable to what had become known as the "five evil customs" (*malos usos*). These were: *intestia*, a death duty of one-third of movables payable in case of intestacy; *exorquia*, another death duty; *cugucia*, one-third or one-half of movables payable in case of a wife's adultery; *arsina*, a fine paid if the farm caught fire accidentally; and *firma d'espoli violenta*, a fine aimed at restricting the raising of a mortgage. These obligations were not new in the fifteenth century, but they had not been universally applicable. It was their generalization and imposition on all peasants liable to *remensas* and the fear of free tenants that they would spread to them which united the Catalan rural population against their lords. This resentment arose as much because these obligations were obvious earmarks of personal servility as because they were economically burdensome. But the search for freedom was, it seems, also exacerbated by a conflict with the lords over abandoned holdings (*casos ronecs*). The question was whether these should be shared among surviving tenants at low rents, or absorbed into demesne or let on lease on short terms at high rents.

Small-scale local revolts against the seigneurial reaction had already begun by the late 1380s, and continued into the early part of the fifteenth century. The *remensas* attempted to have the *malos usos* abolished by the crown, and offered enormous sums for their redemption. Their abolition was accepted by Alphonso V in 1455, under peasant pressure, and it was the refusal of the nobles, led by the Bishop of Gerona and the patricians of Barcelona, which precipitated the war of 1462. In this war the reactionary nobility and the urban patricians found themselves fighting not only the peasants but the king. A renewal of the war in 1483 was due entirely to an attempt by the nobility and the patricians to put the clock back to the pre-1455 situation, but social tensions became critical as a result also of the prolonged crisis of Catalonia's declining economy.

It will be seen that the immediate causes for some of the most serious of the mass movements were actions by landowners or governments, or both together, which altered the customary relationships or disappointed normal expectations, to the detriment of the peasant class as a whole, rich and poor. Although a heavy tax, or a requisition order, or the reversal of a concession might not in itself precipitate a rising, it might do so in the context of the strained social relationships which we find in each of the areas we have considered. This strain is normally seen by the peasants from an apparently conservative standpoint. They cannot accept the abandonment of traditional roles by any one of the orders of the society—whose basic structure they do not, to begin with, challenge. This seems always to be the most important factor, and the significance of precipitating causes (taxes, for example) is that, as they affect all, they unify all—and focus existing resentments.

If we can see common features in the causation of these movements, contrasts rather than similarities appear when we look at the pattern of events and the form of the struggle. The most obvious contrast is the duration of the rebellions. The rising which has bequeathed to history that most familiar name, the Jacquerie, and the supposedly typical charcteristics of peasant rebellion—namely, extreme violence and a hatred of the nobility —was in fact the shortest and worst-organized. The first of the recorded conflicts between peasants and the plundering brigands, the nobles, was at St Leu d'Esserent, near Senlis, on 28 May 1358, though there were probably almost simultaneous outbreaks further west. The destruction of the main peasant army under Guillaume Cale by the King of Navarre near Mello occurred on 10 June and the peasants who were helping the Parisians in their siege of the royalist nobles in the fortress at Meaux were defeated in a fortnight.

On the other hand, the armed revolt of the peasants of maritime Flanders which began in 1323 did not end until June 1328, when the King of France and the Flemish nobility defeated the peasants and artisans at Cassel. The Tuchins began their independent operations as groups of "social bandits" in the mountains of Auvergne in 1363 and were not destroyed as a social force until the summer of 1384. Even after their defeat at Mentières, sporadic bands were operating until the general amnesty of 1381, and there was a brief revival in the early fifteenth century. The struggle of the *remensas* was even longer lived, if we count the earliest sporadic outbreaks as occurring from 1388. The mass campaigns lasted from 1462 until 1471, and from 1484 until 1486—though there is some difficulty here in separating the peasant war for the abolition of the *malos usos* from the civil war which involved the crown, the nobility and bourgeoisie.

It must be due partly to a failure in organization when a mass peasant movement is as quickly suppressed as the Jacquerie: failure to organize according to the needs of the situation, the known strength of the enemy and the reliability of the allies. The Jacques gathered in village groups and operated separately. Owing to the surprise experienced by the nobles at this sudden insubordination, the rebels, with some assistance from the Parisians, managed to destroy a considerable number of castles, along with the records which the owners kept of the peasants' obligations to them. In common with other rural risings, the example of rebellion rapidly spread by word of mouth from village to village, without the separate bands concerting a common policy. Eventually, their most experienced captain, Guillaume Cale, managed to get together a force of several thousands; but this numerical strength gave an illusion of power which Cale tried to dispel. Militarily inexperienced, the fact that they had come together to present a single target for the knights and men-at-arms under Charles of Navarre led to their downfall. Special methods of fighting were needed for peasants to defeat armed horsemen in pitched battle, as the Taborites with their battlewagons made from farm carts were to show after 1420 in Bohemia. Even the successors of the victors of Courtrai were defeated in the end by an army of French chivalry at Cassel, although they had, it seems, succeeded for a time in organizing themselves on the basis of the existing administrative framework of the *ambachten* or castleries.

The most successful peasant military organization (if we put on one side the Hussite armies as not being the product of a specifically peasant movement) was undoubtedly that of the *remensas*. They had already begun to meet in assemblies in the 1440s, in order to discuss the redemption of the *malos usos*, and when the peasant army was eventually organized in the 1460s, their leader Francisco Verntallat did so by recruiting one man from every three households. The removal at the end of the first *remensa* war of peasant garrisons from castles shows that they had learnt the importance of fortification, and a later royal veto, on the eve of the second war, on peasants or artisans having riding horses, shows that they must have learnt, too, this other aspect of medieval armed combat. Above all, the peasant army rested on the basis of sworn association, the *sacramental*, created in the peasant assemblies.

This, then, was one way of organizing: the creation of a military force based on a form of political and social institution, the village or district assembly. It was more successful in Catalonia than in maritime Flanders; but the Tuchins show that it was not the only way in which peasants and plebeians could organize to harass the authorities. Here we return to the more elemental form of organization in small bands, but in the case of the Tuchins there was no attempt to engage in head-on conflict with the military forces of the nobility or the crown. Continuing with their ordinary agricultural or artisan occupations in village or suburb, these **bands of twenty or thirty men, or occasionally more—associates, bound together by terrible oaths—organized themselves for the pillage of livestock, valuables or cash, and for the capture of churchmen, gentry or merchants for the purposes of ransom.** In Auvergne, between the 1360s and the 1380s, the habitual prey of the Tuchins were the English or Gascon *routiers*, who were despoilers of the countryside but whose booty was then looted by the Tuchins like wolves drawn to the sheepfold.

The Tuchins were able to play an intricate political game. Local authorities, such as the consuls of St Flour, made truces with the English in order to be left at peace, while the Tuchins robbed the English, and so embroiled the local notables whom the English suspected of breaking the truce. In the eyes of the royal government, however, such truces were illegal, and the peasant and artisan brigands came almost to appear—quite unintentionally as far as they were concerned—as patriots. The Tuchins kept going as long as conditions favoured them, that is, while disorder created by the operations of the *routiers* and general hostility among peasants and town artisans to the nobles and to the authorities, resulting from the failure to defend them from the Anglo-Gascons and from the excessive taxation of the king's lieutenant, lasted. When relative peace and stability returned, the Tuchins' bands could only prey on the mass of the peasantry, so losing their support.

The Tuchins were not all peasants. Artisans from the suburbs of St Flour and elsewhere were also involved. Furthermore, the leaders of the bands were often members of the nobility. Even so, it is by no means the case that we should not examine the Tuchinat as a peasant movement. For there were, in fact, very few "pure" peasant movements, at any rate on a mass scale, in the sense that the participants and leaders were exclusively of peasant origin. The number of nobles in the leadership of the Tuchins is not difficult to explain. In the first place, they were often outcasts from their own class, sometimes using the Tuchins only for their own purposes, but used by the Tuchins in turn, who found it convenient to employ the military skills of the class which still regarded itself, by profession as well as status, primarily as a warrior class.

Thus, Mignot de Cardaillac, a Tuchin leader in the Paulhac region in the 1360s, was a bastard of a prominent noble family involved in disputes with other nobles over succession to property. Pierre de Brugère (or de Brès), a Tuchin leader during the 1380s, was connected by family ties with many leading families of Auvergne and Languedoc, and probably joined the Tuchins after robbing his relative, the Bishop of Albi, and perhaps because of domestic troubles when his squire became his wife's lover. After Pierre was killed, other gentry leaders appeared, such as the Lord of Pertus and Jean de Dienne. At the fag-end of the Tuchin movement, Jean de Chalus, returning to Auvergne from Agincourt in 1415, was captured by a band of Tuchins and forced to join them, to take part in their assemblies and to bind himself to them by swearing an oath.

The leadership of peasant bands by members of the nobility, even for quite specifically peasant objectives, was not as rare as one might imagine. Even in a movement as frankly hostile to the nobility as a class as the Jacquerie of 1358, some nobles, as well as bourgeois, were engaged on the side of the peasants. The three or four whose names we know from letters of pardon issued afterwards by the king, naturally sought to excuse themselves, alleging that they had been forced to become leaders of the peasants' bands. This may, indeed, have been true, though we can never know what private or political rancours might have determined an individual to abandon his apparent class interest. The interest of the peasants in securing the leadership of locally prominent individuals is more explicable. In the case of the Montmorency district, we even find them asking Simon de Bernes, provost and captain of the county of Beaumont, for permission to choose a leader, a choice which fell on Jacques de Chennevières, who afterwards pretended to have accepted against his wishes and to have attempted to moderate the peasants' violence. As we have already suggested, some peasants may have been conscious of their lack of military expertise. The question also arises as to what extent the concept of the gentry as the natural leaders of the peasants still persisted, even when the conflict of interest between the two classes seemed absolute.

It will not do to overemphasize the part played by gentry in the leadership of peasants' movements. There is the abundant evidence from the earlier period of peasant leadership of small-scale movements which we have already examined, and this source of leaders by no means dried up. Lack of contrary indication would suggest that Guillaume Cale of Mello must have been a well-to-do peasant, and Clais Zannekin, who began to play a leading role in the rising of maritime Flanders from 1324, appears as one of the better-off peasants with a holding of between thirty-five and forty acres of arable land, although it has been suggested that he had property in Bruges. In addition, was not Francisco Verntallat really a peasant, in spite of his poor *hidalgo* ancestors on one side of the family, and his promotion and enrichment by the king after the end of the first war of the *remensas*? And the more radical Père Jean Sala likewise? The same kind of background was probably true of most of the minor leaders in all of the movements. Their names tend not to be recorded. Fewer but more exceptional individuals are mentioned by chroniclers or appear in the records precisely because their participation was unexpected.

A frequently noticed source of outside leaders of peasant and other plebeian movements of the Middle Ages is the clergy, particularly the lesser clergy. Various explanations are given, such as that which states that the participating clerics may have been of peasant origin, and that their lowly position at the bottom of the ecclesiastical hierarchy made them resentful of the existing social order, and that, further, they were influenced by the radical, egalitarian element in the Christian tradition. The lesser clergy, as we have seen, often occupied an important position of leadership in the people's crusades and in heretical movements with peasant and artisan followings. On the whole, the clerics' presence is most frequent where movements have aims going well beyond the satisfaction of immediate social and political demands or the expression of immediate resentment of social oppression. Thus, even if the fight of the Apostles in northern Italy at the beginning of the fourteenth century had any of the characteristics of a peasant movement, by reason of its class composition, its aims were apocalyptic and were inevitably articulated by a man with a clerical background. Similarly, the extreme Taborites or Pikarts around the year 1420 in Bohemia—whatever the temporary practice of a sort of "war communism" might have implied about their social views—were also apocalyptic visionaries, and their leaders tended to be priests, like the Moravian, Martin Huska. Similarly the views of the Taborite centre, of Waldensian inspiration, were articulated by priests such as Jan Zelivsky.

Those movements, however, which we have taken to be typical, where not only was the mass of participants drawn from the peasantry, but where they were reacting against social pressures on them as peasants, and were seeking a peasant solution, had a remarkably weak priestly participation. The one important exception to this is to be found in England in 1381, and will be considered later in detail. Not only were there no priests in the leadership of the rebellion in maritime Flanders, but there is evidence of strong anti-clericalism. The refusal to pay tithes, for example, in the area of Ghent, shows a clear anti-clerical disposition, though this could have been compatible with a certain type of radical clerical inspiration. But under the later leadership of Jacques Peyt, anti-clericalism sharpened. In November 1325 an interdict had been placed on Flanders, and Peyt and his successors had forced priests either to perform their office or to emigrate. Peyt was said to have wished to do away with all priests. Some evidence of a minor participation by a few clerics in the Jacquerie of 1358 can be shown, but there is no leadership. The Tuchins not only had no leaders from the clerical order, but at times show signs of anti-clericalism. In the 1380s, for instance, clerics in Tuchin-dominated areas thought it prudent to disguise themselves as laymen (in areas of military operations it was usually the other way round); a Trinitarian friar so disguised was killed when he was captured.

Nor does the *remensas* movement reveal any clerical participation or direction. It is true that one of the earliest rebellious actions of some of the *remensas* was participation in the anti-Jewish pogroms of 1391, in which there was clerical direction and which assumed a social character unexpected by some of these clerical agitators. *Remensas* were also involved in a jointly anti-semitic and anti-landowner action in Gerona in 1415. But the essential movement against the *malos usos* had no clerical or even religious inspiration. Indeed the historian of the movement, J. V.

Vives, particularly noticed how little religion there was in its ideology. This, he discovered, was mainly of juridical inspiration, namely the idea that by natural law all men are free and have the right to be protected by the king against the nobles. It was the jurisconsult Thomas Mieres, not a cleric, who voiced these views. . . .

In spite of the considerable differences between these late-medieval peasant movements, there was one prominent feature which they had in common: the emergence, among some of the participants, of a consciousness of class. It was, however, a negative class consciousness in that the definition of class which was involved was that of their enemies rather than of themselves: in other words, the nobility. Henri Pirenne, writing about the revolt of maritime Flanders in his introduction to the list of confiscations after Cassel, insisted on its social character. It was, he wrote, "a class war between the peasants and the nobility." This anti-noble characteristic was to the fore already in 1323 in an attack on members of local courts, the *keuriers,* who were of noble or patrician origin. Under the leadership of Jacques Peyt, in 1326, after the reimposition of an indemnity payable to the King of France at the so-called peace of Arques, this deep emotion developed into a terror directed against both the nobility and their supporters. The peasant rebels were said by the official chronicler of the counts of Flanders to have threatened the rich with death, saying to them: "you love the nobles more than you do the commons from whom you live."

This conscious hostility towards the noble class was very prominent during the Jacquerie of 1358. Without any declaration of aims, its existence could be concluded from the fact that the objects of the peasants' attacks were exclusively knights, squires and ladies, along with the castles in which they lived. A recent historian, commenting on the fiscal and other pressures on the peasants which were particularly irksome after the battle of Poitiers, goes so far as to say that "the quick irritation that Jacques Bonhomme experienced in the face of these exactions was nothing compared with his permanent rage against the nobles whom he blamed, as a whole, for not having fulfilled their duty of protection which tradition and mutual obligation demanded of them." Froissart, at the beginning of his account of the Jacquerie, reports a discussion among the peasants (no doubt imagined):

> . . . one of them got up and said that the nobility of France, knights and squires, were disgracing and betraying the realm, and that it would be a good thing if they were all destroyed. At this they all shouted; "He's right! He's right! Shame on any man who saves the gentry from being wiped out."

And again Froissart says (somewhat illogically) that when the peasants were asked the reason for their violent actions, "they replied that they did not know; it was because they saw others doing them that they copied them. They thought that by such means they could destroy all the nobles and gentry in the world, so that there would be no more of them."

Jean de Venette emphasizes the same element of class hatred:

> . . . the peasants . . . seeing that the nobles gave them no protection, but rather oppressed them as heavily as the enemy, rose and took arms against the nobles of France . . . the number of peasants eager to extirpate the nobles and their wives and to destroy their manor houses grew until it was estimated at five thousand.

The social bandit, as compared with the peasants engaged in mass risings, operated mostly with a less precise consciousness of his position of social antagonism to his opponents. Any bird was worth the plucking, and if he did not pluck his own kind it was because there was little or nothing to be had. All the same, awareness of social conflict was not altogether missing. The evidence for the greatest degree of class consciousness comes from the last major phase of Tuchin activity, that of the 1380s, when, according to the life of Charles VI in the St Denis chronicle, the terrible mutual oaths of th Tuchin bands included the promise never more to submit to taxation, but only to keep the ancient liberty of their country (*patrie antiquam servantes libertatem*). The social bandit's chosen prey were men of the church, the nobles, and the merchants. One of their captains, the renegade noble, Pierre de Brugère, gave orders to his lieutenants that no one with smooth, uncalloused hands or who by gesture, clothing or speech showed courtliness or elegance should even be admitted to their company, but rather slain. Such remarks about the Tuchins come from a hostile writer, writing no doubt like Froissart from hearsay evidence. But even taking exaggeration into account, the element of conscious class antagonism which is suggested may well have been present.

The ferocity which, rightly or wrongly, was attributed to the French rebels by the aristocratic chroniclers does not appear in the Catalan wars unless we can glimpse it in the physical demonstrations by some of the *remensas* peasants at the turn of the fourteenth century, when in order to intimidate the landowners, and perhaps unwelcome lessees of the lapsed holdings, they dug ditches and put up crosses and other signs, the *senyals mort*, threatening death. There may have been some diversion from possible class antagonism on the peasants' part by the attitude evinced by the monarchy from time to time, and expressed in its strongest terms perhaps by Queen Maria de Luna in letters to Pope Benedict XIII. In these letters she describes the peasants' servile obligation as "evil, detestable, pestiferous, execrable, and abominable . . . against God and justice, perilous to the soul and leading to the infamy of the Catalan nation." Whether or not such strong words reached the peasants themselves and perhaps counteracted the impression of later more ambivalent royal attitudes to the conflict, the fact remains that the peasants from the beginning made a distinction between rents payable simply for the use of land, which many of them were prepared to pay, and dues which resulted from the special jurisdictional power of the nobles as feudal lords, which they rejected as being "against the natural justice of the liberty of man." In the last phase of the *remensas* war under the leadership of Sala, the most radical demanded the end of all rent and the establishment of absolute peasant property rights. All this implies a generally radical outlook with respect to the institutions which underpinned medieval society, but one without a specific commitment to the eradication of the nobility as a class.

The "moderates" among the Catalan peasants negotiated a settlement by which not only the *malos usos* were to be abolished together with compensation to the lords, but serfdom and the lords' right to impose their will by force (*ius maletractandi*). Perhaps this settlement, like other half-way agreements, would never have been embodied in the *Sentenciae Arbitral de Guadalupe* (1486), had it not been for the pressure of the extremists. The *remensas* became almost peasant-proprietors and for some time enjoyed a relative prosperity, compared with their contemporaries in Aragon and Castile. This success was unique and undoubtedly due to the social and economic crises of fifteenth-century Catalonia and to the need of the crown of Aragon for allies against the Catalan nobility and the patrician government of Barcelona. No other mass-movement, with the possible exception of the English peasants after 1381, achieved a comparable success. We have seen that the Flemish peasants were bloodily defeated, and Flanders entered on a prolonged period of crisis. The peasants of northern France were also crushed in 1358, and were to continue to suffer the main brunt of the Anglo-French wars until the final defeat of the English in 1453. And although we have not found it possible to accept the struggles of the Taborites in Bohemia as other than a national and social movement with peasant support, it must be admitted that in Bohemia in the long run, the position of the peasants, in a society whose structure was not fundamentally changed, worsened rather than improved. The successors of the Taborites adopted a pacifist and quietist position in politics which enabled the lords to bring to Bohemia the deteriorating conditions suffered by peasants all over eastern Europe.

Feudal War in Practice

JOHN KEEGAN

Many books and articles have been devoted to the study of warfare in the Middle Ages and to individual battles and campaigns, but the great majority of these works focus on the art of war rather than on the actual conduct of operations. The military predominance of the heavily armed knight, and the great body of contemporary literature promulgating the ideal of knightly life, have influenced the historiography of warfare so as to emphasize the role of the knight. Medieval chroniclers, too, focused on the aristocratic mounted soldiers, but recent studies show that the major portion of most medieval armies was an infantry force.

Recognition of the composite nature of medieval armies, with its attendant appreciation for the tactics of such forces, does not, however, satisfy the British historian John Keegan. He asserts that historians of modern wars and armies, where the composition of the troops has not been in question, nonetheless give a distorted history of campaigns and battles because they see them from the standpoint of generals and politicians. Keegan points out the defects of this sort of military history and suggests that we will not get a fair view of war unless we look at battles and campaigns against the background of the societies in which they occurred. How violent or sacrificial was the society that produced the army and its generals? What impact did contemporary ideas of mortality have? Questions such as these would enlarge the field of military history and make it part of the general historiography on any period or society. Keegan himself wants to do something more specific, however. He wants to focus on battle itself, but to see it from the standpoint of the common soldier. He asks: What was the common experience of war in medieval and modern Europe? He explains his approach this way: "I do not intend to write about generals or generalship, except to discuss how a commander's physical presence on the field may have influenced his subordinates' will to combat. I do not intend to say anything of logistics or strategy and very little of tactics in the formal sense. And I do not intend to offer a two-sided picture of events, since what happened to one side in any battle I describe will be enough to convey the features I think are salient. On the other hand, I do intend to discuss wounds and their treatment, the mechanics of being taken prisoner, the nature of leadership at the most junior level, the role of compulsion in getting men to stand their ground, the incidence of accidents as a cause of death in war and, above all, the dimensions of the danger which different varieties of weapons offer to the soldier on the battlefield. . . . [M]y purpose [is] . . . to suggest how and why the men who have had (and do have) to face these weapons control their fears, staunch their wounds, go to their deaths. It is a personal attempt to catch a glimpse of the face of battle." (*The Face of Battle*, p. 78). What follows is Keegan's description and explanation of the battle of Agincourt, October 25, 1415, one of the principal battles of the Hundred Years' War.

The army embarked in the second week of August at Portsmouth and set sail on August 11th. It had been gathering since April, while Henry conducted deliberately inconclusive negotiations with Charles VI, and now numbered about ten thousand in all, eight thousand archers and two thousand men-at-arms, exclusive of camp followers. A good deal of the space in the ships, of which there were about 1,500, was given over to impedimenta and a great deal to the expedition's horses: at least one for each man-at-arms, and others for the baggage train and wagon teams. The crossing took a little over two days and on the morning of August 14th the army began to disembark, unopposed by the French, on a beach three miles west of Harfleur. Three days were taken to pitch camp and on August 18th the investment of the town began. It was not strongly garrisoned but its man-made and natural defences were strong, the Seine, the River Lézarde and a belt of marshes protecting it on the south, north and east. An attempt at mining under the moat on the western front was checked by French counter-mines so the small siege train, which contained at least three heavy guns, undertook a bombardment of that section of the walls. It lasted for nearly a month, until the collapse of an important gate-defence, the repulse of a succession of sorties and the failure of a French relieving army to appear, convinced the garrison that they must surrender. After parleys, the town opened its gates to Henry on Sunday, September 22nd.

He now had his base, but was left with neither time nor force enough to develop much of a campaign that year; at least a third of his army was dead or disabled, chiefly through disease, and the autumnal rains were due. Earlier in September he had set to paper his intention of marching down the Seine to Paris and thence to Bordeaux as soon as Harfleur fell; that had clearly become unfeasible, but honour demanded that he should not leave France without making a traverse, however much more circumspect, of the lands he claimed. At a long Council of War, held on October 5th, he convinced his followers that they could both appear to seek battle with the French armies which were known to be gathering and yet safely out-distance them by a march to the haven of Calais. On October 8th he led the army out.

His direct route was about 120 miles and lay cross a succession of rivers, of which only the Somme formed a major obstacle. He began following the coast as far as the Béthune, which he crossed on October 11th, revictualling his army at Arques. The following day he crossed the Bresle, near Eu, having made eighty miles in five days, and on October 13th swung inland to cross the Somme above its estuary. On approaching, however, he got his first news of the enemy and it was grave; the nearest

From John Keegan, *The Face of Battle* (New York: Viking Press, 1976), pp. 81–116.

crossing was blocked and defended by a force of six thousand. After discussion, he rejected a retreat and turned south-east to follow the line of the river until he found an unguarded ford. For the next five days, while his army grew hungrier, the French kept pace with him on the northern bank until on the sixth, by a forced march across the plain of the Santerre (scene of the great British tank battle on August 8th, 1918), he got ahead of them and found a pair of unguarded though damaged causeways at Bethencourt and Voyennes. Some hasty sappering made them fit for traffic and that evening, October 19th, the army slept on the far bank. Henry declared October 20th a day of rest, which his men badly needed, having marched over two hundred miles in twelve days, but the arrival of French heralds with a challenge to fight was a reminder that they could not linger. On October 21st they marched eighteen miles, crossing the tracks of a major French army and, during the three following days, another fifty-three. They were now within two, at most three, marches of safety. All were aware, however, that the French had caught up and were keeping pace on their right flank. And late in the day of October 24th scouts came back with word that the enemy had crossed their path and were deploying for battle ahead of them. Henry ordered his men to deploy also but, as darkness was near, the French eventually stood down and withdrew a little to the north where they camped astride the road to Calais.

The English army found what shelter it could for the night in and around the village of Maisoncelles, ate its skimpy rations, confessed its sins, heard Mass and armed for battle. At first light knights and archers marched out and took up their positions between two woods. The French army, composed almost exclusively of mounted and dismounted men-at-arms, had deployed to meet them and was in similar positions about a thousand yards distant. For four hours both armies held their ground. Henry apparently hoped that the French would attack him; they, who knew that sooner or later he would have to move—either to the attack, which suited their book, or to retreat, which suited them even better— stood or sat idle, eating their breakfasts and calling about cheerfully to each other. Eventually Henry decided to up sticks (literally: his archers had been carrying pointed stakes to defend their lines for the last week) and advance on the French line. Arrived within three hundred yards— extreme bowshot—of the army, the English archers replanted their stakes and loosed off their first flights of arrows. The French, provoked by these arrow strikes, as Henry intended, into attacking, launched charges by the mounted men-at-arms from the wings of the main body. Before they had crossed the intervening space they were followed by the dismounted men-at-arms who, like them, were wearing full armour. The cavalry failed to break the English line, suffered losses from the fire of the archers and turned about. Heading back for their own lines, many riders and loose horses crashed into the advancing line of dismounted men-at-arms. They, though shaken, continued to crowd forward and to mass their attack against the English men-at-arms, who were drawn up in three groups, with archers between them and on the right and left flank. Apparently disdaining battle with the archers, although they were suffering losses from their fire, the French quickened their steps over the last few yards and crashed into the middle of the English line. For a moment it gave way. But the French were so tightly bunched that they could not use their weapons to widen the breach they had made. The English men-at-arms recovered their balance, struck back and were now joined by numbers of the archers who, dropping their bows, ran against the French with axes, mallets and swords, or with weapons abandoned by the French they picked up from the ground. There followed a short but very bloody episode of hand-to-hand combat, in which freedom of action lay almost wholly with the English. Many of the French armoured infantrymen lost their footing and were killed as they lay sprawling; others who remained upright could not defend themselves and were killed by thrusts between their armour-joints or stunned by hammer-blows. The French second line which came up, got embroiled in this fighting without being able to turn the advantage to their side, despite the addition they brought to the very great superiority of numbers the French already enjoyed. Eventually, those Frenchmen who could disentangle themselves from the mêlée made their way back to where the rest of their army, composed of a third line of mounted men-at-arms, stood watching. The English who faced them did so in several places, over heaps of dead, dying or disabled French men-at-arms, heaps said by one chronicler to be taller than a man's height. Others were rounding up disarmed and lightly wounded Frenchmen and leading them to the rear, where they were collected under guard.

While this went on, a French nobleman, the Duke of Brabant, who had arrived late for the battle from a christening party, led forward an improvised charge; but it was broken up without denting the English line, which was still drawn up. Henry had prudently kept it under arms because the French third line—of mounted men—had not dispersed and he must presumably have feared that it would ride down on them if the whole English army gave itself up to taking and looting prisoners. At some time in the afternoon, there were detected signs that the French were nerving themselves to charge anyhow; and more or less simultaneously, a body of armed peasants, led by three mounted knights, suddenly appeared at the baggage park, inflicted some loss of life and stole some objects of value, including one of the King's crowns, before being driven off.

Either that incident or the continued menace of the French third line now prompted Henry to order that all the prisoners instantly be killed. The order was not at once obeyed, and for comprehensible reasons. Even discounting any moral or physical repugnance on the part of their captors, or a misunderstanding of the reason behind the order—that the prisoners might attack the English from the rear with weapons retrieved from the ground if the French cavalry were suddenly to attack their front—the poorer English soldiers, and perhaps not only the poorer, would have been very reluctant to pass up the prospects of ransom which killing the prisoners would entail. Henry was nevertheless adamant; he detailed an esquire and two hundred archers to set about the execution, and stopped them only when it became clear that the French third line was packing up and withdrawing from the field. Meantime very many of the French had been killed; some of the English apparently even incinerated wounded prisoners in cottages where they had been taken for shelter.

The noblest and richest of the prisoners were, nevertheless, spared and dined that evening with the King at Maisoncelles, his base of the previous evening, to which he now returned. En route he summoned the heralds of the two armies who had watched the battle together from a vantage point, and settled with the principal French herald a name for the battle: Agincourt, after the nearest fortified place. Next morning, after collecting the army, marshalling the prisoners and distributing the wounded and the loads of loot among the transport, he marched the army off across the battlefield towards Calais. Numbers of the French wounded had made their way or been helped from the field during the night; those still living, unless thought ransomable, were now killed. On October 29th, the English, with two thousand prisoners, reached Calais. The King left for England at once, to be escorted into London by an enormous party of rejoicing citizens.

These are the bare outlines of the battle, as recorded by seven or eight chroniclers, who do not materially disagree over the sequence, character or significance of events. Of course, even though three of them were present at the scene, none was an eye-witness of everything, or even of very much, that happened. An army on the morrow of a battle, particularly an army as small as that of Agincourt, must nevertheless, be a fairly efficient clearing-house of information, and it seems probable that a broadly accurate view of what had happened—though not necessarily why and how it had happened—would quickly crystallize in the mind of any diligent interrogator, while a popularly agreed version, not dissimilar from it, would soon circulate within, and outside, the ranks. It would seem reasonable therefore to believe that the narrative of Agincourt handed down to us is a good one; it would in any case be profitless to look for a better.

The Battle

What we almost completely lack, though, is the sort of picture and understanding of the practicalities of the fighting and of the mood, outlook and skills of the fighters which were themselves part of the eye-witness chroniclers' vision. We simply cannot visualize, as they were able to do, what the Agincourt arrow-cloud can have looked, or sounded, like; what the armoured men-at-arms sought to do to each other at the moment of the first clash; at what speed and in what density the French cavalry charged down; how the mêlée—the densely packed mass of men in hand-to-hand combat—can have appeared to a detached onlooker, say to men in the French third line; what level the noise of the battle can have reached and how the leaders made themselves heard—if they did so—above it. These questions lead on to less tangible inquiries: how did leadership operate once the fighting had been joined—by exhortation or by example? Or did concerted action depend upon previously rehearsed tactics and corporate feeling alone? Or was there, in fact, no leadership, merely every man—or every brave man—for himself? Less tangible still, what did "bravery" mean in the context of a medieval fight? How did men mentally order the risks which they faced, as we know it is human to do? Were the foot more likely to be frightened of the horses, or of the men on them? Were the armoured men-at-arms more or less frightened of the arrows than of meeting their similarly clad opponents at a weapon's length? Did it seem safer to go on fighting once hard pressed than to surrender? Was running away more hazardous than staying within the press of the fighting?

The answers to some of these questions must be highly conjectural, interesting though the conjectures may be. But to others, we can certainly offer answers which fall within a fairly narrow bracket of probability, because the parameters of the questions are technical. Where speed of movement, density of formations, effect of weapons, for example, are concerned, we can test our suppositions against the known defensive qualities of armour plate, penetrative power of arrows, dimensions and capacities of the human body, carrying power and speed of the horse. And from reasonable probabilities about these military mechanics, we may be able to leap towards an understanding of the dynamics of the battle itself and the spirit of the armies which fought it.

Let us, to begin with, and however artificially, break the battle down into a sequence of separate events. It opened, as we know, with the armies forming up in the light of early morning: whether that meant just after first light, or at the rather later hour of dawn itself—about 6:40 a.m.-—is a point of detail over which we cannot expect the chroniclers to meet Staff College standards of precision. Nor do they. They are even more imprecise about numbers, particularly as they concern the French. For though there is agreement, supported by other evidence, that Henry's army had dwindled to about five or six thousand archers and a thousand men-at-arms, the French are variously counted between 10,000 and 200,000. Colonel Burne convincingly reconciles the differences to produce a figure of 25,000, a very large proportion of which represented armoured men-at-arms. Of these, about a thousand brought their horses to the battlefield; the rest were to fight on foot.

The two armies initially formed up at a distance of some thousand yards from each other; at either end of a long, open and almost flat expanse of ploughland, bordered on each side by woodland. The width of the field, which had recently been sown with winter wheat, was about twelve hundred yards at the French end. The woods converged slightly on the English and, at the point where the armies were eventually to meet, stood about nine hundred to a thousand yards apart. (These measurements suppose—as seems reasonable, field boundaries remaining remarkably stable over centuries—that the outlines of the woods have not much changed.)

The English men-at-arms, most of whom were on foot, took station in three blocks, under the command of the Duke of York, to the right, the King, in the centre, and Lord Camoys, on the left. The archers were disposed between them and also on the flanks; the whole line was about four or five deep. The archer flanks may have been thrown a little forward, and the archers of the two inner groups may have adopted a wedge-like formation. This would have made it appear as if the men-at-arms were deployed a little to their rear. Opposite them, the French were drawn up in three lines, of which the third was mounted, as were two groups, each about five hundred strong, on the flanks. The two forward lines, with a filling of crossbowmen between and some ineffectual cannon on the flanks were each, perhaps, eight thousand strong, and so ranked some eight deep. On both sides, the leaders of the various contingents —nobles, bannerets and knights—displayed armorial banners, under which they and their men would fight, and among the French there was a great deal of tiresome struggling, during the period of deployment, to get these banners into the leading rank.

Deployed, the armies were ready for the battle, which, as we have seen, resolved itself into twelve main episodes: a period of waiting; and English advance; an English arrow strike; a French cavalry charge; a French infantry advance; a mêlée between the French and English men-at-arms; an intervention in the mêlée by the English archers; the flight of the French survivors from the scene of the mêlée; a second period of waiting, during which the French third line threatened, and a small party delivered, another charge; a French raid on the baggage park; a massacre of the French prisoners; finally, mutual departure from the battlefield. What was each of these episodes like, and what impetus did it give to the course of events?

The period of waiting—three or four hours long, and so lasting probably from about seven to eleven o'clock—must have been very trying. Two chroniclers mention that the soldiers in the front ranks sat down and

and ate and drank and that there was a good deal of shouting, chaffing and noisy reconciliation of old quarrels among the French. But that was after they had settled, by pushing and shoving, who was to stand in the forward rank; not a real argument, one may surmise, but a process which put the grander and the braver in front of the more humble and timid. There is no mention of the English imitating them, but given their very real predicament, and their much thinner line of battle, they can have felt little need to dispute the place of honour among themselves. It is also improbable that they did much eating or drinking, for the army had been short of food for nine days and the archers are said to have been subsisting on nuts and berries on the last marches. Waiting, certainly for the English, must then have been a cold, miserable and squalid business. It had been raining, the ground was recently ploughed, many in the army were suffering from diarrhoea. Since none would presumably have been allowed to leave the ranks while the army was deployed for action, sufferers would have had to relieve themselves where they stood. For any afflicted man-at-arms wearing mail leggings laced to his plate armour, even that may not have been possible.

The King's order to advance, which he gave after the veterans had endorsed his guess that the French would not be drawn, may therefore have been generally genuinely welcome. Movement at least meant an opportunity to generate body heat, of which the metal-clad men-at-arms would have dissipated an unnatural amount during the morning. Note, however, when the moment came, that they would have moved forward very fast. An advance in line, particularly by men unequally equipped and burdened, has to be taken slowly if order is to be preserved. The manoeuvre, moreover, was a change of position, not a charge, and the King and his subordinate leaders would presumably have recognized the additional danger of losing cohesion in the face of the enemy who, if alert, would seize on the eventuality as an opportune moment to launch an attack. Several chroniclers indeed mention that on the King's orders a knight, Sir Thomas Erpingham, inspected the archers before they marched off in order to "check their dressing," as a modern drill sergeant would put it, and to ensure that they had their bows strung. The much smaller groups of men-at-arms would have moved as did the banners of their lords, which in turn would have followed the King's.

The army had about seven hundred yards of rain-soaked ploughland to cover. At a slow walk (no medieval army marched in step, and no modern army would have done so over such ground—the "cadenced pace" followed from the hardening and smoothing of the surface of roads), with halts to correct dressing, it would have reached its new position in ten minutes or so, though one may guess that the pace slackened a good deal as they drew nearer the French army and the leaders made mental reckoning of the range. "Extreme bowshot," which is the distance at which Henry presumably planned to take ground, is traditionally calculated at three hundred yards. That is a tremendous carry for a bow, however, and two hundred and fifty yards would be a more realistic judgment of the distance at which he finally halted his line from the French. If, however, his archer flanks were thrown a little forward, his centre would have been farther away; and if, as one chronicler suggests, he had infiltrated parties of bowmen into the woods, the gap between the two armies might have been greater still. Something between two hundred and fifty and three hundred yards is a reasonable bracket therefore.

There must now have ensued another pause, even though a short one. For the archers, who had each been carrying a stout double-pointed wooden stake since the tenth day of the march, had now to hammer these into the ground, at an angle calculated to catch a warhorse in the chest. Once hammered, moreover, the points would have had to be hastily resharpened. Henry had ordered these stakes to be cut as a precaution against the army being surprised by cavalry on the line of march. But it was a sensible improvisation to have them planted on the pitched battlefield, even if not a wholly original one. The Scots at Bannockburn, the English themselves at Crécy and the Flemings at Courtrai had narrowed their fronts by digging patterns of holes which would break the leg of a charging horse; the principle was the same as that which underlay the planting of the Agincourt archers' fence. Though it is not, indeed, possible to guess whether a fence was what the archers constructed. If they hammered their stakes to form a single row, it supposes them standing for some time on the wrong side of it with their backs to the enemy. Is it not more probable that each drove his in where he stood, so forming a kind of thicket, too dangerous for horses to penetrate but roomy enough for the defenders to move about within? That would explain the chronicler Monstrelet's otherwise puzzling statement that "each archer placed before himself a stake." It would also make sense of the rough mathematics we can apply to the problem. Colonel Burne, whose appreciation has not been challenged, estimates the width of the English position at 950 yards. Given that there were a thousand men-at-arms in the line of battle, ranked shoulder to shoulder four deep, they would have occupied, at a yard of front per man, 250 yards. If the five thousand archers, on the remaining seven hundred yards, planted their stakes side by side, they would have formed a fence at five-inch intervals. That obstacle would have been impenetrable to the French—but also to the English archers;* and *their* freedom of movement was, as we shall see, latterly an essential element in the winning of the battle. If we want to picture the formation the archers adopted, therefore, it would be most realistic to think of them standing a yard apart, in six or seven rows, with a yard between them, also

---

*Indeed, they could not have got back *behind* it after they had driven their stakes in.

disposed chequerboard fashion so that the men could see and shoot more easily over the heads of those in front: the whole forming a loose belt twenty or thirty feet deep, with the stakes standing obliquely among them.

What we do not know—and it leaves a serious gap in our understanding of the mechanics of the battle—is how the archers were commanded. The men-at-arms stood beneath the banners of their leaders, who had anyhow mustered them and brought them to the war, and the larger retinues, those of noblemen like the Earl of Suffolk, also contained knighted men-at-arms, who must have acted as subordinate leaders. There is thus no difficulty in visualizing how command was exercised within these fairly small and compact groups—providing one makes allowances for what a modern officer would regard as the unsoldierly habit in the man-at-arms of seeking to engage in "single combat" and of otherwise drawing attention to his individual prowess and skill-at-arms. But if the "officer class," even though the expression has a very doubtful meaning in the medieval military context, was wholly committed to the leadership of a single component of the army, who led the rest? For it is not naive, indeed quite the contrary, to suppose some sort of control over and discipline within the archers' ranks. Had the groupings into twenties under a double-pay "vintenar" and of the twenties into hundreds, under a mounted and armoured "centenar," which we know prevailed in the reign of Edward I, at the beginning of the fourteenth century, persisted into the fifteenth? That would be probable, But we cannot tell to whom the "centenars" were immediately answerable, nor how the chain of command led to the King. We can only feel sure that it did.

Archers versus Infantry and Cavalry

The archers were now in position to open fire (an inappropriate expression, belonging to the gunpowder age, which was barely beginning). Each man disposed his arrows as convenient. He would have had a sheaf, perhaps two, of twenty-four arrows and probably struck them point down into the ground by his feet. The men in the front two ranks would have a clear view of the enemy, those behind only sporadic glimpses: there must therefore have been some sort of ranging order passed by word of mouth. For the archers' task at this opening moment of the battle was to provoke the French into attacking, and it was therefore essential that their arrows should "group" as closely as possible on the target. To translate their purpose into modern artillery language, they had to achieve a very narrow $100°$ zone (i.e. that belt of territory into which *all* missiles fell) and a Time on Target effect (i.e. all their missiles had to arrive simultaneously).

To speculate about their feelings at this moment is otiose. They were experienced soldiers in a desperate spot; and their fire, moreover, was to be "indirect," in that their arrows would not depart straight into the enemy's faces but at a fairly steeply angled trajectory. They need have had no sense of initiating an act of killing, therefore; it was probably their technical and professional sense which was most actively engaged in an activity which was still preliminary to any "real" fighting that might come.

They must have received at least two orders: the first to draw their bows, the second to loose their strings. How the orders were synchronized between different groups of archers is an unanswerable question, but when the shout went up or the banner down, four clouds of arrows would have streaked out of the English line to reach a height of a hundred feet before turning in flight to plunge at a steeper angle on and among the French men-at-arms opposite. These arrows cannot, however, given their terminal velocity and angle of impact, have done a great deal of harm, at least to the men-at-arms. For armour, by the early fifteenth century, was composed almost completely of steel sheet, in place of the iron mail which had been worn on the body until fifty years before but now only covered the awkward points of movement around the shoulder and groin. It was deliberately designed, moreover, to offer a glancing surface, and the contemporary helmet, a wide-brimmed "bascinet," was particularly adapted to deflect blows away from the head and the shoulders. We can suppose that the armour served its purpose effectively in this, the opening moment of Agincourt. But one should not dismiss the moral effect of the arrow strike. The singing of the arrows would not have moved ahead of their flight, but the sound of their impact must have been extraordinarily cacophonous, a weird clanking and banging on the bowed heads and backs of the French men-at-arms. If any of the horses in the flanking squadrons were hit, they were likely to have been hurt, however, even at this extreme range, for they were armoured only on their faces and chests, and the chisel-pointed head of the clothyard arrow would have penetrated the padded cloth hangings which covered the rest of their bodies. Animal cries of pain and fear would have risen above the metallic clatter.

Cavalry versus Infantry

We can also imagine oaths and shouted threats from the French. For the arrow strike achieved its object. How quickly, the chroniclers do not tell us; but as a trained archer could loose a shaft every ten seconds we can guess that it took at most a few minutes to trigger the French attack. The French, as we know, were certain of victory. What they had been waiting for was a tactical pretext; either that of the Englishmen showing them their backs or, on the contrary, cocking a snook. One or two volleys would have been insult enough. On the arrival of the first arrows the two large squadrons of horse on either flank mounted—or had they mounted when the English line advanced?—walked their horses clear of the line and broke into a charge.

A charge at what? The two chroniclers who are specific about this point make it clear that the two groups of cavalry, each five or six hundred strong, of which that on the left hand was led by Clignet de Brébant and Guillaume de Saveuse, made the English archer flanks their target. Their aim, doubtless, was to clear these, the largest blocks of the enemy which immediately threatened them, off the field, leaving the numerically much inferior centre of English men-at-arms, with the smaller groups of their attendant archers, to be overwhelmed by the French infantry. It was nevertheless a strange and dangerous decision, unless, that is, we work on the supposition that the archers had planted their stakes among their own ranks, so concealing that array of obstacles from the French. We may then visualize the French bearing down on the archers in ignorance of the hedgehog their ranks concealed; and of the English giving ground just before the moment of impact, to reveal it.

For "the moment of impact" otherwise begs an important, indeed a vital question. It is not difficult to picture the beginning of the charge; the horsemen booting their mounts to form line, probably two or three rows deep, so that, riding knee to knee, they would have presented a front of two or three hundred lances, more or less equalling in width the line of the archers opposite, say three hundred yards. We can imagine them setting off, sitting (really standing) "long" in their high-backed, padded saddles, legs straight and thrust forward, toes down in the heavy stirrups, lance under right arm, left free to manage the reins (wearing plate armour obviated the need to carry a shield); and we can see them in motion, riding at a pace which took them across all but the last fifty of the two or three hundred yards they had to cover in forty seconds or so and then spurring their horses to ride down on the archers at the best speed they could manage—twelve or fifteen miles an hour.*

So far so good. The distance between horses and archers narrows. The archers, who have delivered three of four volleys at the bowed heads and shoulders of their attackers, get off one more flight. More horses—some have already gone down or broken back with screams of pain—stumble and fall, tripping their neighbours, but the mass drive on and . . . and what? It is at this moment that we have to make a judgment about the difference between what happens in a battle and what happens in a violent accident. A horse, in the normal course of events, will not gallop at an obstacle it cannot jump or see a way through, and it cannot jump or see a way through a solid line of men. Even less will it go at the sort of obviously dangerous obstacle which the archers' stakes presented. Equally, a man will not stand in the path of a running horse: he will run

---

*The horses were probably a big hunter type, not the carthorse of popular belief, and the weight they had to carry some 250 lbs (man 150 lbs, armour 60 lbs, saddle and trappings 40 lbs).

himself, or seek shelter, and only if exceptionally strong-nerved and knowing in its ways, stand his ground. Nevertheless, accidents happen. Men, miscalculating or slow-footed, and horses, confused or maddened, do collide, with results almost exclusively unpleasant for the man. We cannot therefore say, however unnatural and exceptional we recognize collisions between man and horse to be, that nothing of that nature occurred between the archers and the French cavalry at Agincourt. For the archers were trained to "receive cavalry," the horses trained to charge home, while it was the principal function of the riders to insist on the horses doing that against which their nature rebelled. Moreover, two of the eye-witness chroniclers, St. Remy and the Priest of the Cottonian MS, are adamant that some of the French cavalry did get in among the archers.

The two opposed "weapon principles" which military theorists recognize had, in short, both failed; the "missile" principle, personified by the archers, had failed to stop or drive off the cavalry; they, embodying the "shock" principle, had failed to crush the infantry—or, more particularly, to make them run away, for the "shock" which cavalry seek to inflict is really moral, not physical in character. It was the stakes which must have effected the compromise. The French, coming on fast, and in great numbers over a short distance, had escaped the deaths and falls which should have toppled their charge over on itself; the English, emboldened by the physical security the hedgehog of stakes lent their formation, had given ground only a little before the onset; the horses had then found themselves on top of the stakes too late to refuse the obstacle; and a short, violent and noisy collision had resulted.

Some of the men-at-arms' horses "ran out" round the flanks of the archers and into the woods. Those in the rear ranks turned their horses, or were turned by them, and rode back. But three at least, including Guillaume de Saveuse, had their horses impaled on the stakes, thumped to the ground and were killed where they lay, either by mallet blows or by stabs between their armour-joints. The charge, momentarily terrifying for the English, from many of whom French men-at-arms, twice their height from the ground, and moving at ten or fifteen miles an hour on steel-shod and grotesquely caparisoned war-horses, had stopped only a few feet distant, had been a disaster for the enemy. And as they rode off, the archers, with all the violent anger that comes with release from sudden danger, bent their bows and sent fresh flights of arrows after them, bringing down more horses and maddening others into uncontrolled flight.

Infantry versus Infantry

But the results of the rout went beyond the demoralization of the survivors. For, as their horses galloped back, they met the first division of dismounted men-at-arms marching out to attack the English centre.

Perhaps eight thousand strong, and filling the space between the woods eight or ten deep, they could not easily or quickly open their ranks to let the fugitives through. Of what happened in consequence we can get a clear idea, curiously, from a cinema newsreel of the Grosvenor Square demonstration against the Vietnam war in 1968. There, a frightened police horse, fleeing the demonstrators, charged a line of constables on foot. Those directly in its path, barging sideways and backwards to open a gap and seizing their neighbours, set up a curious and violent ripple which ran along the ranks on each side, reaching policemen some good distance away who, tightly packed, clutched at each other for support, and stumbled clumsily backwards and then forwards to keep their balance. The sensations of that ripple are known to anyone who has been a member of a dense, mobile and boisterous crowd and it was certainly what was felt, to a sudden and exaggerated degree, by the French men-at-arms in the face of that involuntary cavalry charge. As in that which had just failed against the archers, many of the horses would have shied off at the moment of impact. But those that barged in, an occurrence to which the chroniclers testify, broke up the rhythm of the advance and knocked some men to the ground, an unpleasant experience when the soil is wet and trampled and one is wearing sixty or seventy pounds of sheet metal on the body.

This interruption in an advance which should have brought the French first division to within weapon's length of the English in three or four minutes at most gave Henry's men-at-arms ample time to brace themselves for the encounter. It also gave the archers, both those in the large groups on the wings and the two smaller groups in the central wedges, the chance to prolong their volleying of arrows into the French ranks. The range was progressively shortened by the advance, and the arrows, coming in on a flat trajectory in sets of five thousand at ten-second intervals, must have begun to cause casualties among the French foot. For though they bowed their heads and hunched their shoulders, presenting a continuous front of deflecting surface (bascinet top, breast-plate, "taces"—the overlapping bands across the stomach and genitals—and leg-pieces) to the storm, some of the arrows must have found the weak spots in the visor and at the shoulders and, as the range dropped right down, might even have penetrated armour itself. The "bodkin-point" was designed to do so, and its terminal velocity, sufficient to drive it through an inch of oak from a short distance, could also, at the right angle of impact, make a hole in sheet steel.

The archers failed nevertheless to halt the French advance. But they succeeded in channelling it—or helping to channel it—on to a narrower front of attack. For the French foot, unlike the cavalry, apparently did not make the archers' positions their objective. As their great mass came on, their front ranks "either from fear of the arrows . . . or that they might more speedily penetrate our ranks to the banners (of the King, the

Duke of York and Lord Camoys) . . . divided themselves into three . . . charging our lines in the three places where the banners were." We may also presume that the return of their own cavalry on the flanks would have helped to compress the infantry mass towards the centre, a tendency perhaps reinforced (we really cannot judge) by the alleged unwillingness of men-at-arms to cross weapons with archers, their social inferiors, when the chance to win glory, and prisoners, in combat with other men-at-arms presented itself. Whatever the play of forces at work on the movement of the French first division, several narrators testify to the outcome. The leading ranks bunched into three assaulting columns and drove into what Colonel Burne, in a topographical analogy, calls the three "re-entrants" of the English line, where the men-at-arms were massed a little in rear of the archers' staked-out enclosures.

Their charge won an initial success, for before it the English men-at-arms fell back "a spear's length." What distance the chronicler means by that traditional phrase we cannot judge, and all the less because the French had cut down their lances in anticipation of fighting on foot. It probably implies "just enough to take the impetus out of the onset of the French," for we must imagine them, although puffed by the effort of a jostling tramp across three hundred yards of wet ploughland, accelerating over the last few feet into a run calculated to drive the points of their spears hard on to the enemy's chests and stomachs. The object would have been to knock over as many of them as possible, and so to open gaps in the ranks and isolate individuals who could then be killed or forced back on to the weapons of their own comrades; "sowing disorder" is a short-hand description of the aim. To avoid its achievement, the English, had they been more numerous, might have started forward to meet the French before they developed impulsion; since they were so outnumbered, it was individually prudent and tactically sound for the men most exposed to trot backwards before the French spearpoints, thus "wrong-footing" their opponents (a spearman times his thrust to coincide with the forward step of his left foot) and setting up those surges and undulations along the face of the French mass which momentarily rob a crowd's onrush of its full impact. The English, at the same time, would have been thrusting their spears at the French and, as movement died out of the two hosts, we can visualize them divided, at a distance of ten or fifteen feet, by a horizontal fence of waving and stabbing spear shafts, the noise of their clattering like that of a bully-off at hockey magnified several hundred times.

In this fashion the clash of the men-at-arms might have petered out, as it did on so many medieval battlefields, without a great deal more hurt to either side—though the French would have continued to suffer casualties from the fire of the archers, as long as they remained within range and the English had arrows to shoot at them (the evidence implies they must now have been running short). We can guess that three factors deterred the antagonists from drawing off from each other. One was the English fear of quitting their solid position between the woods and behind the archers' stakes for the greater dangers of the open field; the second was the French certainty of victory; the third was their enormous press of numbers. For if we accept that they had now divided into three *ad hoc* columns and that the head of each matched in width that of the English opposite—say eighty yards—with intervals between of about the same distance, we are compelled to visualize, taking a bird's-eye viewpoint, a roughly trident-shaped formation, the Frenchmen in the prongs ranking twenty deep and numbering some five thousand in all, those in the base a shapeless and unordered mass amounting to, perhaps, another three thousand—and all of them, except for the seven or eight hundred in the leading ranks, unable to see or hear what was happening, yet certain that the English were done for, and anxious to take a hand in finishing them off.

No one, moreover, had overall authority in this press, nor a chain of command through which to impose it. The consequence was inevitable: the development of an unrelenting pressure from the rear on the backs of those in the line of battle, driving them steadily into the weapon-strokes of the English, or at least denying them that margin of room for individual manoeuvre which is essential if men are to defend themselves—or attack—effectively. This was disastrous, for it is vital to recognize, if we are to understand Agincourt, that all infantry actions, even those fought in the closest of close order, are not, in the last resort, combats of mass against mass, but the sum of many combats of individuals—one against one, one against two, three against five. This must be so, for the very simple reason that the weapons which individuals wield are of very limited range and effect, as they remain ever since missile weapons have become the universal equipment of the infantryman. At Agincourt, where the man-at-arms bore lance, sword, dagger, mace or battleaxe,* his ability to kill or wound was restricted to the circle centred on his own body, within which his reach allowed him to club, slash or stab. Prevented by the throng at their backs from dodging, sidestepping or retreating from the blows and thrusts directed at them by their English opponents, the individual French men-at-arms must shortly have begun to lose their man-to-man fights, collecting blows on the head or limbs which, even through armour, were sufficiently bruising or stunning to make them drop their weapons or lose their balance or footing. Within minutes, perhaps seconds, of hand-to-hand fighting being joined, some of them would have fallen, their bodies lying at the feet of their comrades, further impeding

---

*A category which includes glaive, bill, and similar weapons.

the movement of individuals and thus offering an obstacle to the advance of the whole column.

This was the crucial factor in the development of the battle. Had most of the French first line kept their feet, the crowd pressure of their vastly superior numbers, transmitted through their levelled lances, would shortly have forced the English back. Once men began to go down, however—and perhaps also because the French had shortened their lances, while the English had apparently not—those in the next rank would have found that they could get within reach of the English only by stepping over or on to the bodies of the fallen. Supposing continuing pressure from the rear, moreover, they would have had no choice but to do so; yet in so doing, would have rendered themselves even more vulnerable to a tumble than those already felled, a human body making either an unstable fighting platform or a very effective stumbling block to the heels of a man trying to defend himself from a savage attack to his front. In short, once the French column had become stationary, its front impeded by fallen bodies and its ranks animated by heavy pressure from the rear, the "tumbling effect" along its forward edge would have become cumulative.

Cumulative, but sudden and of short duration: for pressure of numbers and desperation must eventually have caused the French to spill out from their columns and lumber down upon the archers who, it appears, were now beginning to run short of arrows. They could almost certainly not have withstood a charge by armoured men-at-arms, would have broken and, running, have left their own men-at-arms to be surrounded and hacked down. That did not happen. The chroniclers are specific that, on the contrary, it was the archers who moved to the attack. Seeing the French falling at the heads of the columns, while those on the flanks still flinched away from the final flights of arrows, the archers seized the chance that confusion and irresolution offered. Drawing swords, swinging heavier weapons—axes, bills or the mallets they used to hammer in their stakes—they left their staked-out positions and ran down to assault the men in armour.

This is a very difficult episode to visualize convincingly. They cannot have attacked the heads of the French columns, for it was there that the English men-at-arms stood, leaving no room for reinforcements to join in. On the flanks, however, the French cannot yet have suffered many casualties, would have had fairly unencumbered ground to fight on and ought to have had no difficulty in dealing with any unarmoured man foolish enough to come within reach of their weapons. The observation offered by two chroniclers that they were too tightly packed to raise their arms, though very probably true of those in the heart of the crowd, cannot apply to those on its fringes. If the archers did inflict injury on the men-at-arms, and there is unanimous evidence that they did, it must have been in some other way than by direct assault on the close-ordered ranks of the columns.

The most likely explanation is that small groups of archers began by attacking individual men-at-arms, infantry isolated by the scattering of the French first line in the "reverse charge" of their own cavalry or riders unhorsed in the charge itself. The charges had occurred on either flank; so that in front of the main bodies of archers and at a distance of between fifty and two hundred yards from them, must have been seen, in the two or three minutes after the cavalry had ridden back, numbers of Frenchmen, prone, supine, half-risen or shakily upright, who were plainly in no state to offer concerted resistance and scarcely able to defend themselves individually. Those who were down would indeed have had difficulty getting up again from slithery ground under the weight of sixty or seventy pounds of armour; and the same hindrances would have slowed those who regained or had kept their feet in getting back to the protection of the closed columns. Certainly they could not have outdistanced the archers if, as we may surmise, and St Remy, a combatant, implies, some of the latter now took the risk of running forward from their stakes to set about them.*

"Setting about them" probably meant two or three against one, so that while an archer swung or lunged at a man-at-arms' front, another dodged his sword-arm to land him a mallet-blow on the back of the head or an axe-stroke behind the knee. Either would have toppled him and, once sprawling, he would have been helpless; a thrust into his face, if he were wearing a bascinet, into the slits of his visor, if he were wearing a closed helmet, or through the mail of his armpit or groin, would have killed him outright or left him to bleed to death. Each act of execution need have taken only a few seconds; time enough for a flurry of thrusts clumsily parried, a fall, two or three figures to kneel over another on the ground, a few butcher's blows, a cry *in extremis*. "Two thousand pounds of education drops to a ten rupee. . . ." (Kipling, "Arithmetic on the Frontier"). Little scenes of this sort must have been happening all over the two narrow tracts between the woods and the fringes of the French main body within the first minutes of the main battle being joined. The only way for stranded Frenchmen to avoid such a death at the hands of the archers was to ask for quarter, which at this early stage they may not have been willing to grant, despite prospects of ransom. A surrendered enemy, to be put *hors de combat*, had to be escorted off the field, a waste of time and manpower the English could not afford when still at such an apparent disadvantage.

---

*"Soon afterwards, the English archers perceiving this disorder of the advance guard . . . and *hastening to the place where the fugitives came from*, killed and disabled the French. (Author's italics.) Nicolas, *The History of the Battle of Agincourt*, p. 268.

But the check in the front line and the butchery on the flanks appear fairly quickly to have swung the advantage in their favour. The "return charge" of the French cavalry had, according to St Remy, caused some of the French to retreat in panic, and it is possible that panic now broke out again along the flanks and at the front.* If that were so—and it is difficult otherwise to make sense of subsequent events—we must imagine a new tide of movement within the French mass: continued forward pressure from those at the back who could not see, a rearward drift along the flanks of the columns by those who had seen all too clearly what work the archers were at, and a reverse pressure by men-at-arms in the front line seeking, if not escape, at least room to fight without fear of falling, or being pushed, over the bodies of those who had already gone down. These movements would have altered the shape of the French mass, widening the gaps between its flanks and the woods, and so offering the archers room to make an "enveloping" attack. Emboldened by the easy killings achieved by some of their number, we must now imagine the rest, perhaps at the King's command, perhaps by spontaneous decision, massing outside their stakes and then running down in formation to attack the French flanks.

"Flank," of course, is only the military word for "side" (in French, from which we take it, the distinction does not exist) and the advantage attackers enjoy in a flank attack is precisely that of hitting at men half turned away from them. But presumably the state in which the archers found the French flanks was even more to their advantage than that. On the edge of the crowd, men-at-arms were walking or running to the rear. As they went, accelerating no doubt at the sight of the English charging down on them, they exposed men deeper within the crowd who would not until then have had sight of the archers, who were not indeed expecting yet to use their arms and whose attention was wholly directed towards the banging and shouting from their front, where they anticipated doing their fighting. Assaulted suddenly at their right or left shoulders, they can have had little chance to face front and point their weapons before some of them, like those already killed by the English men-at-arms, were struck down at the feet of their neighbours.

If the archers were now able to reproduce along the flanks of the French mass the same "tumbling effect" which had encumbered its front, its destruction must have been imminent. For most death in battle takes place within well-defined and fairly narrow "killing zones," of which the "no-man's-land" of trench warfare is the best known and most comprehensible example. The depth of the killing zone is determined by the effective range of the most prevalent weapon, which, in infantry bat-

---

*The sight of archers killing men-at-arms might either have provoked a counter-attack from the French-men on the flanks or persuaded them individually that Agincourt had become no sort of battle to get killed in. There was no reputation to be won in fighting archers.

tles, is always comparatively short, and, in hand-to-hand fighting, very short—only a few feet. That being so, the *longer* the winning side can make the killing zone, the more casualties can it inflict. If the English were now able to extend the killing zone from along the face to down the sides of the French mass (an "enveloping" attack), they threatened to kill very large numbers of Frenchmen indeed.

Given the horror of their situation, the sense of which must now have been transmitted to the whole mass, the French ought at this point to have broken and run. That they did not was the consequence, once again, of their own superiority of numbers. For heretofore it had only been the first division of their army which had been engaged. The second and the third had stood passive, but as the first began to give way, its collapse heralded by the return of fugitives from the flanks, the second walked forward across the wet and trampled ground to lend it support. This was exactly *not* the help needed at that moment. Had the cavalry, in third line, been brought forward to make a second charge against the archers, now that they were outside the protection of their stakes and without their bows, they might well have achieved a rescue. But they were left where they were, for reasons impossible to reconstruct.* Instead, the second division of infantrymen arrived and, thrusting against the backs of their tired and desperate compatriots, held them firmly in place to suffer further butchery.

From what the chroniclers say, we can suppose most of those in the French first line now to be either dead, wounded, prisoner or ready to surrender, if they could not escape. Many had made their surrender (the Priest of the Cottonian MS cattily reports that "some, even of the more noble . . . that day surrendered themselves more than ten times"); some had not had it accepted: the Duke of Alençon, finding himself cut off and surrounded in a dash to attack the Duke of Gloucester, shouted his submission over the heads of his attackers to the King, who was coming to his brother's rescue, but was killed before Henry could extricate him. Nevertheless, very large numbers of Frenchmen had, on promise of ransom, been taken captive, presumably from the moment when the English sensed that the battle was going their way. Their removal from the field, the deaths of others, and the moral and by now no doubt incipient physical collapse of those left had opened up sufficient space for the English to abandon their close order and penetrate their enemy's ranks.

This advance brought them eventually—we are talking of an elapsed time of perhaps only half an hour since the first blows were exchanged—into contact with the second line. They must themselves have been tiring by this time. For the excitement, fear and physical exertion of fighting

---

*But probably having to do a) with the lack of effective overall command in the French army, b) with the difficulty of seeing from the third line (c. 500 yards from the "killing zone") what was happening at the front.

hand-to-hand with heavy weapons in plate armour quickly drained the body of its energy, despite the surge of energy released under stress by glandular activity. Even so, they were not repulsed by the onset of the second line. Indeed its intervention seems to have made no appreciable impact on the fighting. There is a modern military cliché, "Never reinforce failure," which means broadly that to thrust reinforcements in among soldiers who have failed in an attack, feel themselves beaten and are trying to run away is merely to waste the newcomers' energies in a struggle against the thrust of the crowd and to risk infecting them with its despair. And it was indeed in congestion and desperation that the second line appear to have met the English. The chroniclers do not specify exactly what passed between them, presumably because it was so similar to what had gone on before during the defeat of the first line. Though we may guess that a large number of the second line, as soon as they became aware of the disaster, turned their backs and ran off the way they had come; some were dragged out by their pages or servants.

What facts the chroniclers do provide about this, the culmination of the hand-to hand phase, are difficult to reconcile. The English appear to have had considerable freedom of movement, for they were taking hundreds prisoner and the King and his entourage are reported to have cut their way into the second line (it may have been then that he took the blow which dented the helmet which is still to be seen above his tomb in Westminster Abbey). And yet in at least three places, suggested by the priest's narrative to have been where the enemy columns initially charged the English men-at-arms, the bodies of the French lay piled "higher than a man." Indeed the English are said to have climbed these heaps "and butchered the adversaries below with swords, axes and other weapons."

This "building of the wall of dead" is perhaps the best known incident of the battle. If it had occurred, however, we cannot accept that the King and his armoured followers were able to range freely about the field in the latter stages, since the heaps would have confined them within their own positions. Brief reflection will, moreover, demonstrate that the "heap higher than a man" is a chronicler's exaggeration. Human bodies, even when pushed about by bulldozers, do not, as one can observe if able to keep one's eyes open during film of the mass-burials at Belsen, pile into walls, but lie in shapeless sprawling hummocks. When stiffened by rigor mortis, they can be laid in stacks, as one can see in film of the burial parties of a French regiment carting its dead from the field after an attack in the Second Battle of Champagne (September 1915). But men falling to weaponstrokes in the front line, or tripping over those already down, will lie at most two or three deep. For the heaps to rise higher, they must be climbed by the next victims: and the "six-foot heaps" of Agincourt could have been topped-out only if men on either side had been ready and able to duel together while balancing on the corpses of twenty or thirty others. The notion is ludicrous rather than grisly.

The dead undoubtedly lay thick at Agincourt, and quite probably, at the three places where fighting had been heaviest, in piles. But what probably happened at those spots, as we have seen, is that men-at-arms and archers achieved an envelopment of the heads of the French columns, hemmed in and perhaps completely surrounded groups of the enemy, toppled them over on top of each other with lance thrusts and killed them on the ground. The mounds thus raised were big and hideous enough to justify some priestly rhetoric—but not to deny the English entry into the French position.

The Killing of the Prisoners

Indeed, soon after midday, the English men were "in possession of the field"—by which soldiers would understand that they were able to move freely over the ground earlier occupied by the French, of whom only dead, wounded, and fugitives were now to be seen. Fugitives too slow-footed to reach hiding in the woods, or sanctuary among the cavalry of the still uncommitted third division, were chased and tackled by bounty-hunters; others, greedy for ransom, were sorting through the recumbent bodies and pulling "down the heaps . . . to separate the living from the dead, proposing to keep the living as slaves, to be ransomed." At the back of the battlefield the most valuable prisoners were massed together under guard. They were still wearing their armour but had surrendered their right gauntlets to their captors, as a token of submission (and subsequent reidentification), and taken off their helmets, without which they could not fight.

Henry could not allow each captor individually to sequester his prisoners because of the need to keep the army together as long as the French third division threatened a charge. So while small parties, acting both on their own behalf and that of others still in the ranks, reaped the rewards of the fight, the main bodies of men-at-arms and archers stood their ground—now about two or three hundred yards forward of the line on which they had received the French charge. Henry's caution was justified. Soon after midday, the Duke of Brabant, arriving late, half-equipped, and with a tiny following, charged into these ranks. He was overpowered and led to the rear. But this gallant intervention inspired at least two French noblemen in the third division, the Counts of Masle and Fauquemberghes, to marshal some six hundred of their followers for a concerted charge. They could clearly be seen massing, two or three hundred yards from the English line, and their intentions were obvious. At about the same time, moreover, shouting from the rear informed the English of a raid by the enemy on the baggage park, which had been left almost unguarded.

It was these events which precipitated Henry's notorious order to kill the prisoners. As it turned out, the charge was not delivered and the raid was later revealed to have been a mere rampage by the local peasantry, under the Lord of Agincourt. The signs were enough, however, to convince Henry that his victory, in which he can scarcely have yet believed, was about to be snatched from him. For if the French third division attacked the English where they stood, the archers without arrows or stakes, the men-at-arms weary after a morning of hacking and banging in full armour, all of them hungry, cold, and depressed by the reaction from the intense fears and elations of combat, they might easily have been swept from the field. They could certainly not have withstood the simultaneous assault on their rear, to which, with so many inadequately guarded French prisoners standing about behind them on ground littered with discarded weapons, they were likely also to have been subjected. In these circumstances, his order is comprehensible.

Comprehensible in harsh tactical logic; in ethical, human, and practical terms much more difficult to understand. Henry, a Christian king, was also an experienced soldier and versed in the elaborate code of international law governing relations between a prisoner and his captor. Its most important provision was that which guaranteed the prisoner his life—the only return, after all, for which he would enter into anything so costly and humiliating as a ransom bargain. And while his treachery broke that immunity, the mere suspicion, even if well-founded, that he was about to commit treason could not justify his killing. At a more fundamental level, moreover, the prisoner's life was guaranteed by the Christian commandment against murder, however much more loosely that commandment was interpreted in the fifteenth century. If Henry could give the order and, as he did, subsequently escape the reproval of his peers, of the Church, and of the chroniclers, we must presume it was because the battlefield itself was still regarded as a sort of moral no man's-land and the hour of battle as a legal *dies non.*

His subordinates nevertheless refused to obey. Was this because they felt a more tender conscience? The notion is usually dismissed by medieval specialists, who insist that, at best, the captors objected to the King's interference in what was a personal relationship, the prisoners being not the King's or the army's but the vassals of those who had accepted their surrender; that, at worst, they refused to forgo the prospect of so much ransom money (there being almost no way for a man of the times to make a quick fortune except on the battlefield). But it is significant that the King eventually got his order obeyed only by detailing two hundred archers, under the command of an esquire, to carry out the task. This may suggest that, among the captors, the men-at-arms at any rate felt something more than a financially motivated reluctance. There is, after all, an important difference between fighting with lethal weapons, even if it ends in killing, and mere butchery, and we may expect it to have been all the stronger when the act of fighting was as glorified as it was in the Middle Ages. To meet a similarly equipped opponent was the occasion for which the armoured soldier trained perhaps every day of his life from the onset of manhood. To meet and beat him was a triumph, the highest form which self-expression could take in the medieval nobleman's way of life. The events of the late morning at Agincourt, when men had leapt and grunted and hacked at each other's bodies, behaving in a way which seems grotesque and horrifying to us, was for them, therefore, a sort of apotheosis, giving point to their existence, and perhaps assuring them of commemoration after death (since most chroniclers were principally concerned to celebrate individual feats of arms). But there was certainly no honour to be won in killing one's social equal after he had surrendered and been disarmed. On the contrary, there was a considerable risk of incurring dishonour, which may alone have been strong enough to deter the men-at-arms from obeying Henry's order.

Archers stood outside the chivalric system; nor is there much to the idea that they personified the yeoman virtues. The bowmen of Henry's army were not only tough professional soldiers. There is also evidence that may had enlisted in the first place to avoid punishment for civil acts of violence, including murder. The chroniclers also make clear that, in the heat of combat, and during the more leisurely taking of prisoners after the rout of the French second division, there had been a good deal of killing, principally by the archers, of those too poor or too badly hurt to be worth keeping captive. The question of how more or less reluctant they were to carry out the King's command need not therefore delay us.

But the mechanics of the execution do demand a pause. Between one and two thousand prisoners accompanied Henry to England after the battle, of whom most must have been captured before he issued his order to kill. The chroniclers record that the killers spared the most valuable prisoners and were called off as soon as Henry assured himself that the French third division was not going to attack after all. We may take it therefore that the two hundred archers whom he detailed were heavily outnumbered by their victims, probably by about ten to one. The reason for wanting them killed, however, was that they were liable to re-arm themselves from the jetsam of battle if it were renewed. Why did they not do so when they saw themselves threatened with death, for the announcement of the King's order "by trumpet" and the refusal of their captors to carry it out can have left them in no doubt of the fate he planned for them? And how were the archers able to offer them a match? It may have been that they were roughly pinioned (some contemporary pictures of battle show prisoners being led away with their hands bound); but in that case they offered no proper—or a very much reduced—menace to the army's rear, which in turn diminishes the justification for Henry's order. And even if they were tied, their actual killing is an operation difficult to depict for oneself. The act of surrender is notably accompanied by the onset of lassitude and self-reproach. Is it realistic to imagine, however, these proud and warlike men passively awaiting the arrival of a gang of their social inferiors to do them to death —standing like cattle in groups of ten for a single archer to break their skulls with an axe?

It does seem very improbable, and all the more because what we know of twentieth-century mass-killing suggests that it is very difficult for small numbers of executioners, even when armed with machine-guns, to kill people much more defenceless than armoured knights quickly and in large numbers. What seems altogether more likely, therefore, is that Henry's order, rather than bring about the prisoner's massacre, was intended by its threat to terrorize them into abject inactivity. We may imagine something much less clinical than a *Sonderkommando* at work: the captors loudly announcing their refusal to obey the proclamation and perhaps assuring their prisoners that they would see them come to no harm; argument and even scuffling between them and members of the execution squad; and then a noisy and bloody cattle-drive to the rear, the archers harrying round the flanks of the crowd of armoured Frenchmen as they stumbled away from the scene of fighting and its dangerous debris to a spot nearer the baggage park, whence they could offer no serious threat at all. Some would have been killed in the process, and quite deliberately, but we need not reckon their number in thousands, perhaps not even in hundreds.

The killing, moreover, had a definite term, for Henry ordered it to end when he saw the French third division abandon their attack formation and begin to leave the battlefield. The time was about three o'clock in the afternoon, leaving some two hours more of daylight. The English began at once to spread out over the field looking for prisoners and spoil in places not yet visited. The King made a circuit and, on turning back for his quarters at Maisoncelles, summoned to him the French and English heralds.

The Wounded

The heralds had watched the battle in a group together and, though the French army had left, the French heralds had not yet followed them. For the heralds belonged not to the armies but to the international corporation of experts who regulated civilized warfare. Henry was anxious to hear their verdict on the day's fighting and to fix a name for the battle, so that its outcome and the army's exploits could be readily identified when chroniclers came to record it. Montjoie, the principal French herald, confirmed that the English were the victors and provided Henry with the name of the nearest castle—Agincourt—to serve as eponym.

That decision ended the battle as a military and historical episode. The English drove their prisoners and carried their own wounded back to Maisoncelles for the night, where the twenty surgeons of the army set to work. English casualties had been few: The Duke of York, who was pulled from under a heap of corpses, dead either from suffocation or a heart-attack, and the Earl of Suffolk were the only notable fatalities. The wounded numbered only some hundreds. What were their prospects? In the main, probably quite good. The English had not undergone an arrow attack, so most of the wounds would have been lacerations rather than penetrations, clean even if deep cuts which, if bound up and left, would heal quickly. There would also have been some fractures; depressed fractures of the skull could not be treated—the secret of trepanning awaited rediscovery—but breaks of the arm and lower leg could have been successfully set and splinted. The French wounded enjoyed a much graver prognosis. Many would have suffered penetrating wounds, either from arrows or from thrusts through the weak spots of their armour. Those which had pierced the intestines, emptying its contents into the abdomen, were fatal: peritonitis was inevitable. Penetrations of the chest cavity, which had probably carried in fragments of dirty clothing, were almost as certain to lead to sepsis. Many of the French would have suffered depressed fractures of the skull, and there would have been broken backs caused by falls from horses in armour at speed. Almost all of these injuries we may regard as fatal, the contemporary surgeons being unable to treat them. Many of the French, of course, had not been collected from the battlefield and, if they did not bleed to death, would have succumbed to the combined effects of exposure and shock during the night, when temperatures might have descended into the middle-30s Fahrenheit. It was, therefore, not arbitrary brutality when, in crossing the battlefield next morning, the English killed those whom they found alive. They were almost certain to have died, in any case, when their bodies would have gone to join those which the local peasants, under the supervision of the Bishop of Arras, dug into pits on the site. They are said to have buried about six thousand altogether.

The Will to Combat

What sustained men in a combat like Agincourt, when the penalty of defeat, or of one's own lack of skill or nimbleness was so final and unpleasant? Some factors, either general to battle—as will appear—or more or less particular to this one are relatively easy to isolate. Of the general factors, drink is the most obvious to mention. The English, who were on short rations, presumably had less to drink than the French, but there was drinking in the ranks on both sides during the period of waiting and it is quite probable that many soldiers in both armies went into the mêlée less than sober, if not indeed fighting drunk. For the English, the presence of the King would also have provided what present-day soldiers call a "moral factor" of great importance. The personal bond between leader and follower lies at the root of all explanations of what does and does not happen in battle: and that bond is always strongest in martial societies, of which fifteenth-century England is one type and the warrior states of India, which the British harnessed so successfully to their imperial purpose, are another. The nature of the bond is more complex, and certainly more materialistic than modern ethologists would like to have us believe. But its importance must not be underestimated. And though the late-medieval soldier's immediate loyalty lay towards his captain, the presence on the field of his own and his captain's anointed king, visible to all and ostentatiously risking his life in the heart of the mêlée, must have greatly strengthened his resolve.

Serving to strengthen it further was the endorsement of religion. The morality of killing is not something with which the professional soldier is usually thought to trouble himself, but the Christian knight, whether we mean by that the ideal type as seen by the chroniclers or some at least of the historical figures of whom we have knowledge, was nevertheless exercised by it. What constituted unlawful killing in time of war was well-defined, and carried penalties under civil, military, and religious law. Lawful killing, on the other hand, was an act which religious precept specifically endorsed, within the circumscription of the just war; and however dimly or marginally religious doctrine impinged on the consciousness of the simple soldier or more unthinking knight, the religious preparations which all in the English army underwent before Agincourt must be counted among the most important factors affecting its mood. Henry himself heard Mass three times in succession before the battle, and took Communion, as presumably did most of his followers; there was a small army of priests in the expedition. The soldiers ritually entreated blessing before entering the ranks, going down on their knees, making the sign of the cross and taking earth into their mouths as a symbolic gesture of the death and burial they were thereby accepting.

Drink and prayer must be seen, however, as last-minute and short-term reinforcements of the medieval soldier's (though, we shall see, not only his) will to combat. Far more important, and, given the disparity of their stations, more important still for the common soldier than the men-at-arms, was the prospect of enrichment. Medieval warfare, like all warfare, was about many things, but medieval battle, at the personal level, was about only three: victory first, of course, because the personal consequences of defeat could be so disagreeable; personal distinction in single combat—something of which the man-at-arms would think a great deal more than the bowman; but, ultimately and most important, ransom and loot. Agincourt was untypical of medieval battle in yielding, and then snatching back from the victors the bonanza of wealth that it did; but it is the gold-strike and gold-fever character of medieval battle which we should keep foremost in mind when seeking to understand it.

We should balance it, at the same time, against two other factors. The first of these is the pressure of compulsion. The role which physical coercion or force of unavoidable circumstance plays in bringing men into, and often through, the ordeal of battle is one which almost all military historians consistently underplay, or ignore. Yet we can clearly see that the force of unavoidable circumstances was among the most powerful of the drives to combat at work on the field of Agincourt. The English had sought by every means to avoid battle throughout their long march from Harfleur and, though accepting it on October 25th as a necessary alternative to capitulation and perhaps lifelong captivity, were finally driven to attack by the pains of hunger and cold. The French had also hoped to avoid bringing their confrontation with the English to a fight; and we may convincingly surmise that many of those who went down under the swords or mallet-blows of the English had been drawn into the battle with all the free-will of a man who finds himself going the wrong way on a moving-staircase.

The second factor confounds the former just examined. It concerns the commonplace character of violence in medieval life. What went on at Agincourt appals and horrifies the modern imagination which, vicariously accustomed though it is to the idea of violence, rarely encounters it in actuality and is outraged when it does. The sense of outrage was no doubt as keenly felt by the individual victim of violence five hundred years ago. But the victim of assault, in a world where the rights of lordship were imposed and the quarrels of neighbors settled by sword or knife as a matter of course, was likely to have been a good deal less surprised by it when it occurred. As the language of English law, which we owe to the Middle Ages, reveals, through its references to "putting in fear," "making an affray," and "keeping the Queen's peace," the medieval world was one in which the distinction between private, civil, and foreign war, though recognized, could only be irregularly enforced. Thus battle, though an extreme on the spectrum of experience, was not something unimaginable, something wholly beyond the peace-loving individual's ken. It offered the soldier risk in a particularly concentrated form; but it was treatment to which his upbringing and experience would already have partially inured him.

The Organization of a
Late Medieval City

GERALD STRAUSS

There is a currently prevalent image of the medieval and early modern
city as having crowded, noisy streets, filth, and a lack of sunlight and open space.
This image has been engraved on our minds by films like *Becket* and *Tom Jones*;
the filmmakers took their notion of the city from historians who themselves had
based their descriptions on engravings of cities produced in the sixteenth and
seventeenth centuries. The impression is reinforced when we enter the older
parts of European and some American cities, where the streets are narrow,
crooked, and apparently laid out in a haphazard pattern. Compared with the grid-
like plans favored by modern city planners, these remains of earlier urban life
seem confused and crowded; but the builders of pre-modern cities were not abdi-
cating their duties, and they were not incompetent. The picture of their efforts
should be much brighter than it is painted.

Cities were planned for two purposes—defense and trade. In most cases,
these two functions together determined the plans, but defensibility was the
greater value. Study of most European cities will reveal a plan of streets radiating
out from the central point, which once contained, and sometimes still contains,
the fortress. In some cities, the cathedral usurped the position of the citadel,
since the bishops were the lords of those places. Thus, in Toledo or Chartres or
Durham, the cathedral holds the heights and could, with its strong walls and high
towers, also have functioned as a fortress when necessary.

Not only were medieval cities well planned for their needs, they were also
full of open spaces. The urban population grew rapidly from the twelfth century
on, but houses were built close together, leaving gardens and even pastures within
the city walls. The new urban families came from the countryside (mostly from
the area immediately surrounding the town), and it took some time for them to
lose their penchant for farming. City dwellers supplemented their diets by growing their own vegetables and milking their own cows; "truck farming" was rather
primitive in most places. The open spaces were gradually filled, however, and the
cities became increasingly crowded despite efforts in some places to limit the
population by law. It was only the plague that brought an end to the growth, and
the population decline continued long after the epidemics subsided. It is
estimated, for example, that between 1494 and 1520, one eighth to one seventh
of the houses in the German city of Freiburg were demolished and turned back
into gardens.

City dwellers and city fathers knew that only by careful regulation could
they avoid the hygienic problems of urban life while enjoying its commercial and
cultural advantages. In this selection, Gerald Strauss describes the precautions

taken in Nuremberg to ensure public safety in the city, which was one of the most prosperous in Germany and which exerted great cultural influence in eastern Europe as well as within its own country. At the same time, the selection deals with many topics treated by N. J. G. Pounds in his piece on Rome and Roman cities in Part 1, and it therefore provides a means for assessing both development and continuity in the history of the European city.

"A city is an assembly of men brought together to live happily." Thus said Giovanni Botero in 1588 in his treatise on the place of cities in European society. Botero's definition really illustrates the shift of perspective away from the self-governing commune toward the all-powerful state, which had taken place by the late sixteenth century. To Botero a city was a place where population and money proliferated, where industrial power was gathered, and where a country's economic, social, and cultural resources were concentrated. ("And greatness of a city," he continues, "is termed not the spaciousness of situation or the compass of walls, but the multitude of inhabitants and their power.") There is nothing in Botero's book to suggest that a city should or could have a purpose distinctly its own, different from, perhaps at odds with, the objectives of the territorial state. But for the independent city this is just what the struggle of the past three-and-a-half centuries had been about. A municipal polity and a civic ethic had been created and maintained against king, prince, and baron. Botero did not understand this. He and his book speak for the nascent age of absolutism and mercantilism. A citizen of Nuremberg reading *The Greatness of Cities* in the last decade of the sixteenth century must have put it down with an uneasy apprehension of how times were changing.

Still there is nothing wrong with the statement that men are gathered in cities "to live happily." As an empirical observation of the rewards of civic life it is unobjectionable. By and large, urban life was pleasant, and urban institutions were designed to make it so. No one has ever invented a device for measuring happiness, but where the material conditions were never less than adequate, where society provided not only security but purpose and direction as well, and where work and pleasure coincided, there was bound to be at least contentment. But let us go behind the generalizations and test Botero's statement by trying to find out what it was like to live and work in Nuremberg in the sixteenth century.

For administrative purposes the city was divided into quarters but not, as the name might suggest, into four quarters. Nuremberg had five quarters in the fourteenth century, six in 1400, and from 1449 on, eight:

From Gerald Strauss, *Nuremberg in the Sixteenth Century* (Bloomington, Ind.: Indiana University Press, 1976), pp. 187–92, 194–96, 197–98, 199–200, 208–09.

four each in the Sebald and Lorenz parishes. Originally the quarter organization had served military purposes, and the two quartermasters (*Viertelmeister*) of each of the sections were directly responsible to the three captains general of the city. Their most important duty had always been the mobilization of the residents of their district in the event of siege or attack. But the quarters were used for other civic purposes as well: taxing, census taking, fire fighting, enrolling men for forced labor duty. Quartermasters were helped by street captains, each taking charge of a block of houses. The citizen swore an oath of obedience to his street captain and furnished him with lists of possessions useful to the city in case of emergencies and liable to requisition: arms and ammunition, grain reserves, carts and horses, lanterns, ladders, spare rooms, and so on. The quartermaster coordinated these lists, thus providing the Council with an up-to-date inventory of men and material available when the need arose.

The most dreaded emergency and the most disruptive of civic affairs was, of course, a sudden predatory strike by some rural war lord or a protracted siege by a hostile prince, though Nuremberg's splendid defenses and her reputation for wealth and diplomatic skill discouraged most of the kinds of capricious assaults suffered by lesser cities. But one had to be prepared and Nuremberg was. However, the most frequent use to which the quarter organization was put was not mobilization but fire fighting. News of fires turns up monotonously in the chronicles of the city. Sometimes a single house burned down, often a whole block was reduced to cinders. To the medieval town these fires were anything but ordinary. Every city had its great conflagrations when whole sections of the town were destroyed, with incalculable loss of property and income. In Nuremberg the great fire of 1340 was still remembered after two centuries; starting in the kitchen of a widow's home, it had quickly spread to nearby structures, and two days and nights later more than 400 houses lay in ashes. Next to the dreaded plague, the worst catastrophe that could hit a medieval community was a fire burning out of control. Its destructiveness often remained evident for decades, for, without insurance, few people could put their hands on enough money to rebuild a razed home and workshop. This fact explains the prevalence of clear spaces and garden spots in medieval towns. Houses had once occupied many of these, but fire had gutted them, and the ground had come into the hands of neighbors who preferred to keep it open.

By the fourteenth century most governments had learned to meet the dangers of fire with statutes concerning building materials and space utilization. But little could be done in a country where lumber was cheap and customary and where every householder liked to store his own supplies of wood in his shed and grain under his roof. Not many residences were really well built, and the annals make frequent mention of houses collapsing of their own weight or falling apart when an adjacent structure was damaged. The only practical precaution was to have an effective fire fighting organization. In Nuremberg the quarter administration enabled authorities to call out a large number of men within minutes of the alarm, each prepared to do an assigned job and familiar with the equipment. The public baths were required to keep large vats filled with water mounted on carts ready to go, and every quarter had two hand pumps with adjustable brass nozzles. Fire hooks, leatherbuckets, ladders and axes were mounted on designated houses in each block. Fitted boards to dam up the *Fischbach*, which ran through the center of the city, were in readiness for creating a reservoir from which to deploy bucket brigades. Rewards went to the four carters first to bring water to the scene and to the first three men up the fire ladders. Everything was precisely regulated: responsibility for refilling the vats and cleaning the pumps, guarding the charred site for twenty-four hours, repairing damaged ladders, and so on. The system worked so well in Nuremberg that none of the innumerable isolated fires of which we read became a major conflagration.

The same can be said of security arrangements to control nighttime horseplay and hooliganism. Though these measures were not foolproof, and the courts were kept busy enough sentencing nocturnal brawlers, the worst of the trouble makers were probably discouraged by the precautions taken against them. Once the curfew bell had rung two hours after sunset, everyone was expected to be off the streets unless he had valid business. Patricians were permitted in their *Herrentrinkstube* after dark, and they could also play cards and dice there, but only until the hour before midnight. If legitimately abroad, a man must carry a lighted torch (the streets themselves were dark); failing to do so he was liable to arrest by the city's men at arms who patrolled the streets at night. If upon questioning a person was able to make himself known, he was let go after payment of a fine. "But any citizen, resident, or visitor who cannot establish his identity or provide a credible sponsor will be taken to prison." After midnight the fines doubled, and knives or other weapons found on the suspect, even a lute if he had been out serenading, were confiscated.

Inns closed at sundown, and a traveller lodging for a night could get nothing to drink once the curfew had sounded. If for any reason a tumult got under way, the government was prepared for it. Lanterns and torches were mounted on designated houses, and residents instructed to light them when they heard noise or sensed trouble. Most streets could be blocked off with iron chains drawn across the road from house to house; main thoroughfares were guarded by sets of double or triple chains. Ordinarily these chains were wound on drums enclosed in locked cases, but when trouble began and a crowd gathered, the street captains drew the chains out, making a clatter frightening enough to dishearten at least some of the ruffians. Endres Tucher, the city architect in the 1460's and 1470's . . . lists the location of all these chains. There were 420 of them maintained in good working order, oiled regularly, locks tested, and the drums inspected. No doubt the idea for this system occurred to the Council in the unhappy days of the Rebellion of 1349. It became a standard security device soon after that, always kept in readiness.

The streets themselves were in good condition, well surfaced, and, by and large, clean. This may be a difficult fact for the modern reader to accept, irreconcilable as it is with the commonly held image of mud, filth, and debris in medieval towns. But the evidence to the contrary is conclusive. Nuremberg's unpleasantly wet climate (every visitor complained of the frequent downpours and the ankle-deep mud on country roads) makes it easy to imagine what the city would have looked like had its streets not been properly surfaced. Stone paving was therefore introduced as early as the middle of the fourteenth century and from 1368 on proceeded systematically. The city architect had charge of this work, which was carried on by several paving masters, assisted by journeymen and apprentices and a detachment of day laborers. Streets were paved at public expense to within four feet of the doorstep of a private house. The remaining distance was paved at the home owner's expense. Work was governed by exact regulations. Size and quality of paving stones were determined by the architect, as was the minimum number of blows each stone had to receive from the pounder. The architect noted defective surfaces on his daily tours about the city and ordered immediate repairs.

More difficult was the problem of keeping streets free of trash and refuse, and the most determined measures were required to induce householders to surrender their time-honored right to allow pigs to forage freely on the streets—a practice not only unsightly in itself but also bound to encourage the dumping of garbage onto the streets to feed the scavengers. In 1475 the Council forbade the free circulation of pigs, confining them to sites in front of or behind houses. Once a day they could be driven to the Pegnitz to drink, but their droppings had to be swept up at once and thrown into the river.

The Pegnitz provided a ready receptacle for anything unwanted, from wilted cabbage leaves to cattle carcasses, but here also the Council was determined to prevent the worst of abuses. It ordered the *Fischbach* kept entirely free of refuse, but the very repetition of warnings, threats, and exemplary penalties issuing from the Council Chamber are sad evidence of the inveterate habit of discarding rubbish where most convenient. In the Pegnitz, dumping was permitted only at certain places downstream, set aside for the disposal of the foulest matter, including the contents of the fifty or so public privies located about the city. (Privy cleaning was a job in the hands of skilled technicians called *Nachtmeister* and their helpers, supervised and inspected by the city architect and confined to certain times in the year when the Pegnitz was sufficiently high and swift.) Industrial waste, sweepings from the workshops, and harmful chemicals used by tinsmiths and etchers and others were to be taken to the same spot, and care was urged on apprentices to see that nothing was dropped or spilled on the way. Householders were instructed to keep servants from emptying slops into the street and were held liable for infractions. Carcasses had to be taken to a field beyond the gates and buried there. Building sites were to be tidied as soon as construction had come to an end to keep loose soil and mortar from running into the streets. No great accumulation of trash was permitted in front of houses "so that the rains may not wash it into the streets." Small compost heaps were permitted, but these had to be renewed once a week.

The very punctiliousness of these laws and their constant reiteration suggest that citizens tended to take the Council's warnings lightly. There must certainly have been more dirt around than the regulations allowed... "Bathing money" constituted a regular part of a man's salary, paid weekly, usually on Saturdays. Municipal building workers left work one hour early once a week to go bathing. Like every other profession, the bathing masters had their official *Ordnung*, periodically revised and augmented by Council decrees. Professional bath attendants were trained in the technique of sanitary and medicinal bathing, also in hair cutting and depilation and in simple medical operations, notably blood letting with suction cups. It took three years of apprenticeship to become a journeyman in the craft and seven more years of journeyman's work around the country before one could qualify as a master. During the sixteenth century, Nuremberg had fourteen licensed baths, all located on or near the Pegnitz and the *Fischbach*, whence the water was drawn by means of wooden pipes, then heated over wood fires. Prices of admission to the baths were kept low by Council order so that very nearly every person in the city could go. (Children were admitted free if accompanied by parents.) The usual Council-appointed inspectors went from bath to bath to ensure cleanliness and expert performance. If one paid for the full treatment one was in for an elaborate ritual. It opened with a trumpet or bell signal to indicate that the water was hot and the bath was open. Once inside and stripped of one's clothes, one began with foot washing, then the body was scoured and slapped with a sheaf of twigs, next steam bathing and rubbing to induce perspiration, swatting the skin with wet rags, scratching (for the pleasure of it; bathing masters and employees were obligated to provide this service), hair washing and cutting, combing, lavendering, blood letting, and finally a nap to recuperate from the exertion.

As for medical services, Nurembergers were professionally attended by at least half a dozen doctors, a team of midwives, and several apothecaries. Municipal physicians had practiced in the city since before 1400; they were paid by the Council for the treatment of poor folk, but charged fees for visiting the rich. In the late sixteenth century the medical doctors organized themselves into a *collegium medicum* to suppress quacks and regulate fees; one gulden was charged for the first housecall, a quarter gulden for each subsequent visit, with higher fees for the treatment of infectious diseases. Even in a time of inflation these were high prices, and some kind of free or low-cost medical care was obviously needed. Midwives were salaried, and their activities supervised by several matrons of good family who had a charitable concern for pregnant women, helping out where assistance was called for. Apothecaries were bound by oath to fill prescriptions faithfully. Periodic inspection by two Council members and one or two doctors ascertained that everything was done properly and the scales were accurate.

For the seriously and incurably sick and the very poor, there existed a number of free hospitals, all of them charitable foundations dating back hundreds of years: St. Elisabeth's built by the Johannite Order just outside the walls, near the gate named for it; the so-called "New Hospital" of the Holy Ghost, originally a refuge for the poor but turned into a place for the sick in the 1480's; the Hospital of the Holy Cross in the western part of the city, set aside for syphilitics at the end of the fifteenth century; St. Sebastian's for plague patients and St. John's, St. Leonard's, and St. Jobst's for sufferers from infectious and loathsome diseases. The Hospital of Sts. Peter and Paul accommodated foreign lepers. Persons judged to be mentally ill were incarcerated along with prisoners of war and common criminals in a tower in the *Burg*. . . .

In fact, there was hardly an ill fortune not mitigated by some sort of charitable establishment. Unwanted children found a refuge in privately endowed, but publicly supervised, foundling homes. Nuremberg had one for girls and another for boys. They apparently were decent places. A visitor to the girls' home in 1537 described "a large room wherein I saw forty-six foundling girls, the foundling father and mother, and a few servants. On the walls were racks for drying laundry in winter. Adjacent, a chamber with beds for the children, another for the master and mistress, also a kitchen, a place for firewood, a bath outside, and stables." The children were taught to read and write and kept busy with simple work.

Grown to adolescence, poor children had recourse to several sources of help. Honest girls of poor families could apply to one of a number of foundations for sums up to twenty gulden to buy a trousseau. Serving maids with years of household service behind them might procure a dowry from Andreas Oertel's Marriage Endowment. Older women who had neither prospects of marriage nor sufficient means to enter one of the better convents found a haven in the *Seelhaus* (founded by a well-to-do merchant to speed the salvation of a soul in purgatory). Rehabilitated prostitutes were accommodated in homes maintained, until the Reformation, by the two convents. Other funds provided help for women after childbirth, granted scholarships to poor boys to study at home or abroad, helped men who had met misfortune in business or fallen into debt because of illness. One of the handsomest foundations in the city offered free lodging and board to twelve retired master artisans who had not been able to save enough for a dignified life in their declining years.* And for the really poor there was the so-called Rich Alm, an endowment established privately in 1388, the interest from which bought every Sunday enough bread, meat, flour, herrings, and seasonal vegetables to feed the city's needy during the week. This charity was directly administered by the Council, whose agents compiled fresh lists of the poor and indigent every three months, to make sure that, on the one hand, no one undeserving got on the list and, on the other, no needy person had to do without these basic means to a civilized life.

Occasionally a single case reveals the quality of the Council's concern for its cocitizens. In 1555 the goldsmith Niklas Sailer, despondent over ill health and poor business, made a halfhearted attempt at suicide, but failed. The incident was brought to the Council's attention and investigated. Convinced that the man was at the end of his wits through no moral fault of his own, the Council granted him a weekly subsidy of one gulden, and in order not to humiliate him with this handout, it was arranged that a third person would receive the gulden and turn it over to Sailer without naming the source. The case illustrates the combination of administrative efficiency and personal solicitude characteristic of Nuremberg's government. A similar concern was reflected in the new beggars' regulation of 1522, where special provisions were made for "poor people who feel ashamed to beg and wear the beggar's badge, either because they think it a disgrace to their parents or a dishonor to their craft.". . .

A few observations may illustrate the conditions of material life as enjoyed in Nuremberg at the beginning of the sixteenth century. Almost every family, from patrician to journeyman, had its own house. Statistics from the middle of the fifteenth century show that the largest number of buildings in the city accommodated no more than three or four persons plus a servant girl or two and an apprentice. In time of war, especially when the city was under siege, the picture changed, of course. Rural residents, territorial officials, and even peasants whose farms had been destroyed or occupied sought refuge in the city and were quartered in burgher houses. In fact this need for occasional quartering is one reason for the lack of crowding in normal times: the Council liked to know that space was available for the accommodation of territorial subjects if the need should arise.

Dwellings were places of work as well as of residence. Ground-floor rooms never accommodated living quarters but provided space for workshops, storage, and such. During working hours and unless the weather was inclement, work spilled over into the street; in fact, fire regulations obliged all activities causing sparks or fumes to be carried on

---

*This was Konrad Mendel's *Zwölfbrüderstiftung*, founded in 1388. It was remarkable for its *Memorial Book* containing portraits of nearly all the members through the centuries, showing each at his craft or trade.

outside. Upstairs, even the least pretentious house had enough bedrooms to separate children from parents and servants from their employers. It is interesting to note from the available statistics that the proportion of residents and households to buildings increased as the centuries advanced toward the industrial age. In 1500 few families were crowded close on one another. Tenements did not exist. Even factory workers, the surviving information suggests, were housed in comfortable quarters. To give an example of this: there was a combined copper and iron hammer and flour mill on the bank of the Pegnitz just outside the city. It turned out wire, brass, and metal foil, as well as flour for bread. Workers' residences were attached to the factory, the whole establishment forming a closed rectangle of buildings and sheds. The residences, two rows of attached one-story houses, consisted, each, of a living room, one or two bedrooms, and a kitchen. A small stable for a goat or two and a sty for the inevitable pig were adjacent. All this was provided rent free. Every spring the houses were whitewashed, and stoves and other equipment were maintained at the factory-owner's expense. Workers' widows moved to smaller houses in the colony but could live rent free until their deaths. For the children there was a schoolhouse with a salaried master. Probably not all the workers employed in the city's hammer and paper mills lived quite so nicely. But in general the description accords with local expectations of acceptable conditions of work and residence.

This was true also of the amount and variety of food consumed by Nurembergers. All available information, and there is an enormous lot of it for all periods and for all segments of society, indicates that people ate well and abundantly—superabundantly, if one is to believe the many sermons and verses that portrayed Germans as uncontrollable gluttons and guzzlers. Rich and poor ate differently, of course, then as now, not only because of differences in purchasing power but because each estate had its inherited tastes and preferences and its own occasions for eating. . . .

Life was by no means unremitting toil. There were many holidays, even after the Reformation, for people to enjoy leisure, and enough free entertainment to give everyone something to do. But hard and dedicated work was a way of life for merchant and artisan alike, and it is clear that labor and achievement in one's calling came first in the scale of values. The working day varied in length according to the season, as is only natural where so much work is done outside and where artificial illumination is costly. Nuremberg, along with many south German cities, went by the so-called Great Clock, which counted the hours consecutively from sunrise to sunset: the first hour after daybreak was one hour of the day ("when the clock strikes one"), the first hour after sunset was one hour of the night, the second hour was two of the night, and so on. When the day was shortest it had eight hours, and was reversed. Regiomontanus worked out the system scientifically for Nuremberg in 1488. Before that the days for changing the count had been determined by rule of thumb.

During the day, watchmen went about the city and rang the bells to indicate the hours of the clock. Working hours followed the length of the day, the working day being longer in summer than in winter. To quote from the regulations governing building workers:

> When the clock strikes eight or nine hours in the day [i.e., when the day is eight or nine hours long] be at work when the last hour of the night is over. When it strikes three [i.e., 11 o'clock by the modern clock, the day having begun at 8 a.m.], go to have your midday meal, and return to work at four, until the last hour of the day is over. When the clock strikes fourteen hours in the day, be at work when the clock strikes one [6 a.m.], have your breakfast at three [8 a.m.], return to work at four, take your midday meal at seven [noon], return at eight, have your Vesper at two [3 p.m.], return at eleven, and leave work for the night when it strikes one of the night [7 p.m.].

Thus the shortest work day was seven hours in length, not counting meal times, the longest thirteen. The elongation of the working day to correspond to daylight hours may explain the proliferation of holidays and half-holidays during the Middle Ages. Reformers disapproved of these, not only on theological grounds, but one wonders how the public responded to the cancellation of so many feasts when the change brought abolition of most of the days that could be spent at games or sports while the weather was good. Since so many people were paid by the day and since prices were always on the rise, the grief over missed shooting matches and rope pulls probably was mitigated by the expectation of more pay at the end of the week. But it gives us pause for thought today that a work week of six days and a work day in spring and summer of from twelve to sixteen hours, including mealtimes, left very little occasion for diversion and recreation.

In winter the problem was the reverse: what to do with all the dark hours before bedtime. Most likely people slept much longer in the winter season; there was little else they could do, since no one was expected to be about the streets after it had gotten fully dark. The inns closed down, most convivial occasions were confined to daytime hours, and theatrical plays were not performed in the evenings. Card playing was probably the great favorite for whiling away time; it had been forbidden for some years in the fourteenth century, along with other games of chance, but in the fifteenth, cards reappeared on a list of licit games that also included chess and other board games. Nuremberg had several well-known card makers, artisans who hand painted expensive playing cards and also turned out cheap decks of block-printed cards. Dice throwing was outlawed, as were other means of gambling ("games in which one wins or loses one's pennies" in the official language of the decree), but it is clear from the constant repetition of the ban that it was largely ignored, even though the law specifically included private homes in the injunction.

The Relevance of a University Education in the Late Middle Ages

GUY FITCH LYTLE

In the twentieth century, the position of universities has see-sawed. The steady growth in enrollments and in the importance of university-trained people in American society that can be perceived in the early part of the century ended during the Depression, when graduates found that their education did not open up job opportunities, and when many people could not even afford to enter the university. After the Second World War, growth began again and continued at a very rapid rate until recently. In the past decade, economic problems have again undermined the aspirations of graduates, inflation has put a severe strain on university budgets, and slower population growth has contributed to a decline in enrollments. This pattern of growth and contraction of enrollments can also be seen in the history of the medieval universities, but the nodal points of the rise and decline are spread over centuries rather than decades. In the first two centuries of their existence, the great universities of Paris, Bologna, and Oxford played an important role in society and politics. Kings took an active interest in university affairs and relied on them for the civil servants who built their bureaucratic regimes. University-trained teachers began to dominate the growing educational system of Europe and to participate in the spread of literacy. The universities even acted as arbiters in local and international disputes within the Church, and political issues often affected the internal affairs of the faculty and student organizations. The apex of the universities' political involvement in the Church occurred during the great schism of the late fourteenth century.

The university system also provided an avenue for social mobility in the late medieval community—a community in which the lines of class division were progressively hardening. The values of the educational system cut across economic and social-class boundaries—although it would be wrong to overestimate the egalitarianism of the system. A significant number of poor boys attended the schools and universities, but for individual members of the lower classes, gaining entry to the university must have appeared a formidable task whose successful achievement depended on luck and really extraordinary ability.

Between 1340 and 1430, however, the steady growth in enrollments and increasing influence and wealth of the universities turned around. Study of university records of this period shows that the institutions were in decline —losing students, political and social power, and income and endowment. In this selection, Guy F. Lytle argues that, in England at least, this reversal of fortunes was caused by a lack of jobs for university graduates, and that it led to significant changes in the structure of the universities of Oxford and Cambridge.

Both the semi-autonomy the university enjoyed and the not infrequent official trouble it experienced can be more clearly seen in the light of the overlapping jurisdictions and rival powers of patronage which formed the structure of medieval society. The universities of medieval northern Europe were nurtured originally within the culture of international Christendom, as the special children of a centralizing papacy. As they grew they produced theologians, canon lawyers, and educated priests who could defend and advance both the faith and the church. But if in the early years the papacy was usually a friend to the schools, the bishops often were not. In order to counter this and other localized interference, the universities turned to the king, who responded with a wide-ranging set of exemptions and privileges. As an indirect reward the universities produced anti-papal civil lawyers and chauvinistic bureaucrats and, by the late 15th and early 16th centuries, a class of educated laymen and troubled clerics who would lead in the struggle to redefine the church and state of Reformation Europe.

Oxford found that it could get into trouble with both ecclesiastical and royal patrons when its educational process produced a brilliant heretic, such as John Wyclif, and gave him a forum for his opinions. But more often the university faced the ambiguity of the church (pope, archbishop, or bishop) and the state both appealing to it or threatening it from opposite sides of a conflict. In 1487, and again in 1495, the king demanded that Oxford yield up to his courts a bishop and some students who were using the university as sanctuary while they were seeking justice under its ecclesiastical law. Letters from the university to all the concerned parties show the agony of her indecision, caught in the middle of royal pressure, threats of censure from the church, and the necessity to safeguard her own privileges.

But all of these matters, which might be called the macrostructure of patronage, are well known and yet difficult to analyze briefly. This essay is more concerned with the microstructure: how the attitudes and practices of a society based on patronage affected the internal organization of the university and the careers of its graduates.

Between about 1340 and 1430 in England, there was a serious crisis of patronage for the university and its students which had its roots in demography, war, nationalism, religion, and especially the growing conflict between different types of patrons. At about the same time, Oxford and Cambridge underwent notable institutional changes in which, among other things, *colleges* emerged as the primary administrative, physical, social, and educational focus, at the expense of the older *halls.* There is no

From Guy Fitch Lytle, "Patronage Patterns and Oxford Colleges, c. 1300–c. 1530," in *The University in Society,* Vol. I: *Oxford and Cambridge from the 14th to the Early 19th Century,* ed. Lawrence Stone (Princeton: Princeton University Press, 1974), pp. 112–40.

simple correlation between these complex events; but, by considering them together, the need for, and the contribution of, the colleges becomes somewhat clearer. The colleges provided one important means of solving the patronage crisis for many students, a solution which reflected basic assumptions and realities of English society in the late Middle Ages. It could be argued that their position as dispenser of various kinds of patronage was not by itself a sufficient cause for the rise of colleges to their preeminence within Oxford in the 16th century and later, but the patronage role was certainly a necessary cause, and patronage considerations strongly affected the process by which the change took place...

The Principle of Patronage and English Society 1300–1530

Patronage, in one sense, is simply a matter of who got what jobs for whom and how this was accomplished. As such, the problem can be classified, quantified, and if the data exists, fairly easily determined.

But in another sense patronage may imply a great deal more. In the hierarchical world that was England from the feudal era to the time of Jane Austen and beyond, patronage was the mode in which all society functioned and by which all men, if they could, advanced. As a social principle, however, patronage has always contained numerous ambiguities. On the one hand, it was the working out in practice of the principle and rewards of hierarchy; on the other hand, it was the only counterbalance to hierarchical privilege for those whose ambition exceeded their birth. The patron-client relationship involved a pattern of both exploitation and benevolence on the part of the lord, with the former usually more prominent; but it also established a system which fulfilled many genuine needs for mutual support felt by socially superior men as well as by their inferiors. The client acknowledged subordinance or lack of power (at least in a certain context) in return for material gains and protection. The patron enjoyed a sense of status and munificence, as well as the political influence implicit in large retinues of loyal followers. But perhaps more importantly in the bilateral social relationships which remained as the remnant of an earlier feudal society, lordship implied responsibility. One of the most significant of these obligations was the exercise of the ideal of "public generosity," the distribution of largesse which was demanded by the chivalric ideology and which was institutionalized in patronage.

The many forms and functions of patronage embodied social, political, moral, psychological, legal, religious, and aesthetic realities. They generally acted to bind society together, although abuses were far from being uncommon. Patronage in late medieval society in fact had many of the same attributes that anthropologists find in the "gift-relationship" both in primitive and in sophisticated cultures. Professor Richard Titmuss has described how "in some societies, past and present, gifts to men aim to buy peace; to express affection, regard, or loyalty; to unify the group; to bind the generations; to fulfill a contractual set of obligations and rights; to function as acts of penitence . . . and to symbolize many other human sentiments." Gifts, or patronage, may be economic commodities of some sort which are being used "as vehicles and instruments for realities of another order." One common feature of all these roles is the lack of anonymity. The human relationships were intensely personal (although they produced a feeling of belonging rather than individualism), and neither the patron nor the client could effectively generate a social identity without the other. Another aspect of the social code and structure of chivalry, loyalty, was by these means strengthened.

Patronage both formalized and provided a means for expressing many connections and obligations the society had otherwise imposed. First among these was probably one's duties to his family and kin. Advancement of the family's fortune and honor was a prime consideration in everything from marriage to the need for education, to the appointment of the local vicar; and it would be to a prosperous relative that a youth would most often look for a scholarship or some other patronage. Loyalty to a particular geographical region would often involve a lord, bishop, or official in the advancement of people from that area, and the obligation and satisfaction of this patronage was especially felt when the patron and client were closely allied by reciprocal economic ties, as a landlord and his tenant would be. As we shall se, each of these connections would affect the colleges and their students in the 14th and 15th centuries.

The two greatest sources of patronage were of course the crown and the church. They were approached continuously by suitors, and in turn responded often, since their influence reached every facet of late medieval life. Universities and masters were among the more ardent pleaders, and they received perhaps more than their fair share of the available benefits. University authorities were allowed to control most of the judicial and financial matters in which students and graduates might be involved. Time after time during the Middle Ages the townsmen of Oxford learned, to their discomfort, the extent of these privileges. Not only the members of the university, but also their families, servants, and university employees received special rights. Tax exemptions were forthcoming for students and colleges, and in general the concern shown, and the patronage offered, by the English monarchs for the welfare of the country's scholars was unmatched anywhere in Europe at the time. Nor was the papacy to be outdone in granting favors, and enough immunities and special rulings were issued to set scholars apart as a privileged elite within the already well-protected clergy. . . .

Patronage, as a social principle, always involves a process of reciprocity although the items in that process are usually unequal, intangible, or immeasurable. What would the medieval patron expect and receive? Without going into detail, we can point to service both in war and in peace (chaplains might well serve abroad during times of fighting, just as knights might well represent a lord in Parliament during periods of peace) and to public deference and support as the chief social and political obligations of the client. In the course of the 15th century, many university graduates would find themselves acting as lawyers, secretaries, tutors, chaplains, and administrators in the households of the king, noblemen, and bishops. For this service most of them received ecclesiastical benefices. The reciprocal nature of the arrangement, however, might be carried further. In 1439, the Bishop of Chichester rewarded Thomas Bekynton, a New College graduate and a prominent bureaucrat, with a canonry in his cathedral. Bekynton wrote to the bishop, whom he called his "most beloved father," to thank him for his patronage. No mere words, he said, were sufficient to express his gratitude for the bishop's favor to him, and he desired nothing more than the opportunity to repay these favors. In the meantime, he wished the bishop to know that he had told the king all about the patronage. The patron might receive monetary payment (e.g., from his tenant-clients), but this form of reciprocity did not affect students who had only "human capital" to offer. More common was the proposal of spiritual benefits. Many wills of late medieval Oxford students close by bequeathing the residue of the testator's possessions for the good of his soul and the souls of his benefactors. Many patrons drew up contracts with the recipient of their favors (frequently institutions such as Oxford colleges) both to foster their worldly designs and to assure their own future commemoration.

Finally, we must note that there are many different types of patron-client connections. If "patronage" is to be useful for explaining many of the aspects of medieval history, scholars who use it must distinguish the similarities and differences between, say, a landlord's dealings with a peasant or some other tenant and the same lord's relationship to a knight, a servant, or the local vicar. Almost all of the anthropological literature on patronage has stressed the "dyadic" nature of the contract, the personal tie between two individuals, not between an individual and a collectivity (or an institution). It is clear that this narrow definition will not account for many relationships within medieval society. The undying, corporate lords of the church, such as monasteries, were a serious social and political problem in the eyes of Edward I in the late 13th century. This paper will show how institutions could function not only as direct patrons in a variety of ways, but also as "patronage brokers" to link individuals either with each other (even across several intervening generations) or with the supernatural.

Much research and analysis remains to be done before the precise nature and all the ramifications of medieval patronage become clear. Recent findings, however, have demonstrated that much more than the formal, legal ties of fiefs, *fiefe-rentes*, and indentures must be considered. We must study the many informal patronage connections, with their social, economic, political, personal, and ritual aspects, which acted to coordinate a complex social and cultural system. Only in this way can we gradually supersede our vague vision of "feudal society."

In 1338, the sheriff of Suffolk found that he could not assemble a jury of knights to examine a petition from several lords because there were none in the county who "was not a tenant or of the blood or of the fee or of the robes of one of the aforesaid" lords. As George Holmes has said, "'Bastard feudalism' was well established both as a normal network of relationships and as a possible element in wild disorder." Large retinues made civil war possible. The personal nature both of patronage and a state based on it put great stake in a strong and yet generous monarch; and thus when a weak king such as Henry VI lost control of his patronage, both the opportunity and even the necessity of open conflict emerged. In this paper we are not so much concerned with the more spectacular confrontations such as the "Wars of the Roses," but rather with some of the details of how both the system and the principle of patronage worked with regard to university students.

The Crisis of Patronage, c. 1340–c. 1430

The complaint that unworthy men received promotion while learned doctors and masters were being ignored was one of the commonplace themes of medieval authors. Chaucer's "clerk of Oxenford"

> . . . he was not right fat, I undetake.
> But looked holwe, and thereto soberly.
> Ful thredbare was his overeste courtepy;
> For he hadde geten hym yet no benefice,
> No was so worldly for to have office. . . .

was certainly not the only lean student waiting for a church living in later 14th century England. It is impossible to judge for sure the effect of his own frustration in seeking ecclesiastical promotion on the direction of some of John Wyclif's thought, but certainly he reflects the conflict between lay and papal power over patronage and attacks simony and other related abuses. In a long sermon to the university on the "seven streams of Babylon," Chancellor Thomas Gascoigne discussed absenteeism, pluralism, appropriation of rectories, indulgences, dispensations, and abuses of absolution; but he opened his diatribe with "the unworthy and scandalous ordination and institution of bishops, rectors, and officials which is called promotion," or the various aspects of ecclesiastical patronage.

But few students were as unworldly as Chaucer's clerk, as radical as Wyclif, or as reform-minded as the wealthy Gascoigne. The later Middle Ages in England have been called an "age of ambition," and the universities were competing with warfare, marriage, and trade to be the best avenue of social mobility and thus to attract students. In the early 1400s, a manifesto declared that "knights, esquires, merchants, and the entire community of the realm prefer to make their sons or kinsmen apprentices in some . . . secular craft rather than to send them to the university to become clerks." A proverb, in about 1450, gave as the motive for studying:

> I have heard said in old Romance,
> He that in youth will do his diligence
> To learn, in age it will him advance
> To keep him from all indigence.

was reiterated by Edmund Dudley, an important civil servant under Henry VII, in a book addressed to the aristocracy:

> Favor your cunning clerks and promote them with promotions. . . . Make them your archdeacons and deans, and give them your prebends . . . exhort all others in your diocese that have promotions in likewise to order themselves. . . . How much shall your promoting of virtuous and cunning clerks in great number encourage the students of your universities to take pain and diligence to increase in virtue and cunning.

If a university degree could not assure students of good jobs after they graduated, the institutions faced imminent decline. The figures . . . show that there was a significant decline in the number of university graduates gaining advancement in the church in the later 14th and early 15th centuries. The resulting crisis in the universities caused general alarm.

The dioceses here listed represent a variety of geographical regions and conditions, and yet they clearly indicate a similar pattern of graduate employment. At some point in the second quarter of the 14th century, the percentage of graduates receiving positions turned downward. This trend was accentuated in the latter half of that century, and recovery was slow until the 1430s when the crisis ended. . . .

During this same period, Oxford saw its student body decrease sharply in size: there may have been some 1500 students in the early 14th century and no more than 1000 by 1438. A shrinking of the pool of graduates available to fill the same number of clerical jobs may well explain the pattern, but we must examine the causes of this contraction and not accept too easily a purely demographic explanation for complex social developments.

The demographic and economic changes which affected the whole of Europe after the famines and plagues of the first half of the 14th century undoubtedly had some direct and indirect impact on late medieval Oxford. About 1379, William of Wykeham stated that his foundation of New College was intended to "relieve in part, though in truth we cannot wholly cure, the general disease of the clerical army, which we have seen grievously wounded through want of clergy caused by plagues, wars, and other miseries of the world." Indeed New College was built on a site which had been decimated by plague and which had perhaps served as a plague-pit, or burial ground. Toward the middle of the next century, Gascoigne touched on this cause, among others, for the decline of the state of the church:

> Before the great pestilence in England there were few quarrels among the people and few lawsuits . . . and few lawyers in Oxford, when there were 30,000 scholars at Oxford, as I saw in the rolls of the ancient chancellors of Oxford when I was chancellor there. And the promotion of good men and their residence in their parishes and the fact that churches were sufficiently endowed and not appropriated . . . were the causes why few quarrels then occurred in the parishes and few errors when compared with . . . the errors which occur in the present day.

Gascoigne's statistics are absurd, but the list of causes in the rest of his argument may have substantial merit.

The town of Oxford, situated on the London-Gloucester-Bristol trade route, was certainly hit by plague, but its impact on the university remains an open question. Salter, in an account of his survey of some hall rentals, suggested only a 5 percent falling-off at mid-century; and the general scope of mortality due to the "black death" has been called into question by recent research. In addition, we know that at a later date both the university and the colleges made provisions to carry on academic work away from Oxford in case of plague, and the members of the university never hesitated to disperse at the slightest rumor of a possible outbreak. Unpublished research, however, now indicates that Salter seriously underestimated the decay of the halls and the decline of students, and contemporary founders of colleges usually listed the plague as a cause for the decline of educated clergy. The psychological reactions to the "black death" and the consequent growth in chantry endowments may have been a very significant factor in the ultimate solving of the university patronage crisis. But we cannot allow demographic factors to explain wholly these complex developments, since the chronology of the demographic and patronage curves fails to fit in at least one crucial respect: while the decline may have commenced at roughly the same time in each case, the increase in the percentage of university men finding church positions pre-

ceded the rise in the number of students entering Oxford by one generation and the recovery of population growth in the country as a whole by
two generations.

If we follow Gascoigne, the possibility that changes in patronage patterns explain the fall and rise of student numbers, rather than vice versa,
must be considered. University officials at Oxford were certainly of this
opinion in the 15th century. In 1438, they claimed that, while students
had once flocked there from every country and all the faculties had flourished, now no students came, the buildings were in ruins, and the schools
were in danger of closing. These conditions had been caused by war, scarcity of both food and money, and the lack of adequate reward for merit.
The ignorant were being promoted in the church and elsewhere, while
even those who studied until their old age still could find no positions.
The university cited the example of earlier days, the warnings of the
Bible, and the dangers facing the faith, and then begged the Archbishop of
Canterbury and others for help. In all of this, there was no mention of
plague. Although much less credence can be given to a similar complaint
in 1471, again it was the furious opposition of the world against both
Oxford and the Christian faith, and the continued promotion of unlettered
men instead of graduates, which was said to have kept the university
half-empty. The effects of this situation, according to the officials, were
disastrous for the country, since insubordination and wickedness were
spreading quickly and would destroy the order of the realm. The latter
concluded with a recommendation that, in order to obtain divine favor for
the whole kingdom, special prayers should be widely said for the interces-
sion of Oxford's patron saint, St. Frideswide. Plague and demographic
change, fluctuations in the economy, and extended warfare all were crucial
factors in the social history of late medieval England; but in order to
account fully for the crisis of the universities, it would seem necessary to
pursue further this question of patronage.

Universities and graduates had traditionally looked to Rome to solve
their patronage problems. The papacy had sheltered the nascent *studia
generale* and later used their graduates in its expanding bureaucracy. Since
the popes had supported the growth of the institutions, it was only natural
that their graduates would expect papal patronage. Because of the long
years they had to spend in the schools and away from their local region,
students often lost contact with potential patrons; only when they could
obtain the intervention of the international papal authority were they able
to redress the balance in their favor in the face of "the localization and
preponderance of personal influence in the disposal of benefices." The
universities became even more dependent on the process of papal
patronage when they began to follow the example of other petitioners and
to submit to the pope *rotuli*, or lists of graduates seeking positions or
reservations of benefices. These rolls, which reflect the hierarchy of

university degrees and the hostility of rival faculties, were compiled by the University of Oxford from 1317 until the early 15th century. Even though a successful petition depended as much on luck as on real desert, and while grants became less and less effective as time passed, as late as 1417 Oxford authorities still hoped that the practice might be renewed as an important facet of patronage.

An indication of the role of papal patronage in the careers of some Oxford students can be found in the following figures. Between 1301 and 1350, some 48 percent of those graduates who had careers in the church received at least one papal presentation or reservation. About 26 percent of the graduates had received their *first* known benefice by this means. In the second half of the century, these figures declined to 40 percent and 16 percent respectively. After the final Oxford *rotulus* in 1404, papal patronage virtually ceased. While too much weight should not be placed on these numbers, they do suggest that papal provision was very important in the hopes of students and was perhaps especially important in securing their first job.

During the late 14th and early 15th centuries, direct papal presentations to church livings in England gradually came to a halt, although popes continued their formal provision of bishops and maintained their powers of dispensation. This decline was primarily the result of an increasingly hostile lay public opinion, which was articulated in large part by those groups who were feeling the patronage squeeze in society most severely, the lords and knights, many of whom sat in Parliament. As early as the Parliament at Carlisle in 1307, strong opposition to the pope was being voiced. It had increased further by 1351 when Parliament passed the Statute of Provisors, which greatly limited papal influence on patronage in England. Common themes which ran throughout these documents, as well as those acts which would come later, "the neglect of divine service, hospitality, alms, . . . the frustration of the founders' intentions and the destruction of patrons' rights; the exportation of treasure to enemies; the lack of councillors and betrayal of the kingdom's secrets." They show the growing chauvinism of English attitudes combined with the insistent need to find ways to pay for the new social relationships of the "bastard feudal" or patronage society. Periodic relaxations of these new laws, and the attempts both by Edward III (in 1376) and by Richard II (in 1399) to reach a concordat with Rome, were offset by the passing of a much more stringent Statute of Provisors in 1390 and the annulment by the Lancastrians of Richard II's agreement.

Claims and counterclaims interspersed with years of amiable dealings characterized the relationship between the English rulers and the popes up to the Reformation, but Rome had ceased permanently to be a major patron in the English church. The papal power of patronage, however, had not really collapsed until after 1400; the patronage crisis had begun before 1350 and thus before the first Statute of Provisors, and it was ending just as papal provisions were disappearing.   Certain individuals, and probably certain whole classes of scholars, were adversely affected by this change, but it can hardly have been, as many thought, the sole cause.

The decline of papal patronage should be seen as a symptom or a consequence of a more fundamental social change which was occurring in the later Middle Ages.   To fulfill the obligations of the indentures they had signed, lords needed all the patronage they could muster, and they could not afford to exclude the church from this quest.   It can be proved that many university graduates were involved in this contractual system of secular employment, but contemporary critics often saw that system as detrimental to the advancement in the church of poor but worthy students.   According to John Audelay,

> Now if a poor man sends his son to Oxford to school,
> Both the father and the mother, hindered they shall be;
> And if there falls a benefice, it shall be given a fool,
> To a clerk of a kitchen or of the chancery.

Hoccleve, Dudley, Barclay, and Saint-German, among others repeat this accusation up to the early 16th century.

As the remaining tables in this paper all show, laymen already controlled a significant amount of religious patronage; but as the social system grew in elaboration, so the demands for even more were intensified. Many contemporary letters, petitions, and lawsuits show the king, the queen, the Prince of Wales, royal officials, and other laymen trying to gain control over ecclesiastical presentations.   Monasteries, another source of considerable patronage, could often be bullied or bribed into allowing a layman or the king to dictate a presentation or they might do so to reciprocate for some other favor.   The papacy, however, was less pliable, and it had been only a matter of time until its claims to English patronage were successfully attacked.   It would not be until the middle of the 15th century when the universities had adjusted themselves to the new ways of society (especially by the foundations of more colleges) and when university training and the students it produced were satisfying more of the secular and spiritual needs of their society that graduates found increasingly good markets for employment and ecclesiastical preferment at the hands of new patrons. . . .

Responses to the Crisis

Before this gradual change had reached fruition, individuals and committees of all sorts had suggested and tried a number of specific remedies to aid university graduates.

In 1392, the House of Commons authorized Richard II and his council to modify the Statute of Provisors and requested that they "d'avoir tendrement au coer en ceste Ordinance l'estat & relievement des Universitees d'Oxenford' & de Cantebrigg." In 1400, exemptions were asked both for an individual graduate and for the universities and graduates as a whole. In 1415, the Commons laid the blame for almost all the nation's evils, including rebellion, heresy, and "the extinction of the universities," on the Statute of Provisors, which they acknowledged their own predecessors had devised. Seldom can a university have received such accolade as that which marks the beginning of that Commons' petition to the king. . . . But, the Commons went on, now to the contrary because "l'estatuit de Provision & encountre Provisours fuit fait per Parlement, le Clergie en les ditz Universitees lamentablement est extincte" and because no one had any incentive to study, the church and the realm were falling into ruin for lack of guidance. The king referred the matter to the lords spiritual, the bishops who sat in Parliament.

At times the king intervened personally. In 1399, Richard II granted permission to the Chancellor and graduates of Oxford to seek and accept letters of provision from the pope, notwithstanding all contrary laws, and Henry IV allowed a similar relaxation in 1403, at the special request of his queen. A year earlier, Henry had supported a plan, drawn up by the Convocation of Canterbury at the request of "doctors and other graduates" of Oxford and Cambridge, which required all spiritual patrons to notify a commission composed of the Bishops of Exeter, Hereford, and Rochester of the names, values, and conditions of the benefices in their gift, so that the commission could recommend graduates to the patrons for appropriate promotion. The Bishop of Exeter received the king's Privy Seal letter and passed it on to his vicar-general, but this scheme apparently produced no jobs for the graduates, and it vanished without a further trace from the records. (It is illuminating to notice that when the same vicar-general, Robert Rygge, an Oxford doctor of theology, later wished to make large donations to aid the university and its students, he did so by adding to the endowment of two colleges, Merton and Exeter.)

The church attempted in other ways to relieve the plight of university men. In addition to their responses to the *rotuli* when they were allowed to be sent, popes from time to time issued special directives. In 1382, Urban VI urged the Archbishop of Canterbury to appoint doctors, masters, and bachelors to dignities in the great cathedrals. Churchmen who attended the General Councils like the one at Constance in the early 15th century were consulted, and patronage considerations were high on the agenda for reform. In the list of forty-six articles which Oxford sent to that council, the fourth one contained a plea for the promotion of her graduates; and in a separate list, one Oxford graduate, Richard Ullerston, asked for the special advancement of theologians. The English position was best summed up in the *avisamentum* "de collacionibus beneficiarum pro nacione Anglicana" [concerning the granting of benefices in the English nation]. The *avisamentum* lamented the decline of the church, which it blamed on the lack of good preachers, and then presented a program for making certain that graduates obtained useful benefices. It was more realistic than many of the other remedies proposed, since it very clearly took into account the changing situation and attitudes of both the church and society in late medieval England. It mentioned the pope only once, and rather concentrated on the diocesan bishop as the crucial administrative figure in any new patronage reform. These episcopal patrons were to collate one noncathedral living to every unpromoted graduate with an M.A. or higher degree who had been born in the diocese in question. Whenever there were any graduates born in a bishop's or archbishop's diocese, they were to be given at least one in every four cathedral dignities and canonries; and the universities, to facilitate these presentations, would compile a list of alumni arranged according to place of birth. By focusing directly on one type of powerful patron, and by allowing for the functioning of regional biases which were very strong in that patronage-based society, this proposal ought to have had some chance of success. But the *avisamentum* does not appear in any administrative records, and it therefore seems not to have been implemented.

Similar proposals were discussed by the English clergy themselves in the Convocations of Canterbury in 1417, 1421, and again in 1438. Nothing came of the first two ordinances because of a long-standing conflict between Oxford and the religious orders. In 1438, Pope Eugenius ordered the universities to send delegations to the Council of Ferrara. Oxford alleged that it was too poor to support such a delegation, and the Archbishop of Canterbury was asked to relieve this poverty by a more systematic enforcement of the earlier ordinances for the promotion of graduates. In return for a few concessions from Oxford, Convocation reissued the 1421 plan. All of these schemes put great emphasis on the role of the bishops, and they did in fact become the patrons most favorable toward graduates. In part this can be explained by the rise in the percentage of bishops who were themselves graduates; from roughly 50 percent in the reign of Henry III in the 13th century, to 70 percent under Edward III, to over 90 percent in the 15th century. Moreover, most bishops were very practical men, and they too were using more graduates in their administrations and had to reward them as best they could. As we shall see below, not all graduates had an equal chance to obtain some of this episcopal largesse.

All of these remedies show an awareness by contemporaries of the problem then facing the universities. But most of the responses either answered one small request for one given year or relied on exhortation and other soft pressure. The question remains, therefore, whether in the late 14th and early 15th centuries there was not some firmer, institutional response to the crisis which both aided some pressing university problems and brought the university more into line with prevailing social conditions and attitudes. Clues toward an answer can be found by studying the early history of some colleges founded in that period, especially that of New College.

Oxford Colleges and Patronages, c. 1350–c. 1530

The employment of her graduates was not the only problem facing Oxford in the late Middle Ages and early Renaissance which required new institutional solutions. In nearly every case, the changes which occurred in response to these problems meant that colleges took a more prominent role in the affairs of the university.

To counter the decline in the number of students attending Oxford in the later 14th century, new colleges were founded and older ones were expanded explicitly to recruit new undergraduates, not just to support graduate students as most colleges had previously done. Colleges offered a solution to the problem of financing an education in a period of some economic depression, and this internal patronage of its chosen members has remained the most significant long-term contribution of the colleges. In part because they were not endowed and thus could not fulfill the same patronage role for their students, the number of halls in the university steadily declined from some 120 around 1300 to only 69 in 1444. They fell further to 50 (in 1469), to 31 (in 1501), to 25 (in 1511), to 12 (in 1514), and finally to 8 by 1522. Although in the early 16th century, the halls still housed almost a third of the student body, the surviving halls were large and, since the passage of the various "aulerian" statutes in the 15th century, very collegiate in their structure. A number of colleges annexed or permanently gained control of halls in their immediate area, installed a college fellow as principal of the hall, and used the halls to house what was in effect their new undergraduate population. Because of this change, college men came to dominate the important university jobs, especially those of proctor and scribe. Moreover, as early as 1410, the heads of the colleges were being summoned, along with experts from the faculties, to make an important decision.

Oxford also faced problems in its primary responsibility of teaching. The Regent Master system was no longer producing either enough or the right kind of teachers, and new curricula interests forced many students and scholars to look outside the traditional statutory paths to find alternative methods of gaining and conveying knowledge. The advent of printing was of course crucial in this intellectual transformation, but one must not underestimate the importance of the colleges with their tutorials and endowed lectureships. New College was the first to appoint specific fellows as tutors for other members, but this form of academic and intellectual patronage soon spread to other colleges. New College also established early on a special teacher of Greek, but in this it was soon far surpassed by Magdalen and Corpus Christi.

But we must limit our detailed study of the colleges to the question of their role in ecclesiastical patronage. The university as a corporation tried, but evidently failed, to solve the patronage crisis of its graduates. Even by the middle of the 15th century, it did not hold the advowson, or right to present, to more than one or two livings. The official letter-books (*Epistolae Academicae Oxon.*) are crammed with letters of recommendation for graduates to all conceivable patrons, but, as with other forms of exhortation, these were seldom sufficient to get the person a job. With the cessation of the *rotuli*, not only were graduates obliged to turn away from their reliance on the pope and to look for a local patron, but also the university—the sponsor and compiler of the rolls and thus a collective, corporate lord—lost its only effective patronage function. Oxford tried to overcome this weakness by changing the nature of the chancellorship and substituting a bishop or a nobleman for the often outstanding theologians who had governed the university since the 13th century. This change aided the university as an institution, especially in some of its elaborate building projects, but it did little directly to help graduates secure jobs.

The halls had no answer to this patronage need. In a medieval formulary, there is a testimonial letter by the principal and fellows of a hall on behalf of one of their members. William Swan, a lawyer at the court of Rome in the early 15th century, replied to Master William Dogge's request for a new grace of provision that he would do all he could to help him for the sake of the time they spent together at Oxford in the same "dining hall" (*sala*). But the halls themselves had no patronage to offer and were even less effective than the university.

The colleges did have a solution, at least in part, for the patronage crisis. But in order to understand that solution more fully, we must examine the relationship between the colleges and late medieval society, some evidence of which can be gathered from the motives of the founders. While all colleges had philanthropic aspects, and many can be understood as extensions of a royal, noble, or episcopal "household" or court, all colleges were also chantries of more or less elaboration. All the founders accepted the implicit and explicit relationship between the principle of patronage in late medieval social organization and its spiritual manifestations. Archbishop Chichele demonstrated this attitude quite clearly in his statutes for All Souls College in the early 15th century. He lamented the decayed state of the "unarmed militia of clerics" because of their lack of promotion and their consequent destitutions; he also mourned the "armed militia . . . which has been very much reduced by the wars between the realms of England and France"; and then went on:

> we, therefore, pondering with tedious exercise of thought how . . . we may . . . spiritually or temporally . . . succor each aforesaid soldiery . . . [decided to found] one college of poor and indigent scholars, being clerks, who are constantly bound, not so much to attend therein to the various sciences and faculties, but with all devotion to pray for the souls of glorious memory. . . .

especially those of the House of Lancaster (Chichele's patrons), those who fell in the French wars, and all souls of the faithful departed. Other rubrics of the statutes gave the details on the liturgy to be followed in the masses for the dead. This function of the colleges was increased at the death of almost every fellow, since most graduates would leave money or goods either to specific friends at the college or to the college itself for the celebration of obits and the increase of the college endowment. . . .

In order to fulfill their stated ambitions, the founders had to devise some method not only to educate future priests, but also to find for them effective parish and cathedral positions. The founders came up with an excellent solution: they included as many advowsons as possible in the endowment of the college, which gave the colleges direct control over a substantial amount of ecclesiastical patronage. Of the twenty-one manors which Bishop Wykeham gave to New College, thirteen or fourteen included the advowson of the local church, and two separate advowsons were also included. Although it was wealthier than many other colleges, the pattern of the New College endowment was not untypical. When the college fell into financial difficulties in the 1430s, a former fellow and future bishop, Thomas Bekynton, showed filial loyalty by persuading Henry VI to grant to the college the confiscated property of the alien priory of Longueville. This brought not only six more manors, but also an additional nine units of church patronage. At the Council of Constance there was some reformist pressure to abolish the appropriation of such alien priory possessions to other owners in England. In a letter from New College to Bishop Bubwith, who was at the council, the concern of the college for the manors and the advowsons is evident:

> Some evil people . . . do not shrink . . . from making widows of the colleges and other institutions, established by pious founders, by the deprivation of their privileges and the taking away of their goods. . . . Growling with canine fury at the liberties and privileges granted to us by the Holy Roman Pontiff,

they strive to destroy completely the unions of churches which our lord of holy memory canonically secured at great expense and by licence of the Apostolic See from the alien houses.

All Oxford colleges had much of their endowment in the form of income from the great tithes of impropriated rectories; indeed at their foundation Balliol, Exeter, and Oriel had little else. The income was crucial for the daily operation of the colleges, but the patronage which came with these rectories was also of great importance for starting their graduates on their careers.

PART 5

The Renaissance and Reformation
16th ~ 17th Centuries

Detail from "Birth of the Virgin," by Domenico Ghirlandaio, Santa
Maria Novella, Florence.

The Renaissance and Reformation

The cultural and religious movements that gave their names to the Renaissance–Reformation period occurred against a social background that has become familiar through many historical studies. In Italy, urbanization combined with a rediscovery of classical Greek and Roman literature to create a new view of history and a new sense of national and human identity. Whereas medieval scholars and rulers had extolled the virtues of the Roman Empire and its autocratic government because they saw themselves as its continuators, the Italian humanists, some of whom were both scholars and political figures, rediscovered the Roman Republic and made it their ideal. This shift of political consciousness necessitated a change in historical consciousness, because it made the humanists aware of historical discontinuity. For them, the study of Roman history could not be, as it had been for their medieval predecessors, a study of an earlier age of their own development. Instead, it was the study of a civilization wholly separate from theirs. On the one hand, this historical consciousness led them to attempt a revival of ancient culture. On the other hand, the rediscovery of the Republic brought into vogue republican political values, which were at odds with Roman and medieval imperial ideals, and a new appreciation for urban life.

As the humanists gained sway in the intellectual and artistic world of Europe, their values became dominant in politics and society. Two the articles in this section deal with aspects of these changes. In "Cultural Patronage in Renaissance Florence," Gene Brucker discusses the connection between the powerful urban patriciate and the new intellectuals and artists in the most important of the centers of the new culture. In "Parent and Child in Renaissance Italy," James Bruce Ross reveals the patterns of child-rearing and family life in the urban middle class, which was already becoming the dominant social group in early modern Europe.

Just as the Italian Renaissance can be linked with renaissances of the Middle Ages—although fundamentally different from them—so the Reformation can be seen as yet another medieval movement for ecclesiastical reform, which had a result fundamentally different from that of its predecessors. After Martin Luther's initial attempts to reform the Church and to reformulate its principles of belief, he and other Protestants succeeded in establishing new churches. The Protestant movement may have begun as a reform of the Church as an institution, but it soon turned to a complete reform of the religion itself. To what extent did social changes in late medieval Europe affect the course and the outcome of the Reformation? What were the social consequences of the overhaul of Christianity? Natalie Z. Davis assesses the relationship between religious and social change in "City Women and the French Reformation."

The first article in this section treats a different kind of movement in late medieval and early modern Europe—the movement of microorganisms. The bubonic plague was endemic in Europe from the middle of the fourteenth century to the middle of the seventeenth, and communities had to develop plans and institutions to counter its periodic attacks. Carlo Cipolla describes the new institutions of public health in "A Community Against the Plague."

BIBLIOGRAPHY

On the general problem of plagues and epidemics, see William H. McNeill, *Plagues and Peoples* (New York, 1976). See also Hans Zinsser, *Rats, Lice and History* (Boston, 1935). Every history of the late Middle Ages contains sections on the plague, but for a general survey, see Philip Ziegler, *The Black Death: A study of the Plague in 14th Century Europe* (New York, 1969). Very little has been written about institutions concerned with public health, but see L. F. Hirst, *The Conquest of Plague* (Oxford, 1953).

On the social life and culture of sixteenth-century France, see Natalie Z. Davis, *Society and Culture in Early Modern France* (Palo Alto, Calif., 1975), from which the selection "City Women and the French Reformation" is taken. For general information, see Roland H. Bainton, *Women of the Reformation: In Germany and Italy* (Minneapolis, 1971) and *Women of the Reformation: In France and England* (Minneapolis, 1973). Bainton also wrote a good introduction to the Reformation as a whole, *The Reformation of the Sixteenth Century* (Boston, 1972). See also Robert Kingdon, *Geneva and the Consolidation of the French Protestant Movement* (Madison, Wisc., 1967).

The classic work on Renaissance humanism is Jacob Burckhardt, *The Civilization of the Renaissance in Italy*, 2 vols. (New York, 1951 [originally published in German in 1860]). The more recent classic of Hans Baron, *The Crisis of the Early Italian Renaissance*, rev. ed. (Princeton, 1966), treats specifically the relationship between trends in humanist thought and politics. Denys Hay, *The Italian Renaissance in its Historical Background* (Cambridge, Eng., 1965; 2nd ed., 1977), and L. Martines, *The Social World of the Florentine Humanists* (Princeton, 1963) treat the subject of Brucker's selection, "Cultural Patronage in Renaissance Florence." See also Gene Brucker, *Florentine Politics and Society 1343–1378* (Princeton, 1963). For a penetrating study of humanist thinking, see P. O. Kristeller, *Renaissance Thought* (New York, 1961).

Some of the works cited above also relate to James Bruce Ross's study of the urban family. See, in addition, P. Jones, "Florentine Families and Florentine Diaries in the Fourteenth Century," in *Studies in Italian Medieval History Presented to Miss E. M. Jamison*, ed. P. Grierson and J. W. Perkins (Rome, 1956), pp. 183–205. See the articles in Anthony Molho, ed., *Social and Economic Foundations of the Italian Renaissance* (New York, 1969). For a general survey of life during the Renaissance, see John Gage, *Life in Italy at the Time of the Medici*, ed. P. Quennell (New York, 1968). A new work on the subject of Ross's article is Francis William Kent, *Household and Lineage in Renaissance Florence: The Family Life of the Capponi, Ginori, and Rucellai* (Berkeley, 1978).

A Community Against the Plague

CARLO CIPOLLA

Public health is a prominent national and international issue in the twentieth century. In the United States, every city, county, and state has a large and active public health agency, and the federal government maintains national health centers for research and control of disease, all of them under the giant, cabinet-level Department of Health, Education, and Welfare. The growth of this apparatus for the common good is not the result of modern medical science, but stems from the terrible experience of the late medieval plague epidemics. The plague attacked rural as well as urban areas, but its impact on the close and neighborly populations of the cities far exceeded the toll it took in rural districts. It exposed the vulnerability of life in close quarters, and people fled the cities in hopes of preserving their lives.

The retreat from urbanism was temporary, of course. After the epidemic subsided, people returned to the cities to pick up their careers and settle again into the best life they knew. City dwellers were innovators. They had left the tradition-bound life of the farm and had come to the city to build new lives. Just as they had learned to react to new commercial opportunities and deal with market changes, and just as they had readily received new artistic and intellectual movements, now they responded to the plague and created institutions for public health. In the selection that follows, Carlo Cipolla describes the health institutions of a small Italian city and its environs while telling the story of its battle against the plague epidemic of 1630. His story also reveals the relationship between town and country in late medieval and early modern Italy, and illustrates the hegemony exercised by the great cities—in this case, Florence—over the small ones.

Prato lies in a plain bordered on the west by the pleasant hills of Montalbano and on the north and the east by the "most stony and barren mountaines, which are called Apennine and divide the length of Italy." In that "most pleasant plain" vines and mulberry trees, cypresses and rosemary grew in the harmony of nature. . . .

From Carlo Cipolla, *Cristofano and the Plague* (Berkeley and Los Angeles: University of California Press, 1973), pp. 34, 35, 37–48.

Politically and administratively, Prato was part of the Grand Duchy of Tuscany whose capital was Florence. The town was administered by a Town Council led by the *Priori* and the *Gonfaloniere*. The central authority of the Grand Duke was locally represented by the *Podestà*. The local administration was closely controlled by the central government; however by the early seventeenth century the local administrators were ready to oblige and most willing to prove their deference and obedience to the *Signori* of Florence.

In the first decades of the seventeenth century Prato numbered about 6,000 souls within the walls and about 11,000 souls within its jurisdiction outside the gates. Today Prato boasts a thriving textile industry that exports its products to the four corners of the world. In the fifteenth century Prato was the base of a huge and thriving mercantile firm, the product of the enterprising and managerial genius of Francesco di Marco Datini, "the Merchant of Prato." At the beginning of the seventeenth century the great enterprise of Francesco had long since disappeared and the modern textile industry had not yet started. Robert Dallington visiting Prato in 1596 had a general impression of poverty. . . .

The first official warning of the danger of plague reached Prato toward the end of October 1629: a letter dated the 26th from the Health officers in Florence instructed the local administration to place guards for health controls. Only five days had passed since the news of the outbreak of plague on the northern side of Lake Como had reached Milan and the action of the Health Board in Florence could not have been more prompt.

In the absence of any knowledge about vaccination, the establishment of a sanitary cordon was the only preventive measure people could resort to besides prayers and processions. In response to the letter from Florence, the town Council of Prato, on October 27th promptly appointed four citizens to the position of "*Officiali di Sanità*" (Health officers).

All affairs pertaining to Public Health were placed in their hands and thus the positioning of the guards also. It was customary at the time to have two lines of defence: one at the borders of the territory, at mountain passes and at fords, and the other at the gates of the city. On November 1st, the Officers of Prato wrote to the Officers in Florence that they had complied with the general instructions received on October 26th. On December 27th, in consideration of the very cold weather, the officers ordered the construction of barracks for the guards at three of the five gates and also made provision of one *staio* of embers per day for the guards at each of the five gates. It was a small ration of fuel, but in those days people were accustomed to a harsh life. And so the winter passed.

In May 1630 the news from the north suddenly became very alarming: the plague had been identified in Bologna. The immediate reaction of the Health Board in Florence was to request that all people moving from one place to another should carry health passes. No one without such a certificate could be admitted into the territory of the State or into any walled place. On May 14th the Board instructed the Health officers in Prato to appoint a person who would issue the passes for the local people. Within two days the instructions were carried out.

In the meantime in Bologna the situation had deteriorated tragically, and on June 12th Florence rushed troops to the northern border of the Grand Duchy so that there would be one guard-post every three miles. On the following day, Bologna was put under a total ban, which meant that persons, merchandise and letters could not be received from that city even if accompanied by reassuring health passes. On the 16th all people living close to the border were requested to be on the alert: if they saw strangers close the border where there were no guards they had "to cry in chorus, ring the bells alarmingly and follow the trespassers until they were captured." As fear mounted, the activity of Health offiers both central and local became feverish. June 16th: the officers of Prato added more guards at the gates and increased the wages of the guards as an obvious incentive to them to be more conscientious; June 22nd: the officers in Florence instructed the Health officers of all towns and walled villages of the Grand Duchy to use greater care in the issuing of health passes; July 1st: the Grand Duke rushed thirty horsemen of his personal guard to strengthen border control; July 6th: the officers in Florence instructed local officers to stop all movements of friars of any religious order; July 10th: in Prato the three most frequently used gates—Mercatale, Fiorentina and Pistoiese—were reinforced with barricades. All in vain.

The establishemnt of a sanitary cordon is a necessary but rarely sufficient measure. This was especially so in an age when the microbic enemy was unknown and invisible, when animal vectors were not recognized as such and when the reliability and competence of the guards were questionable.

The precautionary measures of the Health officers did not stop the advance of the enemy. By July, the plague had invaded Trespiano, a village four miles north of Florence on the road to Bologna, and by August it had entered the city of Florence and Tavola, a little village in the jurisdiction of Prato. Both Trespiano and Tavola were isolated, and in Florence a number of houses were quarantined.

There was resistance to the facts. Physicians kept debating whether it was plague or not, and the Health officers in Florence, pending a final decision, distributed reassuring bulletins deluding themselves and others. But day by day the awful truth became more tragically obvious.

During the months of July and August 1630, mortality in Prato seems to have been higher than normal, and in September there were a number of cases of death and illness of a suspicious nature. The local physicians and surgeons were uncertain in their diagnosis: official confirmation of the plague was resisted because of its disastrous implications, yet the local administration grew increasingly nervous. On August 3rd, 1630, the town council decided to raise the number of the Health officers from four to eight, and about one month later the officers wrote to the Health Board in Florence asking for authorization to prepare a pest-house as a precautionary measure. This was an excellent idea but unfortunately the officers in Florence, in their eagerness to prevent panic and avoid the banning of Tuscany by other states, discouraged the initiative. They pointed out that Florence was very close and could easily provide advice and assistance; moreover, the recent rains—they added—by refreshing the air, were bound to have beneficial effects.

Their optimism was ill founded. One man, Niccolò Bardazzi, attendant in the hospital of the Misericordia in Prato, was in charge of those cases of death or sickness which looked suspicious. On September 16th the man fell sick and he died on the 19th. This time the physicians had no doubts: it was the plague. The same day the officers of Prato hurriedly reported the facts to those in Florence. On the following day, September 20th, the Florentine officers promptly responded with a letter of instructions which is exemplary in its precision and conciseness. In its almost telegraphic style one perceives the officers; concern to prevent misunderstanding, to avoid delays, to emphasize the need for precise and effective action:

> you must straightway order that the persons of the family of the deceased be confined to the house. The household items used by the deceased must be separated from the others. You must bar the door of the house from the outside. The family of the deceased must receive victuals through the windows. Make sure that no one comes out. All members of the family have to be provided with victuals for the amount of one *giulio* per day. The money will be paid by the officer who pays the guards at the gates and it will be credited to him. All the above to be ordered and carried out at once. You will inform us of what follows.

Unfortunately what followed was not good. With a letter dated Octoer 2nd, 1630, the Health officers of Prato reported to the Board in Florence that the town was a prey to the plague.

The first round of the battle had been lost. The invisible and pitiless enemy was within the walls claiming lives at a dreadful rate. People were religious and superstitious and they placed much faith in the Divine Providence. Although perfectly aware of how dangerous it was to gather in large groups, they organized processions and other religious ceremonies on October 8th, on October 28th and then again in November. People however, were also practical and while stubbornly hoping for help from God or some other holy Dignitary, they knew that they had to help themselves in their own way.

There were two hospitals in Prato: the hospital *della Misericordia* and the hospital of San Silvestro, both of which were under the same administration. The governor was appointed by the Grand Duke and held office for a period of three years at the end of which he could be reappointed. Over the centuries, these two hospitals had been endowed with property by various citizens and as their income was derived from such properties, their financial situation was largely dependent upon the level of agricultural prices. Around 1630, in normal years, the income of the two hospitals fluctuated around 5,500–7,500 ducats. In a year of exceptionally low agricultural prices, such as 1634, the income of the two hospitals could drop as low as 2,500 ducats.

The hospital regularly received patients for treatment, but this was only incidental. According to an old tradition of medieval origin, the hospitals of Prato like most European hospitals, were devoted to charity at large rather than to the specific task of attending the sick. Between July 1st, 1631 and June 30th, 1632 for example, the two hospitals received 292 patients for a total of 3,692 patient-days, which meant an average permanence of about 13 days per patient. This was approximately equivalent to having had 10 patients for the 365 days of the year. For the 365 days of the year the hospital *della Misericordia* kept 182 abandoned adolescents (128 girls and 54 boys) and also cared for about 100 foundlings. Although the hospital had resident wet nurses, most of the foundlings were given out to non resident wet nurses who of course received compensation for their services. In 1630 the ratio of foundlings kept in the hospital to those given out was 8 to 98. All the above figures conform with a normal pattern, and they clearly show that the vast majority of the resources of the two hospitals was devoted to the care of abandoned youth.

Normally Prato could also count on the services of a number of surgeons and physicians. Early in September 1630, the Health officers of Florence wanted to know the strength of the medical profession in Prato and complying with their request the administration of Prato reported the following:

> . . . The Community of Prato keeps two physicians as *medici condotti.* One is ser Latanzio Magiotti, aged about 40, bachelor, very good doctor, patrician, native of Montevarchi. The other is messer Giobatta Serrati, native of Castiglione Fiorentino, aged 30 with wife and one daughter and is a good doctor. Native of this place is messer Pierfrancesco Fabbruzzi, who has a private practice, is 70 years of age, married with children, a good doctor if he were not so old. In addition there is messer Giuliano Losti, a young man of 25 years of age. He obtained his doctorate in medicine this year and thus far has not put his knowledge into practice. There is also messer Jacopo Lionetti, aged 60, with wife and children who, however, has never practiced.

Although you did not request information about either the quantity or quality of the surgeons, we inform you that there are three surgeons, two of which are in *condotta*: they are Master Michele Cepparelli, native of this place, aged 60, with great experience and without wife or children and Master Antonio Gramigna, native of this place, aged 50, with wife and children, one of whom is at present learning the art from his father. There is also Master Tiburzio, native of this place, who has a private practice, aged 60 with wife and children.

It might be mentioned here that in Italy since the thirteenth century, first in the cities and later also in the villages of some importance, it had become customary to hire physicians and surgeons at the expense of the community. These physicians (and surgeons) were either called *medici* (and *chirurghi*) *condotti* or also *medici* (and *chirurghi*) *del pubblico*. Receiving a regular monthly salary they were to reside in the community, never to leave without permission and to cure without charge all those in need of medical care who could not afford its cost. On occasion, when treating people of some means, they were allowed to receive an extra fee. Besides these doctors and surgeons there were the physicians and surgeons with private practices. According to the report cited above, Prato had two physicians *condotti* and two physicians with private practice as well as one man who held a doctorate but never practiced. Moreover, there were two surgeons *condotti* and one with private practice. This gives a grand total of seven active medical men for a population of about 17,000 souls—definitely a high ratio for the time. Whether a relatively high number of doctors was beneficial to the health of the population is another matter.

When the plague broke out in the town, the ordinary medical structure of Prato had to be reorganized and strengthened. The Health officers of Prato informed the Board in Florence that their town was a prey of the plague on October 2nd; that same day they hurriedly decided to transform one of the two hospitals into a pest-house. Since the hospital *della Misericordia* housed the children, the officers selected the hospital of San Silvestro with the annexed church of San Silvestro. The hospital *della Misericordis* however, had to provide the hospital of San Silvestro with the food, the medicines, the fuel, the beds and the other equipment necessary to operate as a pest-house. The town was to cover the expenses for the personnel.

The officers appointed a confessor, a surgeon and a number of attendants to serve in the pest-house. They also appointed gravediggers, guards, a messenger, a man to deliver the victuals to those confined in their homes and a man to carry the necessities from the hospital *della Misericordia* to the hospital of San Silvestro. Including the physicians, the surgeons, the vice-chancellor who issued the passes, the gravediggers, the chief constable and his men, those who in one way or another fought the plague in Prato under the orders of the Health officers, numbered about twenty-five at the peak of their strength.

The physicians were persons of rank. The surgeons were on a markedly lower social level. At one point, some of the guards at the gates were put in jail, which proves that their conduct was not always exemplary. The gravediggers were an unpleasant and mercenary group and the nicknames given to some of them clearly indicate vulgar and brutal people. On one occasion we know that a convict was enlisted as a gravedigger because of lack of regular help. This was the army which the Health officers led in their fight against the plague—a small army and a very heterogeneous one, which included physicians as well as constables, friars as well as convicts.

It was not easy to keep this small army at full strength. The plague claimed lives among those who served the Public Health as well as among those who were served by it. . . .

City Women and the
French Reformation

NATALIE ZEMON DAVIS

How much did the Reformation revolutionize European life? Clearly, it made a very great difference in the religious life and institutions of Europeans, in their political life, and perhaps in their intellectual life. In the religious sphere, the reformers raised questions about the structure, authority, and beliefs of the universal church of the Middle Ages. Few of these questions were unfamiliar— they had been raised many times by medieval reformers and dissenters— but they now became the foundation for new ecclesiastical structures. These new churches institutionalized the changes desired by their founders, and, presumably, life in such churches differed in significant ways from life in the Catholic Church. The differences were most prevalent in those cities, such as Geneva, where the reformers gained complete political control and established a society organized by the new church— the better to accomplish its goal of salvation. The changes did not, of course, affect the material aspects of life, but they did profoundly alter the relationship between people by changing the authority structure of the ecclesiastical community, by encouraging literacy and the independent reading of the scriptures, and by reviving strong currents of piety and religious feeling in a whole population, making it both more cohesive and less tolerant than it had been under the old Catholic regime.

This selection investigates the effect of the Protestant Reformation on society. Of course, comparison of Protestant and Catholic communities, where one or the other side was overwhelmingly victorious, will not reveal the Reformation experience of most sixteenth-century people. In most places, Protestants and Catholics coexisted, although the coexistence was not usually very peaceful, and it is in these places of contact and conflict that Natalie Z. Davis seeks the answer to the question posed above. The Reformation in France was short-lived, but it split and disrupted ancient communities. Moreover, women had the most to gain from change, so that focusing on them exposes the promise and performance of the reformed communities and churches. Did people join these churches only for theological or religious reasons, or were there other, social grounds? Did the Reformation change people's social position or the quality of their lives?

[I]

The growing cities of sixteenth-century France, ranging from ten thousand inhabitants in smaller places to sixty thousand in Lyon and a hundred thousand in Paris, were the centers of organization and dissemination of Protestantism. The decades in question here are especially those up to the Saint Bartholomew's Day Massacre of 1572—the years when it still seemed hopeful, in the words of a female refugee in Geneva, that the new Christians might deliver their cities from the tyranny and cruelty of the papist Pharaohs. For a while they were successful, with the growth of a large Protestant movement and the establishment in 1559 of an official Reformed Church in France. After 1572, the Huguenot party continued to battle for survival, but it was now doomed to remain a zealous but small minority.

Apart from the religious, almost all adult urban women in the first half of the sixteenth century were married or had once been so. The daughter of a rich merchant, lawyer, or financial officer might find herself betrothed in her late teens. Most women waited until their early twenties, when a dowry could be pieced together from the family or one's wages or extracted from a generous master or mistress.

And then the babies began and kept appearing every two or three years. The wealthy woman, with her full pantry and her country refuge in times of plague, might well raise eix or seven children to adulthood. The artisan's wife might bury nearly as many as she bore, while the poor woman was lucky to have even one live through the perils of a sixteenth-century childhood. Then, if she herself had managed to survive the first rounds of childbearing and live into her thirties, she might well find that her husband had not. Remarriage was common, of course, and until certain restrictive edicts of the French king in the 1560's a widow could contract it quite freely, If she then survived her husband into her forties, chances are she would remain a widow. At this stage of life, women outnumbered and outlived men, and even the widow sought after for her wealth might prefer independence to the relative tutelage of marriage.

With the death rate so high, the cities of sixteenth-century France depended heavily on immigration for their increasing populations. Here, however, we find an interesting difference between the sexes: men made up a much larger percentage of the young immigrants to the cities. The male immigrants contributed to every level of the vocational hierarchy—from notaries, judges, and merchants to craftsmen and unskilled day laborers. And although most of the men came from nearby provinces, some were also drawn from faraway cities and from regions outside the

From Natalie Zemon Davis, *Society and Culture in Early Modern France: Eight Essays by Natalie Zemon Davis* (Stanford: Stanford University Press, 1973)`, pp. 68–83, 86–95.

kingdom of France. The female immigrants, on the other hand, clustered near the bottom of the social ladder and came mostly from villages and hamlets in surrounding provinces to seek domestic service in the city.

Almost all the women took part in one way or another in the economic life of the city. The picture drawn in Renaissance courtesy books and suggested by the quotation from Robert Mandrou—that of women remaining privily in their homes—is rather far from the facts revealed by judicial records and private contracts. The wife of the wealthy lawyer, royal officer, or prosperous merchant supervised the productive activities of a large household but might also rent out and sell rural and urban properties in her own name, in her husband's name, or as a widow. The wives of tradesmen and master craftsmen had some part in running the shops, not just when they were widowed but also while their husbands were alive: a wife might discipline apprentices (who sometimes resented being beaten by a woman's hand), might help the journeymen at the large looms, might retail meats while her husband and his workers slaughtered cattle, might borrow money with her husband for printing ventures, and so on.

In addition, a significant proportion of women in artisanal families and among the *menu peuple* [lower classes] had employ on their own. They worked especially in the textile, clothing, leather, and provisioning trades, although we can also find girls apprenticed to pinmakers and gilders. They sold fish and tripe; they ran inns and taverns. They were painters and, of course, midwives. In Paris they made linen; in Lyon they prepared silk. They made shoes and gloves, belts and collars. In Paris, one Perette Aubertin sold fruit at a stall near the Elise des Mathurins while her husband worked as a printer. In Lyon, one Pernette Morilier made and sold wimples while her husband worked as a goldsmith. And in an extraordinary document from Lyon, a successful merchant-shoemaker confesses that his prosperity was due not so much to his own profits as to those made by his wife over the preceding 25 years in her separate trade as a linen merchant.

Finally, there were the various semiskilled or unskilled jobs done by women. Domestic service involved a surprisingly high number of girls and women. Even a modest artisanal family was likely to have a wretchedly paid serving girl, perhaps acquired from within the walls of one of the orphan-hospitals recently set up in many urban centers. There was service in the bath-houses, which sometimes slid into prostitition. Every city had its *filles de joie*, whom the town council tried to restrict to certain streets and to stop from brazenly soliciting clients right in front of the parish church. And there was heavy work, such as ferrying people across the Saône and other rivers, the boatwomen trying to argue up their fares as they rowed. If all else failed, a woman could dig ditches and carry things at the municipal construction sites. For this last, she worked shoulder to shoulder with unskilled male day workers, being paid about one-half or two-thirds as much as they for her pains.

This economic activity of women among the *menu peuple* may explain in part the funny nicknames that some of them had. Most French women in the sixteenth century kept their maiden names all their lives: when necessary, the phrase "wife of" or "widow of" so-and-so was tacked on. Certain women, however, had sobriquets: *la Capitaine des vaches* (the Captain of the cows) and *la reine d'Hongrie* (the queen of Hungary) were nicknames given to two women who headed households in Lyon; *la Catelle* was a schoolmistress in Paris; *la Varenne*, a midwife in Le Mans; and *la Grosse Marguerite,* a peddler of Orléans. Such names were also attached to very old women. But in all cases, we can assume not only that these women were a little eccentric but also that these names were bestowed on them in the course of public life—in the street, in the marketplace, or in the tavern.

The public life of urban women did not, however, extend to the civic assembly or council chamber. Women who were heads of households do appear on tax lists and even on militia rolls and were expected to supply money or men as the city government required. But that was the extent of political participation for the *citoyenne*. Male artisans and traders also had little say in these oligarchical city governments, but at least the more prosperous among them might have hoped to influence town councillors through their positions as guild representatives. The guild life of women, however, was limited and already weaker than it had been in the later Middle Ages. In short, the political activity of women on all levels of urban society was indirect or informal only. The wives of royal officers or town councillors might have hoped to influence powerful men at their dining tables. The wives of poor and powerless journeymen and day laborers, when their tables were bare because the city fathers had failed to provide the town with grain, might have tried to change things by joining with their husbands and children in a well-timed grain riot.

What of the literacy of urban women in the century after the introduction of printing to Europe? In the families of the urban elite the women had at least a vernacular education—usually at the hands of private tutors—in French, perhaps in Italian, in music, and in arithmetic. A Latin education among nonnoble city women was rare enough that it was remarked—"learned beyond her sex," the saying went—and a girl like Louise Sarrasin of Lyon, whose physician-father had started her in Hebrew, Greek, and Latin by the time she was eight, was considered a wondrous prodigy. It was women from these wealthy families of bankers and jurists who organized the important literary salons in Paris, Lyon, Poitiers, and elsewhere.

Once outside these restricted social circles, however, there was a dramatic drop in the level of education and of mere literacy among city women. An examination of contracts involving some 1,200 people in Lyon in the 1560's and 1570's to see whether those people could simply sign their names reveals that, of the women, only 28 percent could sign their names. These were almost all from the elite families of well-off merchants and publishers, plus a few wives of surgeons and goldsmiths. All the other women in the group—the wives of mercers, of artisans in skilled trades, and even of a few notaries—could not sign. This is in contrast to their husbands and to male artisans generally, whose ability to sign ranged from high among groups like printers, surgeons, and goldsmiths, to moderate among men in the leather and textile trades, to low— although still well above zero—among men in the food and construction trades. Thus, in the populous middle rank of urban society, although both male and female literacy may have risen from the mid-fifteenth century under the impact of economic growth and the invention of printing, the literacy of the men increased much more than that of the women. Tradesmen might have done business with written accounts; tradeswomen more often had to use finger reckoning, the abacus, or counting stones. Only at the bottom of the social hierarchy, among the unskilled workers and urban gardeners, were men and women alike. As with peasants, there were few of either sex who were literate.

And where would women of artisanal families learn to read and write if their fathers and husbands did not teach them? Nunnery schools received only a small number of lay girls, and these only from fine families. The municipal colleges set up in the first half of the sixteenth century in Toulouse, Nîmes, and Lyon were for boys only; so were most of the little vernacular schools that mushroomed in even quite modest city neighborhoods during these years. To be sure, a few schoolmistresses were licensed in Paris, and there were always some Parisian schoolmasters being chided for illegally receiving girls along with their boy pupils. But in Lyon, where I have found only five female teachers from the 1490's to the 1560's, I have come upon 87 schoolmasters for the same decades.

Thus, in the first half of the sixteenth century, the wealthy and well-born woman was being encouraged to read and study by the availability to her of printed books; by the strengthening of the image of the learned lad, as the writings of Christine de Pisan and Marguerite de Navarre appeared in print; and by the attitude of some fathers, who took seriously the modest educational programs for women being urged by Christian humanists like Erasmus and Juan Luis Vives. Reading and writing for women of the *menu peuple* was more likely to be ridiculous, a subject for farce.

All this shows how extraordinary was the achievement of Louise Labé, the one lowborn female poet of sixteenth-century France. From a family of Lyon ropemakers, barber-surgeons, and butchers, in which some of the women were literate and some (including her own stepmother) were not, Louise was beckoned to poetry and publication by her talent and by profane love. Her message to women in 1555 was "to lift their minds a little above their distaffs and spindles . . . to apply themselves to science and learning . . . and to let the world know that if we are not made to command, we must not for that be disdained as companions, both in domestic and public affairs, of those who govern and are obeyed."

[II]

The message of Calvinist reformers to women also concerned reading and patterns of companionship. But before we turn to it, let us see what can be said about the Catholic religious activity of city women on the eve of the French Reformation.

In regard to the sacramental life of the church, the women behaved very much like their husbands. The prominent families, in which the husband was on the parish building committee, attended mass and confession with some regularity. The wealthiest of them also had private chapels in their country homes. Among the rest of the population attendance was infrequent, and it was by no means certain that all the parishioners would even get out once a year to do their Easter duty of confession and communion. (The clergy itself was partly to blame for this. Those big city parishes were doubling and even tripling in size in these decades, and yet the French Church took virtually no steps to increase accordingly its personnel in charge of pastoral functions or even to guarantee confessors who could understand the language and dialect of the parishioners.) Baptism was taken more seriously, however, as were marriage and extreme unction. Every two or three years the husband appeared before the *curé* with the new baby, bringing with him one or two godfathers and up to five godmothers. The wife was most likely at home, waiting till she was ready to get up for her "churching," or purification after childbirth (the *relevailles*). Moreover, the wills of both men and women show an anxious preoccupation with the ceremonial processions at their funerals and masses to be said for the future repose of their souls. A chambermaid or male weaver might invest many months' salary in such arrangements.

In regard to the organizational and social aspects of Catholic piety on the eve of the Reformation, however, the woman's position was somewhat different from the man's. On the one hand, female religious life was less well organized than male religious life; on the other, the occasions in which urban women participated jointly with men in organized lay piety were not as frequent as they might have been.

To be sure, parish processions led by the priests on Corpus Christi and at other times included men, women, and children, and so did the general processions of the town to seek God's help in warding off famine or other disasters. But the heart of lay religious activity in France in the early sixteenth century was in the lay confraternities organized around crafts or around some devotional interests. Here laymen could support common masses, have their own banquets (whose excesses the clergy deplored), and mount processions on their own saints' days—with "blessed bread," music, costumes, and plays. City women were members of confraternities in much smaller numbers than men at this period. For instance, out of 37 confraternities at Rouen in the first half of the sixteenth century, only six mention female members, and these in small proportion. Women were formally excluded from the important Confraternity of the Passion at Paris, and some confraternities in other cities had similar provisions. Young unmarried men were often organized into confraternities under the patronage of Saint Nicholas; young unmarried women prayed to Saint Catherine, but religious organizations of female youth are hard to find.

Even the convents lacked vitality as centers of organization at this time. Fewer in number than the male religious houses in France and drawing exclusively on noble or wealthy urban families for their membership, the convents were being further isolated by the "reform" movements of the early sixteenth century. Pushed back into arid enclosure, the nuns were cut off not only from illicit love affairs but also from rich contact with the women in the neighborhoods in which they lived. Nor in France during the first part of the sixteenth century do we hear of any new female experiments with communal living, work, and spiritual perfection like the late medieval Beguinages or the imaginative Ursuline community just then being created in an Italian city.

Thus, before the Reformation the relation of Catholic lay women to their saints was ordinarily private or informally organized. The most important occasions for invoking the saints were during pregnancy and especially during childbirth. Then, before her female neighbors and her midwife, the parturient woman called upon the Virgin, or, more likely, upon Saint Margaret, patron of pregnant women—that God might comfort her peril and pain and that her child might issue forth alive.

Into this picture of city women separated from their parish clergy and from male religious organizations, one new element was to enter, even before the Reformation. Women who could read or who were part of circles where reading was done aloud were being prompted by vernacular devotional literature and the Bible to speculate on theology. "Why, they're half theologians," said the Franciscan preachers contemptuously. They own Bibles the way they own love stories and romances. They get carried away by questions on transubstantiation, and they go "running around from . . . one [male] religious house to another, seeking advice and making much ado about nothing." What the good brothers expected from city women was not silly reasoning but the tears and repentance that would properly follow a Lenten sermon replete with all the rhetorical devices and dramatic gestures of which the Franciscans were masters.

Even a man who was more sympathetic than the Franciscans to lettered females had his reservations about how far their learning should take them. A male poet praised the noble dame Gabrielle de Bourbon in the 1520's for reading vernacular books on moral and doctrinal questions and for composing little treatises to the honor of God and the Virgin Mary. But she knew her limits, for "women must not apply their minds to curious questions of theology and the secret matters of divinity, the knowledge of which belongs to prelates, rectors and doctors."

The Christian humanist Erasmus was one of the few men of his time who sensed the depths of resentment accumulating in women whose efforts to think about doctrine were not taken seriously by the clergy. In one of his *Colloquies*, a lady learned in Latin and Greek is being twitted by an asinine abbot (the phrase is Erasmus'). She finally bursts out, "If you keep on as you've begun, geese may do the preaching sooner than put up with you tongue-tied pastors. The world's a stage that's topsy-turvy now, as you see. Every man must play his part—or exit."

[III]

The world was indeed topsy-turvy. The Catholic Church, which Erasmus had tried to reform from within, was being split by Protestants who believed that man was saved by faith in Christ alone and that human work had nothing to do with it, who were changing the sacramental system all around and overthrowing the order of the priesthood. Among this welter of new ideas, let us focus here on the new image of the Christian woman as presented in Calvinist popular literature.

We can find her in a little play dated around 1550. The heroine is not a learned lady but a pure and simple woman who knows her Bible. The villain is not a teasing, harmless abbot but a lecherous and stupid village priest. He begins by likening her achievements to those of craftsmen who were meddling with Scripture, and then goes on: "Why, you'll even see a woman / Knock over your arguments / With her responses on the Gospel." And in the play she does, quoting Scripture to oppose the adoration of Mary and the saints and to oppose the power of the popes. The priest can only quote from glosses, call her names, and threaten to burn her.

Wherever one looks in the Protestant propaganda of the 1540's to the 1560's, the Christian woman is identified by her relation to Scripture. Her sexual purity and control are demonstrated by her interest in the Bible, and her right to read the New Testament in the vernacular is defended against those who would forbid it to her, as to such other unlearned persons as merchants and artisans. The author of the pamphlet *The Way to Arrive at the Knowledge of God* put the matter sharply enough: "You say that women who want to read the Bible are just libertines? I say you call them lewd merely because they won't consent to your seduction. You say it's permitted to women to read Boccaccio's *Flamette* or Ovid's *Art of Love.* . who's reading a Bible to the flames. You say it's enough for a woman's salvation for her to do her housework, sew and spin? . . . Of what use then are Christ's promises to her? You'll put spiders in Paradise, for they know how to spin very well."

The message was even put to music during the First Religious War in the 1560's. The Huguenot queen of Navarre sings:

> Those who say it's not for women
> To look at Holy Writ
> Are evil men and infamous
> Seducers and antichrist.
> Alas, my ladies.
> Your poor souls
> Let them not be governed
> By such great devils.

And in reality as well as in popular literature Protestant women were freeing their souls from the rule of priests and doctors of theology. Noble churchmen were horrified at the intemperance with which Protestant females abused them as godless men. The pages of Jean Crespin's widely read *Book of the Martyrs,* based on the real adventures of Protestant heretics, record the story of one Marie Becaudelle, a servant of La Rochelle who learns of the Gospel from her master and argues publicly with a Franciscan, showing him from Scripture that he does not preach according to the Word of God. A bookseller's wife disputes doctrine in a prison cell with the bishop of Paris and with doctors of theology. An honest widow of Tours talks to priests and monks with the witness of Scripture: "I'm a sinner, but I don't need candles to ask God to pardon my faults. You're the ones who walk in darkness." The learned theologians did not know what to make of such monstrous women, who went against nature.

To this challenge to the exclusion of women, the Catholic theologians in mid-century responded not by accommodating but by digging in their heels. It wasn't safe, said an important Jesuit preacher, to leave the Bible to the discretion of "what's turning around in a woman's brain." "To learn essential doctrine," echoed another cleric, "there is no need for women or artisans to take time out from their work and read the Old and New Testament in the vernacular. Then they'll want to dispute about it and give their opinion . . . and they can't help falling into error. Women must be silent in Church, as Saint Paul says." Interestingly enough, when a Catholic vernacular Bible was finally allowed to circulate in France at the end of the sixteenth century, it did not play an important role in the conversion or devotional life of Catholic leaders like Barbe Acarie and Saint Jeanne Frances de Chantal.

Thus, into a pre-Reformation situation in which urban women were estranged from priests or in tension with them over the matter of their theological curiosity, the Protestant movement offered a new option: relations with the priestly order could be broken, and women, like their husbands (indeed *with* their husbands), could be engaged in the pure and serious enterprise of reading and talking about Scripture. The message being broadcast to male artisans and lesser merchants was similar but less momentous. In the first place, the men were more likely already to be literate; and anyway, the only natural order the men were being asked to violate was the separation between the learned and unlearned. The women were also being called to a new relation with men. It is worth noting how different is this appeal to women from that which Max Weber considered most likely to win females over to a new religion. Rather than inciting to orgy and emotion, it was summoning to intellectual activity and self-control.

How was the appeal received? France never became a Protestant kingdom, of course, and even in cities where the movement was strong only one-third to one-half of the population might be ardent Calvinists. City men who became caught up in Protestantism ranged from wealthy bankers and professionals to poor journeymen, but they were generally from the more skilled and complex, the more literate, or the more novel trades and occupations. A printer, a goldsmith, or a barber-surgeon was more likely to disobey priests and doctors of theology than was a boatmaster, a butcher, or a baker.

What of the Calvinist women? As with the men, they did not come from the mass of poor unskilled people at the bottom of urban society, although a certain percentage of domestic servants did follow their masters and mistresses into the Reformed Church. The Protestant women belonged mostly to the families of craftsmen, merchants, and professional men, but they were by no means exclusively the literate women in these circles. For all the female martyrs who answered the Inquisitors by citing Scripture they had read, there were as many who could answer only by citing doctrines they had heard. It is also clear that in Lyon in the 1570's, more than a decade after the Reformed Church had been set up, a significant percentage of Reformed women still could not write their names. For this last group, then, the Protestant path was not a way to express their new literacy but a way finally to associate themselves with that surge of male literacy already described.

But there is more that we can say about city women who turned Protestant. A preliminary examination of women arrested for heresy or killed in Catholic uprisings in many parts of France, of women among the

Protestant suspects in Toulouse in 1568–69, and of a very large sample of Protestant women in Lyon (about 750 women) yields three main observations. First, there is no clear evidence either that the wives mainly followed their husbands into the movement or that it worked the other way around.* We can find women converted by their husbands who became more committed than their men; we can find wives who converted while their husbands remained "polluted in idolatry" and husbands who converted while their wives lagged behind. Second, the Protestant women seemed to include more than a random number of widows, of women with employ of their own—such as dressmakers, merchants, midwives, hotel-keepers, and the like—and of women with the curious nicknames associated with public and eccentric personalities. But finally, the Protestant movement in the sixteenth century did not pull in the small but significant group of genuinely learned women in the city—neither the patronesses of the literary salons nor the profane female poets. Louise Labé, who pleaded with women to lift their heads above their distaffs, always remained in the church that invoked the Virgin, although one of her aunts, a female barber, joined the Calvinists.

What do these observations suggest about the state of life of city women before their conversion to the new religion? They do not indicate a prior experience of mere futility and waste or restrictive little family worlds. Rather, Protestant religious commitment seems to have complemented in a new sphere the scope and independence that the women's lives had already had. Women already independent in the street and market now ventured into the male preserve of theology. And yet the literary woman, already admitted to the castle of learning, does not seem to have needed the Religion of the Book. A look at developments with the Reformed Church will indicate why this should have been so.

[IV]

After 1562 the Reformed Church of France started to settle into its new institutional structures and the promise of Protestantism began to be realized for city women. Special catechism classes in French were set up for women, and in towns under Huguenot control efforts were made to encourage literacy, even among all the poor girls in the orphanages, not just the gifted few. In certain Reformed families the literate husbands finally began teaching their wives to read.

*Nancy Roelker found a different pattern among Huguenot noblewomen, who more often than their husbands took the first step toward conversion ("The Appeal of Calvinism to French Noblewomen in the Sixteenth Century," *The Journal of Interdisciplinary History* 2 [1972]: 402). Class differences help explain this contrast, such as the more significant roles in public life enjoyed by noblewomen that those allowed to city women.

Some Protestant females, however, had more ambitious goals. The image of the new Christian woman with her Bible had beckoned them to more than catechism classes or reading the Scriptures with their husbands. Consider Marie Dentière. One-time abbess in Tournai, but expelled from her convent in the 1520's because of heresy, Dentière married a pastor and found her way to Geneva during its years of religious revolution. There, according to the report of a nun of the Poor Clare order, Marie got "mixed up with preaching," coming, for instance, to the convent to persuade the poor creatures to leave their miserable life. She also published two religious works, one of them an epistle on religious matters addressed to Princess Marguerite de Navarre. Here Dentière inserted a "Defense for Women" against calumnies, not only by Catholic adversaries but also by some of the Protestant faithful. The latter were saying that it was rash for women to publish works to each other on Scriptural matters. Dentière disagreed; "If God has done the grace to some poor women to reveal to them by His Holy Scriptures some good and holy thing, dare they not write about it, speak about it, and declare it, one to the other? . . . Is it not foolishly done to hide the talent that God has given us?"

Dentière maintained the modest fiction that she was addressing herself only to other females. Later women did not. Some of the women prisoners in the French jails preached to "the greater consolation" of both male and female listeners. Our ex-Calvinist jurist Florimond de Raemond gave several examples, both from the Protestant conventicles and from the regular Reformed services as late as 1572, of women who while waiting for a preacher to arrive had gone up to pulpits and read from the Bible. One *théologienne* even took public issue with her pastor. Finally, in some of the Reformed Churches southwest of Paris—in areas where weavers and women had been early converts—a movement started to permit lay persons to prophesy. This would have allowed both women and unlearned men to get up in church and speak on holy things.

Jean Calvin, Théodore de Bèze, and other members of the Venerable Company of Pastors did not welcome these developments. The social thrust of the Reformation, as they saw it, was to overthrow the hierarchical priestly class and administer the church instead by well-trained pastors and sound male members of the Consistories. That was enough topsy-turvy for them. And like Catholic critics who had quoted Paul's dictum from I Corinthians that "women keep silence in the churches" against Protestants who were reading and talking about the Bible, now the Reformed pastors quoted it against Protestant women who wanted to preach publicly or have some special vocation in the church. Pierre Viret explained in 1560 that the elect were equal in that they were called to be Christian and faithful — man and woman, master and servant, free and serf. But the Gospel had not abolished within the church the rank and order of nature and of human society. God created and Christ confirmed that order. Even if a woman had greater spiritual gifts than had her husband, she could not speak in Christian assembly. Her task, said Pastor Viret, was merely to instruct her children in the faith when they were young; she might also be a schoolteacher to girls if she wished. . . .

[V]

An examination of a few other areas of Protestant reform reveals the same pattern as in reading Scripture and preaching: city women revolted against priests and entered new religious relations that brought them together with men or likened them to men but left them unequal.

The new Calvinist liturgy, with its stress on the concerted fellowship of the congregation, used the vernacular—the language of women and the unlearned—and included Psalms sung jointly by men and women. Nothing shocked Catholic observers more than this. When they heard the music of male and female voices filtering from a house where a conventicle was assembled, all they could imagine were lewd activities with the candles extinguished. It was no better when the Protestant movement came into the open. After the rich ceremony of the mass, performed by the clergy with due sanctity and grandeur, the Reformed service seemed, in the words of a Catholic in Paris in the 1560's, "without law, without order, without harmony." "The minister begins. Everybody follows— men, women, children, servants, chambermaids. . . . No one is on the same verse. . . . The fine-voiced maidens let loose their hums and trills ... so the young men will be sure to listen. How wrong of Calvin to let women sing in Church."

To Protestant ears, it was vey different. For laymen and laywomen in the service the common voice in praise of the Lord expressed the lack of distance between pastor and congregation. The Catholic priests had stolen the Psalms; now they had been returned. As for the participants in the conventicles, the songs gave them courage and affirmed their sense of purity over the hypocritical papists, who no sooner left the mass than they were singing love songs. The Protestant faithful were firmly in control of their sexual impulses, they believed, their dark and sober clothes a testimonal to their sincerity. And when the women and men sang together in the great armed street marches of the 1560's, the songs were a militant challenge to the hardened Catholics and an invitation to the wavering listeners to join the elect.

For the city women, there was even more novelty. They had had a role smaller than men's in the organized lay ceremonial life of the church, and the confraternities had involved them rather little. Previously, nuns had been the only women to sing the office. Now the confraternities and the convents would be abolished. The ceremonial was simplified and there was only one kind of group for worship, one in which men and women sang together. For Protestant tradesmen, many of whom were immigrants to the city, the new liturgical fellowship provided religious roots they had been unable to find in the inhospitable parishes. For Protestant women, who were not as likely to have been immigrants, the new liturgy provided roots in religious organizations with men.

But this leveling, this gathering together of men and women, had its limits. Singing in church did not lead women on to preaching or to participating in the Consistory any more than Bible-reading had. Furthermore, there was some effort by the pastors to order the congregations so as to reflect the social order. In Geneva, special seats were assigned to minimize the mingling of the sexes. And in some Reformed churches the sexes were separated when communion was taken: the men went up first to partake of the Holy Supper.

Psalms were added to the religious life of the Protestants and saints were taken away—from prayer, image, and invocation. Here the matter of sex was indifferent: Saint Damian departed as did Saint Margaret; Saint Nicholas departed as did Saint Catherine. Protestant men and women affirmed before the Inquisition that one must not call upon the Virgin, for, blessed though she was, she had no merit. And when the magistrates were slow to purify the churches of their idolatrous statues, zealous members of the *menu peuple* smashed the saints. Females were always included in these crowds. Indeed, like the armed march of the psalm-singers, the iconoclastic riot was a transfer of the joint political action of the grain riot into the religious sphere.

But the loss of the saints affected men and women unequally. Reformed prayer could no longer be addressed to a woman, whereas the masculine identity of the Father and Son was left intact. It may seem anachronistic to raise the matter of sexual identity in religious images during the Reformation, but it is not. Soon afterward, the Catholic poet Marie le Jars de Gournay, friend and editor of Montaigne, was to argue in her *Equality of the Sexes* that Jesus' incarnation as a male was no special honor to the male sex but a mere historical convenience; given the patriarchal malice of the Jews, a female savior would never have been accepted. But if one were going to emphasize the sex of Jesus, then it was all the more important to stress the perfection of Mary and her role in the conception of our Lord. So, if the removal from Holy Mother Church cut off certain forms of religious affect for men, for women the consequences for their identities went even deeper. Now during their hours of childbirth—a "combat," Calvin described it, "a horrible torment"—they called no more on the Virgin and said no prayers to Saint Margaret. Rather, as Calvin advised, they groaned and sighed to the Lord and He received those groans as a sign of their obedience.

Obedience to the Lord was, of course, a matter for both men and women. But women had the additional charge of being obedient to their husbands. The Reformed position on marriage provides a final illustration of the pattern "together but unequal."

The Protestant critique of clerical celibacy involved first and foremost a downgrading of the concept that the male had a greater capacity than the female to discipline his sexual impulses. Since the time of the Greeks, physicians had been telling people that physiology made the female more lustful, the more uncontrollable sex. As Doctor François Rabelais put it, there are many things a man can do, from work to wine, to control "the pricks of venery"; but a woman, with her hysteric animal (the womb) within, could rarely restrain herself from cuckolding her husband. Given these assumptions, clerical celibacy for the superior sex had been thought a real possibility whereas for the female it had appeared an exceptional achievement.

The Reformers' observation that continence was a rare gift of God and their admonition "Better to marry than to burn" were, then, primarily addressed to the numerous male clergy and less to the small fraction of female religious. Indeed, sermons on clerical marriage stressed how the groom would now be saved from fornication and hellfire but said little of the soul of the bride. It is surely significant, too, that male religious joined the Reformation movements in proportionately larger numbers than did female. The nuns were always the strong holdouts, even when they were promised dowries and pensions. Though some of them may have been afraid to try their chances on the marriage market, many simply preferred the separate celibate state and organizations. When Marie Dentière tried to persuade the nuns of the Poor Clare order at Geneva to end their hypocritical lives and marry, as she had, the sisters spat at her.

The argument for clerical marriage, then, equalized men and women somewhat in regard to their appetites. It also raised the woman's status by affirming that she could be a worthy companion to a minister of God. The priest's concubine, chased from his house in ignominy by Catholic reformers and ridiculed as a harlot by Protestants, could now become the pastor's wife! A respectable girl from a good city family—likely, in the first generation to be the daughter of a merchant or prosperous craftsman —would be a helpful companion to her husband, keeping his busy household in order and his colleagues entertained. And she would raise her son to be a pastor and her daughter to be a pastor's wife.

Since marriage was now the only encouraged state, the Reformers did what they could to make it more tolerable according to their lights. Friendship and companionship within marriage were stressed, as many historians have pointed out, although it is a mistake to think that this was unique to Protestant thought. Catholic humanist writers valued these relations within marriage as well. In other ways, the Reformed position was more original.* A single sexual standard would now be enforced rather than talked about; and the victorious Huguenot Consistories during the Wars of Religion chased out the prostitutes almost as quickly as they silenced the mass. The husband would be compelled insofar as possible to exercise his authority, in Calvin's words, "with moderation and not insult over the woman who has been given him [by God] as his partner." Thus, in a real innovation in Christian Europe, men who beat their wives were haled before Consistories and threatened with denial of communion. The men grumbled and complained—"I beat my wife before and I'll beat her again if she be bad," said a Lyon typecaster—but the situation had improved enough in Geneva by the end of the century that some called it "the women's Paradise."

But despite all this, the Reformed model of the marriage relation subjected the wife to her husband as surely as did the Catholic one. Women had been created subject to men, said Calvin, although before the fall "this was a liberal and gently subjection." Through sin, it had become worse: "Let the woman be satisfied with her state of subjection, and not take it amiss that she is made inferior to the more distinguished sex." Nor was this view restricted to pastors. There are many examples from sixteenth-century France of Protestant husbands instructing their wives, "their dear sisters and loyal spouses," telling them of their religious duties, telling them of their responsibilities toward their children, warning them that they must never do anything without seeking advice first. And if Protestant wives then told their husbands to go to the devil or otherwise insulted them so loudly that the neighbors heard, the women might soon find themselves brought before the Consistories and even punished (as the criminal records of Geneva reveal) by three days in prison on bread and water.

---

*It does not seem justified to argue, as does Roelker, that Calvin's position on divorce "advanced women to a position of equality with their husbands." "By permitting wives as well as husbands to instigate divorce proceedings," she maintains, "Calvin elevated their dignity and increased their legal rights. Enacted into Genevan law, this could not help but raise the position of women to a higher level" ("The Appeal of Calvinism," p. 406). The institution of divorce with permission to remarry in cases of adultery or very prolonged absence was, of course, an important innovation by Calvin and other Protestant reformers. But this change did not remedy an *inequality* in the existing marriage law. The canon law had long allowed either male or female the right to initiate proceedings in an ecclesiastical court for separation in case of the partner's adultery, as well as for annulment and dissolution in certain circumstances. What determined whether men and women in fact had equal access to separation or divorce before or after the Reformation was, first, the informal operation of the double standard, which tolerated the husband's adultery more readily than the wife's, and, second, the relatively greater economic difficulty faced by the single woman supporting herself and her children in the interval before she was able to remarry. For all but the very wealthy man or woman, divorce or legal separation was an unlikely possibility. In any case, the exhaustive research of René Stauffenegger has shown that divorces were very rarely granted in Geneva in the late sixteenth and early seventeenth centuries—pastors and Consistory always pressing for couples to solve their disputes. See Keith Thomas, "The Double Standard," *Journal of the History of Ideas* 20 (1959): 200–202; John T. Noonan, Jr., *Power to Dissolve* (Cambridge, Mass., 1972), chaps. 1–3, 7; R. Stauffenegger, "Le mariage à Gene͏̈eve vers 1600," *Mémoires de la société pour l'histoire du droit* 27 (1966): 327–28.

Undoubtedly there were many Reformed marriages in commercial and artisanal circles where the husbands and wives lived together in peace and friendship. And why not? Women had joined the Reformation to rebel against priests and pope, not to rebel against their husbands. Although they wanted certain "masculine" religious activities opened to them, Calvinist wives—even the most unruly of them—never went so far as to deny the theory of the subjection of women within marriage. The practice of subjection in individual marriages during those heroic decades of the Reformation may have been tempered by two things: first, the personaity of the wife herself, which sustained her revolt against priestly power and her search for new relations with books and men; and second, the common cause of reform, which for a while demanded courageous action from both husbands and wives.

And what could a city woman accomplish for the cause if she were not rich and powerful like a noblewoman? On a Catholic feast day, she could defy her Catholic neighbors by sitting ostentatiously spinning in her window. She could puzzle over the Bible alone or with her husband or with Protestant friends. If she were a printer's wife or widow, she could help get out a Protestant edition to spread the word about tyrannical priests. She could use her house for an illegal Protestant conventicle or assembly. She could put aside her dissolute hoop skirts and full gowns and start to wear black. She could harangue priests in the streets. She could march singing songs in defiance of royal edicts. She could smash statues, break baptismal founts, and destroy holy images. She could, if persecution became very serious, flee to London or Geneva, perhaps the longest trip she had ever taken. She could stay in France and dig the foundations for a Reformed temple. She could even fight—as in Toulouse, where a Huguenot woman bore arms in the First Religious War. And she could die in flames, shouting to her husband, as did one young wife of Langres, "My friend, if we have been joined in marriage in body, think that this is only like a promise of marriage, for our Lord . . . will marry us the day of our martyrdom."

Many of these actions, such as Bible-reading, clearly were special to Protestant city women. A few were not. The Catholic city women in Elizabethan England, for instance, hid priests in their quarters and, if captured, went to the "marriage" of martyrdom as bravely as did any Huguenot. It was the same among the radical Anabaptists. One kind of action, however, seems to have been special to Catholic city women (as also to the radical Quaker women of the seventeenth century): organized group action among women. On the highest level, this was expressed in such attempts to create new forms of common life and work among females as the Ursulines and the Sisters of Charity and the Christian Institutes of Mary Ward. On the lowest level, this was reflected in the violent activity of all-female Catholic crowds—throwing stones at Protestant women, throwing mire at pastors, and, in the case of a group of female butchers in Aix-en-Provence, beating and hanging the wife of a Protestant bookseller.

These contrasts can point the way to some general conclusions about the long-range significance of the Reformed solution for relations between the sexes. In an interesting essay, Alice Rossi suggests three models for talking about equality. One is assimilationist: the subordinate group is somewhat raised by making it like the superior group. A second is pluralistic: each group is allowed to keep its distinctive characteristics but within a context of society at large that is still hierarchical. The third is hybrid (or, better, transformational), involving changes within and among all groups involved. Whatever transformations in social relations were accomplished by either the reformation or the Counter-Reformation, it seems that as far as relations between the sexes go the Reformed solution was assimilationist; the Catholic solution, with its female saints and convents, was pluralistic. Neither, of course, eliminated the subject status of women.*

Is one position clearly better than the other? That is, within the context of the society of the sixteenth and seventeenth centuries did one solution seem to offer greater freedom to men and women to make decisions about their lives and to adopt new roles? One important school of sociologists always answers such questions in favor of Protestantism. It is the superior sect: its transcendent and activist Father, less hierarchical religious symbolism, and this-wordly asceticism all make for a more evolved religion, facilitating the desacralization of society. More different choices are also facilitated, so this argument goes, and more rapid social change.

Certainly it is true that the Reformed solution did promote a certain desexualization of society, a certain neutralizing of forms of communication and of certain religious places so that they became acceptable for women. These were important gains, bringing new tools to women and new experience to both sexes. But the assimilationist solution brought losses, too. This worldly asceticism denied laymen and laywomen much of the shared recreational and festive life allowed them by Catholicism. It closed off an institutionalized and respectable alternative to private family life: the communal living of the monastery. By destroying the female saints as exemplars for both sexes, it cut off a wide range of affect and activity. And by eliminating a separate identity and separate organization for women in religious life, it may have made them a little more vulnerable to subjection in all spheres.

As it turned out, women suffered for their powerlessness in both Catholic and Protestant lands in the late sixteenth to eighteenth centuries

---

* The same point can be made in regard to class relations within the two Reformations, the Reformed Church assimilating artisans and even peasants upward in styles of religious behavior and the Catholic allowing greater scope to "peasant religion." Although Calvinism reduced the levels of angelic and ecclesiastical hierarchy, neither church challenged the *concept* of social hierarchy.

as changes in marriage laws restricted the freedoms of wives even further, as female guilds dwindled, as the female role in middle-level commerce and farm direction contracted, and as the differential between male and female wages increased. In both Catholic France and Protestant England, the learned lady struggled to establish a role for herself: the female schoolteacher became a familiar figure, whether as a spinster or as an Ursuline; the female dramatist scrambled to make a living, from the scandalous Aphra Behn in the seventeenth century to the scandalous Olympe de Gouges in the eighteenth.

Thus it is hard to establish from a historical point of view that the Reformed assimilationist structure always facilitated more rapid and creative changes in sex roles than did the relatively pluralistic structure found in the Catholicism of the sixteenth and seventeenth centuries. Both forms of religious life have contributed to the transformation of sex roles and to the transformation of society. In the proper circumstances, each can serve as a corrective to the other. Whatever long-range changes may be achieved, the varied voices heard in this essay will have played their part: the immodest Louise Labé telling women to lift their minds a little above their distaffs, the servant Marie Becaudelle disputing with her priest, the ex-num Marie Dentière urging women to speak and write about Scripture, and yes, the Catholic Marie le Jars de Gournay reminding us that, after all, it was only a historical accident that our Lord Jesus Christ was born a male.

Cultural Patronage in Renaissance Florence

GENE BRUCKER

How do artists and intellectuals get the time and freedom to pursue their crafts, and is such time and freedom justified? This question is perennial. It calls for an assessment of the cultural ideals and institutions of the society about which it is asked, and it has special importance when the society in question has had a particularly brilliant cultural life, as did Periclean Athens, Augustan Rome, twelfth- and thirteenth-century Paris, and Renaissance Florence. In all these times and places, hardheaded men of commerce and politics invested in the patronage of artists and scholars. The additional question must always be asked: Why then and not at other times? In part, the answer may be found by reference to historical conditions. It is not surprising that art and intellect do not flourish in times of war, migration, or severe deprivation. The civil wars following Julius Caesar's murder, the Germanic invasions, the dislocations caused by Viking and Magyar attacks were not conducive to patronage of artistic and intellectual culture, which costs a great deal in materials and in the manpower of the most talented members of society. Yet, once we have noted that high culture requires relative peace and prosperity, we must still explain why Athens and not Corinth, why Paris and not London or Mainz, why Florence and not Milan, became centers where artists and intellectuals found patrons.

In the following selection, Gene Brucker examines the relationship between the leaders of Florentine commercial and political life and the artistic and intellectual community they supported.

Foundations and Premises

For two centuries, from the age of Dante and Giotto to that of Machiavelli and Michelangelo, Florence was one of Latin Europe's most dynamic and creative centers of intellectual and artistic activity. This chapter will attempt to define the nature of that cultural achievement, and to relate it to the city's institutions and values, and to her experience. Perhaps no problem of historical analysis is so challenging and provoca-

From Gene Brucker, *Renaissance Florence* (New York: John Wiley & Sons, 1969), pp. 213, 215–18, 220–30.

tive, and so beset with pitfalls, as the attempt to explain the relationship between social and cultural phenomena. Every student of Florentine history is confronted by these questions. Why was this society so creative, and so receptive to change and innovation? Of all the major Italian cities, why did Florence—and not Milan or Genoa or Venice—achieve the greatest distinction in art and learning during these centuries? . . .

The most distinctive feature of Florentine intellectual life was not its variety and complexity—which was matched, to some degree, by Milan, Venice, and Naples—but rather the unusually close rapport between these cultural traditions. Contributing to this atmosphere of free communication was the social structure, perhaps the most flexible of any major Italian city. But another important factor was the towering figure of Dante Alighieri. The poet represented a crucial stage in the fusion of the universalist, hierarchical ideals of classic-Christian tradition with the parochial values and interests of the local milieu. In the Florentine schools and *studia* (and perhaps also at the University of Bologna), Dante had absorbed those universal ideals which had been summarized so brilliantly by Thomas Aquinas. The poet wrote scholastic treatises, and he also composed essays praising the Christian virtues. His political ideas, his veneration for the Empire and the values of ancient Rome, were likewise universal and hierarchical. Yet his *Divine Comedy* was written in the local Tuscan dialect, not in Latin. And although this work contains the universal concepts of the classical and Christian traditions, it is also a Florentine poem, replete with the particular values, emotions, and concerns of that community. The poet did not succeed in reconciling all the contradictions between the two traditions, but his genius enabled him to surmount these discordant elements, and to create a magnificent synthesis combining ideal and reality, the universal and the particular. He also established a lofty standard of excellence, to serve as challenge and inspiration for later generations of Florentine intellectuals.

In the realm of the visual arts, Giotto di Bondone (d. 1337) filled a role similar to Dante's in literature. Giotto's subject matter was traditionally Christian; he learned to paint in the Byzantine style of the thirteenth century. His great contribution to fresco painting was to humanize the wooden, stylized figures of Byzantine art, to create scenes that were naturalistic and lifelike, but also grandiose and monumental. His fresco cycle in Padua of Christ's life and the scenes in S. Croce [Florence] from the life of St. Francis are supreme statements of these qualities in Giotto's art, worthy of comparison with the *Divine Comedy.* Certain attempts have been made to identify the sources of Giotto's inspiration and genius, for example, in the Franciscan emphasis upon Christ's humanity, and the striving for a more intense religious experience. Rather less persuasive is that interpretation which depicts him as a representative of the Florentine bourgeoisie, whose monumental human figures reflect the self-confidence of a rising social class, emancipating itself from subjection to the church and the feudal nobility. Giotto's fame during his lifetime was enormous, although his reputation declined during the second half of the fourteenth century. But his frescoes made a profound impact upon the revolutionary generation of Florentine artists in the early Quattrocento, who recovered Giotto's sense of the monumental, which had disappeared from the Florentine art of the preceding age.

Complexity of social structure, variety of intellectual interests, a history of fruitful intercourse between different traditions—these are some factors which fostered cultural vitality and innovation in Florence. The aristocracy did not merely patronize art and learning; it was actively involved in the city's cultural life. Nearly every prominent family counted a lawyer and a cleric among its number; and by the middle of the fifteenth century, many houses—Strozzi, Corbinelli, Rossi, Medici, Davanzati, Alessandri—could also boast of a humanist scholar. The intellectual interests of many Florentines cut across cultural and disciplinary barriers. Cosimo de' Medici is a good example: banker, statesman, scholar, a friend and patron of humanists (Bruni, Niccoli, Marsuppini, Poggio), artists (Donatello, Brunelleschi, Michelozzo), and learned clerics (Ambrogio Traversari, Pope Nicholas V). The library of a wealthy merchant, Piero di Duccio Alberti, was inventoried in 1400; it contained a large number of business papers and ledgers, a book of hours, several Latin grammars and works by the classical authors Aesop, Cicero, Seneca, Eutropius, and Vigentius. A notary, Ser Matteo Gherardi, died in 1390, leaving a collection of legal treatises (decretals, commentaries, works on canon law), but also a nucleus of religious works (a book of homilies, a psalter, a prayer collection, and a Bible), and the writings of Aesop and Boethius. Lapo Mazzei's letters to Francesco Datini contain references to the Bible and to Christian authors (St. Augustine, St. Bernard, St. Francis, St. Thomas Aquinas), to ancient writers (Cicero, Seneca, Sallust, Hoarce, Livy, Vergil, Valerius Maximus, Boethius), and to the vernacular works of Dante, Jacopone da Todi, and the Vallombrosan hermit Giovanni dalle Celle. In a treatise on the subject of fortune written about 1460, Giovanni Rucellai incorporated citations from an unusually wide range of classical, Christian, and Italian authors: Aristotle, Epictetus, Sallust, Cicero, Seneca, St. Bernard, Dante, Petrarch, and a Florentine theologian, Leonardo Dati.

Communication between merchants, politicians, artists, and scholars was also facilitated by certain attitudes and conventions, to some degree institutionalized, of this society. Wealthy banker and poor artisans sat together as equals in the Signoria, a political tradition which must have facilitated intellectual discourse between aristocratic patrons and the sculptors, painters and other craftsmen they employed to build their palaces and decorate their chapels. The open and candid discussions about the problems of cathedral construction (in which bankers, lawyers, friars, and craftsmen participated) also cut across social and professional barriers.

Among the citizens invited to counsel the Signoria were men representing all of the major professions and occupations (with the sole exception of theology). These included the lawyers Filippo Corsini, Lorenzo Ridolfi, and Giuliano Davanzati; the physician Cristofano di Giorgio; the humanists Leonardo Bruni, Pall Strozzi, and Agnolo Pandolfini, who were thus provided with an arena for voicing their political opinions and publicizing ideas and perspectives derived from their disciplines. This forum may have stimulated interest in classical antiquity, and thus contributed to Florence's precocious adoption of humanism as a moral and educational system.

Another device for promoting communication between men of diverse disciplines and cultural interests was the Florentine version of the salon. One of these meetings was described in the *Paradiso degli Alberti* by Giovanni da Prato; other groups gathered around the Augustinian friar Luigi Marsili, the humanist chancellor Coluccio Salutati, and the Camaldolese prior of S. Maria degli Angeli, Ambrogio Traversari. Scholars have also discovered references to an informal gathering which met in the early 1400s under the Tettoio dei Pisani, a pavilion adjacent to the Piazza della Signoria, and another two decades later organized by Augustinian scholars, Fra Evangelista of Pisa and Fra Girolamo of Naples. . . .

The Florentine sense of quality was a product of the city's craft tradition and the exceptional skills of her artisans. The industrial and craft guilds had developed a system of quality control to protect their trades; every Florentine realized that the maintenance of high standards benefited the city's economy. This appreciation of quality, and a corresponding disdain for the shoddy and inferior, became a characteristic feature of the Florentine mentality and mode of perception. It is revealed in this letter written by a lawyer, Rosso Orlandi, to a friend in Venice, Piero Davanzati, about a very small problem, the purchase of a piece of cloth:

I received your letter in which you instruct me to buy and send you twelve yards of good blue cloth. One of my neighbors is a good friend and a cloth expert. First we looked around in the cloth factories, where occasionally one may find some nice remnants at a discount, but we didn't see anything we liked. Then we visited all of the retail shops which sell for cash. It is not their custom to allow buyers to examine and compare the cloth of one shop with that of another. However, we did find a way to examine the finest and most beautiful cloth in each shop, and we also seized the opportunity to compare these prices side by side. From them all, we chose a cloth from the shop of Zanobi di Ser Gino. There were none that were better woven or more beautifully dyed. Furthermore, the cloth was nearly a foot wider than the others, even after it had been washed and trimmed. Since Florentine shearers do better work than those in Venice, I have had the cloth washed and trimmed here. When you see it, I believe that you will be pleased with it. You will like it even better after you have worn it for several months; for it is a cloth which will wear extremely well.

The Florentine esthetic sense was derived from this appreciation for quality; it is stamped upon the physical city and upon the rural landscape, fashioned by generations of men who prized beauty. It is revealed too in contemporary writing, for example in a letter from a banker, Jacopo Pazzi, to his friend Filippo Strozzi in Naples (1464), thanking him for a consignment of gold coins: "They are so beautiful that they give me great pleasure, because I love coins which are well designed; and you know that the more beautiful things are, the more they are cherished." Writing in his diary in the 1460s, Giovanni Rucellai described "the most attractive and pleasing aspects" of his villa at Quarachi, a few miles west of Florence near the Arno. He mentioned the house, the garden planted with fruit trees, the fish pond surrounded by fir trees, and another wooded grove at the edge of the garden adjacent to the road. "This park is a source of great consolation," Rucellai wrote, "not only to ourselves and our neighbors, but also to strangers and travelers who pass by during the heat of summer . . . who can refresh themselves with the clear and tasty water. . . . And no traveler passes who does not stop for a quarter of an hour to view the garden filled with beautiful plants. So I feel that the creation of this park . . . was a very worthy enterprise." Also illustrating the Florentine concern for esthetic values is a document in the files of the republic's diplomatic correspondence. During a crucial period of the Milanese war (December 1400), the Signoria wrote to the general of the Camaldolese order concerning the sale of a grove of fir trees which were to be cut down, near the ancient monastery of Camaldoli in the Apennines. Expressing their shock and dismay at this vandalism, the priors reminded the general that the trees had been planted and nourished by his predecessors "for the consolation of the hermits and the admiration of the visitors." Four years later (September 1404) the commune again raised this issue, urging the general to cease the despoliation of the monastic patrimony, whose beauty was as pleasing to God as to man.

Florentines were usually sensitive to physical environment, and they possessed a rare talent for communicating their perceptions. They were also intensely aware of other men: their features and habits, their character, their virtues and vices. This curiosity led them ultimately to develop an introspective interest in themselves. Professor Kristeller has noted that humanist writing is characterized by "the tendency to express, and to consider worth expressing, the concrete uniqueness of one's feelings, opinions, experiences and surroundings. . . ." These qualities are displayed in Latin treatises and letters, and also in the diaries and private correspondence of ordinary Florentines. Even such prosaic documents as tax declarations are frequently couched in very expressive language, as they describe the topography of a hill farm or the antipathetic character of a surly peasant. This appreciation of the concrete, the specific, and the unique was fostered not only by the literature of antiquity, but also by the social and intellectual climate of Renaissance Florence.

Cultural Patronage in Renaissance Florence:
Structures, Motivations, Trends

Renaissance culture, so the textbooks assert, was subsidized by a new social class, the urban bourgeoisie. Replacing the nobility and the clergy as the dominant group in society, the bourgeoisie also supplanted them in their traditional role as patrons of culture. With the wealth gained from their mercantile, banking, and industrial enterprises, they were able to hire the poets, scholars, and artists whose brilliant achievements brought fame and glory to them and their city. Through these intellectuals and artists, their employees and agents, the bourgeoisie were able to express their own ideals and values. Stated so simply and crudely, this analysis is valid, but it does require elaboration, qualification, and refinement. One must examine the methods and techniques by which this society encouraged and nourished—materially and psychologically—its intellectuals. How was talent recognized and merit rewarded? What were the peculiar and unique opportunities Florence offered for creative achievement? How effectively were the city's intellectual resources exploited, and how much talent was attracted from abroad? Finally, how were changes in the structure and values of the society reflected in different forms of patronage?

Intellectual activity in medieval and Renaissance Florence was predominantly—almost exclusively—functional; it was related to specific vocational and professional purposes, and directed toward the satisfaction of social needs. The educational system was organized to train some boys for mercantile careers and others for professional careers in law, the notarial discipline, medicine, and theology. In his statistical survey of Florence prior to the Black Death, Giovanni Villani cites some interesting figures on school enrollment. In a population of approximately 100,000, between 8000 and 10,000 youths were enrolled in the city's private schools. While the majority attended elementary schools, which taught the rudiments of the vernacular, 1000 advanced students went to special schools to learn the mathematics necessary for a business career, and another 500 enrolled in preprofessional academies which taught Latin grammar, rhetoric, and logic. Although these figures may be inflated, they do indicate the great value attached to education in Florence, and also the unusually high literacy rate, perhaps one-fourth or one-third of the male population. A basic knowledge of reading, writing, and arithmetic was an essential prerequisite for a business career, even in one of the artisan trades. An incident described in the protocols of the Merchants' Court illustrates this recognition of the value of education among the city's underprivileged. A young emigrant from the Perugian *contado*, Antonio di Manno, instituted a lawsuit for the recovery of a gold florin which he had paid in advance for some elementary instruction. Antonio worked as an apprentice in a shoemaker's shop where a fellow employee,

Miniato, agreed to teach him reading and writing for a year, but then broke his promise when he left the shop.

The size and quality of Florence's educational system (which included conventual *studia* and a university as well as primary and secondary schools) was one factor in the city's ability to attract talent from abroad. Alongside the institutions which provided formal schooling were the guilds with their system of instruction for apprentices. Young artists like Giotto from the Mugello and Masaccio from S. Giovanni Valdarno came to Florence to study in the workshops of the great masters, to live and work in a stimulating intellectual environment, and to gain wealth and fame in a community which subsidized the arts. The city's attraction for men with professional training is documented by the unending flow of petitions from foreign lawyers, notaries, and physicians who sought Florentine citizenship. In 1381 a young physician, Ugolino of Montecatini, had just begun his professional career in Pisa, where he had a small practice and a lectureship in the university. He was then invited to become the town physician of Pescia in the Valdinievole. The most compelling reason for abandoning his teaching post at Pisa to accept this offer was the opportunity to take part in disputations, and to enlarge his experience. Ugolino admitted that the move to Pescia would not redound to his honor, but he believed that it would benefit his career. Apparently, his ultimate goal was to practice medicine in Florence and lecture in the university, but he was realistic about the difficulties confronting him. It required years to build a medical reputation, and then the physician had to endure the jealousy of his colleagues. But Ugolino was willing to accept the challenge of the metropolis, aware that "our profession is one of those influenced by fortune." In 1429, a young Lucchese lawyer, Filippo Balducci, was contemplating a move to Florence from Siena, where he taught and practiced law. To a Florentine acquaintance he wrote: "Since I have always had a great affection for that magnificent and glorious city, which I consider one of the three [greatest] in the world, I would rather be there than here, even though I will earn less."

Public recognition of the distinguished achievement in Florence took various forms. The most tangible mark of distinction was the bestowal of a public office, a university professorship, or an artistic commission upon the meritorious, and these were distributed quite generously to prominent scholars and artists. In 1375, Coluccio Salutati became the first humanist chancellor of the republic; his successors in that office were men of great learning and reputation: Leonardo Bruni, Poggio Bracciolini, Carlo Marsuppini. In 1300, the commune granted a tax exemption to the architect Arnolfo di Cambio, "since this master is the most renowned and the most expert in church construction of any other in these parts; and that through his industry, experience and genius, the Florentine commune . . . from the magnificent beginning of this church . . . hopes to have the most beautiful and the most honorable cathedral in Tuscany." A century and a half later, Leonardo Bruni and Poggio Bracciolini obtained similar exemptions; Poggio had claimed that "he cannot pay the assessments levied against citizens who have profited from trade and the emoluments of public service, since he plans to devote all of his energies to study. . . ." Although Filippo Brunelleschi obtained no tax exemption from the state, he did receive a rare public acknowledgment of his talent. Described in a provision of June 1421 as a "man of the most perspicacious intelligence and admirable industry," he was granted a three-year patent on a boat he had invented, which apparently reduced the costs of transporting goods on the Arno. In reserving all benefits for this invention to Brunelleschi, the law stated that its objective was to prevent "the fruits of his talents and virtue from accruing to another," and also "to stimulate him to greater activity and even more subtle investigations. . . ."

During his lifetime, Dante Alighieri received no accolades from his native city, but after the poet's death, the Florentines made some belated gestures of apology. Giovanni Villani wrote that "because of the virtues and knowledge and worthiness of this citizen, it seems proper to grant him perpetual memory in our chronicle, even though his own noble works, which he has left to us in writing, bear witness to him and bring renown to our city." Giovanni Boccaccio's appointment (1373) as the commune's official lecturer on the *Divine Comedy* was an unprecedented sign of Dante's exalted reputation. Twenty-three years later, the councils passed a law authorizing the officials in charge of the cathedral to arrange for the return of the bodies of five illustrious Florentines who had died and been buried abroad. Munificent tombs were planned for these men in the cathedral, where no other interments were to be permitted. Four of the charter members of this Pantheon—Dante, Petrarch, Boccaccio, and Zanobi da Strada—were literary men, and the fifth was a distinguished lawyer named Accursius (d. 1260?) who taught for many years in the University of Bologna. This project failed completely, for the guardians of these bodies refused to surrender them. In 1430, the Signoria again appealed to the lord of Ravenna for Dante's remains. "Our people," so the official letter read, "harbor a singular and particular affection for the glorious and undying memory of that most excellent and renowned poet, Dante Alighieri; the fame of this man is such that it redounds to the praise and splendor of our city. . . ."

Not every distinguished citizen remained home to adorn his native city with his talents. Petrarch was never attracted to Florence, nor was Boccaccio an enthusiastic admirer of the city. After 1400, however, the pendulum swung quite decisively in Florence's favor, and during the first half of the Quattrocento, her cultural magnetism was particularly intense. Native artists and writers—Masaccio, Brunelleschi, Ghiberti, Manetti—stayed home and made only brief excursions abroad, while their ranks were supplemented by foreigners: Bruni, Poggio Bracciolini, Gentile da Fabriano. S. Croce, not the cathedral, became Florence's Pantheon, and the tombs in that Franciscan basilica are visual evidence of the magnitude of Florentine genius, and also of the city's inability to retain and exploit that genius fully. Dante, Petrarch, and Boccaccio are still missing, although Dante is commemorated by an ugly modern cenotaph. From an esthetic viewpoint, the two most noteworthy tombs are those of the humanist Bruni and Marsuppini, both of whom received imposing state funerals. Lorenzo Ghiberti, Niccolò Machiavelli, and Michelangelo are all buried in S. Croce, although Michelangelo died where he had lived and worked, in Rome. His body was spirited away to Florence by agents of Duke Cosimo I. Some distinguished Florentines of the Quattrocento are not interred in S. Croce. These include Palla Strozzi, who died in Padua while living in involuntary exile, Leon Battista Alberti, who died in Rome in 1472, and Leonardo da Vinci, who abandoned both Florence and Italy to spend his last years at the French court of Francis I.

The official recognition of intellectual and artistic distinction was one aspect of the collective, public nature of artistic and scholarly patronage in early Renaissance Florence. The great architectural monuments of the fourteenth and fifteenth centuries were supervised by commissions of *operai* selected by the guilds. In 1402, Lorenzo Ghiberti won a commission for the Baptistery doors in a public competition organized by the consuls of the Calimala guild, and judged by a special committee of thirty-four painters, sculptors, and goldsmiths. In the realm of letters and scholarship, official patronage was also important and useful, generally assuming the form of a communal office or a university professorship. The bestowal of the chancellor's office upon distinguished humanists like Salutati and Bruni was a reward for their fame and reputation, as well as payment for services rendered to the republic. By the middle of the fifteenth century, however, public subsidy of culture was declining, and the role of the private patron, and of culture created exclusively for private needs, now assumed greater importance than before. This trend can be charted in two quite different contexts: in the history of the Florentine Studio, and in Medicean patronage of the arts.

The fortunes of the city's major institution of higher learning provide a valuable corrective to the idealized picture of this society as totally committed to intellectual distinction, and willing to make heavy sacrifices to achieve and maintain excellence. From the beginning, Florence's efforts to create a university of the first rank met with very limited success. In 1321, a *studium generale* was established by the commune; it never flourished and ceased to function in the 1330s. But even before the Black Death had run its course, a courageous and imaginative Signoria enacted a decree (August 26, 1348) which authorized the reopening of the Studio, and bravely proclaimed that "from the study of the sciences, the city of Florence will receive an increase in honors and a full measure of wealth. . . ." Although the circumstances of its foundation could not have been less promising, the university did survive and gradually developed a modest reputation. But its existence was never secure, and it limped along on the rather meager resources which the commune grudgingly provided. Records of the deliberations on the university's budget in the 1360s reveal that some citizens doubted whether the school was worth its cost. During its most flourishing period, in the 1380s, the university operated with a substantial budget of 3000 florins, which paid for a staff of twenty-four professors. But one consequence of the debilitating wars with Giangaleazzo Visconti was the closing of the university in 1406; it did not reopen again until 1413. Thereafter, its budget was repeatedly cut during the Milanese wars of the 1420s; it was finally reduced to 200 florins in 1426. Four years later, the Studio governors candidly admitted that the university was in a parlous state. "It grieves us sorely," they announced, "that this glorious republic, which had surpassed the rest of Italy and all previous centuries in beauty and splendor, should be surpassed in this one respect by some of our neighboring cities, which in every other way are inferior to us."

This failure of the university to achieve the distinction which its founders and supporters envisaged is perhaps the crucial factor in the reluctance of Florence's ruling class to provide adequate and sustained support. The solid reputations of Bologna and Padua were never really challenged by the Studio, and shrewd politicians may have realized that no amount of money would change that fact. Patrician interests were not affected adversely by the mediocre quality of Studio instruction; wealthy citizens could send their sons to other Italian universities, and particularly to Bologna, to acquire the skills and the degrees needed to further their professional careers. Also contributing to the declining importance of the university was the tendency, in Florence and elsewhere, for humanistic studies—rhetoric, moral philosophy, poetry—to flourish outside of the university. Although these subjects were offered regularly in the Studio, occasionally by such distinguished scholars as Chrysoloras, Filelfo and Marsuppini, most teaching in the humanities occurred in a private context; tutors instructing students in their homes, scholars assembling in monasteries or in private palaces to discuss classical texts. Like other facets of patrician life in Quattrocento Florence, learning and education were becoming more private, aristocratic, and exclusive.

The most renowned institution of higher learning in Florence in the second half of the fifteenth century was not the Studio, but the Platonic Academy, an informal coterie of scholars and students united by an interest in Platonic philosophy. Its leader was Marsilio Ficino, whose translations of Platonic writings were subsidized by the Medici. The Academy had a geographical focus in Ficino's villa at Careggi outside of Florence, but it possessed no formal organization, nor did it provide any regular instruction. Its only scheduled events were irregular lectures by Ficino and occasional banquets and symposia held infrequently at the Careggi villa. Ficino did provide loose and informal guidance to his disciples and to visiting scholars like Pico della Mirandola and Jacques Lefèvre d'Étaples. But the essential qualities of this community were privacy, intimacy, and learning pursued for its own sake, without any concern for vocational or practical benefits.

This shift in the form and object of patronage from the public-corporate to the private sphere also occurred in he plastic arts. Communal and guild patronage was at its height between 1375 and 1425, when the Loggia dei Lanzi and the cathedral dome were built, when guilds were commissioning Baptistery doors and statues for Orsanmichele and erecting new headquarters for themselves. In these decades, too, private subsidy of the arts was largely (although not exclusively) directed toward public enterprises. The first architectural projects financed by Cosimo de' Medici were reconstructions of churches and monasteries: S. Lorenzo, S. Marco, the Badia of Fiesole, and the church of S. Francesco in Bosco in the Mugello. This pattern was sanctioned by tradition, and so too was its collective form, since other families were involved in several of these projects. If only because of his superior resources, Cosimo's voice in these collective enterprises tended to predominate; S. Lorenzo, for example, was finally completed with Medici money twenty years after the project had been initiated. Cosimo's reluctance to finish this work earlier was apparently due to his unwillingness to appear too bold and ambitious as a patron. His plan to rebuild S. Marco was thwarted when other families with burial rights in the convent refused to surrender them.

Despite these limitations imposed upon Cosimo's patronage by community sentiment and tradition, and by his own sense of propriety, his total contribution was impressive. His greatest achievement was, of course, the palace on the Via Larga, and it was within the confines of that structure that later Medici generations satisfied their esthetic needs. Lorenzo was recognized as the premier connoisseur of the arts in Italy, and his advice on painters and architects was sought by princes throughout the peninsula. As one dimension of his foreign policy, he sent Florentine artists to work for those rulers whose favor he desired. But Lorenzo's material subsidy of the arts in Florence was niggardly. Most of his money for this purpose was spent not on ecclesiastical or civic projects, but on his private collection of precious gems and antique art. This had been assembled for his enjoyment, and for that of close friends and visiting dignitaries, whose appreciation of the gesture might be politically advantageous as well as personally gratifying. Lorenzo's collections of *objets d'art* was the esthetic counterpart of the Platonic Academy.

Parent and Child in Renaissance Italy

JAMES BRUCE ROSS

Before the development of modern psychology, before it was fashionable to collect children's verses, artwork, and opinions, our only knowledge of childhood and the perceptions and experiences of children was derived from the recollections of adults. In the earlier selection on parents and children in the Middle Ages, Mary Martin McLaughlin relied on the reminiscences of Guibert of Nogent and on biographical works (saints' lives) that probably preserve some recollections by their subjects themselves. In addition, McLaughlin found occasional contemporary admonitions to parents that, by implication at least, give us some idea about how children were treated and what was expected of them. By a bit of imagination, the historian can describe the child's experience of such expectations and treatment, but the skimpiness of our knowledge is all too plain. In dealing with parent and child in the civilization of Renaissance Italy, James Bruce Ross has used sources similar to McLaughlin's, but the literate urbanites of the sixteenth century produced many more reminiscences than did medieval people. The relatively rich sources make it possible for Ross to construct a fairly complete portrait of children's experience in that period. He can describe the system of child-rearing, establish a general chronology of young life, and present contemporary ideas about family life, because many treatises and personal letters dealing with these subjects survive.

A brief review of the history of the family in medieval Europe will serve as background for Ross' article and as reflection on McLaughlin's article. We sometimes speak of the emergence of the family in the fifteenth and sixteenth centuries—a way of speaking that may seem rather strange. After all, medieval society derived from Germanic and Roman society, both of which were wholly based on the family. But the growth of feudalism during the Middle Ages had a profound effect on the family. The family system of primitive Germanic society broke down as feudalism became the organizing principle of European society. Feudal lords could effectively control the political position of the family by controlling the marriage of their vassals. Likewise, feudal law restricted the role of families in the system of power by insisting on primogeniture: Although younger sons could receive fiefs from their fathers, and daughters could be given dowries, there were strict limitations on the size of these donations. A man could not disinherit his eldest son, nor could he leave his heir so little land that the heir could not fulfill his obligations to his lord.

Families did, of course, occasionally gain a powerful position within the feudal hierarchy. The famous Clares of England used the favor of the English kings to spread through the baronage of the kingdom. Their success is indicated by their position within the party of rebellious barons that won the Magna Carta from King John in 1215. Of the twenty-four barons chosen to look after the royal government on behalf of the rebels, sixteen were members of the Clare family. Yet it is significant that the power of the family consisted in its success in infiltrating the feudal structure rather than opposing it. One Clare, for example, married the great William Marshal (see "The Training of a Knight" in Part 3). Feudal rank, not family connections, determined a person's place in the community.

Another indication of the declining importance of the family in medieval England is found in the common law of property. Progressively during the twelfth and thirteenth centuries, family rights of property—and the concomitant inability of the head of the family to alienate property—devolved on the paterfamilias. In 1225, the royal court decided that a man could alienate land and deprive his heirs of any right to it. Family rights of property had become individual rights.

Cases before the royal court did not much affect life in the peasant villages, which was in all likelihood much more traditional and therefore more family-oriented than life among the upper classes. Yet the conclusions to be drawn from the documents of the upper classes are strikingly confirmed by another sort of evidence that was more popular, or at least more public, in character. The art of the cathedrals often portrayed aspects of everyday life, especially peasant life, but the family did not figure in these representations.

It can be argued that these medieval representations only reveal the life of the rural aristocracy and peasants, and that we should not take them as a reflection of urban family life. This is true; the rural society of feudal barons set the standards of medieval social and family life. In turning to look at the families of Renaissance Italy, we see a life style similar to that of medieval urban populations; but now middle-class urbanites were becoming the dominant group in European society. The difference in focus between McLaughlin's and Ross' articles is not merely the result of the historian's personal interest or the survival of particular sources; it represents an actual, major change in early modern society.

"I called to mind when, the exact hour and moment, and where and how he was conceived by me, and how great a joy it was to me and his mother; and soon came his movements in the womb which I noted carefully with my hand, awaiting his birth with the greatest eagerness. And then when he was born, male, sound, well-proportioned, what happiness, what joy I experienced; and then as he grew from good to better, such satisfaction, such pleasure in his childish words, pleasing to all, loving towards me his father and his mother, precocious for his age."

Giovanni Morelli

From James Bruce Ross, "The Middle-Class Child in Urban Italy, Fourteenth to Early Sixteenth Century" in *The History of Childhood*, ed. L. deMause (New York: The Psychohistory Press, 1974), pp.183–216.

What was it like to be a middle-class child in the urban centres of northern and central Italy in the period of "the Renaissance," from about 1300 to the early sixteenth century? The life of the peasant child and of the proletarian urban child remains almost wholly obscure, but thanks to the articulate impulses of the mercantile and professional classes, and the remarkable number of their extant records, we can gain some understanding of the upbringing of their children. Although no voices of children reach us directly, we can hear them, faintly and imperfectly to be sure, through the media of those who controlled their lives or observed their development. Fathers of families sometimes recall their own early years and usually record with care the vital data of their offspring; moralists and preachers admonish parents in traditional Christian terms; educators create an ideal ethic of pedagogy, from classical sources; physicians and artists observe and comment upon the child in particular ways. A few exceptional individuals write their own life history, transmuting their childhood experience in their old age. All of these adults draw from the accumulated wisdom of the past but reflect as well the power of prevailing custom and the peculiar strains of an aggressive and competitive society subject to physical disasters, plague, famine and flood, as well as civil violence and war.

In pursuit of evidence for this elusive subject the modern scholar must search widely, examining masses of diverse materials, published and unpublished, in order to find even a few fragments or tessera with which to construct some kind of mosaic. The shapes that emerge will be faulty, the colors dim, but perhaps the whole may make some sense to the modern student of childhood, past and present. Deeper psychological insight, more lively historical imagination, as well as the fruits of contemporary quantitative studies, will enrich and doubtless modify the tentative conclusions of this short essay, but the evidence presented, almost wholly from the sources, will, I hope, remain valuable to the future inquirer.

Because the Tuscans, and especially the Florentines, were more articulate than any other people in Italy at this time and their records richer and more accessible than those of other areas, their voices are heard most clearly in this essay. The political fragmentation of the peninsula of Italy, only a geographical expression until the mid-nineteenth century, precludes the characterization of any child as "Italian," and the uneven cultural development of the major parts makes questionable any generalization beyond the limits of a single territorial entity. It seems valid, however, to consider as a whole the experience of the middle-class child in central and northern Italy. "The City" (Rome) was distinct in every way, and "The Kingdom" (Naples, with or without Sicily) was overwhelmingly rural, retarded in social and cultural development, and therefore relatively inarticulate for our purposes.

The First Two Years: Mother or Nurse?
The Balia: Ideal and Actual

What were the infant's first contacts with the world outside the womb? Birth in the parental bed, bath in the same room, and baptism in the parish church were followed almost at once by delivery into the hands of a *balia* or wet-nurse, generally a peasant woman living at a distance, with whom the infant would presumably remain for about two years or until weaning was completed. Immediate separation from its mother, therefore, was the fate of the new-born child in the middle-class families of urban Italy in the period of our study. It became wholly dependent for food, care and affection upon a surrogate, and its return to its own mother was to a stranger in an alien home, to a person with whom no physical or emotional ties had ever been established. Clearly the *balia* looms large in any discussion of the young child in Italy.

The antiquity of the institution of the wet-nurse is well known to all students of pediatrics. Of interest to us here is the continuity of a body of injunctions concerning the choice of a wet-nurse and the performance of her basic functions, especially as they had been formulated by the physician Soranus of Ephesus (96 – 138 A.D.). This core of material seems to be the source of most of the didactic treatises on the care of infants that were written in our period although the lines of transmission are not clear. Of equal interest in these Italian writings is the persistence of the advocacy of maternal feeding, but in ambivalent terms similar to those of Soranus:

> Other things being equal, it is better to feed the child with maternal milk; for this is more suited to it, and the mothers become more sympathetic towards the offspring, and it is more natural to be fed from the mother after parturition, just as before parturition. But if anything prevents it one must choose the best wet-nurse, lest the mother grow prematurely old, having spent herself through the daily suckling. . . . The mother will fare better with a view to her own recovery and to further child-bearing, if she is relieved of having her breasts distended. . . .

Among the Italian writers of the fourteenth century the wet-nurse is accepted as a matter of course. For example, the mother is relegated to a minor role by the leading authority on the subject, the poet-notary, Francesco da Barberino, who urges that the wet-nurse be as much like the mother as possible, and that if she falls sick, she should take the infant to its mother, "who, if she wishes and it is convenient, will be able to suckle it with fine milk; though it is true that in the beginning the milk of another is better than hers." Much the same attitude is shown by the Tuscan merchant Paolo da Certaldo in his collection of moral admonitions written after 1350. Not mentioning the mother at all, he calls for great care in the choice of a wet-nurse:

She should be prudent, well-mannered, honest, not a drinker or a drunkard, because very often children draw from and resemble the nature of the milk they suck; and therefore be careful the wet nurses of your children aren't proud and don't have other evil traits. . . .

The fate of the child put out with a *balia* depended upon many variables including the duration of the stay. Supposedly it lasted for two years or until weaning, which was obviously abrupt in many cases; Barberino says about two years and warns against sudden weaning. Actually it varied considerably, as a few examples will show. A girl child in the Florentine Sassetti family was returned in 1370 after twenty-nine months by her *balia* with whom the parents remained on good terms "although the child was in rather poor shape, but in truth more from illness than from poor care." The fortunate illegitimate daughter of Datini (by a slave-girl) was taken in by his wife in 1395 and brought "home" at six years from her *balia* whose husband wrote saying that he and his wife had loved her like a daughter, and "because she is a good girl and very fearful," he hoped they would be kind to her. The father of Giovanni Morelli was left by his father with a *balia* in the country until he was "ten or twelve," perhaps because his parent "had so many grown children, or because his wife being dead and he an old man, he didn't want the trouble of bringing up the child, or the expense." The grown man remembered this *balia* as "the most awful bestial woman that ever was," who had given him so many blows that the mere thought of her so enraged him that he would have killed her if he could have laid hands on her. A branch of the Adriani family of Florence in 1470 received their son back from his *balia* at fifteen months and were told he had been "eight days without the breast" because she had become pregnant.

In general, it seems clear that the pregnancy of the *balia* more frequently terminated the stay than the early death of the child. The causes of the latter are rarely made clear. Did illegitimate infants die more frequently and earlier than legitimate babies in the care of a *balia*? Infanticide veiled as "smothering may well have occurred more frequently than we know though there were more humane ways of disposing of unwanted children, legitimate and illegitimate. The foundling hospitals received a steady stream of the latter. But the danger of "smothering" is made clear by Barberino's injunction: "don't let the baby lie with you in such a way that you might roll over on top of him." (It is worth noting that the "layettes" sent with infants by Rustichi and others included a cradle with coverlet and pillow.)

Few explicit references to "smothering," however, have been found. Among the many deaths of young children noted by Morelli in his review of three generations, only one, a nephew, was thought to have been "suffocated" at the home of the *balia*; the great killer in this family was the Black Death in the recurrent waves of 1363, 1374, 1400. Another instance is found in an early life of the humanist Marsiglio Ficino; his grandmother appeared to his mother in a dream, grieving, on the seventeenth day after the birth of a child, and "the next day countrymen brought back her child suffocated by her nurse." And a few days after Cellini visited his natural son he received word the child was dead, "smothered" by his nurse. The question arises, however, why a *balia* would deliberately "smother" a child or carelessly run the risk of doing so. The child's death would mean the end of an arrangement profitable to her and to her husband. And the penalties for infanticide might be harsh.

The Return of the Native: From About Two to Seven
Child and Mother: Care in Theory and Practice

The return of the child to its native home after some two years forced upon him another severe adjustment; now displaced from the only "mother" he had ever known he must find his true mother in the midst of a strange household, an urban "family" which might be large and complex in composition. If the trend may have been towards the smaller "nuclear" family there is plenty of evidence of the persistence of the large "family" in the fourteenth and fifteenth centuries, that is, in the sense defined by Alberti as "children, wife, and other members of the household, both relatives and servants. . . . I would want all my family to live under one roof, to warm themselves at one hearth and to seat themselves at one table."

A few examples of the size and composition of households may be helpful.

One of the Peruzzi, Florentine merchants, notes in his "secret book" for 1314 the expenses incurred for half of the cost of "the house and family" which he had in common with his brother; he himself had twelve children. Two other merchants in the Florentine tax records of 1427 claim substantial reductions on the basis of large households, one noting a household of fifteen members, including two married sons and their families, as well as five adolescent sons, the other listing twelve dependents, wife, sister and nine children. In praising his wife in the late fourteenth century another merchant, Velluti, says she is a big, beautiful woman of fifty, wise, understanding, tireless, and splendid as a nurse, "and that's not to be wondered at, considering how many she's had to manage, husbands, sons, brothers and other persons." A mixed household under the roof of a widow is described in 1442 as containing her husband's two natural children, her own three sons, her daughter, the wives of two sons and three children of one of them. A similar composite household is that of Paoli Niccolini, wool merchant of the mid-fifteenth century; it included his children by two wives, the sons of one wife by her first husband and two of his sons by a slave whom he freed and kept in residence.

Discord in such households was inevitable. San Bernardino notes what a bride might expect on arrival in her new home, such as the enmity of step-children: ". . . and she has no love for them and can scarcely bear for them to have enough to eat. And they are often so knowing as to perceive that she doesn't wish them well and would like for her to have nothing at all to eat." And if she finds another daughter-in-law in the house, "there will soon be an end to peace and concord," and if a mother-in-law, "I'll say no more!" Morelli describes admiringly the way in which his sister "Mea," married at fifteen into a large, disorderly and quarrelsome household, imposed peace upon old and young by her grace and virtue.

The child returning from the *balia*, therefore, might have to compete for the attention of his mother, or some adult woman, not only with his own siblings but with half-brothers and sisters, legitimate or illegitimate, some obviously of alien blood, or with cousins under the tutelage of their fathers. Illegitimate children were sometimes even brought home from overseas, as in the case of Gregorio Dati, who, in 1391 had a child by a Tartar slave in Valencia, whom he sent back to Florence to be reared at three months. A member of the Velluti family brought back from Sicily in 1355 his dead brother's illegitimate daughter, age ten, although he was at first dubious about her parentage, "and I welcomed her, and I and my family . . . treated her as though she were my own daughter." The numbers of children might even be augmented by little slave-servants, especially girls of eleven or twelve, Tartars, Slavs, or "Arabs," whom Datini and other merchants bought to use as household drudges or little nurses. These children were distinguished from the others by looks, speech, manners and the clothes they were required to wear, marked with black, as were the older slave-servants in the house.

If it was difficult for the returning child to win a place in his mother's affections in such households, perhaps he attached himself at first to an older sister or brother, to an uncle or an aunt or grandparent living in the house. When a well-known Florentine widow was looking for a bride for one of her sons, she commented favorably on a girl who was "responsible for a large family (there are twelve children, six boys and six girls) and the mother is always pregnant and is not very competent." The grandmothers in the Medici family seem to have been active in the upbringing of children in that restless clan as they moved from city to villa, villa to villa, to escape the plague, bad weather and other troubles. In a well-known picture, Ghirlandaio conveys the feeling of intimacy which a child might develop towards a grandfather.

We shall never know what impressions of his family a child actually formed but some early adult memories, recorded in different ways, may be helpful. A study of Leonardo da Vinci, an illegitimate child who was successively part of several family groups, makes suggestive use of the drawings of heads, mostly in profile, dating perhaps from as early as the artist's sixteenth year. By means of verbal portraits the Florentine Giovanni Morelli in his private journal, written mostly in his thirties, evokes vivid images of those whom he loved most in the family constellation, treating as shadowy figures the others. He idealizes his father, whom he lost at three years, as a "poor abandoned boy," left at the *balia's* until ten or twelve years, who never saw his father, but who by courage and virtue triumphed over paternal neglect and fraternal indifference to become head of the family. Married at twenty-eight to Telda, "thirteen and beautiful," he sired five children before he died in the plague of 1374, leaving four surviving children, two girls, nine and six, and two boys, four and three, at the mercy of "a cruel mother" who soon remarried and turned them over to her parents. For a brief period an heroic young cousin served as a father figure to the child in a large family group which fled to Bologna to escape the plague but this admirable young man who skilfully managed the large household soon died. The child's next attachment was to his older sister, Mea, beautiful, gifted and gay, but she married at fifteen and died in childbirth at twenty-two. For Giovanni the loss of his father was irreparable, "so great is the benefit the child receives from a living father," his hourly guidance and good counsel; his first duty should be to insure that in case of his death the wife does not remarry and leave their children, "for there is no mother so bad that she isn't better for her children than any other woman.". . .

In Alberti's dialogue on the family, the characters, married and unmarried, place upon the father the weight of responsibility for the upbringing of children after infancy, "that tender age . . . more properly assigned to women's quiet care." They debate the balance of paternal joys and sorrows and seem to ignore or denigrate the mother's role, stressing the father's love as "more unshakable, more constant, more vast, more complete" than any other. Even they, however, reveal certain circumstances which diminished his role and enhanced the mother's, such as his absences from home and his greater age. Recent demographic studies, especially of the Florentine area, have established statistically a striking disparity in age between husband and wife and a consequent remoteness of the father from the child. Some social and cultural implications of the close proximity of mother and child have also been suggested.

The relative closeness in age of the young mother to the child was often enhanced by frequent absences, even prolonged, of mercantile fathers, and by political exile following upon sudden reversal of party controls, such as the return of the Medici to Florence in 1434. San Bernardino sharply warns against the long absences of merchants and encourages wives to try to force them to return: "I'm not speaking of a week or two weeks or even a month . . . but to stay two years or three is not rational and hence displeasing to God." Such practices, a normal aspect of mercantile activity, were probably more disruptive of family life than political exile. Many young women of prominent families, however, were made "widows" by the exile of their husbands. Vespasiano, the Florentine book-seller and biographer, pays tribute to some of these illustrious women, noting their careful administration of the household, their solicitude for their children; he admires especially those who, as real widows, remained celibate and devoted themselves wholly to their souls and their children.

"Young widows" were, in fact, a common social phenomenon and concern for their welfare, fiscal and moral, and that of their children pervades many kinds of sources. The preacher-prophet of Florence, Savonarola (1452–1498), devotes a whole treatise to widowhood in which he analyzes the motives for remarrying or remaining chaste. He does not condemn those young widows who remained unmarried not for love of God but "rather for human reasons such as the love of their children," from whom they cannot bear to separate themselves. San Antonino of Florence (1389–1459), in his letters of guidance to a young widow, urges her to try to be both father and mother to her children, "a father in punishing and training them, a mother in nourishing them, not with dainties or too many indulgences as do carnal mothers but not spiritual ones; for children need both bread and blows." And San Bernardino, "let the widow learn to rear her family" and be especially watchful of daughters.

Anxiety for the welfare of children whose widowed mothers remarry is expressed in many ways. Paolo da Certaldo urges fathers

> to avoid like fire leaving your goods and children only in the hands of your wife. . . . In many ways and for many reasons, it may happen that she'll leave your children and rob them of their patrimony or treat them badly or see someone else abuse them and remain silent. . . .

The provisions of many wills contain a clause "if she remains a widow and lives with her children" qualifying legacies to daughters and wives. In his history of his family, Morelli, abandoned at four by a "cruel mother," notes in every case whether a widow remarried or stayed with her children. He gives elaborate directions to his heirs how to ensure in their wills that the mother should not leave the offspring, listing several provisions which he grades in terms of the husband's confidence in his wife's devotion to their children. . . .

The age between two and about seven was the period when the child of either sex must have known most closely the mother's care and developed its first emotional bond with her, a bond which might be enhanced by the youth of the mother, the age and absences of the father, or the widowhood of the mother. Perhaps the earlier deprivation suffered by both child and mother deepened this relationship and helps to explain the sustained devotion of many adult males to their mothers. It is doubtful whether this period was at first one "full of delight and accompanied by general laughter at the child's first words," as Alberti suggests. San Bernardino evokes a different kind of welcome when he attacks the odious "putting out" system: "and when he comes home to you, you say, 'I don't know whom you are like, certainly none of us!'" But time tempered the strangeness on both sides, and San Bernardino shrewdly notes the different qualities with which a mother looks at her own children ("with the eye of the heart"), those of her neighbor ("with pleasant mien"), and those of her enemies ("with a stern eye and scowl").

The predominant role of the mother is implicit in the treatise of the Dominican Giovanni Dominici (c. 1356 to c. 1420), himself the son of a widow, written for a lady who was "almost a widow," to advise her about the daily life of the child as well as its moral training: "one can effectively control children until they are grown up to about the age of twelve, then they begin to throw off the maternal yoke." The mother should adorn the house with pictures and statues "pleasing to childhood," such as "a good representation of Jesus nursing, sleeping in His mother's lap or standing courteously before Her," or one in which "he sees himself mirrored in the Holy Baptist . . . a little child who enters the desert, plays with birds" or "of Jesus and the Baptist pictured together. . . ." She should dress both sexes simply, in decent attire and modest colors; "from three years on" the son is to

> know no distinction between male and female other than dress and hair. From then on let him be a stranger to being petted, embraced and kissed by you until after the twenty-fifth year. Granted that there will not take place any thought or natural movement before the age of five . . . do not be less solicitous that he be chaste and modest always and, in every place, covered as modestly as if he were a girl.

As for sleeping, she should not allow him after three years to "sleep on one bed or on one pillow with his sisters or romp too much with them during the day." Rear them separately if possible. "He should sleep clothed with a night shirt reaching below the knees. . . . Let not the mother nor the father, much less any other person, touch him."

"Do not forbid them to play games. . . . Growing nature makes the child run and jump." As long as they play these simple games "you play with them and let them win." If they hurt one another, chide the wrongdoer but moderately so the injured one won't delight in revenge.

To prepare them for adversity the mother should inure them to hardships, putting the boy to sleep sometimes dressed, "once a week on a couch, occasionally on a chest, and with the windows open," treating him "somewhat as if he were the son of a peasant." And "accustom them to eat bitter things, such as peachstones, horehound, strong herbs and fritters" and occasionally "certain harmless little remedies like purgatives" to prepare them for future sickness.   And in anticipation of poverty, "children should be accustomed to eat coarse food, to wear cheap and common clothing, to go on foot. . . ."

From other kinds of sources it is clear that Dominici's prescriptions reflect religious attitudes and sexual fears more than the secular reality he observes and deplores:

> At present how much you work and strive to lead them about the whole day, to hug and kiss them, to sing them songs, to tell them foolish stories, to scare them with a dozen bogies, to deceive them, to play hide and seek with them and to take pains in making them beautiful, healthy, cheerful, laughing and wholly content according to the sensual!

His advice raises many questions, few of which can be answered.   How was it possible to separate boys and girls at such an age, to prevent them from seeing and touching one another as they romped in the confines of an urban house and courtyard?   The everyday garment of both sexes in the early years seems to have been a short tunic of wool, loose or belted, with little underneath.

Close relations between the sexes in childhood are evident in some sources, for example, in Morelli's account of trying to marry a young girl whom he had wanted for a wife from the time she was a tiny child.   Also, a member of the Valori family in 1452 chose as his wife the one of two sisters whom he knew well "because up to the age of twelve we had been brought up almost together."   A mixed group of lively children is pictured in a letter of Piero, age eight, to his father, Lorenzo de' Medici, in 1479:

> We are all well and studying.   Giovanni [four] is beginning to spell. . . . Giuliano [the baby] laughs and thinks of nothing else, Lucrezia [nine] sews, sings and reads.   Maddalena [six] knocks her head against the wall. . . . Luisa [two] begins to say a few little words.   Contessina [over a year] fills the house with her noise.

Spontaneous play by young children is recognized as natural even by the austere Dominici who sees no good in toys, such as "little wooden horses, attractive cymbals, imitation birds, gilded drums, and a thousand different kinds of toys, all accustoming them to vanity."   In pictures of the period, little children playing spontaneously are most often shown in the persons of the Christ Child and Little St. John, reaching out to each other, sometimes embracing, sometimes with a lamb, lively and responsive.   They are also represented in dozens of ways, singly, in two's and larger groups, as tiny "angel-children," called *putti* or *amorini*, usually winged, nude, appealing.   One of the most playful groups is that of the very young and chubby, winged male *amori* by Agostino di Duccio who are frantically engaged in a variety of activities on land and sea, shooting, boating, swimming on sea monsters, playing musical instruments. More realistic, perhaps, is the representation of seven nude *putti* in a drawing by Raphael who are acting out with glee a specific game, "judge and prisoner."

But all these *putti* are ideal, not real, infants inspired clearly by classical forms though doubtless influenced by observation of living children; their robust forms, angelic faces, fantastic activities, can hardly be considered as typical of actual children. And the same is true of the most famous examples of older children, some adolescent, on the two singers' pulpits created for the cathedral in Florence. The grace and dignity of the classically clad, almost sexless children of Luca della Robbia in their dancing and music-making convey the character of a heavenly, not earthly, choir, though the faces may resemble those of Tuscan boys, then and now. And the almost Bacchic abandon of the winged wreath dancers in Donatello's frieze seems even more remote from the homes and streets of Italian cities. What did these ideal children mean to those who created them or those who looked at them, children and adults? What were real children doing at these ages in the home, or school or shop? About the homely activities of the child, where and how he ate, slept, defecated, played, we know very little. Even surviving domestic architecture reveals little about the use of living space for intimate purposes.

The moralists tell us little, the *ricordi* almost nothing. Paola da Certaldo is succinct, as always: "Feed the boy well and dress him as well as you can, I mean in good taste and decently. . . . Dress the girl well but as for eating, it doesn't matter as long as it keeps her alive; don't let her get fat."

And Dominici, with future poverty in mind:

> Children should be accustomed to eat coarse food, to wear cheap and common clothes. . . . They should also learn to wait on themselves, and to use as little as possible the services of maid or servant, setting and clearing the table, dressing and undressing themselves, putting on their own shoes and clothes and so forth.

Did children eat, standing up, scraps from the table, while serving or later? (Seated children are generally seen only in school-room scenes.) Filarete, the humanist-architect, writing in the 1460's about an "ideal school," warns that children should not eat too much; let them be given tough meat so they won't bolt their food, and, up to the age of twenty, stand to eat while one child reads aloud. They should not sleep more than six to eight hours. If one may judge from the slender young children in the family portraits of the age, even the children of the rich were not over-fed; though well-formed they look less amply fed than the chubby babies or the plump *putti* of the artists.

In general, the didactic treatises of the humanist educators, inspired by classical authorities, call for a regime of austerity tempered by reason and concern for the individual. The most celebrated teacher of the age, Vittorino da Feltre (1378–1446), wrote no treatises but put the prevailing principles of classical-Christian education into effect in his boarding school for children of the ruling family of Mantua and other deserving children of varying ages, some as young as six or seven. "The Pleasant House" was governed by the ever-watchful ascetic eye of the celibate master who permitted no coddling in habits of eating, clothing or sleeping, obviously guided by sexual fears. Few mothers of busy households could have supervised the daily habits of the children as effectively as Vittorino. . . .

From Father to Master: The Father's Role
Discipline and Instruction

During the younger years of the child the father's responsibility seems to have been limited primarily to periods of illness and disaster except where the poor health of the mother or poverty made made his attention indispensable. One of the married Alberti family members speaks of the anguish of the father during the first period of life which "seems to be almost nothing but attacks of smallpox, measles, and rose rash. It is never free of stomach trouble, and there are always periods of debility." These and dozens of other kinds of diseases of children are described in the Italian medical treatises of the sixteenth century but few are clearly identified in the sources. In the *ricordi* the fact of death is usually simply stated and dated by the father, especially with reference to cases of very early mortality at the home of the *balia*.

Morelli, in reviewing his own life, notes his "illness" at four years, "long serious illness" at seven, "smallpox" at nine, and a grave illness and fever at twelve. He describes much more fully the mortal illness of his son, Alberto, in 1406:

> He fell ill with a flow of blood from the nose. It happened . . . three times before we noticed that he had fever, and then Monday morning when he was at school, the fever seized him, the blood burst from his nose and stomach and body, and, as it pleased God, he lived sixteen days . . . in great torment and agony. . . .

Further details of the child's suffering make it clear that Alberto's father rarely, if ever, left the child during this time; he includes his wife, however, in this account and in the description of their common grief that followed.

Strenuous efforts to keep alive a baby of six months, the illegitimate son of Datini, were made by his friends in Prato in communication with the father in Florence. The child, afflicted by "seizures," perhaps due to the "humidity," and fever, died after a few days despite the use of medicines, ointments and "incantations"; the "beaver's fat" sent from Florence by his father arrived too late. He had been removed from the house of his *balia* so that he might receive better care. Lapo Mazzei writes to Datini that he took his little son afflicted with epilepsy into his own bed with him.

The harsh treatment received by the young Cardan from both parents perhaps intensified the night terrors and sweats from which he suffered, as well as the hallucinations he experienced from four to seven and found agreeable while resting in bed until his father permitted him to get up. His treatment of his own children seems to have been little better; his older son was given out to a dissolute *balia* and barely survived the illnesses of his third and fourth years. . . .

In theory the father was considered to be directly responsible for the son's education but even the members of the Alberti family agree that "if the father is not himself capable of teaching, or is too busy with more important tasks (if anything is more important than the care of one's children)," let him find a tutor. Seven is often termed the suitable age at which to begin formal education but Palmieri, and similarly Rucellai, suggest starting earlier to teach the child his letters at home, making use of little devices such as forming letters in fruits and sweetmeats and giving them to him if he can recognize S, O, C and other letters. Dominici also mentions the value of little inducements or rewards, such as new shoes, an inkstand, a slate and so on. Vegio stresses parental responsibility in the early years of schooling, proposing the use of a relative or older brother as a mentor and the participation of the parents in hearing the child recite what he has supposedly learned.

Most middle-class children first encountered formal instruction at the age of seven or earlier in the schools of the commune. These "common schools" were deplored by Dominici as places where "a multitude of wicked, dissolute persons assemble, facile in evil or difficult to control"; all the parents could do was to fortify the child morally. Vegio sees a positive advantage in sending the child out of the home for his schooling, among his peers and away from women and servants, but the parents should get to know the teachers, pay them well and beware of overcrowded classrooms and frequent changes of teachers.

Some records of actual experience may prove useful. A succinct account of his education is given by a member of the Valori family of Florence, born 1354:

In 1363, when the plague stopped, I Bartolomeo, was put to learn grammar at the school of Master Manovello and I stayed there up to 1367 through the month of May. And then in June of the same year I was put to learn abacus to know how to keep accounts, with Master Tomaso . . . , and I stayed there up to February, 1368. And on the same day I was sent to the bank of Bernardo. . . .

Though his schooling was delayed by the plague, this boy went through the three stages which were the normal progression in a mercantile society, learning to read, learning to do accounting and then apprenticeship in a bank or shop.

Morelli, without a father's guidance, went to school at five where he suffered "many blows and frights" in subjection to his master. At eight he was put under a master in the house whose discipline by day and night he found "displeasing to childish freedom." And at eleven to twelve after a severe case of smallpox, he suffered from a master of unusual harshness. His little son, Alberto, was more precocious; at four he wanted to go to school, at six he knew "Donatus" (primary Latin grammar), and at eight the Psalter, at nine he studied Latin and learned to read mercantile letters. The father reproaches himself bitterly after the child's death for having "worn him out at school and with many and frequent harsh blows."

Antonio Rustichi recorded the early education of his sons as conscientiously as their births. He sent Lionardo at five and Stefano at four to primary school in 1422, changed them to a second master in 1423, and soon shifted to a master in the house, who was given his keep but "no salary, or shoes or clothes." The latter lasted only a few weeks, going off to Pisa to study. In 1425 Antonio sent Stefano (seven), and Marabottino (four) to a teacher at Or San Michele "to learn to read," adding a third son in 1427. But he shifted all three to another master in 1428 because the teacher "was not instructing them well." They were moved again "to learn to read" in 1431, and in 1432 sent to learn the abacus. And so on. This over-burdened father clearly tried to find not only the most economical way of educating his sons, sending them in groups and experimenting with a house tutor, but was also determined that they should be well taught. The frequent changes of teachers recall the similar shifts of *balias* from which his children had suffered earlier. . . .

In summary, the life of the ordinary urban middle-class child in the period of the Renaissance seems to have been marked by a series of severe adjustments, both physical and emotional. The first and most significant of these was the almost immediate displacement of the infant from its mother's bosom to that of a *balia*; the second was the return of the young child, after some two years of absence, to a strange mother and an unknown home; the third was the projection of the boy of about seven into the classroom, and later the shop, and of the young girl at nine or ten into a nunnery or, often before sixteen, into marriage. These major displacements of the child might be supplemented by minor ones, of flight with one's family from the plague into another house, to the country or to another city, or departure from the native city with one's exiled father.

Disturbing as these changes might be they did not require separation of the child from the mother as did the first displacement or as the remarriage of the mother might do.

In the first period of its life the child, handed over to a surrogate, was deprived of the love and care of both parents; in the next period he was probably drawn most closely under the mother's wing; in the next the boy came under the tutelage of the father and his surrogate, the master, while the girl remained under the mother's close supervision until her fate was determined. The first stage seems to me the most crucial and the least recognized or understood. It poses an historical question of absorbing interest: how could the deprived and neglected infants of the middle classes develop into the architects of a vigorous, productive and creative era which we call "the Renaissance"? The enigma will probably remain with us but at least we are asking new questions and devising new methods of inquiry. It seems likely to me that the approach of the psychologist and psychoanalyst will prove most fruitful in illuminating the long-range consequences of emotional deprivation.

For the social historian the best focus of attention may be the second stage, the young child's life from about two to about seven years when circumstances forced upon him an extraordinary adjustment to a strange environment. For this period a greater volume of positive evidence can be found through the use of unpublished materials and the critical reexamination of what we already have at hand. Although the walls of the *balia* house will stand forever between us and the swaddled infant, perhaps we can learn how to look more sharply through the doors and windows of the urban home and see the child in his intimate activities and relationships. In our efforts we can make fuller use, among other materials, of the vast resources left to us by Italian architects, painters, sculptors and craftsmen whose work has rarely been subjected to psychohistorical analysis.

B 4
C 5
D 6
E 7
F 8
G 9
H 0
I 1
J 2